THE RIGHT OF NONUSE

The Right of Nonuse

Jan G. Laitos

OXFORD
UNIVERSITY PRESS

OXFORD
UNIVERSITY PRESS

Oxford University Press, Inc., publishes works that further Oxford University's objective of excellence in research, scholarship, and education.

Oxford New York
Auckland Cape Town Dar es Salaam Hong Kong Karachi Kuala Lumpur Madrid Melbourne
Mexico City Nairobi New Delhi Shanghai Taipei Toronto

With offices in
Argentina Austria Brazil Chile Czech Republic France Greece Guatemala Hungary Italy
Japan Poland Portugal Singapore South Korea Switzerland Thailand Turkey Ukraine
Vietnam

Published by Oxford University Press, Inc.
198 Madison Avenue, New York, New York 10016

Library of Congress Cataloging-in-Publication Data

Laitos, Jan.
The right of nonuse / Jan G. Laitos.
p. cm.
Includes bibliographical references and index.
ISBN 978-0-19-538606-6 ((hardback) : alk. paper)
1. Natural resources—Law and legislation. 2. Natural resources—Government policy. I. Title.
K3478.L35 2012
346.04′4—dc23
2011048643

9 8 7 6 5 4 3 2 1
Printed in the United States of America on acid-free paper

Note to Readers
This publication is designed to provide accurate and authoritative information in regard to the subject matter covered. It is based upon sources believed to be accurate and reliable and is intended to be current as of the time it was written. It is sold with the understanding that the publisher is not engaged in rendering legal, accounting, or other professional services. If legal advice or other expert assistance is required, the services of a competent professional person should be sought. Also, to confirm that the information has not been affected or changed by recent developments, traditional legal research techniques should be used, including checking primary sources where appropriate.

(Based on the Declaration of Principles jointly adopted by a Committee of the American Bar Association and a Committee of Publishers and Associations.)

This is for two important people in my life,

Erik and Carrie

Acknowledgments

MANY AIDED AND ENCOURAGED me while this book was being considered, and then written. Most of the chapters within Part II were originally published as an article by the University of Oregon *Journal of Environmental Law and Litigation*, in Volume 25(2). That article was coauthored by Professor Catherine M. H. Keske, who was the lead in many of the resource economics and game theory arguments and analyses that appear in Part II. Heather Joyce helped me with the research that went into Part II. Within Part IV, Ashley Barr became expert in evolutionary biology and privacy rights as she worked with me on Chapter 13, "The Biology of Resource Nonuse"; Greg Angstadt tapped into his extensive physics and chemistry background to help out with Chapter 14, "The Science of Resource Nonuse"; and Joanna Thompson was an invaluable resource for the game theory discussion that appears in Chapter 15, "The Economics of Resource Nonuse." Three others were of great assistance in Part V. Much of Chapter 16, "The Problem of Government Regulation: The Emerging Shift from Anthropocentric to Ecocentric Nonuse Laws," was originally published as an article by the American Planning Association's *Journal of Planning and Environment*, in Volume 63(1). That article was coauthored by Andrew Swan. Diane Burkhardt found for me many of the references cited in Chapter 17,"The Problem of Rights Creation: Can Natural Resources Have Legal Rights?" Chapter 18,"The Problem of Standing: May Natural Resources Raise Their Own Right of Nonuse?," was benefitted by the good work of Hermine Kallman. As a general matter, I received valuable critical feedback from the Society of Environmental Law and Economics, particularly Professor Shi-Ling Hsu. Professor Dan Cole was both an educator and supporter during the early stages of the book, and Professor Kerry Krutilla offered valuable insight that I have tried to incorporate into Chapter 1, "The Nature of Nature." Professor J. B. Ruhl's writings opened my eyes to the significance of ecosystem services and natural capital. Professor Christopher Stone's still-seminal article "Should Trees Have Standing?" was both visionary and, as they say, "spot on." He saw it all long before anyone else. Thanks also to Chris Collins and Izzy Pizarro, who wanted my idea to be published, and who helped make this book happen. Professor Corrada offered helpful advice on choosing a publisher. Finally, I have to recognize Michelle Slaton, Diane Bales and Anne Beblavi, who toiled over draft after draft after draft. Their persistence and competence permitted all this research and thought to finally make its way to these pages.

Contents

PART I

Introduction

1. The Nature of Nature

NATURE IS COMPRISED of natural and environmental resources. These are living things, substances and compounds that support life, systems that permit the biosphere to evolve, and non-living things that make up the ecosystems and baseline preconditions for life. Human beings are unique in that they are living organisms who are part of the living Earth, but they are also the only life forms that are fully capable of affecting, and affecting adversely, all other living organisms on the planet. When these modern humans use, and over-use, natural and environmental resources, they can jeopardize both these resources and their ecological context.

This human penchant towards excessive resource use not only exhausts natural resources, and contaminates environmental resources, it also destroys an integral "nonuse" quality held by all of the Earth's components. This nonuse dimension of all natural goods thrives when humans have not used, or do not use, natural and environmental resources. When humans either did not exist, or when they existed in paltry numbers in a non-industrial state, resources were not used by humans to the point where nature was harmed. In such a state of balance, the natural systems that sustain life arose, and over time all living things emerged.

By the time modern *Homo sapiens* evolved, and began migrating across the planet, they did so in an environment that was oxygen-rich, climate regulated, and greenhouse gas balanced. Virtually all living natural resources they encountered were sustainably renewable. This living Earth arose because nature's nonuse qualities had not yet been impaired by human use activities. As a result, these nonuse dimensions of nature permitted life-producing processes to emerge, and living organisms to arise, that became the ingredients of the current living Earth. But, when humans over-used resources, they first depleted them and then polluted them. Now humans are chipping away at the very nonuse features of resources that permitted both life, and humans, to come into being in the first place.

Nature is not just a fixed quantity of environmental matter, or a set amount of natural systems, that is utilized, and eventually consumed, by this most voracious and predatory and destructive of all living things, humans. Nature is also a repository of nonuse qualities, which, if left alone by humans, is capable of giving and nourishing life. The relentless natural ills of this world are not due solely to too much human use, which exhausts and poisons nature. The decline of the systems, species, and substances that make up life on this planet is equally due to grave injuries to nature's nonuse components. Use begets over-use, which in turn circles back to inflict harm on all of nature's nonuse abilities. It is the erosion and corruption of Earth's essential nonuse functions that is the major environmental threat.

1 The Nature of Nature

THIS BOOK WILL advance three central arguments. First, it will assert that the planet Earth is in trouble. It will note that there is growing evidence that nature, consisting of living organisms, natural resources, and environmental goods, is experiencing extinction, exhaustion, and pollution at an alarming rate. Second, the book will argue that, by and large, humans have been unsuccessful in reversing or even slowing this trend. This failure of response has been due to two mistakes: (1) the selection of the wrong normative standard by which to assess threats to natural resources, and (2) an insensitivity to an integral "nonuse" facet of nature and natural resources. Third, the book will suggest that policy makers and lawmakers should, and ultimately will need to, recognize and legitimate the intrinsic, nonanthropomorphic value of nature and its many resources when *not used* by humans. This nonuse function may be best acknowledged by conferring on natural resources a legal right of nonuse, which is basically a right to be left alone. When humans do not overuse nature, and when nature is allowed to operate without human intervention, it may then perform the natural functions that originally permitted this planet to become the platform for the rise of all living things, including humans.

A list of planetary maladies could go on and on. Such a list would include, but not be limited to, habitat loss, species extinctions, ecosystem alteration, release of vast quantities of fossil carbon that the planet took hundreds of millions of years to store away, warmer global climate, melting arctic ice and mountain glaciers, higher sea levels, increase in the amount of nitrogen fixed on land, and atmospheric carbon-dioxide levels that are expected to remain high for thousands of years.

Unlike previous planetary changes, this transformation of the natural environment has been largely brought about by one source—the humans who populate the earth. These humans are not merely residents of the planet: They are now critical to its workings. They are shaping and affecting, and affecting adversely, most every aspect of the natural world.[1]

Humans, particularly biologists, earth scientists, and policy makers, are not unaware of the troublesome, if not catastrophic, environmental and ecological changes that are the inevitable consequence of relentless human activity.[2] However, the environmental and resource-protective fixes that humans have added to their laws, rules, and legal requirements do not seem to be working. The planet still experiences anthropomorphic assaults on its natural objects, organisms, and systems. Despite a promiscuous array of both proposed and adopted government standards for saving the planet, there has been a continuous deterioration of nature, natural resources, and environmental goods.[3] Humans have caused the troubles with the planet's natural and environmental resources, but our legal and institutional responses have been unable to reign in our own activities that create these problems.

There are two central reasons for this failure of response. One explanation involves the normative standard that the United States and most nations have selected for judging the worth or effectiveness of these legal and institutional responses to natural resources depletion and contamination. That normative standard has been built upon an instrumentalist human welfare valuation. Resource conservation and environmental laws have traditionally been adopted only when problems with nature have negatively impacted humans in some way. Laws have been advanced and judged according to a normative stance that reflects a strong anthropocentric component—the issue has not been whether the laws have improved the health and viability of *nature*, but whether they have adequately protected the future welfare of *humans*.

---

[1] *The Anthrocene: A Man-Made World*, Economist (May 26, 2011).

[2] *See, e.g.*, James Gustove Speth, The Bridge at the End of the World: Capitalism, the Environment, and Crossing from Crisis to Sustainability (2008); Tyler Volk, CO^{2} Rising: The World's Greatest Environmental Challenge (2008); John M. Broder, *Bigger Toolkit Needed to Manage Climate Change*, N.Y. TIMES, 11 (Dec. 11, 2011); Abby Goodnough, *Scientists Say Cod are Scant; Nets Say Otherwise*, N.Y. TIMES 20 (Dec. 11, 2011); Justin Gillis, *Forests Across the World Dying Off as Climate Warms*, N.Y. Times, Oct. 1, 2011; Pete Spots, *Climate Change: Species Climbing Higher and Migrating North, Study Says*, Christian Sci. Monitor, Aug. 19, 2011 (organisms are responding to human-caused climate change at a rate much faster than scientists estimated a decade ago, according to a new study in the journal *Science*); Jeremy B. Jackson et. al., *Historical Overfishing and the Recent Collapse of Coastal Ecosystems*, 293 Sci. 629 (2001); Sing S. Chew, *World Ecological Degradation: Accumulation, Urbanization, and Deforestation*, 3000 B.C.–A.D. 2000 (2001).

[3] *See, e.g.*, Shi-Ling Hsu, *The Case for a Carbon Tax: Getting Past Our Hang-Ups to Effective Climate Policy* (2011); Alyson C. Flournoy, *The Case for the National Environmental Legacy Act*, *in* Beyond Environmental Law (A. Flournoy & D. Driesen eds., 2010); Richard P. Hiskes, The Human Right to a Green Future: Environmental Rights and Intergenerational Justice (2009); Ted Nordhaus & Michael Shellenberger, Break Through: Why We Can't Leave Saving the Planet to Environmentalists (2009); J.B. Ruhl, Steven E. Kraft & Christopher L. Lant, The Law and Policy of Ecosystem Services (2007).

It is one of the central theses of this book that this anthropocentric standard is too limited. An alternative ethical imperative is now needed, one that gives equal countervailing weight to the needs and intrinsic nonanthropocentric value of nature and natural resources. The normative standard by which to judge legal and governmental responses to environmental problems should also reflect the worth of nature and natural systems *irrespective of humans*.[4]

Another explanation for the failure of laws and government initiatives to address the problems of natural resource loss and pollution lies in a stubborn refusal to decipher the codebook of nature. To understand the workings of this planet, one must recognize a heretofore-ignored universal law of nature: All natural resources—the atmosphere, the waters, the wildlife, the vegetation, the land—have two essential components, a use and nonuse function.

Humans have, historically, only been interested in the "use" component of resources. From the time that *Homo sapiens* emerged on this earth, nature's wealth has been perceived to have value only if it is used. This strictly utilitarian view carried into our laws. The law of private property, for example, holds that one of the most essential features of the property right is the right for the owner to use the property.[5] Nonuse, by contrast, was grounds to divest the owner of a property interest.[6] Even environmental protective laws were adopted because we began to realize that environmental goods had human health value when we used them as something other than a sink in which to dump our garbage. Resource protective laws were similarly adopted to regulate human activities that depleted commodity goods, such as forests, or destroyed preservation landscapes, such as wilderness. In both cases, humans wanted to use the now-safeguarded resource, either for future development or aesthetic purposes.

But what has been overlooked in most of the legal responses to environmental damage or resource eradication has been the equally important *nonuse* component of natural resources. This dimension of all resources is vital to the planet when humans do not actively use the resource. When we leave them alone, natural resources perform services and play roles essential to the earth's vitality. In other words, when humans do not use a resource, it is not without worth; it is then able to serve functions essential to the viability of the natural world. It is, after all, the future of this natural world that is at risk, and this world should be our focus, not just the humans who now happen to inhabit it.

The earth's workings created the virtual Garden of Eden that *Homo sapiens* encountered when they emerged as the planet's dominant species. It was the nonuse component that created the conditions that allowed all life to come forth. One reason for the failure of our legal response to combat resource and environmental

---

[4] Mark Sagoff, Price, Principle, and the Environment (2004); Frederic L. Bender, The Culture of Extinction: Toward a Philosophy of Deep Ecology (2003); Arne Naess, *The Shallow and the Deep, Long-Range Ecology Movement: A Summary*, 16 Inquiry 95 (1973).

[5] 1 William Blackstone, Commentaries 138 (1765–1769).

[6] *See e.g.*, Jenkins v. State, Dep't. of Water Resources, 647 P.2d 1256 (Idaho 1982).

assaults has been the absence of laws that first acknowledge and then empower this nonuse part of all natural resources.[7]

If the twin causes of a persistent failure to address serious threats to natural and environmental resources are (1) our traditional anthropocentric focus when legal responses are fashioned, and (2) our omission of the nonuse component of resources when considering how best to protect the planet, then what is needed now would be a nonanthropocentric response that legitimates the nonuse value of natural resources. What is needed, and what is proposed in this book, is the creation of a legally recognized *right of nonuse,* held not by humans, but by the natural resources themselves.[8] The purpose of this book is to lay out, through multiple disciplines, the reasons for, and the operation of, such an unprecedented right.

Part II below considers the social and economic history of how natural resources have traditionally been used by humans, and how lately humans have valued resource nonuse when it suits their limited anthropocentric purpose. Part II relies on game theory to explain why and how humans used resources, protected resource nonuse when it suited their anthropogenic purposes, and should now legitimate purely ecocentric resource nonuse values. Part III is a history of how laws, legal institutions, and government bodies have responded first to resource use demands, and then to calls for resource nonuse when humans will be benefited. Part IV argues, using the disciplines of evolutionary biology, science, and economics (primarily game theory) that the nonuse component of natural resources is not only an inherent part of all natural resources, but a feature of nature that may bring about a more optimal result for the planet, if it is recognized and legitimated by legal institutions. Part V discusses the practical parameters of such a right of nonuse. The chapters in Part V review how current laws are beginning to reflect nonanthropocentric nonuse values, how a workable "right" of nonuse might be created, and how natural resources would be empowered to assert their own right of nonuse.

---

[7] *See, e.g.* Jan G. Laitos & Andrew Swan, *The Growing Role of Nonuse Values in Land Use Planning and Environmental Law*, 63 PLANNING & ENVIR. LAW 3 (Jan. 2011).

[8] *See, e.g.*, Jan G. Laitos & Catherine M.H. Keske, *The Right of Nonuse*, 25 J. ENVTL. LAW & LITIG. (2011); Christopher Stone, *Should Trees Have Standing?—Toward Legal Rights for Natural Objects*, 45 SO. CAL. L. REV. 450 (1972); Sierra Club v. Morton, 405 U.S. 727, 749 (1972) (Douglas, J. dissenting); Clare Kendall, *A New Law of Nature*, GUARDIAN, Sept. 24, 2008.

PART II

A Social - Economic History of Resource Use and Nonuse

HUMANKIND IS ON a path of inefficient and unsustainable resource use and exploitation. As a result, the earth and its resources are now facing irreversible disruptions that have the potential to affect multiple generations.[1] These disastrous global effects are not caused only by excessive resource use. Rather, accelerated human use of resources also has the devastating consequence of impairing the purely ecocentric benefits that follow when humans do not use resources. When resources are left alone by humans, when they are not exploited or developed, their nonuse is beneficial for the entire biosphere, of which humans are only a part. The destruction of this critical nonuse component of natural resources is creating many of the alarming environmental changes that are so disturbing to the planet. One may create a series of analytical arguments founded in economic game theory, which illustrate that sustainable resource use can only be achieved if legal rights are bestowed upon not just human resource users, or humans who benefit themselves from resource nonuse, but upon the resource itself. This may be defined as the resource's "right of nonuse." Establishing a "right of nonuse" effectively privatizes a resource, facilitating a cooperative game that is among three kinds of players: human resource users, humans who selfishly prefer resource nonuse, and the resource itself. An analysis under this three-player game, which at last includes the natural resource itself as a critical actor, provides a framework for moving toward an efficient, sustainable path of resource conservation.

[1] Among the most obvious of these disruptions are diminishing energy supplies and usable natural resources, adverse climate change, and accelerating loss of biodiversity. THOMAS L. FRIEDMAN, HOT, FLAT, AND CROWDED 37–47 (2008); Justin Gillis, *Panel Finds Climate Change Behind Some Extreme Weather*, N.Y. TIMES A5 (Nov. 19, 2011) (the Intergovernmental Panel on Climate Change, a high-profile United Nations body assigned to report on developments in climate research, has concluded that some weather extremes seen around the world are consequences of human-induced climate change, which can be expected to worsen in the coming decades); Leao Serva, *An Assault on the Amazon*, N.Y. TIMES (Nov. 17, 2011) (almost 20 percent of the Amazon rainforest has been destroyed, and, according to the World Wildlife Fund, at current rates of deforestation, 55 percent of the Amazon rainforest could be gone by 2030); *see also* P.C.D. Milly et al., *Stationarity is Dead: Whither Waste Management*, 319 SCI. 573, 573 (2008) (arguing that the customary belief that natural systems fluctuate within a narrow, predictable range is no longer true, due to "substantial anthropogenic change" of the earth's climate); Robert J. Diaz & Rutger Rosenberg, *Spreading Dead Zones and Consequences for Marine Ecosystems*, 321 SCI. 926, 926 (2008) ("Dead zones in the coastal oceans have spread exponentially since the 1960s [and are] . . . fueled by riverine runoff of fertilizers and the burning of fossil fuels.").

2 Defining Natural Resource Use and Nonuse

A. Natural Resource Use and Nonuse Values

All natural resources consist of both a use and nonuse component, summarized in Table 2.1,[1] below. The use dimension in turn is divided into two classes: direct use and indirect use. Direct use occurs when humans utilize, exploit, or otherwise disturb a resource. We value this direct use component when we extract, develop, cultivate, or change some natural raw material for human ends.[2] The use component of resources is exploited when we deposit our waste directly into the natural environment, using the atmosphere, hydrosphere, and the earth's soils as sinks for our pollutants.[3] Returns from direct use can be measured rather easily through market

[1] Information in Table 1 is adapted from IAN HODGE, JESSICA DUNN & ECONOMIC AND SOCIAL RESEARCH COUNCIL, RURAL CHANGE AND SUSTAINABILITY: A REVIEW OF RESEARCH 139 (1992) and JONATHAN A. LESSER, DANIEL E. DODDS & RICHARD O. ZERBE, JR., ENVIRONMENTAL ECONOMICS AND POLICY 268–82 (1997).

[2] *See generally* JAN G. LAITOS, SANDRA B. ZELLMER, MARY C. WOOD & DANIEL H. COLE, NATURAL RESOURCES LAW 724–1158 (2006) (discussing laws applying to the human uses of land, timber, minerals, and water).

[3] John R. McNeill, *Resource Exploitation and Over-Exploitation: A Look at the 20th Century, in* EXPLOITATION AND OVER-EXPLOITATION IN SOCIETIES PAST AND PRESENT 51, 55 (Brigittta Benzing & Bernd Herrmann eds., 2003); *see also* JOHN S. APPLEGATE, JAN G. LAITOS, JEFFREY GABA & NOAH SACHS, THE REGULATION OF TOXIC SUBSTANCES AND HAZARDOUS WASTES (2d ed. 2011) (discussing regulatory definitions and regulations of hazardous waste under the Resource Conservation and Recovery Act).

TABLE 2.1

Examples of Use, Option, and Existence Values

Use Values	
Direct Use	Indirect Use
Harvesting plants	Carbon sequestration
Extraction of petroleum	Clean air
Extraction of minerals	Clean water
	Uncontaminated soils
Nonconsumptive uses	
Wildlife viewing	
Passive recreation	
Nonuse Values	
Option Values	Existence Values
Conservation of topsoil	Natural areas (intrinsic value)
Grasslands preservation	Pristine wilderness
Petroleum reserves	Natural wetlands
Future recreation	Wild and scenic waters
Ecosystems	Intrinsic value for natural objects
	Wildlife
	Historical objects

activity, such as price and quantity sold or other economic measures. Direct uses may also include nonconsumptive uses, such as visiting a national park for wildlife viewing.[4] These uses may not appear to be outwardly destructive, but human visitation in great enough numbers can both harm wildlife and reduce the benefit humans experience from viewing animals in the wild. Many direct uses are quasi-public or congestible public goods. They are nonrivalrous and nonexclusive at low levels of consumption, but become congested at high levels of use. Resource use may also encompass "indirect uses" derived from a resource or an ecosystem, such as carbon sequestration, clean air, or clean water.[5] Indirect uses can provide life-giving services and functions to this planet (including to humans) when humans do not directly use the resource.[6]

---

[4] Ruth DeFries & Stefano Pagiola, *Analytical Approaches for Assessing Ecosystem Condition and Human Well-Being, in* ECOSYSTEMS AND HUMAN WELL-BEING: CURRENT STATE AND TRENDS 54 (Rashid Hassan, Robert Scholes & Neville Ash eds., 2005).

[5] For the sake of clarity, and unless otherwise mentioned, the term *use* refers strictly to direct resource use.

[6] J.B. RUHL, STEVEN KRAFT & CHRISTOPHER LANT, THE LAW AND POLICY OF ECOSYSTEM SERVICES 27–32 (2007).

In contrast, nonuse benefits arise when humans want to maintain the option of using a resource in the future (otherwise known as *option value*), or to preserve a resource for the sake of its existence, such as carbon sequestration, clear air, or clean water (otherwise known as *existence value*).[7] Nonuse values can also produce global ecosystem services that permit sustainable life on the earth, even if there are no humans or if a resource is untouched by humans.[8] Resource nonuse provides for the indirect resources that are received and enjoyed by humans. Both indirect use and existence nonuse values can also be measured, but it can be tricky to do so.[9]

Within each resource on the earth, the use and nonuse components exist within a closed system;[10] this means that if humans "use" a resource, that use diminishes the resource's nonuse potential.[11] The human rate of resource use has changed over time, and the current levels are unsustainable to humankind in the long run. Central to this thesis is the belief that a resource's nonuse value can directly facilitate the resource's indirect uses that are necessary for human life.[12]

---

[7] John V. Krutilla, *Conservation Reconsidered*, 57 AM. ECON. REV. 777, 779–82 (1967). There are differences in opinion among economists as to whether option value is a subcategory of nonuse or whether it should comprise a third category by itself. *See also* LESSER ET AL., *supra* note 1, at 268–82.

[8] *See generally* NATURE'S SERVICES: SOCIETAL DEPENDENCE ON NATURAL ECOSYSTEMS (Gretchen C. Daily ed., 1997) (providing an overview of the services nature provides that benefit humans, as well as those that sustain life in general); HERMAN E. DALY & JOSHUA FARLEY, ECOLOGICAL ECONOMICS: PRINCIPLES AND APPLICATIONS 77–110 (2004) (describing the relationship among resources, their consumption and nonconsumption, the economy, and ecology); Gordon B. Bonan, *Forests and Climate Change: Forcings, Feedbacks, and the Climate Benefits of Forests*, 320 SCI. 1444 (2008) (explaining the beneficial effects of forests, when not removed by humans, on climate). On the other hand, human overuse of resources can dramatically adversely affect the earth's nonuse value. *See generally* Richard A. Kerr, *How Urgent is Climate Change?*, 318 SCI. 1230 (2007) (explaining that human-produced greenhouse gases could transform 40% of existing global ecosystems by the year 2100).

[9] LESSER ET AL., *supra* note 1, at 268–82.

[10] Resource economists generally agree that there is a finite resource base of exhaustible resources. *See, e.g.*, DALY & FARLEY, *supra* note 8, at 77–88; JOHN E. TILTON, ON BORROWED TIME? ASSESSING THE THREAT OF MINERAL DEPLETION 101–23 (2003). Although the base itself is finite, economically viable reserves of exhaustible resources such as oil frequently increase with improvements in technology. *See, e.g.*, DALY & FARLEY, *supra* note 8, at 78; TILTON, *supra*, at 101–05. Price signals rise to indicate presence of scarcity, which will mean that oil extraction will become prohibitively expensive before the last drop of oil is actually extracted. However, mineral economists have had difficulty projecting when these reserves will become uneconomical to maintain. *See* TILTON, *supra*, at 101–23. Renewable resources require more sophisticated modeling, and the success of replenishing these resources depends upon a number of variables, including initial stock, rate of use, regeneration rate, and resource-carrying capacity. For an excellent depiction of renewable resource modeling, readers are recommended to consult JON M. CONRAD, RESOURCE ECONOMICS (1999) and JON M. CONRAD & COLIN W. CLARK, RESOURCE ECONOMICS: NOTES AND PROBLEMS (2002 reprt. ed.).

[11] All natural resources conform to the laws of thermodynamics. Consistent with the first law—the law of conservation of matter—any activation of a resource's use dimension will also have a depressing effect on that resource's nonuse qualities. And, consistent with the second law—the law of increased entropy—human use of a resource converts usable energy into unusable energy, deteriorating the resource's ability to generate nonuse benefits. *See generally* DONALD HAVME, BIOLOGICAL THERMODYNAMICS (2001).

[12] For example, the nonuse value of air is the following: When it is not polluted by humans, air provides critical components to the biosphere, such as oxygen, that confer on humans and other species an important indirect use value. Humans may place value on the existence of clean air for the support of species other than humans.

When hominids first emerged, demands on the resource nonuse component dominated because these early humans were not yet sufficiently numerous or technologically sophisticated to directly affect the earth's resource use base.[13] Indeed, some resource features, such as naturally occurring abrupt climate changes, threatened our species' very survival during the Pleistocene Epoch.[14] But, from the Pleistocene-Holocene boundary about 11,500 years ago[15] to the present time, anthropogenic use decisions have created a significant human footprint, which has in turn diminished the nonuse value and indirect use value of the planet's resources.[16] As a result, we face an unprecedented time when human exploitation of the use component of resources so degrades the nonuse component that the extinction of these human users is now a realistic possibility.[17]

This part provides a taxonomy of the influences that have guided our choices about resource use and nonuse. Initially, human survival behaviors, organizing institutions, changing legal regimes, and assumptions about relative resource abundance, drove human decisions that eventually caused inefficient use of resources. These humans, past and present, then realized that their ability to improve their quality of life with respect to resources depended on what other humans wanted to do with these same resources. This interdependence means that human choices to use or not use resources became, in effect, a game of strategy.[18] The outcome of this resource game depended on how the players acted in response to the actions of other players. It is best to rely on game theory to examine how and why the relevant resource players, and their assumptions about resource use and nonuse, have affected the earth's resource base over time in different ways.

As different resource players emerged throughout human history, so did the outcome of their "games," as well as their likelihood of achieving equilibrium among

[13] Leendert P. Louwe Kooijmans, *Archaeological Approaches to the Long-Term History of the Landscape, in* Exploitation and Over-Exploitation in Societies Past and Present 63, 64, 69 (Brigittta Benzing & Bernd Herrmann eds., 2003) (explaining that early hunters and foragers had little impact on the environment, as they survived with subsistence activities).

[14] Harvey Weiss, *Beyond the Younger Dryas: Collapse as Adaptation to Abrupt Climate Change in Ancient West Asia and the Eastern Mediterranean, in* Environmental Disaster and the Archaeology of Human Response 75, 75 (Garth Bawden & Richard Martin Reycraft eds., 2000).

[15] The Pleistocene-Holocene boundary is generally considered a major transitional point in human social evolution. *See id.*; Rolf Peter Sieferle, *Sustainability in a World History Perspective, in* Exploitation and Over-Exploitation in Societies Past and Present 123, 128 (Brigittta Benzing & Bernd Herrmann eds., 2003). Prior to that boundary, highly variable climates and environments made agriculture impossible, while afterward more complex and coordinated agricultural societies could emerge. Sieferle, *supra*, at 128.

[16] *See* Mark Serreze & Julienne Stroeve, *Standing on the Brink*, Nature Reps. Climate Change (Oct. 8, 2008), http://www.nature.com/climate/2008/0811/full/climate.2008.108.html; Richard A. Kerr, *Global Warming Is Changing the World*, 316 Sci. 188, 188 (2007).

[17] *An Epidemic of Extinctions: Decimation of Life on Earth*, Independent, May 16, 2008, *available at* http://www.independent.co.uk/environment/nature/an-epidemic-ofextinctions-decimation-of-life-on-earth-829325.html; Kenneth R. Weiss, *25 Percent of Mammals May Face Extinction*, Denv. Post, Oct. 7, 2008, at 13A, *available at* http://www.denverpost.com/search/ci_10654051.

[18] Douglas G. Baird, Robert H. Gentner & Randal C. Picker, Game Theory and the Law 21 (1994).

the players. At first the games were between two classes of resource users—those who owned the right to use the resource and those who did not yet possess such a use right, but who wanted to acquire it. Then, as these user-use games created havoc in the resources market, a new nonplayer emerged—the person or group of people who believed they would be better off if resources were not used. Their interests increasingly needed legal recognition and official "resource player" status before there could be an optimal outcome. When laws and legal institutions granted resource nonusers the right to assert their anthropocentric interests in resource nonuse, the user and nonuser players strategized against each other over time in a different resource game between resource users and nonusers.

It is the central thesis of Part II that this game, which characterizes virtually all resource disputes in the 21st century, is doomed to fail. It will never achieve an optimal level of sustainable resource use, an adequate protection of resource nonuse values, or a cooperative game among the critical resource players. This failure is because the current resources game excludes a key player—the natural resource itself. Only that resource can adequately assert its own nonanthropocentric interests in not being used by humans. The resource nonuse values that are now asserted in resource games are primarily interests raised by human players who themselves would benefit anthropogenically by the resource nonuse. The natural resource's purely ecocentric interests in nonuse—in being left alone by humans—are not part of these resource games. The creation of a legally acknowledged right of nonuse, held by the natural resource itself, would permit resource games to become cooperative games, and achieve an optimality that is impossible when the only players with legal rights are human users and nonusers. This argument is further advanced in Chapter 15.

B. Natural Resource Use and Nonuse over Time

We have so far experienced four distinct "eras" of resource use and nonuse. The first of these eras, which can be called the Age of Human Survival, occurred tens of thousands of years ago during the Pleistocene Epoch. During Era I, the players were semiautonomous, and their relationship to resources was simply one of trying to survive in the face of nature's raw and threatening power.[19] The second era ran from the time human populations organized themselves into complex societies until roughly the 18th century, as the decentralized free market gradually emerged as the chief resource-production-allocating mechanism.[20] In Era II, which can be called the Age of the Market, resource users were the primary players. Their goal was to quickly tap the

[19] David S. Gutzler, *Human Response to Environmental Disruption*, *in* Environmental Disaster and the Archaeology of Human Response 213, 215–16 (Garth Bawden & Richard Martin Reycraft eds., 2000) ("[G]igantic pre-Holocene warming and cooling events . . . must have had profound effects on life (including humans).").

[20] *See generally* Adam Smith, An Inquiry into the Nature and Causes of the Wealth of Nations (Kathryn Sutherland ed., Oxford University Press 1993) (1776).

seemingly endless resource use benefits before another competing user did so. In this race for resources, any rudimentary resource games were either between those who wished to use the same resource for the same purpose, or between those who wished to use a given resource for different purposes.

From the 18th century until the middle of the 20th century, the concept of a property right in a resource allowed owners to fully control and exploit the use component of their resources. Property interests became the engine for distributing diminishing resources in the face of escalating demands.[21] During this time there was also an emerging movement for "resource conservation," which in the United States established federal agencies to ensure a sustainable path of resource use on public lands. Although agencies such as the U.S. Forest Service, which was created in 1905, and the National Park Service, founded in 1916, eventually grew to protect nonuse values,[22] the charter of these agencies was to ensure the availability of resources for future human use.[23] During Era III, the Age of Property, the players were primarily resource users of competing uses who had no interest in the nonuse component of the resource they exploited. The two classes of players during Era III resource games were users with a property interest in the resource—both public and private owners—and would-be users without a property interest.

In Era IV, from the 1950s until the present, human anthropogenic decisions and activities resulted in dramatic reductions in the natural resource base, as well as increasing rates of pollution.[24] These human actions so affected the use component of resources that the very nature of the earth's biosphere not only became controlled

---

[21] Leonard Zobler, *An Economic-Historical View of Natural Resource Use and Conservation*, 38 ECON. GEOGRAPHY 189, 190 (1962). At the beginning of Era III, the specter of a depleted European resource base led to the exploration and colonization of North America, South America, and Africa. *See id.* at 189–90.

[22] *About Us*, U.S. NAT'L PARK SERVICE, http://www.nps.gov/aboutus (last visited Nov. 16, 2010).

[23] *See* Organic Administration Act of 1897, ch. 2, 30 Stat. 11 (codified as amended at 16 U.S.C. §§ 473–482, 581) (2006). Era III also witnessed an early movement for preservation and advocacy of resource nonuse, as opposed to conservation. Prominent activists during this era included the naturalist John Muir, and Aldo Leopold (founder of the Wilderness Society). Muir's conflict with the first chief of the U.S. Forest Service, Gifford Pinchot, and advocacy of sustainable managed forestry became legendary. John M. Meyer, *Gifford Pinchot, John Muir and the Boundaries of Politics in American Thought*, 30 POLITY 267, 267–68 (1997).

[24] Wangari Maathai, *World in Focus: The Seeds of Peace*, 2006 WLNR11744115 (July 8, 2006) ("[E]nvironmental degradation . . . and over-consumption continue to threaten the planet . . . ."); Tini Tran & John Heilprin, *Brown Clouds A Growing Risk*, DENV. POST, Nov. 14, 2008, at 14A, *available at* http://www.denverpost.com/headlines/ci _10978201 (commenting on "atmospheric brown clouds" covering vast areas of Asia, the Middle East, and Southern Africa). Of course, human damage to resource nonuse services did not first begin in the 1950s. Anthropogenic actions had been devastating landscapes and ecosystems long before the 20th century. *See* David Rains Wallace et al., *Not How, But Why? Beyond Proximate Cause for Environmental Degradation*, 6 CONSERVATION IN PRACTICE 42, 42–43 (2005) (reviewing JARED DIAMOND, COLLAPSE: HOW SOCIETIES CHOOSE TO FAIL OR SUCCEED (2005)); Malcolm Gladwell, *The Vanishing*, NEW YORKER, Jan. 3, 2005, at 70–73, *available at* http://www.newyorker .com/archive/2005/01/03/050103crbo_books (reviewing DIAMOND, *supra*). What occurred in the 20th century is that we first began to realize the scope and extent of these nonuse damages.

by one species, but its integrity and sustainability were also compromised.[25] This realization, combined with loss of natural areas untouched by humans, led to laws that legitimated a new third player: humans who value resource nonuse.[26] These Era IV laws that address the harmful impact of excessive resource use and loss of nature tend to focus on the use's impact on individual humans, rather than on the resource or its environment.[27] Indeed, the new third player empowered by these laws—the nonuser—often champions indirect and nonuse interests primarily because of the anthropocentric benefits that result from leaving resources alone.[28]

Humans now so thoroughly dominate the earth, and are so pervasively the beneficiaries of its institutions, that our current Era IV may be termed the "Anthrocene" Age.[29] There will not be a socially optimum equilibrium among three players (users, nonusers, and resource and land managers)[30] to adequately sustain the human population in the future in Era IV games.[31] This is because resource use is competitive,

---

[25] For example, anthropogenic emissions of greenhouse gases seem to be a contributing factor as to why the earth has entered a new period of significant climate change. Richard B. Alley et al., Intergovernmental Panel on Climate Change, *Summary for Policymakers, in* CLIMATE CHANGE 2007: THE PHYSICAL SCIENCE BASIS 10 (Susan Solomon et al. eds., 2007), *available at* http://www.ipcc.ch/pdf/assessment-report/ar4/wg1/ar4-wg1-spm.pdf.

[26] *See* Clean Air Act, 42 U.S.C. § 7401(b)(1) (2006) ("[T]he purposes of [this Act] are . . . to protect . . . the Nation's air resources so as to promote the public health and welfare and the productive capacity of its population."); Ocean Dumping Act, 33 U.S.C. § 1401(b) (2006) ("[I]t is the policy of the United States to regulate the dumping of all types of materials into ocean waters . . . to prevent . . . any material which would adversely affect human health or . . . economic potentialities."). Also, Era IV witnessed the emergence of subdisciplines of economics—such as environmental economics, resource economics, and experimental economics—that allowed us to better understand human interactions with, and preferences for, the environment and natural resources. *See, e.g.*, JOHN VON NEUMANN & OSKAR MORGENSTERN, THEORY OF GAMES AND ECONOMIC BEHAVIOR (3rd. 1953); John F. Nash, Jr., *The Bargaining Problem*, 18 ECONOMETRICA 155 (1950).

[27] *See, e.g.*, Friends of the Earth, Inc. v. Laidlaw Envtl. Servs., 528 U.S. 167, 181 (2000) ("The relevant showing for purposes of Article III standing, however, is not injury to the environment but injury to the plaintiff."); National Environmental Policy Act, 42 U.S.C. § 4331(a) (2006) ("[T]he continuing policy of the Federal Government . . . [is] to use all practicable means and measures . . . in a manner calculated to . . . maintain conditions under which man and nature can exist in productive harmony, and fulfill the . . . requirement of . . . future generations of Americans."); *see also* Gunther Handle, *Human Rights and Protection of the Environment, in* ECONOMIC, SOCIAL AND CULTURAL RIGHTS 303, 304–05 (Asbjørn Eide, Catarina Krause & Allan Rosas eds., 2d rev. ed. 2001).

[28] In 1997, the economic benefit of the nonuse "ecosystem services" provided to humans by productive natural systems unaffected by human interference was valued at between 16 and 54 trillion dollars. Robert Constanza et al., *The Value of the World's Ecosystem Services and Natural Capital*, 387 NATURE 253, 259 (1997).

[29] ANDREW REVKIN, GLOBAL WARMING: UNDERSTANDING THE FORECAST 55 (1992). Some have more recently termed this era the "Anthropocene Age." *See The Anthropocene: A Man-Made World*, ECONOMIST (May 26, 2011).

[30] AVIWASH K. DIXIT & BARRY J. NALEBUFF, THINKING STRATEGICALLY: THE COMPETITIVE EDGE IN BUSINESS, POLITICS, AND EVERYDAY LIFE 77 (1991) (explaining that even if some equilibrium is reached among the players that may be best for those players, this result may not necessarily be best for society as a whole).

[31] *See* Roger B. Myerson, *Nash Equilibrium and the History of Economic Theory*, 38 J. OF ECON. LITERATURE 1067, 1069–70 (1999).

which can be modeled as a noncooperative game that yields a Nash Equilibrium. In other words, each resource player maximizes its welfare given the best predicted strategy of the others. In the case of resource use, this results in a poor outcome for all.[32] As a specific example, the suboptimal allocation of resources is due in part to government provisioning of public goods such as wildlife habitat or open space that may crowd out the altruistic behavior of private individuals, who might be willing to supply such nonmarket goods.[33] Era IV laws give individuals, organizations, and governments the ability to raise their interests in resource nonuse or indirect uses. Even though nonuse values may be prioritized by some players, the resulting noncooperation leads to suboptimal resource use at a high rate.

A natural resource's nonuse component should be given legal stature—a right of nonuse—so that the resource can act as its own player, or agent, in resource games. When the resource is actually given legal rights, we will enter Era V, a new Age of Ecocentrism, where a sustainable social outcome can be reached. In Era V, a resource's own nonuse interests can be considered credible by all other resource players: owner-users, nonowner would-be users, and nonusers wishing to protect resource nonuse for their own anthropocentric objectives. And because these players represent virtually all the relevant resource interests on this planet, establishing a right of nonuse effectively facilitates a cooperative game that will lead to an efficient, sustainable path of resource conservation.[34]

---

[32] *Id.*

[33] An excellent summary of this literature is presented in a seminal article by Theodore Bergstrom, Lawrence Blume & Hal Varian, *On the Private Provision of Public Goods*, 29 J. PUB. ECONS. 25, 25–49 (1986), exploring the implications of private provisioning of public goods through a descriptive model and comparative statics.

[34] These players would not necessarily be engaged in a simultaneous multi-player game. Rather, it will be seen below that all resource players throughout the various eras have typically participated in a series of separate two-player, and occasional three-player, simultaneous and sequential games. Because owner-users and nonowner would-be users are essentially users of resources, most of the games in Era IV, the current time, have been between two players: users and nonusers, where the nonusers wish for the resource to be left alone for their own anthropocentric ends. Era V would introduce a critical third player, the resource itself. The games that would emerge in Era V would be among users, human nonusers, and the resource.

3 Era I—The Age of Human Survival

MODERN HUMANS EMERGED during a time called the Pleistocene Epoch, roughly tens of thousands of years ago. The first few early humans struggling to exist then were rather sparsely distributed and had little aggregate impact on the use component of resources.[1] Our ancestors exploited easily accessible natural resources in order to gain a toehold in an environment that was harsh and threatening to this new species.[2] Small groups of hunter-gatherers eked out a tenuous existence in highly variable environments and climates. The earth's natural dimension proved to be a two-edged sword. On the one hand, resource stress was so frequent and dramatic that these populations constantly had to alter their behavior and locations to survive.[3] On the other, their very survival depended on nature's ecosystem services and benefits that provided them with the essentials of life.[4]

---

[1] *See generally* Peter J. Richerson & Robert Boyd, *Built for Speed: Pleistocene Climate Variation and the Origin of Human Culture, in* 13 PERSPECTIVES IN ETHOLOGY 1 (Francois Tonneau & Nicholas S. Thompson eds., 2000).

[2] Catherine Delano Smith, *Late Neolithic Settlement, Land-Use and* Garigue *in the Montpellier Region*, France, 7 MAN 397, 404 (1972) (addressing forest clearance and vegetation degradation); Coralie M. Mills et al., *Neolithic Land-Use and Environmental Degradation: A Study from the Western Isles of Scotland*, 78 ANTIQUITY 886, 892–93 (2003) (discussing stripping of turf for shelter insulation and removal of peat for fuel).

[3] Brian Hayden, *Research and Development in the Stone Age: Technological Transitions among Hunter-Gatherers*, 22 CURRENT ANTHROPOLOGY 519, 520 (1981). This cultural instability meant that larger, more organized and cooperative societies could not yet arise.

[4] The ecosystems that were not yet affected by human use built the planet's biomass (vegetation and wildlife) and abiotic resources (soil and water) that supported the sustainability of human life. *See generally*

During this time, humans depended upon group cooperation for individual survival. Because competition for resources was maladaptive, hunter-gatherers emphasized resource sharing between and within groups.[5] The social rule among these hunting and gathering societies was egalitarianism, so as to ensure that no individual or group appropriated a disproportionate share of food. However, nomadic societies living in scattered small groups with limited cooperation could never enjoy the level of resource reliability and population organization necessary to create stable, complex social institutions with relatively minor, dispersed environmental impacts.[6]

At the end of Era I, roughly 11,500 years ago, the climate became much less variable, permitting agricultural subsistence systems to emerge over a large fraction of the earth's surface.[7] This marks a major transition point in human social evolution. The formation of institutions had previously been impossible because of dramatically changing climate conditions. With climate stability came resource reliability, domestication, and agriculture, as well as human cooperation, coordination, and division of labor.[8] The greater efficiency of agriculture also meant that agricultural populations competed with, and eventually overwhelmed, hunter-gatherer populations.

As agriculture and plant-intensive resource strategies became dominant in all but the most marginal environments, human population densities rose and more complex social organizations developed.[9] Because resources needed for survival seemed plentiful, these communities tolerated, for the first time in human experience, status competition, wealth control, and social ranking.[10] Humans no longer lived in small, atomized egalitarian groups where resources were shared. Instead, new social institutions evolved, and resources for the most part were allocated by barter and trade, and commodity money, which reflects value inherent in the good itself.[11]

The human relationship to resources during Era I can be understood by reference to individual decision theory. A fundamental principle of economics is that individuals maximize their own welfare. With the assumption that individuals were rational decision makers who chose actions regarding resources with the aim of

---

Norman L. Christensen et al., *The Report of the Ecological Society of America Committee on the Scientific Basis for Ecosystem Management*, 6 ECOLOGICAL APPLICATIONS 665 (1996).

[5] Hayden, *supra* note 3, at 527, 542.

[6] *See* Peter J. Richerson & Robert Boyd, *Institutional Evolution in the Holocene: The Rise of Complex Societies*, *in* THE ORIGIN OF HUMAN SOCIAL INSTITUTIONS 197, 197–204 (W.G. Runciman ed., 2001), *available at* http://www.des.ucdavis.edu/faculty/Richerson/evolutioninstitutions.pdf.

[7] BRUCE D. SMITH, THE EMERGENCE OF AGRICULTURE 19–20 (1995).

[8] *See generally* Harvey Weiss, Beyond the Younger Dryas: Collapse as an Adaptation to Abrupt Climate Change in Ancient West Asia and the Eastern Mediterranean, in ENVIRONMENTAL DISASTER AND THE ARCHAEOLOGY OF HUMAN RESPONSE 75 (Garth Bowden & Richard Mortin Reycraft eds., 2000). Richerson & Boyd, *supra* note 6, at 197; Hayden, *supra* note 3, at 523, 530.

[9] *See generally* RICHARD MANNING, AGAINST THE GRAIN: HOW AGRICULTURE HAS HIJACKED CIVILIZATION (2004).

[10] PETER A. CORNING, THE SYNERGISM HYPOTHESIS: A THEORY OF PROGRESSIVE EVOLUTION (1983). *See generally* MANNING, *supra* note 9.

[11] Leonard Zobler, An Economic-Historical View of Natural Resources Use and Conservation, 38 ECON. GEOGRAPHY 189, 191 (1962) Richerson & Boyd, *supra* note 6, at 202.

furthering individual interests, the limited resources during Era I meant that individual decisions revolved around basic human survival.[12] The crux of most Era I decisions was that an individual chose only one action toward a resource—for example, to plant crop A or crop B, to harvest now or delay until later, or to completely deforest the land or halt timber cutting. The choice had to be made in light of the consequences of alternatives and the chances of these consequences occurring. Typically, Era I humans did not need to take into account the actions of other humans. Over time, humans could successfully predict the likely immediate outcomes that would play out when decisions were made to use and exploit resources.[13]

During the Age of Survival, early humans had little understanding of and only limited control over nature's production processes. There existed a huge stock of relatively untouched natural resources, but humans still lacked the skills to tap the use potential of these resources. The discount rate was very high—humans were necessarily more concerned about their survival in the moment, rather than maintaining resources for future use. With a seemingly endless supply of resources, forests were burned to increase grazing areas,[14] turf was stripped to remove peat,[15] and soils were exhausted, degrading the natural nutrients of the soil system.[16] There were no laws or legal institutions to regulate these resource use decisions, or their impact on future uses.[17] But a new organizing institution, the market, was slowly beginning to emerge.[18]

In Era I, bartering was a common means for transactions to occur, but other basic market transactions also evolved, including the recording and repayment of debts through various forms of accounting, commodity money, and fiat money such as shells and beads.[19] The market eventually became the chief mechanism influencing the resource use decisions of growing numbers of people who formed egalitarian communities, and who enjoyed the returns that followed from agricultural subsistence. These populations, with their agriculture and their complex, market-based social organizations, increasingly settled many parts of the world, overwhelming native populations with less efficient subsistence and less complex social institutions. A new era arose, lasting thousands of years—the Age of the Market.

---

[12] *See* Michael D. Resnik, Choices: An Introduction to Decision Theory 4 (1987); J. Morgan Jones, Introduction to Decision Theory 2, 5 (1977).

[13] *See generally* David Rindos, The Origins of Agriculture: An Evolutionary Perspective (1984).

[14] Hayden, *supra* note 3, at 519.

[15] Mills et al., *supra* note 2, at 893, 894.

[16] Leendert P. Louwe Kooijmans, Archaeological Approaches to the Long-Term History of the Landscape, in Exploitation and Over-Exploitation in Societies Past and Present 63, 73 (Brigitta Benzing & Bernd Hermann eds., 2003).

[17] *See* MARSHALL SAHLINS, STONE AGE ECONOMICS 1–39 (1972).

[18] *See generally* Adam Smith, *An Inquiry into the Nature and Causes of the Wealth of Nations* (Kathryn Sutherland ed., Oxford University Press 1993) (1776).

[19] *See generally* Rafael Gasson, *Quiripas and Mostacillas: The Evolution of Shell Beads as a Medium of Exchange in Northern South America*, 47 ETHNOHISTORY 581, (Summer-Fall 2000).

4 Era II—The Age of the Market[1]

AS HUMANS GRADUALLY organized themselves into increasingly complex social systems, they realized that interconnection among other humans often led to a status that was superior to what resulted when they remained isolated from each other. Although international trade was known to exist for thousands of years, as time progressed and human population centers began to build, exchange and transactions between individuals became more common. The institution that seemed to best reflect these interchanges was the classic free market associated with Adam Smith.[2]

Compared to previous eras, societies, especially after 1000 A.D., were characterized by extreme decentralized governments, and they formed the foundation of today's market system. Markets evolved from predominant bartering and commodity money to formalized monetary systems. Price discovery processes enabled more exchanges, trades, and agreements among resource users. When buyers and sellers receive more information on the scarcity of the good, its relative value to society, and the prices that the other side of the market is willing to pay (or accept), more transactions

[1] The Age of the Market is the period between ancient times, roughly the second century B.C., through the early modern times of the late 1700s. This is the period in world history before property laws became dominant, where goods were exchanged among resource actors, and contract law was the primary legal mechanism for ensuring that bargains, exchanges, and deals could be credible.

[2] Adam Smith, *An Inquiry Into the Nature and Causes of the Wealth of Nations* (Kathryn Sutherland ed., Oxford University Press 1993) (1776); *see* Arun Agrawal, *Common Resources and Institutional Sustainability*, *in* THE DRAMA OF THE COMMONS 41, 42 (Elinor Ostrom et al., Committee on the Human Dimensions of Global Change eds., 2002).

may occur. Perhaps most important, these transactions can take place without the intervention of government or a third-party negotiator.[3] In Era II, natural resources seemed limitless, and technological advances improved access to these resources. Use of this abundant resource base helped bring about the rise of Western European nations as global economic powers. These nations dominated the planet's economy between 1500 A.D. and the Industrial Revolution two-and-a-half centuries later.[4]

As resource users consumed vast quantities of raw materials, they found that they increasingly had to compete among themselves to secure the riches of the world's resource base. Era I decisions involved humans seeking resources, while Era II decisions involved humans competing with other humans for resources. This shift brought about an important behavioral change, both economically and legally. With the advent of markets, individual decisions about resources were slowly replaced with group decisions.[5] Individual resource users realized that they could form groups for mutual benefit. The expectation was that by working together, they might be able to improve their results overall and the payoffs to the members of the group.[6] These kinds of interactive decisions among resource users are understood in light of one branch of game theory—cooperative games.[7]

During Era II, potential resource users had a choice—appropriate the resource as an individual, or cooperate with other potential users, so that the group of individual users would arrive at a better resource allocation. Appropriation was redistributive; one user benefited at the expense of another. Cooperation assumed that individuals would accept and commit to offers or exchanges by other users that would make them better off than they would have been by individual action. However, for cooperative games to succeed, agreements and promises among resource users in a market had to be enforceable. Legal doctrine needed to arise in the form of contract law that enabled market players to have the capacity for credible commitment.

Exchanges occurring over time involve more risk to both players, especially when the completion of the transaction depends on both parties promising to complete the exchange. Repetitious exchanges do not necessarily lead to cooperation or an optimal equilibrium, because players may have incentives to cheat, particularly if a player knows that his or her opponent is not likely to cheat. For example, if one player makes an investment based on a second player's promise to deliver goods in exchange, the promise maker may not feel compelled to complete the transaction after the investment is made. The investing player may therefore be better off not investing because there is no consequence to the other player for simply appropriating

---

[3] *See generally* RONALD H. COASE, THE FIRM, THE MARKET AND THE LAW 15 (1988); ROBERT C. ELLICKSON, ORDER WITHOUT LAW: HOW NEIGHBORS SETTLE DISPUTES (1991).

[4] *See generally* KENNETH POMERANZ, THE GREAT DIVERGENCE: EUROPE, CHINA, AND THE MAKING OF THE MODERN WORLD ECONOMY (2000).

[5] *See generally* Roderick M. Kramer & Marilynn B. Brewer, *Effects of Group Identity on Resource Use in a Simulated Commons Dilemma*, 46 J. PERSONALITY & SOCIAL PSYCHOL. 1044 (1984).

[6] ALLEN W. JOHNSON & TIMOTHY EARLE, THE EVOLUTION OF HUMAN SOCIETIES: FROM FORAGING GROUPS TO AGRARIAN STATE (1987).

[7] John Von Neumann & Oskar Morgenstern, *Theory of Games and Economic Behavior* 15 (3d ed. 1953).

		Player 2	
		Cooperate/invest	Defect/appropriate
Player 1	Initiate transaction	0.5 0.5	−1.0 1.0
	Do not initiate transaction	0 0	0 0

FIGURE 4.1 Without contract.

that investment. Under these circumstances, a cautious player may not invest for fear of loss without a remedy. No market transaction will then occur.

This normal form game scenario is reflected below in Figure 4.1. This matrix summarizes the bargaining possibilities where there is no contract or enforceable agreement between players who have complete information about one another's payoffs and how the game is played.[8] By receiving the investment, Player 2 possesses the dominant strategy,[9] because that player acquires the investor's money in exchange for a mere promise of delivery at a later date, which is referred to as a "deferred exchange." Because the exchange is deferred, the dominant strategy for Player 2 is to appropriate the investment and not to deliver to the investing player, Player 1. In other words, Player 2 profits from not delivering on a promise. Therefore, in the absence of a cooperative and enforceable agreement, Player 1 will not invest, and will not enter into the arrangement knowing that it is credible and likely for the other player to appropriate the investment. However, if Player 1 does not invest, neither player can benefit. In this case, both players will receive a payoff of zero.

Note that the number in each box on the left is Player 1's payoff; the number on the right is Player 2's payoff. The box containing the solution is highlighted.

Figure 4.1 illustrates that both players will reach the optimal result only when they cooperate. If both players cooperate, then each will receive a payoff of .5 (top left box) because both actors will split the profits (1.0/2 = .5). If Player 2 defects and takes payment but does not deliver the goods, then the payoff is 1.0, while Player 1 loses the entire investment (top right box). Because Player 1, the investor, is aware of Player 2's dominant strategy, a higher payoff for defection, Player 1 will decline to enter into an agreement. Neither gain from this activity, and each receive a payoff of zero because there is no transaction.

[8] Robert Cooter & Thomas Ulen, Law and Economics 197–98 (4th ed. 2004).

[9] Dominant strategies provide the highest payoff compared to any other strategies for any other players. Philip D. Straffin, Game Theory and Strategy 3–31 (6th prtg. 2006).

The addition of an enforceable agreement changes the payoffs and benefits for both players. Only if the cautious investor can be assured that the other player will perform will that investor initiate the transaction. An enforceable contract ensures a remedy if Player 2 appropriates and keeps the goods. Because Player 1 is assured compensatory payment if Player 2 defeats and appropriates, both will cooperate and divide the payoffs evenly. Cooperation thereby produces productivity: When both parties cooperate with each other, then they share in the transaction and both benefit. The enforceable contract transforms a game with a noncooperative solution into one with a cooperative solution.

Figure 4.2 highlights the outcomes for players when they enter into a binding contract. Players 1 and 2 will form a contract where there is complete information, and when Player 2 agrees to cooperate with Player 1, in exchange for investment. When both cooperate, they each receive an equal payoff of .5 (top left box). In contrast to the scenario presented in Figure 4.1, if Player 2 appropriates the investment, the agreement made between the parties is enforced and the investing player, Player 1, is awarded the contract payoff of .5. Player 2 then pays for the breach, making Player 2 worse off than simply fulfilling the contract. If Player 2 breaches, this will yield a payoff of -0.5 (top right box). Player 1, the investing player, now has the assurance needed to enter into a contract, and if Player 2 appropriates the investment, Player 1 receives a payoff of .5. The contract facilitates productivity and the players' participation in a cooperative game. If neither player enters into a contract, the first player will not initiate the transaction, and the payoffs remain zero for both players. The best solution is therefore to enter into a contract and engage in a productive transaction.

Note that the number in each box on the left is Player 1's payoff; the number on the right is Player 2's payoff. The box containing the solution is highlighted.

		Player 2	
		Cooperate/invest	Defect/appropriate
Player 1	Initiate transaction	0.5 0.5	0.5 0.5
	Do not initiate transaction (because no contract)	0 0	0 0

FIGURE 4.2 With contract.

A. The Rise of the Market as an Organizing Institution

In Era II, after the transition to agricultural societies, global economic development appeared to remain at a standstill for many centuries. This long period of little economic growth had two causes—exceptionally modest population expansion and diminishing factors of production, such as natural resources. This time of stalled population growth, lasting until around 1000 A.D., has been called the period of "Malthusian stagnation."[10] Some regions experienced a resource collapse stemming from human exploitation and eventual exhaustion of natural resource use potential, which concomitantly destroyed the natural systems that had enabled early human civilizations to arise.[11]

Sometime after 1000 A.D., expanded international trade, primarily by various Islamic states and the Sung Dynasty in China, ushered in a period of global population growth that lasted through the 16th century.[12] With increased international trade, Western Europe, which had at best performed only a peripheral role in the initial emergence of the new world economy, slowly rose to become the dominant player of Era II global trade.[13] There were two reasons Western Europe was able to leap ahead of competing world economic powers—first, the discovery, acquisition, and use of cheap natural resources, and second, the formalization of an expanded international economy.

Initially, demand rose for indigenous resources with high immediate utilitarian value, such as timber, wool, fish, grain, and minerals, which catered to a rising population. The discovery and use of coal as a cheaply available energy resource in 18th-century Northwestern Europe also helps explain why Europe, and not China, was the epicenter of the Industrial Revolution and eventual world economic dominance.[14] But it was the historical accident of the discovery of the New World, with its cornucopia of natural resources, that permitted Western Europe to become the world's central power by the end of Era II. The ability to tap new resources in the Americas with high use potential allowed Western European states to thrive long after their own natural resources had been spent.[15]

---

[10] Oded Galor & David N. Weil, *From Malthusian Stagnation to Modern Growth*, 89 AM. ECON. REV. 150, 150–54 (1999).

[11] *See, e.g.*, James A. Brander & M. Scott Taylor, *The Simple Economics of Easter Island: A Ricardo-Malthus Model of Renewable Resource Use*, 88 AM. ECON. REV. 119, 121–22, 131–32 (1998) (describing the collapse of the Mayan civilization due to deforestation and soil erosion, the demise of the Mesopotamian civilizations due to soil salinization, and the decline of the Chaco Anasazi in the southwestern United States due to soil degradation).

[12] Richerson & Boyd, *supra* note 1, at 19.

[13] *See generally* Ronald Findlay, *The Emergence of the World Economy*, *in* CONTEMPORARY ECONOMIC ISSUES: PROCEEDINGS OF THE ELEVENTH WORLD CONGRESS OF THE INTERNATIONAL ECONOMICS ASSOCIATION, TUNIS, at 82 (1998).

[14] *See generally* POMERANZ, *supra* note 4.

[15] Ronald Findlay, *The Roots of Divergence: Western Economic History in Comparative Perspective*, 82 AM. ECON. REV. 158, 158–61 (1992); Guido di Tella, *Economics of the Frontier*, *in* ECONOMICS IN THE LONG VIEW: ESSAYS IN HONOUR OF W.W. ROSTOW 210–27 (W.W. Rostow, Charles Poor Kingleberger & Guido di Tella eds., 1982).

Europe had another enormous advantage. Throughout much of Era II there existed no uniform authority that could halt bourgeoning trade and commercial development from taking place. As a result, decentralized, unsupervised markets arose, providing order and organization for the trades, exchanges, and transactions that were occurring, largely in natural resources.[16] Gradually, most of the regimes of Europe adopted a market economy. They provided the market with protection, legitimation, and nonarbitrary laws such as the law of contract, so that market players could make enforceable bargains and agreements. The efficient use of money and other commercial tools were also a hallmark of Era II markets.[17] The use of money replaced exchanges in a barter system, which lowered the considerable transaction costs involved in trade.[18]

The dominant market system that emerged in Era II swiftly replaced Era I community, tribal, and cultural norms.[19] Moreover, government regulation and centralized planning were not necessary for this economic system to function in an orderly way.[20] Instead, individuals and groups were free to make their own choices about the production, use, distribution, and consumption of natural resources, where economic decisions were made by buyers and sellers of goods and services. In such a competitive system, production tended to flow toward what societies valued most, which was resource use and development.[21] This drive to use resources occurred either when individuals acted alone, or when they discovered the synergistic potential of cooperation, coordination, and division of labor. Natural resources were exploited because entrepreneurs and other market participants sought to maximize profits, wealth, and individual welfare in the short run, often at an unsustainable rate for the long run.[22]

---

[16] Paul Kennedy, The Rise and Fall of the Great Powers: Economic Change and Military Conflict From 1500–2000, at 20–21 (1988).

[17] Douglas C. North & Robert Paul Thomas, The Rise of the Western World: A New Economic History 54–55 (1973).

[18] A person wishing to buy something in a barter system has to find someone who has the sought-after item and who wishes to convey it away, and who also wants something processed by the buyer. This is referred to as a "double coincidence of wants." Sreekala Kochugovindan & Nicolaas J. Vriend, *Is the Study of Complex Adaptive Systems Going to Solve the Mystery of Adam Smith's "Invisible Hand"?* 3 Ind. Rev. 53, 53–66 (1998). A search for that exact combination is not only costly, it will prevent many beneficial exchanges from occurring at all. The use of money, by contrast, facilitates the drawing up of contracts, and reduces the quantity of goods that need to be held for purposes of exchange.

[19] *See generally* Karl Polanyi, The Great Transformation: The Political and Economic Origins of Our Time (2001).

[20] When Era II cultures attempted to manage resources through central planning, the result too often was cultural and resource collapse. Vernon L. Scarborough, *Resilience, Resource Use, and Socioeconomic Organization, in* Environmental Disaster and the Archaeology of Human Response 195, 205 (Garth Bawden & Richard Martin Reycraft eds., 2000).

[21] Richerson & Boyd, *supra* note 6, at 18; Tom Tietenberg, *The Tradable Permits Approach to Protecting the Commons: What Have We Learned, in* The Drama of the Commons 197, 200 (Elinor Ostrom et al., Committee on the Human Dimensions of Global Change eds., 2002); Leonard Zobler, *An Economic-Historical View of Natural Resource Use and Conservation,* 38 Econ. Geography 189, 192 (1962).

[22] Alan M. Taylor & Jeffrey G. Williamson, *Capital Flows to the New World as an Intergenerational Transfer*, 102 J. Pol. Econ. 348, 348–49 (1994).

Basic economic theory dictates that private landowners have an incentive to use resources at a rate that will allow them future use also.[23] However, during Era II, market failures contributed to resource depletion. Imperfect information resulting from gaps in scientific knowledge and awareness of resource regeneration rates led to suboptimal resource use, and in some cases, species extinction.[24] Price information must be allowed to clearly communicate scarcity so that rational actors can adjust their consumption accordingly.

Dispersed populations did not always facilitate the adequate transfer of price information. Another market failure, open access—also known as the commons problem—reflected the fact that most resources were not owned by any one person (*res nullius*), and were therefore subject to capture and use by those who somehow were able to seize control of natural goods.[25] Open access leads to inadequate resource allocation because there are diminishing marginal returns to each individual who subsequently uses the resource. Individuals have incentive to use more of a resource than what may be desirable for the greater good.[26] Resource overuse results when individuals cannot be excluded from using a resource. In other words, the resource is rivalrous, meaning no one can be excluded from using the resource, but there is competition for the resource itself. Examples of open access, or commons, prevalent during Era II included grazing livestock, harvesting timber, and catching fish. Such open access problems can be corrected by predictable and transferable property rights for all relevant commodities in the marketplace.[27] Throughout Era II, property rights in natural resources were nonexistent or ill-defined.[28]

B. The Theory of Games: Cooperative Games in the Age of the Market

When trying to capture the dynamics of a time when individuals by and large seemed to rely on the marketplace as an organizing institution for their resource choices, it is important to articulate the assumptions that must be made to understand market behavior and the rationale for the persistence of market failures. Under a classic Adam Smith *Wealth of Nations* market model, individuals make calculations based on the assumption that all agents behave rationally. The market model then presumes that if "societal" rules do not interfere with such individual actions, the

[23] *See generally* William J. Baumol & Wallace E. Oates, The Theory of Environmental Policy (2d ed. 1998).

[24] The hunting of whales nearly into extinction for the use of whale oil for energy is one such example of resource overuse. Ugo Bardi, *Prices and Production over a Complete Hubbert Cycle: The Case of the American Whale Fisheries in the 19th Century*, Energy Bull. (Nov. 24, 2004), http://www.energybulletin.net/node/3338.

[25] *See* Pierson v. Post, 3 Cai. 175, 178 (N.Y. Sup. Ct. 1805); Carol M. Rose, *Possession as the Origin of Property*, 52 U. Chi. L. Rev. 73, 73–74 (1985).

[26] Garrett Hardin, *The Tragedy of the Commons*, 162 Sci. 1243 (1968); Shi-Ling Hsu, *What Is a Tragedy of the Commons? Overfishing and the Campaign Spending Problem*, 69 Alb. L. Rev. 75, 77 (2005).

[27] Aviwash K. Dixit & Barry J. Nalebuff, *Thinking Strategically: The Competitive Edge in Business, Politics, and Everyday Life* 223–25 (1991); Roger B. Myerson, *Nash Equilibrium and the History of Economic Theory*, 38 J. of Economic Literature 1067, 1080 (1999).

[28] *See generally* Terry L. Anderson & Peter J. Hill, *The Race for Property Rights*, 33 J.L. & Econ. 177, (1990).

so-called "invisible hand" will promote the larger interests of the individual's society and the amount of a good consumed will be efficiently allocated for the future.[29]

However, if everyone in a relevant market does what is best for the individual, they might wind up with the worst result from their collective viewpoint. This is the lesson from the standard "prisoner's dilemma game," where self-interest and an inability to coordinate behavior or enforce prior agreements yields an outcome for each prisoner that is inferior compared to a strategy of mutual cooperation.[30] In a similar fashion, during Era II, it became increasingly apparent that the outcome for any individual actor depended not only on that actor's own rational and self-interested actions, but on the independent actions of others. Simply put, individuals maximize their own welfare, given the predicted behavior of other players.[31] Because game theory concerns the rational behavior of decision makers or players[32] whose decisions affect one another, it has been suggested that "interactive decision theory" might be a more descriptive name for the dynamic that became prominent in Era II—individuals dealing with other individuals with an interest in resources. This multiparty dynamic contrasts with Era I, where individuals usually made noninteractive—that is, unilateral—decisions about resources.[33]

Era II players had choices when confronting other players interested in using resources. A player attempting to maximize self-interest could independently compete for the resource to achieve individual control. Or, when there was more than one player coveting a resource, players could coordinate their strategies and form coalitions. Players choosing cooperation over appropriation were, in effect, deciding that the outcome of cooperation would yield more than acting alone.[34] By contrast, acting

---

[29] SMITH, *supra* note 20, at 292 ("And he is in this led by an invisible hand to promote an end which was no part of his intention. By pursuing his own interest, he frequently promotes that of the society . . . .").

[30] In the familiar prisoner's dilemma game, there are two prisoners and each is informed that the prisoner will receive a modest sentence if neither prisoner informs on the other; that the prisoner will be let free if that prisoner alone informs on the other prisoner, while the other prisoner will get a maximum sentence; and that both will receive a significant sentence short of the maximum if both inform on the other. Behaving rationally and selfishly, each will become an informant because, regardless of what the other prisoner does, each can reduce his or her sentence by being an informant. But, the potential superior outcome is that both remain silent, and thus both receive modest sentences. This outcome is not possible because the two prisoners cannot coordinate their behavior. This game was first defined by Merrill Meeks Flood and Melvin Dresher as part of a 100-trial game experiment at RAND Laboratories. MERILL M. FLOOD, A PREFERENCE EXPERIMENT (SERIES 2, TRIALS 2, 3, 4) (1952). In the 1950s, mathematician Albert Tucker coined the game "prisoner's dilemma," a name by which it is known today. T. Kippenberger, *The Prisoner's Dilemma*, 2 THE ANTIDOTE 8, 8–11 (1997).

[31] Baird et al., *supra* note 18, at 11. Game theory is the general analytical framework for doing rational choice analysis without the traditional market structures of goods and prices. A rational player in a game will choose an outcome that that player prefers, given what that player expects the other players in the game to do. Myerson, *supra* note 27, at 1068.

[32] The *decision theory model* assumes that individuals are rational decision makers who make decisions with the aim of furthering individual interests. *See* RESNIK, *supra* note 12, at 5 and accompanying text.

[33] Robert Aumann, *Game Theory*, *in* 3 THE NEW PALGRAVE 529 (Steven N. Durlauf & Lawrence E. Blume eds., 2008).

[34] A cooperative game is akin to a branch of decision theory that focuses on individuals making group decisions. With a group decision, an effort is made to not simply reflect what an individual does in a game to further that individual's own goals, but also to develop a policy that is applicable to all the participants. RESNIK, *supra* note

alone in order to appropriate the resource for just one player was redistributive—the player who acquired the resource was benefitted at the expense of competing players. Throughout Era II, and up to the present time, players for resources sometimes collaborated, cooperated, and made agreements with others out of self-interest.[35] When they did so, they were engaged in what game theoreticians call a "cooperative" game.[36]

Many Era II interactions can be characterized as cooperative games because first, the players were able to make credible agreements. Second, the cooperating players arranged themselves according to the amount of value each placed on a particular strategy. Third, stable resource use groups arose because the players realized that they would not do better by defecting to individual strategies.[37]

Such cooperative games required the players to make commitments to carry out particular strategies. Any commitment made in a cooperative game needed to be considered credible—that is, binding and enforceable—to the other players in the game. Credible agreements can be made if strong social norms are in place to urge players to keep their promises.[38] The invention of contracts, enforceable by a third party such as a court, helped the participants in a cooperative game to make truly credible commitments to cooperative strategies.[39]

Games in which the participants can make credible, enforceable agreements can yield a "cooperative solution" where the outcome of the game is best for all of the players who participate in the game. For an individual player, the agreement with the other players should not place that player in a position inferior to the position the player would be in absent the agreement. For the group, the agreement should

---

32, at 5 ("Unfortunately, it is frequently difficult to tell . . . when several individuals are choosing, whether they are involved in a [cooperative] game or in a group decision.").

[35] *See* Peter J. Richerson, Robert Boyd & Brian Paciotti, *An Evolutionary Theory of Commons Management*, *in* THE DRAMA OF THE COMMONS 403, 404–06 (Elinor Ostrom et al., Committee on the Human Dimensions of Global Change eds., 2002); ROBERT L. HEILBRONER, THE WORLDLY PHILOSOPHERS 27, 174–75 (6th ed. updated 1992) (discussing Francis Edgeworth's realization in the 19th century that people did not always behave according to market theory—in a purely independent competitive fashion—but instead formed groups that made agreements among their members). For a modern example of resource users entering into a cooperative game, see Sandra Zellmer, *The Anti-Speculation Doctrine and Its Implications for Collaborative Water Management*, 8 NEV. L.J. 994 (2008).

[36] CONTRIBUTION TO THE THEORY OF GAMES 13–42 (R.D. Luce & A.W. Tucker eds., 1959) (providing a translation of John von Neumann's introduction to cooperative games).

[37] *See generally* Theodore L. Turocy & Bernhard von Stengel, *Game Theory*, *in* ENCYCLOPEDIA OF INFORMATION SYSTEMS (2002); VON NEUMANN & MORGENSTERN, *supra* note 7. During Era II, cooperative games were perhaps best reflected by the amount of trade in natural resources that emerged. Before trading could occur, participants in the trade needed to cooperate as part of the transaction. *See generally* Ronald Findlay, *The Terms of Trade and Equilibrium Growth in the World Economy*, 70 AM. ECON. REV. 291 (1980); CARLO CIPOLLA, BEFORE THE INDUSTRIAL REVOLUTION: EUROPEAN SOCIETY AND ECONOMY 1000–1700 (1976).

[38] LEE BOLDEMAN, THE CULT OF THE MARKET: ECONOMIC FUNDAMENTALISM AND ITS DISCONTENTS, 245–68 (2007); ALAN WATSON, ROMAN LAW AND COMPARATIVE LAW 127–28 (1991).

[39] ROBERT COOTER & THOMAS ULEN, LAW & ECONOMICS 198 (4th ed. 2004) ("The first purpose of contract law is to enable people to cooperate by converting games with noncooperative solutions into games with cooperative solutions.") (emphasis omitted).

maximize the total possible utility produced by the agreement.[40] In other words, the outcome of the agreement should represent some Pareto optimal condition in which no party can be made better off without adversely affecting another party.[41]

One can illustrate how a cooperative game can be used to overcome an open access market failure when two users access a resource for the same purpose.[42] In this game, two shepherds each have a flock of sheep that graze on an unowned open access pasture. Each shepherd grazes sheep as often as possible and increases the size of the flock as frequently as possible. Initially, the two shepherds incur no additional cost for each sheep added to the flock, so both have an incentive to increase their respective flocks in order to increase their profits. The shepherds are not concerned about the other's flock until the total number of sheep grazing exceeds the feeding capacity of the pasture. Once the pasture is overgrazed, each sheep gains less weight because less feed is available, making the sheep less valuable at market.

Both shepherds eventually realize that the additional sheep reduced the grass available for the sheep each already owns. To improve the value of their flocks, the shepherds will realize that the number of sheep has to decrease. However, because neither shepherd has the right to exclude the other from the pasture, one shepherd is unlikely to reduce flock numbers unless the other shepherd does the same. They will therefore agree to a maximum number of sheep in each flock that will not deplete the pasture grass. One or the other may be tempted to breach this agreement. However, neither should breach if both shepherds communicate and each knows if the other breaches. In other words, if both shepherds have complete information, there should be no breach because user defection by both parties destroys the pasture, which is the resource each user needs to raise marketable sheep and to maintain livelihood. Because each realizes that the breach by one will bring about the breach of the other, leading to an overgrazed pasture, each shepherd's payoff will remain highest if neither breaches.

Figure 4.3 illustrates this cooperative game. If both users share the resource, both will benefit by receiving payoffs equal to 100. When one defects at the expense of the other, the defecting user gains more than a fair share, 110, while the nondefecting user loses, receiving -1, because the defecting user's sheep will eventually reduce the value of the herd of the nondefecting user, driving the herder from the pasture. When both defect, neither user profits because overuse destroys the resource. Such mutual defection results in a payoff of zero for both players. When both users cooperate according to the agreement, both receive the highest possible payoff; when neither cooperates, the ultimate payoff is zero. Although the equilibrium value is for

---

[40] Jules L. Coleman, Markets, Morals and the Law 102–03 (1988); Steven Shavell, Foundations of Economic Analysis of Law 293 (2004).

[41] Different negotiated agreements in a cooperative game may achieve a Pareto optimal result and maximize the total possible utility between the players, but distribute different amounts of gain among them. There is likely no one preferred negotiated distributional outcome between bargaining players achieving Pareto optimality in a cooperative game. 1 Brian Barry, A Treatise in Social Justice: Theories of Justice 33–41 (1989).

[42] *See* Daniel H. Cole & Peter Z. Grossman, *Institutions Matter! Why the Herder Problem Is Not a Prisoner's Dilemma*, 69 Theory & Decision 219, 224–29 (2010).

		Shepherd Two	
		Use/cooperate	Defect
Shepherd One	Use/cooperate	100 100	–1 110
	Defect	110 –1	0 0

FIGURE 4.3 Open access resource use: competitive grazing.

both shepherds to defect, the Pareto optimal solution is cooperation. A Pareto optimal solution is also likely because this game, often described as the Herders' Problem, can be iterative and take place over multiple time periods. The iterative nature allows herders to communicate and reach this solution.[43]

Note that the first shepherd's payoff is listed on the left of each box, while the second shepherd's payoff is listed on the right of each box. The box containing the Pareto optimal solution is highlighted.

The other common resource situation during Era II occurred when users had an interest in utilizing a resource for differing purposes. Similar to the game above, the users can cooperate and agree to share the resource, defect on the agreement and try to get more of the resource than the other user, or refuse to cooperate and try to use as much of the resource as possible, leading to the resource's destruction. Of the possible solutions to the problem, the users are better off if they choose to cooperate and share the land between them. When the users keep this agreement, Pareto optimality can be achieved and the users attain the highest collective payoff.

In this game, there is one parcel of unowned land. One user would like to graze livestock, while the other would like to grow wheat. One cannot graze livestock where the other is growing wheat. Both users want to maximize their production from the parcel of land in order to increase profit, and each user would therefore like to use the whole parcel of land. If one postpones using the resource for a season, the other user will use the unowned land for personal economic gain. Conflict between the two users arises when both express the desire to exploit the land resource for different purposes—grazing and wheat growing. Both users have an incentive not to cooperate with each other. Each user wants to take as much of the open land as fast as possible to maximize profit from either growing wheat or grazing. However, as neither user can exclude the other from the land, they may decide to share it. Both will then have the certainty of some profit at market.

[43] Elinor Ostrom, Governing the Commons: The Evolution of Institutions for Collective Action 58–102 (1990).

		Player 2: Livestock Producer	
		Use/cooperate	Defect
Player 1: Wheat Grower	Use/cooperate	100 100	–1 110
	Defect	110 –1	0 0

FIGURE 4.4 Resource use for different purposes.
Note that the number in each box on the left is the wheat grower's payoff; the number on the right is the livestock producer's payoff. The noncooperative solution is highlighted.

Alternatively, with no agreement to cooperate, the users risk reducing the land's productivity by simultaneously overgrazing on the wheat fields and destroying grazing land to grow wheat. Because the payoff for cooperation is better than the payoff for mutual defection, the users cooperate. Mutual defection destroys the land for both users, so by cooperating the users accomplish the best outcome.

In Figure 4.4, cooperation among the wheat grower and the livestock producer yields a Pareto optimal outcome (100 and 100). If one defects and tries to use more resource than the agreed amount, one user will then lose and the other will gain, but the payoff is not optimal (110 for the one defecting, and -1 for the one abiding by the agreement, because the defecting user destroys the nondefecting user's share of the land). As one player's overuse is the other's loss, when both overuse, neither attains any payoff because the resource becomes depleted.

Note that the number in each box on the left is the wheat grower's payoff; the number on the right is the livestock producer's payoff. The noncooperative solution is highlighted.

C. The Problem of Open Access and the Law of the Rush

Although cooperative games in the Age of the Market were an efficient way for resource players to allocate land and stock commodities among competing users, there were serious impediments that prevented such games from becoming the dominant structure of allocation. Cooperative games form spontaneously through ad hoc contracting where parties renegotiate inefficient entitlements to achieve an optimally efficient allocation.[44] Such collective action is more likely when the property rights are clearly defined, when the number of parties is small, when the parties

[44] *See generally* Ronald H. Coase, *The Problem of Social Cost*, 3 J.L. & ECON. 1 (1960).

have similar expectations regarding the net gains of agreement, when there is little uncertainty regarding the size and distribution of costs and benefits, and when the aggregate gains of taking action are large relative to the costs.[45] This is often referred to as a "Coasian bargain."[46] Perhaps even more important, the sought-after common resource was likely to be of high value, subject not only to contract law, but to a system of predictable property rights, whether informal or formal, group or individual.[47]

During the Age of the Market, resources were often commodities such as forage and grasslands that were part of open access or common pool regimes.[48] When there is a lack of clear property rights to resources, open access tends to prevail. In such a situation, resource users do not bear the full costs of their actions, aggregate short-term production and use levels are too high, and competing users inflict costs on one another with externalities.[49] Cooperation gives way to a competitive rush to exploit the resource before another user gets there and uses it first. As group size grows, transaction, information, and compliance and enforcement costs rise, and resource users find that they cannot negotiate with each other to constrain wasteful behavior. In "tragedy of the commons" settings, there are few price signals to reveal opportunity costs, and free riding and other forms of strategic behavior become common, thus preventing efficient bargains.[50] It is one striking characteristic of open access—the inability of any user (or group of users) to enforce their management decisions against any other user—that prevents conservation of the resource for future use.[51]

During Era II, when property rights to natural resources were unformed or incomplete, there often was a race to capture previously unclaimed land and resources.[52] Moreover, when many individuals are competing to establish some kind of possessory use interest in a natural resource, they typically incur high costs in claiming and securing their possessory rights. Distracted by the need first to capture land and resources, and then to enforce boundaries, Era II resource players likely often failed to consider the advantage of cooperation and coordination as an alternative to the "law of the rush." Resource quality problems associated with the resulting resource overuse—for example, declining productivity of an estuary, increased soil erosion

---

[45] *Id.*

[46] These conditions characterize successful negotiating efforts among relatively homogeneous small groups. Elinor Ostrom, *Self-Governance of Common-Pool Resources*, *in* 3 THE NEW PALGRAVE DICTIONARY OF ECONOMICS AND THE LAW 424–32 (Peter Newman ed., 1998).

[47] Steven N. S. Cheung, *The Structure of a Contract and the Theory of a Non-Exclusive Resource*, 13 J.L. & ECON. 49, 52–54 (1970).

[48] S.V. Ciriacy-Wantrup & Richard C. Bishop, *"Common Property" as a Concept in Natural Resources Policy*, 15 NAT. RESOURCES J. 713, 718–19 (1975).

[49] Hsu, *supra* note 26, at 77.

[50] Hardin, *supra* note 26, at 1244–46; Amitai Aviram, *A Paradox of Spontaneous Formation: The Evolution of Private Legal Systems*, 22 YALE L. & POL'Y REV. 1, 10 (2004).

[51] JAMES WILLARD HURST, LAW AND THE CONDITIONS OF FREEDOM IN THE NINETEENTH CENTURY UNITED STATES 7 (1956); Ciriacy-Wantrup & Bishop, *supra* note 48, at 718–19; DANIEL H. COLE, POLLUTION AND PROPERTY 6 (2002).

[52] Poorly defined property rights, as existed during Era II, are classically viewed as a contributing factor to open access resources. *See, e.g.*, James A. Brander & M. Scott Taylor, *International Trade and Open-Access Renewable Resources: The Small Open Economy Case*, 30 CAN. J. ECON. 526, 529 (1997).

due to unchecked grazing practices, or damage to public goods such as watershed quality—were also prominent.[53]

As a consequence, Era II was a time when natural resource entrepreneurs both consumed vast quantities of stock natural resources and accelerated consumption rates of renewable resources.[54] So great was the alteration of the natural world during this time that some have recommended that we speak of a "second nature" that occurred at the end of Era II: a time when the interactions of humans with the natural environment were so profoundly anthropogenic that the pristine nature of our collective imagination was forever transformed.[55] For example, deforestation was rampant during Era II, in part because of a growing need for agricultural land and timber for fuel and building.[56] Equally, there was regional depletion of essential natural resources—such as minerals, arable land, and fresh water—which caused out-migration and the collapse of established civilizations.[57]

It increasingly became apparent that there was a need to update rules and applicable laws to adapt to changing needs and expectations for natural resources. The law of contract had limited benefit for increasing social coordination in this respect. Gradually, resource overuse and depletion by growing populations unable to solve the effects of open access conditions by cooperative games alone led to an endogenous process of property rights establishment.[58]

Where people lived and worked together and shared a sense of identity and belonging, and where they shared some level of dependence on a natural resource, collective action was possible and common property regimes initially arose.[59] As contrasted with non-property or open access situations, where a resource initially has no owner and no one has a right to exclude anyone else, *common property* refers to collective ownership arrangements. With common property, the owners cannot exclude each other from the commons but can exclude outsiders.

Eventually, as new market actors gained access to resources, including common pool resources, they began to seek to privatize such resources to ensure the value of their claims.[60] By the end of Era II, the privatization of the commons and the

---

[53] C.C. Gibson & C.D. Becker, *A Lack of Institutional Demand: Why a Strong Local Economy in Western Ecuador Fails to Protect its Forest*, *in* PEOPLE AND FORESTS: COMMUNITIES, INSTITUTIONS AND GOVERNANCE 135–61 (Clark C. Gibson et al. eds., 2000).

[54] Zobler, *supra* note 21, at 192.

[55] *See generally* Alan L. Kolata, *Environmental Thresholds and the "Natural History" of an Andean Civilization*, *in* ENVIRONMENTAL DISASTER AND THE ARCHAEOLOGY OF HUMAN RESPONSE 163 (Garth Bawden & Richard Martin Reycraft eds., 2000).

[56] Mark G. Macklin, Clive Bonsall, Fay M. Davies & Mark Robinson, *Human-Environment Interactions During the Holocene: New Data and Interpretations from the Oban Area, Argyll, Scotland*, 10 HOLOCENE 118–19 (2000), *available at* http://hol.sagepub.com/content/10/1/109.full.pdf.

[57] Linda Cordell, *Aftermath of Chaos in the Pueblo Southwest*, *in* ENVIRONMENTAL DISASTER AND THE ARCHAEOLOGY OF HUMAN RESPONSE 179, 189 (Garth Bawden & Richard Martin Reycraft eds., 2000).

[58] *See generally* Terry L. Anderson & Peter J. Hill, *The Race for Property Rights*, 33 J.L. & ECON. 177 (1990).

[59] *See* Michael Taylor & Sarah Singleton, *Common Property, Collective Action and Community*, 4 J. THEORETICAL POL. 309 (1992); OSTROM, *supra* note 43, at 68–98.

[60] *See generally* William Ascher & Robert Healy, NATURAL RESOURCE POLICY MAKING IN DEVELOPING COUNTRIES: ENVIRONMENT, ECONOMIC GROWTH, AND INCOME DISTRIBUTION (1990).

conversion of resources into valuable saleable commodities was becoming the norm. A new body of law developed to protect such individual resource claims: the law of private property. Individuals with private property held rights to use, to dispose, and to exclude others from the resource. With the advent of private property, the tragedy of the commons was partially corrected, although this type of market failure continued within some groups.

Era I was a time when there were, in effect, a series of one-person games, or games where a single player made decisions about survival in nature and the use of natural resources. Formal laws were largely nonexistent, and societal norms and customs guided behavior. Individual Era I decisions about resources could be analyzed using decision theory.[61] In Era II, individuals continued their acquisitive relationship with natural resources, but their interactions increasingly involved other individuals engaged in making strategic decisions about resources. Sometimes arrangements between individuals interested in resources could be negotiated by contract and bargain, where the resulting agreement could be likened, in game theoretic terms, to a cooperative game.[62]

Despite the fact that such games could yield a collectively optimal result, implementation problems drew Era II individuals away from the cooperation that would have, in the long run, served them best. With open access resources such as land, timber, minerals, fish, and wildlife, if the costs of cooperating with competing users are high,[63] rational self-interest encourages independent noncooperative behavior.[64] The assumption becomes that any one user can do better either by not cooperating initially, or by defecting from a cooperative agreement.[65] When natural resources are overconsumed or exploited, the indirect and nonuse values are compromised.[66]

---

[61] *See generally* RESNIK, *supra* note 32.

[62] *See* NORTH & THOMAS, *supra* note 17, at 9 ("In one sense [Era II] may be defined as an arrangement of society based on contract, expressed or implied.") (quoting C.W. PREVITE ORTON, THE SHORTER CAMBRIDGE MEDIEVAL HISTORY 418–19 (1952)).

[63] *See* OSTROM, *supra* note 46, at 424–32; Cheung, *supra* note 47, at 52–54.

[64] *See* H. Scott Gordon, *The Economic Theory of a Common-Property Resource: The Fishery*, 62 J. POL. ECON. 124, 128–35 (1954); Hardin, *supra* note 26, at 1244–47; Hsu, *supra* note 26, at 77; LEN FISHER, ROCK, PAPER, SCISSORS: GAME THEORY IN EVERYDAY LIFE 4–5 (2008).

[65] Fisher, *supra* note 64.

[66] For example, if the earth's atmosphere is not polluted by anthropogenic greenhouse gases, the resulting indirect use value associated with an unpolluted atmosphere moderates temperatures, sea levels, precipitation patterns, glacial and sea ice melting, and so forth. Human use of that open access resource in the form of atmospheric emissions has likely adversely impaired the naturally occurring indirect uses of atmospheric gases. *See* Peter M. Vitousek, Harold A. Mooney, Jane Lubchenco & Jerry M. Melillo, *Human Domination of Earth's Ecosystems*, 277 SCI. 494 (1997). However, our efforts to resolve this threat of climate change and global warming will be hampered by the same logic that encouraged resource overuse and noncooperation during Era II—polluting nations will logically believe there is little incentive to control their carbon emissions so long as other nations with access to the resource continue to pollute. *See* Geoffrey Lean, *A World Dying, But Can We Unite to Save It?* INDEPENDENT U.K., Nov. 18, 2007, *available at* http://www.independent.co.uk/environment/climate-change/a-world-dying-but-can-we-unite -to-save-it-400847.html. Even Garrett Hardin recognized that the absence of property rights can lead to pollution and the degradation of resource nonuse values. Hardin, *supra* note 80, at 1245.

5 Era III—The Age of Property

COMPETITIVE NATURAL RESOURCE use, coupled with a rudimentary awareness of suboptimal consumption, ultimately led to a paradigm shift that ushered in a new era, Era III. This era witnessed the rise of legally protected ownership rights to the natural world and the emergence of the Age of Property. Although the idea of property in land and natural resources had been manifested in different European countries for centuries,[1] the practice became firmly embedded as an integral part of successful economies, including the United States, by the 19th century.[2] From the early 19th century through the middle of the 20th century, the concept of a property right in a resource both moderated the effect of the open access tragedies experienced in Era II and allowed the owner to fully exploit the use component of the resource now under the owner's control.[3]

During the Age of Property, there was no single, centralized decision maker. Instead, there were many asset owners and entrepreneurs who released the use potential of resources by exercising their individual use choices through the market. In such a system, legal rights needed to be assigned to market actors who could use the resources

---

[1] DOUGLAS C. NORTH & ROBERT PAUL THOMAS, THE RISE OF THE WESTERN WORLD: A NEW ECONOMIC HISTORY 19–24 (1973).

[2] David Feeny, *The Development of Property Rights in Land: A Comparative Study*, *in* TOWARD A POLITICAL ECONOMY OF DEVELOPMENT: A RATIONAL CHOICE PERSPECTIVE 272 (Brain Barr et al. eds., 1988); Harold Demsetz, *Toward a Theory of Property Rights*, 57 AM. ECON. REV. 347, 350–53 (1967).

[3] Leonard Zobler, *An Economic-Historical View of Natural Resource Use and Conservation*, 38 ECON. GEOGRAPHY 189, 190 (1962).

most productively, and the costs of transfers needed to be low enough to encourage exchanges that placed the resource in the hands of one who would optimize use. This result could occur only if there was an appropriate system of property rights.[4]

Although the advent of property helped to stem the rush to exploit unowned open access resources, other laws and legal institutions increased the discount rate, which in turn encouraged resource exploitation.[5] As a result, resource development slowly intensified during Era III. The rate of exploitation was often greater than regeneration rates, and resource substitutes were often available, as was the case for substituting coal for wood as a source of energy.[6] Although property rights could facilitate an efficient Coasian bargain, such rights were often not clearly defined for large resources such as watersheds or air space. As a result, resource use also created negative externalities for large groups, where users imposed costs upon a larger group that had a stake in the resource. For example, water pollution and soil erosion resulting from unsustainable agricultural practices or acid mine drainage often contaminated the indirect use and ecological qualities of water.[7] Other resources were exploited because they were public goods incapable of being owned, such as the atmosphere, where individual firms could pollute the good's indirect use and natural nonuse capacities.[8] Some resources were prone to overuse because they were congestible goods, such as rangelands, capable of being shared at a low marginal cost until a certain congestion point was reached.[9] The reality is, then, that the development of property in Era III did not bring about conservation of resources; resources were still used, and overused, despite the removal of most open access conditions.

Another collateral consequence of property regimes is that conflicts emerged among competing classes of property interests. Resources became owned by individuals and groups subject to two basic property regimes: Common property (*res communes*) refers to collective ownership situations, in which the owners of the resource cannot exclude each other but can exclude outsiders. Private property (*res privatae*), on the other hand, describes resources owned by individuals who can use, transfer, and exclude others.[10] When these different regimes had an interest in the same

---

[4] Ronald H. Coase, Nobel Prize Lecture: The Institutional Structure of Production (Dec. 9, 1991), NOBEL LECTURES, ECONOMICS 1991–1995 (T. Persson ed., 1997).

[5] James Willard Hurst, *Law and Conditions of Freedom in the Nineteenth Century United States* 7 (1965) ("[Nineteenth century Americans] had in common a deep faith in the social benefits to flow from a rapid increase in productivity; all shared an impatience to get on with the job by whatever means seemed functionally adapted to it, including the law.") (footnote omitted).

[6] CAROL A. DAHL, INTERNATIONAL ENERGY MARKETS: UNDERSTANDING PRICING, POLICY, AND PROFITS 16–37 (2004).

[7] *See, e.g.,* PIERS BLAIKIE, THE POLITICAL ECONOMY OF SOIL EROSION IN DEVELOPING COUNTRIES (1986). The alarm over human impairment of nature's nonuse benefits was raised much earlier, in Era III, in GEORGE PERKINS MARSH, MAN AND NATURE: OR, PHYSICAL GEOGRAPHY AS MODIFIED BY HUMAN ACTION (1864).

[8] DANIEL H. COLE & PETER Z. GROSSMAN, PRINCIPLES OF LAW & ECONOMICS 316 (2005).

[9] *See generally* Terry L. Anderson & Peter J. Hill, *The Evolution of Property Rights: A Study of the American West*, 18 J.L. & ECON. 163 (1975).

[10] DANIEL W. BROMLEY, ENVIRONMENT AND ECONOMY: PROPERTY RIGHTS AND PUBLIC POLICY 31 (1991).

resource, such as water or land in the New World, some system needed to arise to sort out relative priorities among them.

A parallel property rights conflict occurred when private property interests were created. Private ownership of a resource meant that two classes of interests in a resource were necessarily created: owners who could exclude others from using the resource, and nonowners. Nonowners, in turn, were comprised of two groups. First, a nonowner could be one who might have wished to use the resource now controlled by the owner, for either a similar or different purpose, but as a nonowner was precluded by law from doing so. Second, a nonowner could be one who did not wish to directly use the resource, but who could receive indirect use benefits, such as clean water, from the owner's property, but could not because of the owner's use. Such a nonowner was harmed by the use, and would have benefitted from the owner's nonuse.

When owners and nonowners came into conflict over the appropriate or preferred use or nonuse of resources, "resource popularity conflict" emerged.[11] Such a conflict might arise if a resource was deemed valuable for uses similar to the owner's, for uses different than the owner's, or for not being used at all. A system needed to be created to permit owners and nonowners to work through their different—and sometimes clashing—interests in land and resources.

In the Age of the Market, resource players were sometimes able to make enforceable agreements with other players, resulting in a cooperative game. If the transaction costs were sufficiently low to permit a cooperative game, then players could as a group fully commit themselves to specific resource-use strategies. In contrast, in the Age of Property, holders of legally protected property interests in land and resources usually had no need to make a collective commitment to some resource strategy. The process of making resource use or nonuse choices was relatively simple for those with a private property interest—the choices were made out of their own self-interest, irrespective of the interests of other property owners, or nonowners—especially nonowners who were somehow harmed by the owner's use. The resulting games were noncooperative, and an understanding of Era III resource strategies is best studied in light of noncooperative game theory.[12]

A. The Rise of Property

In Europe, and then in America, the idea of property was grounded in several assumptions. One was advanced by John Locke, who argued that ownership over a

---

[11] *See* Jan G. Laitos & Rachael Gamble, *The Problem with Wilderness*, 32 HARV. ENVTL. L. REV. 503, 506, 527–31 (2008) (explaining that a resource popularity conflict exists when there is more than one group that wishes to use an area, the groups wish to use it—or not use it—in different and incompatible ways, and applicable law permits one group of users but excludes others); *see, e.g.*, PAUL GATES, HISTORY OF PUBLIC LAND LAW DEVELOPMENT 466–68 (1968) (discussing conflicts between stockmen who acquired a property right in rangelands for their cattle and settlers who wanted to use that same land to homestead and farm).

[12] Aviwash K. Dixit and Barry J. Nalebuff, *Thinking Strategically: The Competitive Edge in Business, Politics, and Everyday Life* 70–76 (1991); Alvin E. Roth, *Editor's Introduction and Overview*, *in* GAME-THEORETIC MODELS OF BARGAINING 1–2 (Alvin E. Roth ed., 1985).

resource—particularly land—could arise through individual labor.[13] But perhaps the most central assumption involves the workings of a market-based economic system. One may presume that such a system will permit market actors to exercise rights to perform certain actions with resources—and to negotiate exchanges regarding resources—but only if there are zero or de minimis transaction costs. In a real world of positive and often high transaction costs, individuals in the market can take steps to increase the value of resources and of resource production if rights are assigned to those who can use them most productively, with incentives that induce them to do so, and the costs of rights transference to others are relatively low. Only an appropriate system of property rights, legitimized and enforced by the law, can bring about this result.[14] The kind of property interest that is most consistent with a perfectly functioning market is a private property right to land and resources, encompassing the right of the owner to use this property to the exclusion of others, with the ability to transfer it to another.[15]

Private property was not necessarily the first type of property interest to rise out of open access. Common or communal property, involving the exclusion of all but a group of insiders from access to some common resource, was probably the first kind of property regime to emerge.[16] There were, however, several problems with common property systems. If the multiple owners did not have any internal structure of governance, they competed with one another for resource appropriation, resulting in an overuse of the resource similar to what had occurred on a smaller scale when open access was the norm. Although the owners could have agreed upon some rules of use by engaging in a cooperative game, there was always a tendency to defect from any agreement, especially if individual self-interest suggested a better short-term outcome.[17] Even if the initial transaction costs of cooperation were surmountable,

---

[13] William B. Scott, In Pursuit of Happiness: American Conceptions of Property from the Seventeenth to the Twentieth Century 31 (1977). Locke also advocated the position that property was not necessarily something exclusively created by government, and that, indeed, property rights existed prior to government. John Locke, Two Treatises of Government (Peter Laslett ed., 1988). Of course, other Era III philosophers, such as Jeremy Bentham, did not share Locke's views on the origin of property. Bentham, for example, insisted that property cannot exist without government. Ellen Frankel Paul, Moral Revolution and Economic Science 50 (1979). Debates about the true origins of property rights continue to this day. *See, e.g.*, Saul Levmore, *Two Stories about the Evolution of Property Rights* 31 J. Legal Stud. S421 (2002); Katrina Miriam Wyman, *From Fur to Fish: Reconsidering the Evolution of Private Property*, 80 N.Y.U. L. Rev. 117 (2005). Irrespective of the exact source of property rights, only rights to resources that have been given official recognition by formal legal instrumentalities will likely be sustained if challenged in an administrative or judicial setting. Edella Schlager & Elinor Ostrom, *Property-Rights Regimes and Natural Resources: A Conceptual Analysis*, 68 Land Econ. 249, 252 (1992) (contrasting *de jure* property rights, which are acknowledged by government institutions, with *de facto* rights that originate among property owners who cooperate to define rights themselves).

[14] Ronald H. Coase, *The Institutional Structure of Production*, *in* Nobel Lectures: Economic Sciences 1991–1995, at 11–20 (Torsten Persson ed., 1997).

[15] NORTH & THOMAS, *supra* note 1, at 91.

[16] Thráinn Eggertsson, *Open Access versus Common Property*, *in* Property Rights: Cooperation, Conflict, and Law 74–82, 84–85 (Terry L. Anderson & Fred S. McChesney eds., 2003).

[17] Len Fisher, *Rock,Paper, Scissors: Game Theory in Everyday Life* 4–5 (2008).

post-agreement enforcement and monitoring costs must have been considerable. Moreover, trespassing from outsiders would have increased the uncertainty about appropriate use levels for joint owners.[18]

Common property regimes typically were successful when the resource was a common-pool resource such as a pasture or a fishery.[19] Even then, certain contextual and historic conditions had to be present before the communal property was enduring.[20] What instead distinguished the Age of Property was the balkanization and privatization of land, resources, and natural assets. Ownership in Era III became individual, not shared, and the dominant property interest became private, not common.[21]

The division of a commons or open-access resource into individual parcels occurred in different ways in different parts of the world. In America, the law of property tended to reward individual initiative; ownership went to those who seized and claimed the resource. This notion of capture, similar to Locke's labor theory, slowly transformed open-access conditions into a multitude of private ownership interests. Individuals acquired, by possession and use, property rights in land,[22] and to natural resources such as minerals,[23] water,[24] forage,[25] and even wild game.[26] Applicable laws legitimated these interests, providing their owners with security and enforcement mechanisms should claim jumpers and competitors emerge.[27]

For most natural resources, especially land, the property interest consisted of several operational rights held by the owner. Among the most important were the right to defined *boundaries* around the owned interest, the right to *access* and *use* the resource, the right to *exclude* others from it, and the right of alienation (i.e., sale, transfer, and lease). In common property regimes, different individual owners could possess some, but not all, of these rights.[28] With private property, an owner

---

[18] S.V. Ciriacy-Wantrup & Richard Bishop, *"Common Property" as a Concept in Natural Resources Policy* 15 NAT. RESOURCES J. 713 (1975); Michael Taylor, *The Economics and Politics of Property Rights and Common Pool Resources*, 32 NAT. RESOURCES J. 633 (1992).

[19] *See, e.g.*, Robert McC. Netting, *Of Men and Meadows: Strategies for Alpine Land Use*, 45 ANTHROPOLOGICAL Q. 132, 139–41 (1972); Wyman, *supra* note 13, at 126.

[20] Elinor Ostrom, *Governing the Commons: The Evolution of Institutions for Collective Action* 90–102 (1990); DANIEL H. COLE, POLLUTION & PROPERTY 112–20 (2002).

[21] *See* Yoram Barzel, *Property Rights in the Firm, in* PROPERTY RIGHTS: COOPERATION, CONFLICT, AND THE LAW 43, 43–57 (Terry L. Anderson & Fred S. McChesney eds., 2003); Demsetz, *supra* note 2, at 355–57.

[22] *See, e.g.*, Homestead Act of 1862, ch. 75, 12 Stat. 392 (repealed 1976).

[23] John Umbeck, *Might Makes Rights: A Theory of the Formation and Initial Distribution of Property Rights*, 19 ECON. INQUIRY 38, 40–43 (1981); General Mining Act of 1872, ch. 152, 17 Stat. 91.

[24] Anderson & Hill, *supra* note 9, at 176–78.

[25] *See generally* TERRY L. ANDERSON & PETER J. HILL, THE NOT SO WILD, WILD WEST: PROPERTY RIGHTS ON THE FRONTIER (2004).

[26] William T. Hornaday, *The Extermination of the American Bison, in* U.S. NATIONAL MUSEUM: ANNUAL REPORT 493 (1887) *microformed on* Western Americana: Frontier History of the Trans-Mississippi West, 1550–1900 No. 2661; 4 ERNEST T. SETON, LIVES OF GAME ANIMALS 451 (1937).

[27] NORTH & THOMAS, *supra* note 1, at 7 ("[G]overnments [in Era IV] were able to define and enforce property rights at a lower cost than could voluntary groups, and . . . these gains became even more pronounced as markets expanded.").

[28] OSTROM, *supra* note 20, at 250–54.

typically held all of these rights, with the rights of use and exclusion being the most critical.[29]

As a private property owner was not only given the right to exclude all others, but the exclusive use of the property interest, two implications followed. First, with private property came two classes of individuals interested in natural resources—owners and nonowners. Second, the exact nature and extent of the resource use was subject to the sole discretion of the owner. In Era III, where resource use was to dominate, owners and nonowners typically agreed that a resource should be used. If there was disagreement, it would likely have been over competing uses, not over whether the resource should be used at all. Similarly, as ownership and resource use were basically coterminous, there were little or no limits within the property right itself to deter overuse.

B. Resource Overuse and Large Group Externalities

It is an irony of private property that its creation was in part based on the assumption that open access resources would be unsustainably exploited unless some property regime was imposed for their protection.[30] However, rational property owners in Era III not only failed to conserve resources, they tended to knowingly exploit them.[31] There were, and still are, several reasons for an owner's urge to use land and resources. First, most property rights are inherently use rights, giving the owner the freedom to exploit the resource's use component for his or her own benefit.[32] Second, consistent with standard economic theory, it would be entirely rational for owners of renewable resources (e.g., range, pasture, timber, fish, or game) to use their properties up to the point of resource extinguishment and exhaustion when the discount rate sufficiently exceeds the maximum reproductive potential of the resource, and an immediate profit can be made from harvesting the last remaining resource.[33] Third, owners often have a relatively high discount rate, encouraging them to discount future costs and benefits quite heavily. High discount rates lead to exploitation and eventual loss of natural resources, particularly when the science behind resource renewal rates is not

---

[29] Barzel, *supra* note 21, at 43; Richard Stroup & John Baden, *Property Rights and Natural Resource Management*, 2 Literature of Liberty: A Review of Liberal Thought 5–7 (1979), http://www.econlib.org/library/essays/LtrLbrty/strbdPR1.html (explaining that the right to use and the right to exert control over a resource is an important feature of a property right). The right of exclusion allows owners to decide who may enter a resource, which means they can capture for themselves (and for their offspring) the benefits from investments they undertake in a resource. Richard Posner, *Economic Analysis of Law*, *in* Economic Foundations of Property Law 12, 12–13 (Bruce A. Ackerman ed., 1975).

[30] Hardin, *supra* note 26, at 1247.

[31] Daniel W. Bromley, Environment and Economy: Property Rights and Public Policy 171 (1991); Thomas Michael Power, Lost Landscapes and Failed Economics: The Search for a Value of Place 138 (1996).

[32] 1 Richard R. Powell, Powell on Real Property § 11.01 (Michael Allen Wolf ed. 2007); Eric T. Freyfogle, *Context and Accommodation in Modern Property Law*, 41 Stan. L. Rev. 1529, 1530 (1989).

[33] Colin W. Clark, *The Economics of Overexploitation*, 181 Sci. 630, 630 (1973); Schlager & Ostrom, *supra* note 13, at 256.

known or readily available.[34] The slow but steady depletion of the resource use component during Era III, while not socially optimal, was consistent with the wishes of the private property owners—to maximize private but not social benefits.

The law of private property was developed and then adopted in large part to permit the owner of a potentially valuable property to have exclusive use rights, free from other competing use interests.[35] Although owners could, in theory, not use the resource they owned, that option was rarely exercised, either because there was no perceived value in an unused resource or because it was flatly discouraged by applicable legal doctrine.[36] As a matter of economic reality, a high Era III demand for raw materials rewarded decisions that maximized short-term profits for private entrepreneurs.[37] With some renewable resources such as fish, it even seemed rational for users to extinguish rather than conserve the resource.[38]

The Era III resource use path, coupled with a failure to protect nonuse values, led to three environmental consequences. First, the world began to deplete its stock natural resources, especially energy fuels and industrial minerals.[39] The main driver of this resource demand was the need of rapidly industrializing European economies, as well as the burgeoning economy of the United States,[40] to exploit the seemingly plentiful natural resources of the New World.[41] The strength of the international market meant that natural resources that were not being used within the parent country could be transformed into other forms of capital by being traded to countries that needed them for economic growth.[42]

Second, renewable biological resources such as fisheries, forests, and pasturelands became exploited. As a result of intensifying fishing efforts, one marine fishery after

---

[34] Colin W. Clark, *Profit Maximization and the Extinction of Animal Species*, 81 J. POL. ECON. 950, 951 (1973); Bruce A. Larson & Daniel W. Bromley, *Property Rights, Externalities, and Resource Degradation: Locating the Tragedy*, 33 J. DEV. ECON. 235 (1990).

[35] *See generally* Robert C. Ellickson, *Property in Land*, 102 YALE L.J. 1315, 1356 (1993).

[36] For example, western water law was and is characterized by a use-it-or-lose-it mentality that encouraged needless use in order to maintain rights, and punished conservation and nonuse, as saved water was often forfeited. *See, e.g.*, Colorado Water Conservancy Dist. v. Shelton Farms, Inc., 529 P.2d 1321 (Colo. 1974); Stephen F. Williams, *The Requirement of Beneficial Use as a Cause of Waste in Water Resource Development*, 23 NAT. RESOURCES J. 7 (1983).

[37] Zobler, *supra* note 3, at 190, 192.

[38] H. Scott Gordon, *The Economic Theory of a Common-Property Resource: The Fishery*, 62 J. POL. ECON. 124 (1954); Clark, *supra* note 34, at 950–51.

[39] John R. McNeil, *Resource Exploitation and Over-Exploitation: A Look at the 20th Century*, *in* EXPLOITATION AND OVER-EXPLOITATION IN SOCIETIES PAST AND PRESENT 51, 53–55 (Brigetta Benzing & Bernd Herrmann eds. 2003).

[40] The United States, spurred on by the nation's dreams of Manifest Destiny, also consumed its own land and natural resources on an unprecedented scale during Era III. Sandra Zellmer, *Sustaining Geographies of Hope: Cultural Resources on Public Lands*, 73 U. COLO. L. REV. 413, 425 (2002).

[41] Era III is often referred to as the "Golden Age of Resource-Based Development." EDWARD B. BARBIER, NATURAL RESOURCES AND ECONOMIC DEVELOPMENT 81–83 (2005); Alan Green & M.C. Urquhart, *Factor and Commodity Flows in the International Economy of 1870–1914: A Multi-Country View*, 36 J. ECON. HIST. 217, 247 (1976); Zobler, *supra* note 3, at 190.

[42] Ronald Findlay & Mats Lundahl, *Natural Resources, "Vent-For-Surplus," and the Staples Theory*, *in* FROM CLASSICAL ECONOMICS TO DEVELOPMENT ECONOMICS 68 (G. Meier ed. 1994).

another collapsed in Era III.[43] Forests and woodlands shrank, accounting for perhaps half of the net deforestation in world history.[44] Massive forest clearance reduced biodiversity, added carbon to the atmosphere, and exposed millions of square miles of soil to erosion. Rangelands and pasturelands become overgrazed, degrading or destroying naturally occurring grasslands along with the considerable ecological values provided when these resources are not used as a commodity.[45]

Third, raw population growth, worldwide industrialization, and increasing combustion of fossil fuels for energy use required that the inevitable waste products of this resource use and consumption be deposited somewhere. The atmosphere, the hydrosphere, and the earth's underground soils accepted the wastes and pollution of Era III. Because in most situations these naturally occurring resources were not owned (and in the case of air and many waters, not capable of ownership), the market's pricing mechanism did not provide useful signals to those seeking a free depository for the growing amount of pollution that was being produced.[46] As a result, pollutants accumulated faster than they could be absorbed, recycled, or dissipated. As Era III closed out in middle of the 20th century, environmental goods with enormous nonuse value—such as the atmosphere, hydrosphere, and even the earth itself—were receiving overloads of pollutants, with increasingly disturbing consequences for both ecosystems and humans.[47]

Resource owners and users in Era III were predictably acting in their own self-interest. Unfortunately, in overconsuming or overusing their resources, or exploiting public environmental goods such as the atmosphere, they imposed externalities upon a larger group that also had some stake in the resource. An externality occurs when some market activity, such as resource use, affects third parties who are not participants in that market activity, and there is an imposed cost on an outside party. In other words, an externality is more formally defined as an "unintended spillover effect," where the costs or benefits of the activity are not adequately reflected in the price of the good. When numerous parties experience the spillover effect but are not responsible for the harm-producing activity, the result is a large group negative externality.[48]

---

[43] *See* Jeremy B.C. Jackson et al., *Historical Overfishing and the Recent Collapse of Coastal Ecosystems*, 293 SCI. 629 (2001). *See also* McNeill, *supra* note 39, at 58 ("Since the late 1980s, all marine fisheries have been exploited at or above sustainable levels.").

[44] SING C. CHEW, WORLD ECOLOGICAL DEGRADATION: ACCUMULATION, URBANIZATION AND DEFORESTATION, 3000 B.C.–A.D. 2000, AT 3 (2001); J.R. MCNEILL, SOMETHING NEW UNDER THE SUN: AN ENVIRONMENTAL HISTORY OF THE TWENTIETH CENTURY WORLD 229–37 (2000); DAVID EVANS, A HISTORY OF NATURE CONSERVATION IN BRITAIN 57 (2d ed. 1992).

[45] COLE, *supra* note 20, at 97 (explaining that in the early 20th century, Great Britain "had the smallest percentage of forested land—just 3 percent—of any country in Europe"); *see generally* Joseph M. Feller & David E. Brown, *From Old-Growth Forests to Old-Growth Grasslands: Managing Rangelands for Structure and Function*, 42 ARIZ. L. REV. 319 (2000); LAITOS ET AL., NATURAL RESOURCE LAW 464–65 (2006).

[46] COLE, *supra* note 20, at 2 ("In the absence of property rights to protect them, environmental goods have been abused, sometimes to the point of destruction.").

[47] McNeill, *supra* note 39, at 55–56.

[48] COLE & GROSSMAN, *supra* note 8, at 14; Hsu, *supra* note 26, at 78.

In Era III, the large group externality affected nonowners. They were either nonowners who wanted to use the resource in a way different than the owner's use (or at another point in time), or who would have preferred that the resource not be used at all. For the first of these classes, the externality generated by the owner's use negatively impacted the interests, or presumed profits, of the nonowner, the would-be user of the resource. An example of this kind of externality is evident when an owner of subsurface minerals extracts them and negatively affects the surface use of the land for agriculture. For nonowners who benefitted from the resource in its natural state, the externality generated by the owner's use was the resulting degradation of nonuse values and benefits from indirect use.

There was a large group temporal externality as well, because a suboptimal rate of resource use also imposed negative costs on future resource users, who lost future access to resources such as virgin forests. Although commentators have pointed out that domestication of nature took place over thousands of years,[49] the rate by which the human footprint affected natural settings intensified greatly during Era III. Such unprecedented human use forces future generations to engage in resource-protective practices in order to maintain ecosystem service benefits. Heightened resource management, particularly in agricultural areas, perpetuated a profound long-term cycle of necessary management of human-altered ecosystems by means of controlling fire, pests, and invasive species. The human imprint shifted the balance of the ecosystem, creating a new burden on future generations to continue these land management strategies.[50]

The two most immediate large group externalities to arise in Era III involved the exploitation of renewable biological resources and the pollution of public goods such as the atmosphere and hydrosphere. Deforestation, overfishing, drained wetlands, and grasslands removal had short-term effects on nonowners who otherwise would have benefitted from the indirect services and existence value provided by healthy forests,[51] sustainable fisheries,[52] functioning wetlands,[53] and natural rangelands.[54] Air and water pollution, as well as the toxic contamination of land, had very real health effects on individuals who did not own, and therefore had no control over, the enterprises responsible for the waste disposal practices.[55] The consequences

[49] *See* Peter Kareiva et al., *Domesticated Nature: Shaping Landscapes and Ecosystems for Human Welfare*, 316 SCI. 1866, 1866–67 (2007); *see also* Eric W. Sanderson et al., *The Human Footprint and the Last of the Wild*, 52 BIOSCIENCE 891, 892 (2002).

[50] *See generally* Fred P. Miller, *After 10,000 Years of Agriculture, Whither Agronomy?*, 100 AGRONOMY J. 22 (2008).

[51] JOHN COPELAND NAGLE & J.B. RUHL, THE LAW OF BIODIVERSITY AND ECOSYSTEM MANAGEMENT 435–41 (2d ed. 2006).

[52] McNeill, *supra* note 39, at 58.

[53] James Boyd & Lisa Wainger, *Measuring Ecosystem Service Benefits for Wetland Mitigation*, 24 NAT'L WETLANDS NEWSL. 11, 11–15 (2002).

[54] *See generally* DEBRA L. DONAHUE, THE WESTERN RANGE REVISITED: REMOVING LIVESTOCK FROM PUBLIC LANDS TO CONSERVE NATIVE BIODIVERSITY (1999).

[55] The most serious resource exploitation involved the use of the atmosphere, hydrosphere, and soils as sinks for all manner of pollutants, because there are no substitutes for human uses of air, water, and earth. McNeill, *supra* note 39, at 51.

of stock resource depletion were not as immediately experienced because new sources seemed to be constantly discovered.[56] However, the relentless removal of fossil fuels and valuable minerals would eventually adversely affect nonowners in Era IV, because by then newly discovered sources were far less plentiful, which meant that diminished supply and higher prices would become the norm.

C. Resource Popularity Conflicts and Noncooperative Games

The ubiquitous nature of private property law gradually divided the universe of parties interested in land and natural resources into two classes: owners and nonowners. Nonowners, in turn, consisted of those who also wished to use the owner's resource but could not do so, and those who held nonuse values for a resource. During Era III, owners typically were authorized, even encouraged, to use their property for their own short-term self-interest.[57] When an owner's use of a resource created conflict with nonowners who also wished to use that resource, these conflicts were usually sorted out by private property law.[58] The owner who held a property right to land or some natural resource had the legal right to use that resource and exclude nonowner would-be users from it. Owners could also erect boundaries to keep this class of nonowners away, and to protect the owner's interests in a wide range of uses.[59]

If a nonowner wished to use an owner's property, in theory, the nonowner could engage in a cooperative game in order to produce a socially optimal result,[60] where, by contract and agreement, the nonowner would be able to purchase and acquire some ownership or use interest from the owner.[61] However, the size of the group of nonowners affected by owners' resource use could potentially have been so large and diffuse that coordinating strategies between owners and nonowners would have been practically impossible. Because owners had a legally protected right to use their own resources, and because Era III positive law did not penalize use of environmental public goods as pollution sinks, owners likely were unwilling to engage in a strategy of mutual cooperation with nonowners that would have reduced the rate of resource use.[62] As a result, nonowners were often affected by an owner's resource use strategy, but they had no legal recourse to influence or deter the owner. Nonowners and nonusers were not players in the Era III resource use game.

---

[56] Kenneth S. Deffeyes, Hubbert's Peak: The Impending World Oil Shortage 1–13 (2001); Vaclav Smil, Energies: An Illustrated Guide to the Biosphere and Civilization 136–37 (1999).

[57] James Willard Hurst, Law and Economic Growth: The Legal History of the Lumber Industry in Wisconsin, 1836–1915, at 105, 127 (1984).

[58] Livestock grazing is a prominent resource use example where a nonowner of land, such as a livestock owner, might desire to use the property of another, such as the land owner, to feed his cattle.

[59] Henry E. Smith, *Exclusion Versus Governance: Two Strategies for Delineating Property Rights*, 31 J. Legal Stud. S453, 454–56 (2002).

[60] *Id.*

[61] *See supra* Chapter 4, Era II—The Age of the Market.

[62] McNeill, *supra* note 39, at 51.

Owners could safely ignore the plight of these nonowners because those who were affected by resource overuse were powerless to halt, slow, or influence an owner's choices regarding resources. Unfortunately, nonowners either harmed by or benefitting from the owner's resource use were unable to engage in even noncooperative games in Era III. Although there were large group negative externalities experienced by these nonowners,[63] applicable law did not provide them with any effective legal recourse to halt an owner's exploitation of either an owned natural resource or an unowned environmental public good.[64] It was not until laws and legal institutions in Era IV gave legal stature to the nonuse interests of nonowners that they could become players in the resource game.

The suboptimal rate of resource use that dominated Era III was the result of information failures about stock depletion in the case of nonrenewable resources, the carrying capacity of the land, and the rate of regeneration for renewable resources. The rush of private landowners to produce commodities and short-term profits (along with considerable externalities) can be illustrated by a simplistic noncooperative game theory model.[65] If the participants in a resource game are either unable or unwilling to coordinate their behavior (in this case, to achieve resource conservation), and if they instead choose their strategies regarding the resource independently, then the resulting game becomes a noncooperative game.[66] In a noncooperative game, like a cooperative game, every player is assumed to be rational; a rational player will choose an action that leads to the outcome that player prefers, given what that player expects the other players to do.[67] Unlike a cooperative game, a noncooperative game does not require coordination among the players, and there are no cooperative enforceable agreements made between players that will allow them to maximize their gains collectively.[68]

Players engaged in a noncooperative game are not necessarily doomed to experience chaos.[69] In 1950, Nobel Prize laureate Dr. John Nash proved that even noncooperative games can yield a equilibrium between the players.[70] This is now called

---

[63] *See supra* notes 39–50 and accompanying text.

[64] Era III laws available to those adversely affected by an owner's overuse of a resource usually consisted of either common law nuisance doctrine or primitive antipollution regulations. These were rarely effective in curbing an owner's use preferences. *See generally* Jan G. Laitos, *Legal Institutions and Pollution: Some Intersections between Law and History*, 15 Nat. Resources J. 423 (1975).

[65] Of course, specific local or state laws could facilitate different noncooperative game scenarios. For the purpose of illustration, we have selected a simple model with the most basic economic assumptions of a game theory model. Variations of different noncooperative game models can be adapted to reflect nuances in property law. Furthermore, assigning probabilities to different strategies and relaxing assumptions may yield different equilibriums. These variations are voluminous and beyond the scope of this chapter.

[66] Larry Samuelson, Evolutionary Games and Equilibrium Selection 1, 10 (1998).

[67] *See generally* Tim Harford, The Logic of Life: The Rational Economics of an Irrational World (2008).

[68] Scott Borg, *Finding Sanity with Game Theory*, Strategy & Business 2, *available at* http://www.strategy-business.com/article/8527?gko = e6930.

[69] *See generally* James W. Friedman, *A Noncooperative Equilibrium for Super Games*, 38 Rev. Of Econ. Stud. 1 (1971).

[70] John F. Nash, Jr., *The Bargaining Problem*, 18 Econometrica 155 (1950); John F. Nash, Jr., *Equilibrium Points in n-Person Games*, 36 Proc. Nat'l Acad. of Sci. 48 (1950).

a Nash equilibrium. When players find themselves in a noncooperative game, there is either a unique solution or a set of available solutions that will produce maximum payoffs for each player in the game, given the likely strategies of the other players.[71] In a Nash equilibrium, each player is informed of the others' strategies, and each player makes the optimal choice given what the other players might choose. There is no further benefit for a player to change strategies if the strategies of the other players remain unchanged.[72] In other words, a Nash equilibrium does not necessarily coincide with Pareto optimality; a Nash equilibrium is defined as the best strategy for that player when all other players in the noncooperative game are playing their best strategy. There is not necessarily a unique Nash equilibrium and it is not uncommon for multiple Nash equilibria to exist.

Resource owners in Era III engaged in a high rate of resource consumption that can be explained by a classic game of "chicken." Like the game of chicken, each resource player recognizes that his or her continued course of action may have detrimental consequences. However, the short-term gain of winning is so high that players are deterred from their hazardous, high-consequence course of action. The game has been heavily studied and adapted in several contexts to explain brinkmanship that pushes noncooperative behavior to the point of near disaster.[73] In the game of chicken, the Nash equilibrium is that of suboptimal use.[74] Consider a situation where the players drive toward each other on a single track at a high speed until one "chickens out," and swerves off the track to avoid colliding. The player who swerves gains nothing, and the player who stays on the track gains everything. Neither player wants to yield to the other. Given the strategies of the other player in the game and the fact that players cannot communicate their intentions, the best strategy for each player is to select the course opposite of their opponent. Because both players assume that their opponent is rational and would prefer not to have a head-on collision, the Nash equilibrium strategy is to select the opposite of an opponent's course. The opponents are "deadlocked" because both assume that the other will back down.

The game played between owner-users in Era III is analogous to the chicken game. Two resource owner-users—suppose they are foresters—have incentive to clear-cut and supply as much wood to the market as possible to gain financial rewards. Although it would be socially optimal to conserve the wood production in order to sustain the forest, each producer has incentive to clear-cut and gain market share if the opponent chooses conservation. The nonuser, who may have an interest in the existence value of the forest for its beauty, or who would benefit from forest nonuse because then it would supply oxygen, is not even a player in this game. But the nonuser would experience the negative externality of clear-cutting.

The payoffs and Nash equilibrium are illustrated in Figure 5.1. Forester 2 may either conserve (upper left box), or clear-cut (upper right box). If Forester 2 conserves,

---

[71] *Id.*

[72] DIXIT & NALEBUFF, *supra* note 12, at 77.

[73] AVINASH K. DIXIT & SUSAN SKEATH, GAMES OF STRATEGY 457 (1999).

[74] Evolutionary biology has been likened to a game of chicken. *See* J. Maynard Smith & G.R. Price, *The Logic of Animal Conflict*, 246 NATURE 15 (1973).

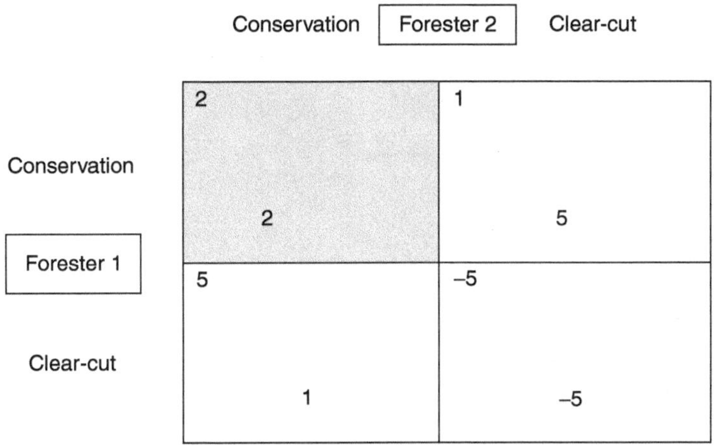

FIGURE 5.1 Game of chicken.

Forester 1 experiences a high payoff (5) from clear-cutting the forest, while Forester 2 experiences a much lower payout (1) due to Forester 1's market domination. Likewise, if Forester 1 conserves, Forester 2 experiences a high payoff (5) from clear-cutting the forest, while Forester 1 experiences a much lower payout (1) due to Forester 2's market domination. If both clear-cut, there will be a negative payout to both. But because this is a noncooperative game, both foresters will clear-cut the forest, even though this strategy produces the least desirable result for the two players and for society.

Note that the number in each box on the left is the Forester 1's payoff; the number on the right is Forester 2's payoff. The Nash equilibrium solution is highlighted.

The owner-user foresters are deadlocked in trying to anticipate their opponent's strategy. As a result, there is an endless bout of suboptimal resource use. The foresters, nonusers, and ecosystem suffer as a result.

6 Era IV—The Anthrocene Age

BY THE MIDDLE of the 20th century, a new era had swept much of the planet and its legal institutions. Era IV may be called the Anthrocene Age because of the prominent role played by human anthropogenic decisions.[1] Era IV, which continues to the present, has three prominent anthropocentric characteristics: (1) continued suboptimal use of some resources, (2) laws requiring individuals and entities to comply with regulations in order to protect indirect resource values that provide human benefit, and (3) new laws that for the first time recognize and uphold human preferences for nonuse values. Throughout Era IV, the resource economy increasingly came under political and governmental control; however, these 20th century laws were anthropocentric and designed to protect resource indirect use and nonuse values primarily for the benefit of humans.[2]

---

[1] *See* Daniel H. Cole, *Climate Change, Adaption, and Development*, 26 J. ENVTL. L. 1 (2008); ANDREW REVKIN, GLOBAL WARMING: UNDERSTANDING THE FORECAST 55 (1992); *see generally* Michael Williams, *Forests*, *in* THE EARTH AS TRANSFORMED BY HUMAN ACTION: GLOBAL AND REGIONAL CHANGE OVER THE PAST 300 YEARS 179 (B.L. Turner II et al. eds., 1990).

[2] *See, e.g.*, Friends of the Earth v. Laidlaw Envtl. Servs., 528 U.S. 167, 181 (2000) ("The relevant showing for purposes of Article III standing, however, is not injury to the environment but injury to the plaintiff."); The National Environmental Policy Act, 42 U.S.C. § 4331(a) (2006) ("[T]he continuing policy of the Federal Government [is] . . . to use all practicable means and measures . . . in a manner calculated to . . . maintain conditions under which man and nature can exist in productive harmony, and fulfill the . . . requirements of future generations of Americans."); *see also* Gunther Handle, *Human Rights and Protection of the Environment*, *in* ECONOMIC, SOCIAL, AND CULTURAL RIGHTS 304–05 (Asbjørn Eide, Catarina Krause & Allan Rosas eds., 2001).

During Era IV, scientific knowledge emerged to document the human benefits gained from indirect resource benefits such as clean air and clean water. Most Western countries, particularly the United States, enacted environmental protection laws that undermined absolutist notions of property rights prevalent in Era III. In Era IV, unlike Era III, ownership of natural resources no longer conferred unchecked authority over their extraction and development. The creation of scientifically grounded Best Management Practices (BMPs) and other science-based environmental standards resulted in regulations aimed to limit the external costs and deleterious effects on indirect uses imposed by an individual's private resource use.[3] Furthermore, the Era III preservation movement, ignited by prominent writings and activism of naturalists from this time period, gained momentum and popularity in Era IV, particularly in the last decade of the 20th century.[4] Human preferences for resource existence values were validated in Era IV by the passage of several laws to protect resource nonuse values. For example, the U.S. Forest Service, which manages multiple use lands, is mandated to consider ecosystem integrity and use and nonuse values (such as forestry, grazing, recreation, and wilderness).[5]

Increased government presence yielded two principal results: first, legislation and government enforcement that aimed to reduce negative externalities imposed by direct uses, and second, increased government ownership of public lands. Governments also gained momentum in acquiring public ownership interests in valuable resources, including land, in order to reduce exploitation of unowned public goods.[6] Increased scientific knowledge and changing public preferences led to an affirmative duty imposed on Era IV public land managers to protect indirect and nonuse values threatened by use demands,[7] and to impose nonuse values on certain lands that might otherwise have seemed important only for use potential.[8] These new Era IV laws restricted or prevented direct resource use. They also advanced the anthropocentric goals of protecting indirect uses (e.g., public goods healthy for humans), and nonuse values (e.g., option and existence values).

Era IV laws have created, and given legal power to, an important new interest to be reckoned with when considering our relationship to natural resources: resource indirect use and nonuse for the benefit of humans. These laws give individuals,

---

[3] Robert Gottlieb, Forcing the Spring: The Transformation of the American Environment Movement 113 (1993); Wash. State Dep't of Natural Res. v. Browning, 199 P.3d 430 (Wash. Ct. App. 2008) (upholding state agency stop-work orders prohibiting timber owner from harvesting trees).

[4] John M. Meyer, *Gifford Pinchot, John Muir and the Boundaries of Politics in American Thought*, 30 Polity 267 (1997).

[5] John B. Loomis, Integrated Public Lands Management (2d ed. 2002).

[6] *See e.g.*, Massachusetts v. Envtl. Prot. Agency, 127 S. Ct. 1438 (2007) (emission of greenhouse gases released into the atmosphere contribute to global warming, which is experienced by both those who emit these gases, and those who do not).

[7] *See* 16 U.S.C. § 1132 (2006) (future protection of roadless areas within national forests); 43 U.S.C. § 1782(a) (2006) (protection of wilderness study areas within U.S. Bureau of Land Management lands); Endangered Species Act of 1973, 16 U.S.C. § 1531 (2006).

[8] *See e.g.*, Antiquities Act of 1906, 16 U.S.C. § 431 (2006); Wild and Scenic Rivers Act of 1968, 16 U.S.C. §§ 1271–1287; Wilderness Act of 1964, 16 U.S.C. §§ 1131–1136.

organizations, and even governments that value indirect use and nonuse of resources the legal ability to directly challenge both private and public resource use decisions that compromise the human interest in nonuse values.[9] Those asserting anthropocentric indirect use and nonuse interests have taken on resource use interest in three settings: private resource owners who use, or wish to use, resources under their control;[10] public resource owners who use, or authorize private use of, resources owned by some government entity;[11] and users who exploit an unowned resource.[12]

Despite the ubiquity of laws authorizing resource nonusers to challenge resource use decisions for anthropocentric ends, the harsh reality is that the world's resource base continues to diminish below suboptimal levels,[13] and natural systems continue to degrade and disappear.[14] There are, of course, many asserted and demonstrated reasons for the world's persistent pursuit of the use values associated with resources.[15] These range from exponentially increasing populations, to ever-increasing demand for raw materials from developing countries and certain sectors of the American economy that see their survival linked to resource use, to the human tendency to discount the value of future benefits associated with present conservation.

Market failures, such as unowned public goods, and government failures stemming from the management of these public goods, also yield a suboptimal level of natural systems and natural resources in Era IV, much like they did in Era III. Ironically, increased government intervention itself has yielded government failures, an overcorrection stemming from attempts to address market imperfections. Government command and control policies mandating compliance with air and water quality standards do not provide incentives to jointly improve productivity, and typically lead to further inefficiencies and mislaid incentives to protect use, indirect use, and nonuse interests.[16] Furthermore, government intervention explicitly

---

[9] Richard J. Lazarus, The Making of Environmental Law 80–83 (2004). Era IV laws also permit those interested in the nonuse component of land to create an ownership interest in that component. *See also* Elizabeth Byers & Karin Marchetti Ponte, The Conservation Easement Handbook (2d ed. 2005).

[10] *See, e.g.*, Davis v. Agua Sierra Res., L.L.C., 174 P.3d 298 (Ariz. Ct. App. 2008) (challenging the withdrawal of percolating groundwater by the overlying landowner).

[11] *See* Sue Major Holmes, *Judge Backs BLM Plan on Gas Drilling in N.M.*, Denv. Post, Oct. 10, 2008, at B2 (describing an environmental challenge to a Bureau of Land Management plan contemplating ten thousand new gas wells in northern New Mexico).

[12] *See* El Comite Para El Bienestar v. Warmerdam, 539 F.3d 1062 (9th Cir. 2008) (citizen group challenge to emissions of volatile organic compounds into California's atmosphere).

[13] Don Hinrichsen et al., Consequences of Overuse and Pollution, XXVI Population Reports, ch. 4 (Population Info. Program ed., 1998); Elisabeth Rosenthal & Andrew C. Revkin, *Science Panel Calls Global Warming "Unequivocal,"* N.Y. Times, Feb. 3, 2007, at A1; William McKibben, The End of Nature 51 (2006).

[14] *See* Thomas L. Friedman, *In the Age of Noah*, N.Y. Times, Dec. 23, 2007, *available at* http://www.nytimes.com/2007/12/23/opinion/23friedman.html; Michael Shellenberger & Ted Nordhaus, The Death of Environmentalism: Global Warming Politics in a Post-Environmental World (2004), *available at* http://www.thebreakthrough.org/images/Death_of_Environmentalism.pdf.

[15] *See* Shellenberger & Nordhaus, *supra* note 14.

[16] Eric W. Orts, *Reflexive Environmental Law*, 89 Nw. U.L. Rev. 1227, 1236 (1995).

developed to conserve resource use has also crowded out the private provisioning of public goods, such as open space.[17] Ultimately, this public action can yield a suboptimal production of environmental goods.[18]

Put in terms of game theory, Era IV laws legitimized a new player in natural resources games. This player had preferences for indirect uses and nonuses, and was legally empowered to resist user interests. Instead of the simple user-versus-user games so prevalent in Eras II and III, in Era IV the games increasingly involved humans who believed their indirect use and nonuse interests would be harmed by resource use. Resource users were private resource owners, public resource owners who either used resources directly or who authorized private use, or users of unowned public good resources. The new player, a resource nonuser, was a protector of natural systems for human-centric reasons. Not to be confused with nonuse values, which are essentially existence values, resource nonusers included individuals with preferences for (1) indirect use benefits that followed from a clean, unpolluted environment; (2) option values for possible future nonconsumptive use, such as low-impact recreation; and (3) nonuse interests, such as existence values realized when humans left a resource alone. Resource nonusers were individuals, resource-protective organizations, and government entities empowered to enforce new Era IV laws.

Although motivations differed, the commonality is that nonusers demonstrated anthropocentric ambitions. Even nonusers with existence values presented anthropocentric preferences that furthered the rights of humans. Although nonusers and users may have approached the resource differently, the anthropocentric focus resulted in suboptimal, unsustainable resource use, regardless of whether the game was cooperative or noncooperative. Achieving cooperation requires considerable coordination, often imposing high transaction costs and requiring agency-based collaborative facilitation.[19] As noted in Part IV, Chapter 15, noncooperative games do not yield agreements between players that will allow them to maximize their gains collectively.[20] Such games, because they are refereed by proscriptive laws between two opposing interests, usually lead to a win-lose outcome. Such an outcome is neither a collectively optimal result nor an efficient result for the players.[21]

A. Resource Use and Anthropogenic Harm

Throughout Eras I and II, humans viewed nature, and natural resources, as either a source of cheap or free exploitable wealth, or a virtually costless dumping ground for wastes. Common law doctrine and resource-use friendly government agencies and

---

[17] *See* Theodore Bergstrom et al., *On the Private Provision of Public Goods*, 29 J. PUB. ECON. 25, 25–49 (1986).

[18] *See generally* Richard Cornes & Todd Sandler, *Easy Riders, Joint Production, and Public Goods*, 94 ECON. J. 580, 580–98 (1984).

[19] *See generally* Holly Wise Bender & Wade E. Martin, *Modeling Conflict Using Spatial Voting Games: An Application to USDA Forest Service Lands*, 12 INT'L J. ENV'T & POLLUTION 217 (1999).

[20] *See* Larry Samuelson, *Evolutionary Games and Equilibrium Selection* (1998).

[21] *See* Samuelson, *id.* at 1, 10; Tim Harford, *The Logic of Life: The Rational Economics of an Irrational World* (2008).

courts validated human enterprises using resources for economic gain.[22] Nonuse interests were largely silent, in large part due to an absence of legal legitimacy for nonuse values.[23]

By Era IV, this unchecked use had been spurred on by an accelerated demand for raw materials. The earth's population was increasing almost exponentially. Economic growth among Western countries was the norm, developing nations such as China and India put new demands on natural resource products, and resources were both the fuel for this growth and a free waste receptacle for growth's discarded by-products.[24] Human resource use patterns fundamentally reshaped the earth; the planet was human-dominated and permanently altered.[25] Much of this mid-20th-century transformation had serious negative effects on resource availability and viability.

Era IV laws did have some effect on some dimensions of resource pollution and depletion. However, by the 21st century other indicators of environmental quality had declined.[26] Notably, carbon dioxide and other greenhouse gases had increased.[27] This change resulted in what many scientists believed to be anthropocentrically induced global climate change.[28] These deleterious impacts on resources eventually alarmed humans, who began not only to take note of a diminished resource base, but also feared human health threats from environmental pollution.[29] Eventually, fears

---

[22] *See, e.g.*, Ebbetts Pass Forest Watch v. Cal. Dep't of Forestry, 183 P.3d 1210, 1226 (Cal. 2008) (approving timber harvesting plans despite concerns about environmental impacts); Adaven Mgmt., Inc. v. Mountain Falls Acquisition, Corp., 191 P.3d 1189, 1192–96 (Nev. 2008) (discussing "anti-speculation" doctrine in western water law, which ensures that property right in water is put to "beneficial use"); Karl Vick, *Secret Deal May Speed Development of Forest Land*, DENV. POST, July 6, 2008, at 7A (timber company approved by the U.S. Forest Service to build homes on forest land).

[23] *See supra* Chapter 4, ERA II—The Age of the Market

[24] Leonard Zobler, *An Economic-Historical View of Natural Resources Use and Conservation,* 38 ECON. GEOGRAPHY 189, 190 (1962).

[25] Peter M. Vitousek et al., *Human Domination of Earth's Ecosystem*, 277 SCI. 494, 498 (1997). *See also* Peter Kareiva et al., *Domesticated Nature: Shaping Landscapes and Ecosystems for Human Welfare*, 316 SCI. 1866 (2007) (we have converted roughly "50 percent of the world's surface . . . to grazed land or cultivated crops").

[26] According to the theory of the environmental Kuznets curve, which is based on the work of Simon Kuznets, environmental quality is expected to increase as per capita income increases. *See generally* Simon Kuznets, *Quantitative Aspects of the Economic Growth of Nations, VIII: The Distribution of Income by Size*, ECON. DEV. & CULTURAL CHANGE, Jan. 1963, at 1.

[27] Elaborations and laboratory experiments have since documented that improvements in environmental quality with increases in average income may not be the case in practice. Specifically, greenhouse gases do not actually decline when worldwide per capita income increases, implying that wealthier nations may reduce pollution in some areas, but greenhouse gas emissions may increase. *See generally* David I. Stern et al., *Economic Growth and Environmental Degradation: The Environmental Kuznets Curve and Sustainable Development*, 24 WORLD DEV. 1151–60 (1996).

[28] RICHARD N.L. ANDREWS, MANAGING THE ENVIRONMENT, MANAGING OURSELVES: A HISTORY OF AMERICAN ENVIRONMENTAL POLICY 353 (1999); ANDREW GOUDIE, THE HUMAN IMPACT ON THE NATURAL ENVIRONMENT 167 (4th ed. 1994).

[29] HERMAN E. DALY & JOSHUA FARLEY, ECOLOGICAL ECONOMICS PRINCIPLES AND APPLICATIONS (2004); Edella Schlager & Elinor Ostrom, *Property-Rights Regimes and Natural Resources: A Conceptual Analysis*, 68 LAND ECON. 249, 279 (1992); *see also Developing Nations Balk at Climate Plan*, DENV. POST, July 10, 2008, at 7A (the five main developing nations—China, India, Brazil, Mexico, and South Africa—rejected a

about environmental degradation raised doubts about humankind's very survival. These anthropocentric fears caused us to turn to laws and legal institutions to address the growing exploitation of open access resources and the onslaught of negative environmental externalities.[30]

Apart from concerns about how resource overuse might adversely affect humans, evidence was also mounting that natural resources played an important ecological and biological role when they were not being exploited by humans. Just as exploitation of resources produced large group negative externalities, it was becoming equally clear that, when left alone and not used, certain natural resources generated positive externalities.[31] For example, naturally occurring wetlands, whether unowned or privately owned, perform and provide several valuable ecosystem services, such as flood control and pollution filtration.[32] Because the market normally does not take into account such nonuse benefits when decisions are being made about resource use,[33] methodologies were developed in Era IV to attempt to measure such values, such as contingent valuation.[34]

B. Anthropocentric Laws Protecting Resource Human Indirect Use and Nonuse Values

As resource exploitation posed growing threats to both humans and ecosystems, new Era IV laws began to legitimate and empower resource nonusers. This player had been largely powerless in Era III,[35] but now it had a battery of statutory weapons to resist harmful resource use when the use adversely affected human nonuse values.[36] Era III laws had embraced largely absolutist notions of private property rights, which assumed that ownership conferred upon owners plenary authority to engage in maximum resource appropriation and exploitation.[37] By contrast, the core premise of

goal for reducing global emissions of greenhouse gases, "since it is wealthier countries that have [already] created most of the environmental damage").

[30] San Antonio Conservation Soc'y v. Tex. Highway Dep't, 400 U.S. 968, 969–71 (1970) (Black, J., dissenting). *See also* Pannaro Energy, Inc. v. Mont. Bd. of Envtl. Review, 199 P.3d 191, 194 (Mont. 2008) (agency concerned that water produced from privately owned coal bed methane gas had a harmful effect on soils and stream life).

[31] Ironically, once domesticated and managed, many natural resources require active management by humans to maintain positive benefits. Prominent examples are the infiltration of invasive plant species in former pasturelands and years of wildfire mitigation that have led to wildfires in the urban-rural interface. Human disturbance often yields a necessary cycle of land management, making the return to a truly natural system very difficult to achieve.

[32] J.B. Ruhl, Steven Kraft & Christopher Lant, *The Law and Policy of Ecosystem Services* 64–65 (2007).

[33] Andrew Balmford et al., *Economic Reasons for Conserving Wild Nature*, 297 Sci. 950, 952–53 (2002).

[34] Marino Gatto & Giulio A. De Leo, *Pricing Biodiversity and Ecosystem Services: The Never-Ending Story*, 50 Bioscience 347 (2000) (Revealed that preference or hedonic pricing are other methods that try to capture the worth of a resource's nonuse values. These impute some of the value of one good or service traded in the market to the presence of another attribute that is not traded.).

[35] *See supra* Chapter 5, ERA III—The Age of Property.

[36] *See* Lazarus, *supra* note 9, at 47–113.

[37] Robert Gottlieb, Forcing the Spring: The Transformation of the American Environmental Movement 7–8 (1992).

many Era IV laws was that the sovereign's police power could regulate private activities, including the natural environment that adversely affected human health and welfare.

Governments in two ways asserted public rights protecting anthropocentric values threatened by excessive resource use. First, they claimed resources—often open access resources—as publicly owned property. Most Western countries did this by establishing national forests, national parks, national rangelands, and other public lands.[38] Second, governments imposed public rights through the regulation of private resource use. Governments did this by regulating both private use of open access[39] and privately owned resources.[40]

Although perceived threats to human health were primary drivers for the adoption of these laws, another motive for this unparalleled government intervention lay in our gradual realization that natural systems generate positive spillovers, indirect uses, and nonuse values for the benefit of humans. This recognition of unused nature justified restrictions on private use decisions regarding resources. Humans also discovered that they cared deeply about preserving from development and alteration certain locations characterized as wildlands,[41] wildlife, and endangered species and their habitats.[42] Part of this benefit involved the personal, sometimes mystical feelings people had toward nature.[43] Some of the benefit was due to a realization that humans and their natural environment are closely linked and mutually interdependent.[44] Ecologists and economists have tried to estimate the quantitative value to the world's economic well-being that was provided by productive natural systems—a 1997 publication in *Nature* concluded that the total annual global value of ecosystem services was between 16 and 54 trillion dollars.[45]

Such psychological, ecological, and economic factors influenced lawmakers, who in Era IV found themselves under pressure to acknowledge values of the natural world. However, throughout Era IV, the laws and legal doctrine that sought to protect the indirect use and nonuse components of resources did so for largely anthrpocentric ends. It was the public's right to the benefits of resource nonuse

---

[38] Daniel H. Cole & Peter Z. Grossman, *Principles of Law and Economics* 325–26 (2005).

[39] *See, e.g.*, Clean Air Act of 1970, 42 U.S.C. § 7401 (2006) (imposing a system of public rights and private duties regarding the atmosphere); State ex rel. State Eng'r v. Comm'r of Public Lands, 200 P.3d 86, 99 (N.M. Ct. App. 2008) (under federal reserved rights doctrine, federal government may impliedly reserve water and exempt it from appropriation under state law).

[40] *See, e.g.*, Home Builders Ass'n of Cent. Ariz. v. Kard, 199 P.3d 629 (Ariz. Ct. App. 2008) (home builders challenging state air quality permits required for earth-moving operations on privately owned lands).

[41] *See, e.g.*, Wilderness Act of 1964, 16 U.S.C. §§ 1131–1136 (2006).

[42] *See, e.g.*, Endangered Species Act of 1973, 16 U.S.C. § 1531 (2006); Tenn. Valley Auth. v. Hill, 437 U.S. 153 (1978); Nat'l Wildlife Refuge Improvement Act of 1997, 16 U.S.C. §§ 668dd–668ee (2006).

[43] *See, e.g.*, Wallace Stegner, *Why We Need Wilderness*, Mother Earth News, Aug./Sept. 2004, at 64, 65.

[44] Dan Tarlock, *The Nonequilibrium Paradigm in Ecology and the Partial Unraveling of Environmental Law*, 27 Loy. L.A. L. Rev. 1121, 1126–27 (1994).

[45] Robert Constanza et al., *The Value of the World's Ecosystem Services and Natural Capital*, 387 Nature 253, 259 (1997).

that became legally protected; it usually was not the resource's right to remain in a natural state.[46] The new statutes and regulations focused on the harmful impacts that resource use decisions had on individual humans, rather than on the natural environment itself.[47] American environmental laws enacted in the latter half of the 20th century seemed little concerned about the injuries to natural resources caused by overuse. Instead, these laws were more intent on the threats to personal health and welfare that followed from environmental degradation.[48] This anthropocentric emphasis is particularly evident with laws addressing overuse of open access resources.[49] Even under the National Environmental Policy Act (NEPA), when federal resource use actions are proposed, an impact statement must be prepared only if the action might affect "the quality of the *human* environment."[50] Many federal natural resources laws enacted in Era IV also emphasized the need for publicly owned lands to be conserved and preserved because of "the anthropocentric virtues of wild lands."[51]

The law of standing similarly evolved to ensure that courts will not hear from plaintiffs raising the interests of natural resources; rather, it is only through the transformation of such interests into harms to persons that violations of environmentally protective laws can be remedied by courts.[52] Under Article III of the U.S. Constitution, if some resource nonuse attribute is threatened or harmed by a resource use decision, those wishing to challenge that action in court must claim that they have somehow been injured.[53] To satisfy standing requirements the injury must be to the human plaintiff,[54] and it is irrelevant that the underlying harm is to some otherwise

---

[46] There were some exceptions to the law's inclination to acknowledge and protect nonuse values so as to primarily advance strictly human ends. *See* Just v. Marinette Cnty., 201 N.W.2d 761, 768 (Wis. 1972); 42 U.S.C. § 9607(f) (2006) (for certain hazardous waste disposal sites subject to cleanup under CERCLA, a federal or state "trustee" may be designated to assess damages to natural resources); Katrina M. Wyman, *The Property Challenges in Marine Fisheries*, 50 Ariz. L. Rev. 511, 513–15, 528–29 (2008) (discussing "no take areas" for certain marine fisheries, where extractive uses are prohibited and nonuse values are preserved).

[47] Gunther Handl, *Human Rights and Protection of the Environment: A Mildly "Revisionist" View*, *in* Human Rights, Sustainable Development and the Environment 117 (Antonio Trindade ed., 1992).

[48] Lazarus, *supra* note 9, at 59.

[49] The 1970 Clean Air Act, 42 U.S.C. § 7409(b) (2006), requires that national ambient air quality standards be established for the protection of public health. The 1972 Clean Water Act, 33 U.S.C. § 1251(a)(2) (2006), requires that the waters of the United States be fishable and swimmable. Amendments to the Resource Conservation and Recovery Act, 42 U.S.C. § 6924(a) (2006), call for disposal regulations for hazardous waste "as may be necessary to protect human health." The Comprehensive Environmental Response, Compensation, and Liability Act of 1980 (CERCLA), 42 U.S.C. §§ 9601 et seq. (2006), requires the cleanup of abandoned and inactive hazardous waste sites containing substances that could be toxic or harmful to humans.

[50] 42 U.S.C. § 4332(2)(c) (emphasis added).

[51] Sandra Zellmer, *A Preservation Paradox: Political Prestidigitation and an Enduring Resource of Wildness*, 34 Envtl. L. 1015, 1040 (2004); Wilderness Act of 1964, 16 U.S.C. § 1131(b), (c) (2006); Lazarus, *supra* note 9, at 93.

[52] *See* Friends of the Earth, Inc. v. Laidlaw Envtl. Servs. (TOC), Inc., 528 U.S. 167, 181 (2000). See also Chapter 18.

[53] Sierra Club v. Morton, 405 U.S. 727, 734–35 (1972).

[54] *See* Weaver's Cove Energy v. R.I. Dep't of Envtl. Mgmt., 524 F.3d 1330, 1333 (D.C. Cir. 2008).

protected natural resource.[55] Even in environmental lawsuits brought under the generous review provisions of the Administrative Procedure Act, it is the human plaintiff's interests in protecting and preserving resource nonuse from use that is the focus of a court's initial inquiry.[56] Yet the overuse of a resource that impairs that resource's nonuse component itself rarely attaches to identifiable humans, even when human plaintiffs allege "concrete and particularized" harm sufficient to satisfy standing requirements in court.[57]

An anthropocentric focus also affects cost-benefit analysis undertaken as a condition of environmentally protective legal action. If the cost of excessive resource use is only measured in human lives lost or human health impaired, the staggering nonuse values that are lost to the planet may be overlooked.[58] If one seeks to measure the benefits of nonuse, the accounting scope required to monetize the value to the earth for leaving a resource alone is monumental and will likely present much controversy.[59]

C. The Rise of a New Player in the Resource Game

In Era II, disputes over resources were typically between users who may have wished to use the same resource. With the emergence of contract law, these Era II users could sometimes engage in cooperative games, presented earlier in Figure 4.2. At times, such agreements resulted in cooperation and win-win solutions to the conflict. In Era III, with the arrival of private property law, the two competing users were often owner-users and nonowners who wanted to use the resource. Because owner-users had the weight of property ownership justifying their use, few cooperative games were played with nonowner would-be users. Also, during Era III another player arose—the nonowner who was harmed by resource use by experiencing negative externalities and by losing the positive nonuse values that were degraded by excessive resource use. But throughout most of Era III, this third player had no legal stature and therefore could largely be ignored by resource users.

All this changed in Era IV.[60] Users either had ownership rights permitting use (e.g., when the user was either a private or public owner), or in the case of an unowned

---

[55] Lujan v. Defenders of Wildlife, 504 U.S. 555, 563 (1992) ("But the 'injury in fact' test requires more than an injury to a cognizable interest. It requires that the party seeking review be . . . injured." (quoting *Sierra Club*, 405 U.S. at 734–35).

[56] Bennett v. Spear, 520 U.S. 154, 167–68 (1997); Salmon Spawning & Recovery Alliance v. United States, 532 F.3d 1338, 1347 n.7 (Fed. Cir. 2008).

[57] Shi-Ling Hsu, *The Identifiability Bias in Environmental Law*, 35 FLA. ST. U.L. REV. 433, 467 (2008).

[58] *See, e.g.*, James Salzman, Barton H. Thompson, Jr. & Gretchen C. Daily, *Protecting Ecosystem Services: Science, Economics, and Law*, 20 STAN. ENVTL. L.J. 309 (2001).

[59] Sidney A. Shapiro & Christopher H. Schroeder, *Beyond Cost-Benefit Analysis: A Pragmatic Reorientation*, 32 HARV. ENVTL. L. REV. 433, 456 (2008); *see, e.g.*, Entergy Corp. v. Riverkeeper, Inc., 129 S. Ct. 1498, 1509 (2009) (discussing how the "non-use benefits" of national air quality performance standards would be of "indeterminate value").

[60] Sometimes Era IV laws were activated by agencies, such as the U.S. Environmental Protection Agency, that relied on such laws to protect nonusers from the effects of resource use.

resource, confronted no market barriers to resource exploitation. By contrast, nonusers had the ability to deploy Era IV laws, which gave them the legal power to curb or halt harmful use of both owned and unowned resources.[61] Users and nonusers with opposing interests often went toe-to-toe with equally viable legal support, and the frequent and often anticipated conflict made it difficult to predict whether the resulting game would be cooperative or noncooperative.

This uncertainty was particularly the case for collaborative decision-making sessions when stakeholders (either users or nonusers) had incentives to engage in a sophisticated game to disguise their preferences, and form a voting block to misrepresent their interests and to further their objectives.[62] Studies have shown that a number of variables can complicate a process in which users and nonusers, whose interests may support either indirect or nonuse values, met to vote on policy options. Examples of these complexities include ordering of status quo alternatives on the agenda during a voting process, degree of required majority for a win to secure an alternative (i.e., simple majority or super majority), and transferable utility, which means that a nonuser would be willing to sacrifice the nonuse of a particular parcel of land if the nonuse is transferred to another parcel.[63]

Such complex strategies during Era IV made it difficult to predict whether a cooperative or noncooperative game would actually take place. Noncooperative situations arise when self-interested players either are unwilling or unable to communicate, or cannot or do not trust each other, and so cannot make credible commitments to cooperative strategies. Throughout Era IV, users and nonusers found themselves in exactly this situation. Involvement from a governmental agency tasked with supporting multiple uses within the constraints of ecosystem service-carrying capacities often yields options that trump the preferences of the other players. In other words, agency multiple use policies such as U.S. Forest Service lands policies that permit multiple activities often yield a compromise that allocates some use to each party. However, this result does not necessarily mean that the players are pleased—the outcome may lead to malcontent. Regardless of whether the game is cooperative or noncooperative, when government agencies are involved the end result is still usually an overall suboptimal allocation of environmental goods with respect to indirect use value or

---

[61] *See, e.g.*, Babbitt v. Sweet Home Chapter, 515 U.S. 687, 708 (1995) (finding that the Endangered Species Act prohibition against "taking" a species encompasses destruction or modification of the habitat of the red-cockaded woodpecker and northern spotted owl).

[62] Bender, *supra* note 19 ("Although mandated to include the public in its decisions, the USDA Forest Service (USFS) can choose to undertake different types of public involvement. More recently, the USFS has embraced a collaborative (i.e., cooperative) decision-making process, which focuses on bringing stakeholders together for intensive education, communication and mediation to come to a consensus decision. In contrast, the purpose of the more traditional noncooperative National Environmental Policy Act (NEPA) process is solely to educate interested parties about USFS activities and solicit information about the public's desires. These models focus on comparing the results of non-cooperative public involvement models with the cooperative or collaborative models.").

[63] *Id.*

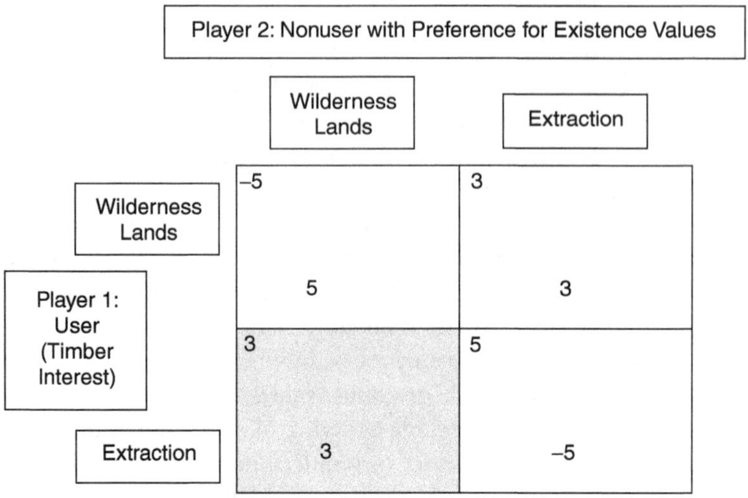

FIGURE 6.1 Multiple use for Forest Service lands.

nonuse values. Government provisioning of environmental goods crowds out the private provisioning of these same goods.[64]

Figure 6.1 demonstrates how a noncooperative solution between two players defaults to a suboptimal multiple use plan that encourages both extraction and wilderness use. Imagine in this particular scenario that the U.S. Forest Service is evaluating a proposal to permit timber extraction in a national forest within an area well-known for its scenic vistas and wildlife viewing.

The extraction proposal has triggered the need for an analysis of the environmental impacts under NEPA, which initiated considerable public involvement. For purposes of simplicity, we can break the groups into users who prefer the extraction option because it offers the potential to increase regional job availability and economic development, and nonusers—ardent environmentalists who truly prioritize existence values. In other words, environmentalists prioritize the nonuse values of these U.S. Forest Service lands, and these nonusers would prefer to see the area return to a natural state, to the point of closing visitor use even for hiking. The U.S. Forest Service, which is tasked with managing multiple uses, must consider all of these uses within the constraints of the ecosystem.[65] In this noncooperative game, the Nash equilibrium of the U.S. Forest Service multiple use mandate facilitates both use and nonuse, but to a degree that does not fully satisfy either group.[66]

Note that the number in each box reflects Player 1's (timber interest) payoff on the left; the number on the right reflects Player 2's payoff. The box containing the noncooperative solution for agency multiple use is highlighted.

[64] Bergstrom et al., *supra* note 17.

[65] *See, e.g.*, Multiple Use Sustained Yield Act of 1960, 16 U.S.C. §§ 528–531 (2006).

[66] For the sake of simplicity, this game is modeled using pure strategies, where players do not assign probabilities to the outcome of the play.

In Figure 6.1, payoffs are based upon the number of acres of U.S. Forest Service lands that are allocated for each purpose: extraction and nonuse. Player 2 demonstrates considerable nonuse values for large wilderness areas (5). The wilderness area is compromised if extraction takes place, but Player 2 would prefer to see some wilderness maintained (3), even if less wilderness acreage is ultimately available. Player 1, with a timber interest, would prefer to see the lands converted to extraction (5). Maintaining the lands as wilderness areas would result in considerable profit losses to Player 1 (-5); however, Player 1 receives some benefit (3) from multiple use.

The Nash equilibrium occurs when Player 1 extracts and Player 2 enjoys some wilderness, reflected in the lower left box. This set of strategies also demonstrates multiple use and a Pareto optimal solution in terms of acreage allocated toward each use. Those who value wilderness benefit from the nonuse designation, and the timber harvester benefits by the ability to cut some timber. However, due to the nature of the use and nonuse activities, there is still room for externalities and conflict between users and nonusers, as well as within these groups. For example, clear-cutting produces spillover effects such as excessive runoff on the adjacent wilderness lands.

Conversely, the timber harvesters are frustrated by the wilderness designation because they are unable to maximize profits from the available resource next door. Government ownership of a resource does not necessarily yield a socially optimal result.[67]

D. Private Provisioning of Nonuse Environmental Goods

Although a public ownership solution to the conflict between use and nonuse seemed elusive regarding lands and resources, so too did market-based solutions for the provisioning of environmental goods, common in the latter part of the 20th century and early 21st century. Cap-and-trade programs were implemented in the mid-1990s to cap the total output of smog-inducing air emissions such as nitrous oxides (NOx) and sulfur oxides (SOx). These cap-and-trade programs allowed firms to either buy or sell the right to emit pollution as appropriate for their manufacturing practices while the industry as a whole was required to reduce total emissions. Firms were able to provide an environmental good, clean air, while deciding on the appropriate manufacturing processes to manage emissions and maximize profits.[68] Although these cap-and-trade practices were imperfect in implementation, economists and other professionals applauded them as market-based solutions, and the SOx cap-and-trade guidelines seemed to reduce this pollutant.[69] The trading of

[67] Daniel H. Cole, *Pollution and Property*, 39–40 (2002) (discussing public mismanagement of publicly owned "multiple use" resources); Thomas Borcherding, *Natural Resources and Transgenerational Equity*, *in* ECONOMICS AND THE ENVIRONMENT: A RECONCILIATION 95–115 (Walter Block ed., 1990) (public ownership of resources sometimes merely converts the tragedy of open access into the "tragedy of the political commons").

[68] Jonathon A. Lesser, Daniel E. Dobbs & Richard O. Zerbe, Jr., *Environmental Economics and Policy* 156–159 (1997).

[69] COLE, *supra* note 67; Byron Swift, *The Acid Rain Test*, 14 ENVTL. FORUM 17 (1997); Barry Wallerstein, Letter to the Editor, *Our Cap and Trade NOx the SOx Off*, WALL ST. J., April 25, 2009, at A10.

greenhouse gases such as carbon dioxide also emerged in the 21st century. Although such carbon markets were mandated in the European Union,[70] the creation of the Chicago Climate Exchange—the first voluntary market for the trading of greenhouse gases—showed promise for trade in the United States.[71]

In Era IV, other laws sought to provide private firms and landowners financial incentives to reduce externalities and to create public goods on their private property. Most notably, conservation easements evolved into one of the most common tools for protecting private lands that provide public goods possessing nonuse value, such as wildlife habitat, aesthetic views, or historical significance.[72] With a conservation easement, land remains in private ownership, but the landowner enters into a contractual agreement to place restrictions on development or use of the land in return for benefits, which may include tax benefits and other forms of remuneration.[73] In order to implement a conservation easement, a landowner must work with a conservation organization, usually a land trust, which enforces the agreement and agrees to ensure protection of the nonuse conservation values of the land. In the case of a donated conservation easement, the land trust facilitates the conservation easement contract, but does not directly pay the landowner. Not to be confused with transferable development rights, the conservation easement contract effectively extinguishes the land's development use rights in perpetuity, regardless of whether the property is transferred at a future point in time to another owner.[74]

Like emissions trading practices, conservation easements represented a market-based solution to a market failure. While emissions trading reduced the negative externality (air pollution) imposed upon the public from private industry, conservation easements sought to correct a positive externality. Without the corresponding tax breaks, the landowners with such easements are uncompensated for keeping land undeveloped and providing public goods such as wildlife habitat and scenic views.[75] Conservation easements and emissions trading were considered two rather successful market-based programs to provide landowners with a financial incentive to internalize the externalities and to supply a more optimal quantity of environmental goods and nonuse benefits. Although other similar trading programs, such as water

---

[70] *See* Emissions Trading System—Policies, EUROPEAN COMMISSION CLIMATE ACTION, http://ec.europa.eu/environment/climat/emission/index_en.htm (last updated Nov. 15, 2010) (summarizing cap and trade requirements in the European Union).

[71] CHICAGO CLIMATE EXCHANGE, http://www.chicagoclimatex.com (last visited Nov. 26, 2010).

[72] John C. Bergstrom, B.L. Dillman & J.R. Stoll, *Public Environmental Amenity Benefits of Private Land: The Case of Prime Agricultural Land*, 17 S.J. AGRIC. ECON. 139, 139–49 (1985); J. Wyerman, *Private Land Conservation in U.S. Soars*, LAND TRUST ALLIANCE (2006), http://www.landtrustalliance.org/events-news/alliance-news/private -land-conservation-in-u.s.-soars (last visited Nov. 16, 2010).

[73] Parkinson v. Bd. of Assessors, 495 N.E.2d 294 (Mass. 1986) (tax abatements permitted for valid conservation easements on taxpayer's property).

[74] J.A. GUSTANSKI, PROTECTING THE LAND: CONSERVATION EASEMENTS PAST, PRESENT, AND FUTURE 1–14 (2000).

[75] *See generally* CATHERINE M. KESKE, RENTS, EFFICIENCY, AND INCOMPLETE MARKETS: THE EMERGING MARKET FOR PRIVATE LAND PRESERVATION AND CONSERVATION EASEMENTS (2008).

markets, proved to be less successful and did not gain momentum due to information failures and high transactions costs,[76] emissions trading and conservation easements showed that the market could in some cases act as an incentive for industry and private landowners to protect nonuse values from resource use.

By the 21st century, however, concerns about the irreversibility of environmental damage and the rate of change in environmental quality in emerging economies such as India and China called into question whether the market could react quickly enough to provide nonuse benefits and environmental goods in the United States and worldwide.[77] If the market had the potential to protect the environment and nonuse values in some cases, such as emissions trading programs and conservation easements, then why was there still a suboptimal level of environmental goods? A number of factors have contributed to this outcome: different discount rates between developed and developing nations,[78] variability in the preferences for environmental goods within a nation,[79] and differences of opinion between scientists about the level of existing environmental degradation.[80] Publicly owned resources have also produced suboptimal levels of nonuse benefits. As shown by Figure 6.1 above, although government may allocate use and nonuse values on public lands, there is still not enough land and resources to meet everyone's desires.[81]

Failures of the market, limitations associated with government empowerment of individuals raising nonuse interests, and suboptimal results yielded by government ownership of public goods all lead to this conclusion: The only way to achieve an optimal amount of resource use is for humans to actually privatize the resource itself and bestow upon the resource legal rights so that the resource becomes its own player in a game of strategy. What seems to be needed is the legal formalization of the private provisioning of a public good in order to prevent free-riding behaviors. This can

---

[76] Janis M. Carey, David L. Sunding & David Zilberman, *Transaction Costs and Trading Behavior in an Immature Water Market*, 7 Env't & Dev. Econ. 733, 733–750 (2002); J.M. Carey & D.L. Sunding, *Emerging Markets in Water: A Comparative Analysis of the Central Valley and Colorado-Big Thompson Projects*, 14 Nat. Resources J. 283, 283–328 (2001).

[77] Tyler Volk, Co2 Rising: The World's Greatest Environmental Challenge (2009); Kerry Emanuel, What We Know about Climate Change (2009); James Gustave Speth, The Bridge at the End of the World: Capitalism, the Environment, and Crossing from Crisis to Sustainability, 17–45 (2008).

[78] *See* Sebastian Edwards, *Country Risk, Foreign Borrowing, and the Social Discount Rate in an Open Developing Economy*, Nat'l Bureau of Econ. Research, Inc., Working Paper Number 1651 (1986).

[79] Lynne Koontz & Dana L. Hoag, U.S. Geological Survey, Fort Collins Science Center, Analyzing Stakeholder Preferences for Managing Elk and Bison at the National Elk Refuge and Grand Teton National Park: An Example of the Disparate Stakeholder Management Approach Open-File Report 1224 (2005).

[80] Yuko Heath & Robert Gifford, *Free Market Ideology and Environmental Degradation* 38 Env't & Behavior 48, 48–71 (2006).

[81] John B. Loomis & Catherine M. Keske, *Mountain Substitutability and Peak Load Pricing of High Alpine Peaks as a Management Tool to Reduce Environmental Damage: A Contingent Evaluation Study*, 90 J. Envtl. Mgmt. 1751, 1751–60 (2009).

be done by collective action or formation of small groups.[82] Instead of relying on Era IV laws that create rights in people and institutions to raise nonuse values in resources for human-oriented ends, laws should give legal stature and protection to the resource itself so that its nonanthropocentric, ecocentric interests may be advanced in a resource game.[83] Through a series of elegant mathematical and economic models, several authors have shown that reliance on government alone to protect and assert nonuse values simply crowds out private solutions to relentless use activities threatening resource nonuse values.[84]

---

[82] *See generally* MANCUR OLSON, THE LOGIC OF COLLECTIVE ACTION: PUBLIC GOODS AND THE THEORY OF GROUPS (1965).

[83] Peter G. Warr, *Pareto Optimal Redistribution and Private Charity*, 19 J. PUB. ECON. 131, 131–38 (1982); Peter G. Warr, *The Private Provision of a Public Good Is Independent of the Distribution of Income*, 13 ECON. LETTERS 207, 207–11 (1983).

[84] Theodore Bergstrom et al., *supra* note 17; Steven J. Eagle, *Reflections on Private Property, Planning, and State Power*, 61 PLAN. & ENVTL. L. 3 (2009); Harold Demsetz, *Information and Efficiency: Another Viewpoint*, 12 J.L. & ECON. 1 (1969).

7 Era V—The Age of Ecocentrism

DESPITE THE UBIQUITOUSNESS of Era IV laws, which gave individuals, organizations, and governments the ability to raise their human-based interest in resource nonuse, the Anthrocene Age still experienced escalating human demands on resource nonuse services.[1] The questions that arise from this failure are: Why are these laws and legal institutions unable to protect resource nonuse values? And what must be done to secure effective protection of the endangered nonuse component of resources?

The answer to the first question in large part lies in the fact that Era IV laws, while purporting to protect resource nonuse values, in reality gave humans and their institutions the right to assert their own anthropocentric interests in resource nonuse.[2] This human-centered focus has in turn been based on the standard economic assumption that environmental and resource policies should be assessed exclusively in terms of their effects on the well-being and preferences of individuals.[3] The answer to the second question follows from the answer to the first: If laws that permit humans to raise their interests in resource nonuse cannot adequately deter human assaults on the planet's natural resource base, then perhaps laws should give legal status to the resource itself so that its nonanthropocentric, ecocentric interests may be protected.

---

[1] *See, e.g.*, CLIMATE CHANGE: WHAT IT MEANS FOR US, OUR CHILDREN, AND OUR GRANDCHILDREN (JOSEPH F.C. DIMENTO & PAMELA M. DOUGHMAN EDS., 2007); HARVEY BLATT, AMERICA'S ENVIRONMENTAL REPORT CARD: ARE WE MAKING THE GRADE? (2005);.

[2] *See supra* Chapter 6, section B.

[3] Jonathon A. Lesser, Daniel E. Dobbs and Richard O. Zerbe, Jr., *Environmental Economics and Policy*, 40–43 (1997).

The establishment of a right of nonuse held by natural resources would permit resources to assert a legally acknowledged right to be left alone when threatened by human use desires. Such a right would also empower a third player in the natural resources game: the resource itself and its nonuse component. When the resource's own nonuse interest must be reckoned with by the other two legally recognized resource players—users and nonusers raising human interests—the resulting resources game may finally yield a cooperative solution and an equilibrium that is a collectively optimal result.

A. Resource Endangerment despite Era IV Laws

Most of the resource nonuse laws put in place during Era IV rested on two pillars of standard microeconomic theory. First, based on the groundbreaking work of welfare economist A. C. Pigou, policy makers realized that pollution was an externality or social cost of production that required some non-market response to an otherwise intractable market failure.[4] Era IV pollution control laws were in turn designed to constrain the health risks that one person may impose on another. These laws were also meant to internalize externalities when resources such as air, water, and land are used as free dumping grounds for waste, thereby impairing the indirect use value that humans enjoy from unpolluted public environmental goods.[5] Second, based on the insight of John Krutilla and others that people value natural objects simply because they are natural when unused, policy makers also recognized that markets fail to respond to the nonuse value of natural objects that people want to preserve, but may not ever use, consume, or experience.[6] As a consequence of this realization, statutes were enacted that preserved natural landscapes, landmarks, and living things such as endangered wildlife.[7]

All these pollution prevention and resource preservation laws no doubt have helped to reduce the rate of pollution of public environmental goods and the degradation and destruction of natural objects. However, by the first decade of the 21st century it was becoming apparent that they had not been able to prevent four potentially catastrophic environmental threats. These drivers of planetary collapse include climate crisis,[8]

---

[4] *See generally* A.C. Pigou, The Economics of Welfare 172–203 (4th ed. 1932).

[5] *E.g.*, Clean Air Act, 42 U.S.C. §§ 7401–7671q (2006); Noaki Schwartz, *60 Percent in Nation Live in Dirty Air*, Denv. Post, April 29, 2009, at 6A, *available at* http://www .denverpost.com/search/c:_12249820.

[6] *See generally* John V. Krutilla, *Conservation Reconsidered*, 57 Am. Econ. Rev. 777 (1967).

[7] *See e.g.*, Wilderness Act, 16 U.S.C. §§ 1131–1136 (2006); Endangered Species Act, 7 U.S.C. § 136, 16 U.S.C. §§ 1531–1544; Antiquities Act, 16 U.S.C. §§ 431–433 (1906).

[8] *See generally* Tyler Volk, *CO2 Rising: The World's Greatest Environmental Challenge* (2009); Mark Lynas, Six Degrees: Our Future on a Hotter Planet (2007); Kerry Emanuel, *What We Know About Climate Change* (2009); *Remember Kyoto? Most Nations Don't*, N.Y.TIMES 10 (Dec. 4, 2011) (from 1990 to 2009, global emissions of carbon dioxide, them ain greenhouse gas produced by burning fossil fuels, rose by 38 per cent); Gillian Gotora, *Climate Change Intensifies Struggles of African Farmers*, The Denver Post 16A (Nov. 27, 2011); Dan Vergano & Doyle Rice, *"Game Changer": Report on Climate Change Urges Action*, USA Today, June 17, 2009, at 6D, *available at* http://www.usatoday.com/weather/climate/globalwarming/

natural systems destruction,[9] diminution of biomass productivity,[10] and species extinction.[11] Unlike pollution and impairment of natural objects, these four particular perils do not just threaten human welfare, they jeopardize the earth's entire biosphere, irrespective of human preferences or needs.[12] Passage of more Era IV-like pollution prevention and resource preservation laws seems doomed.[13] After all, the four threats to planetary survival arose despite the existence of such laws. What is called for is something new—some response that does what existing law does not.

B. From Human Harm to Eco-Harm

The distinguishing characteristic of Era IV laws was that they acknowledged a human preference that certain resources not be used, because the converse—resource use—was interfering with various human nonuse values. For example, use of public environmental goods as pollution sinks was thought to impair human health values, while use and development of wild lands and species habitat as economic commodities was thought to impair the existence value of natural objects people wanted to preserve. The laws that responded to these resource nonuse preferences were thereby either explicitly or implicitly anthropocentric.[14] These laws assumed that the harms sought to be redressed were harms to humans, but not necessarily to the natural resource being overused by humans.[15]

2009-06-16 -Climate_change_damage_n.htm; Mark Jaffe, *Developing World's Impact Rises in Ozone*, DENV. POST, Feb. 19, 2009, at 12A, *available at* http://www.denverpost.com/headlines/ci_11738042.

[9] *See generally* JAMES LOVELOCK, THE REVENGE OF GAIA: EARTH'S CLIMATE CRISIS AND THE FATE OF HUMANITY (2006); TYLER VOLK, GAIA'S BODY: TOWARD A PHYSIOLOGY OF EARTH (2003); Ruhl et al., *supra* note 6; REED F. NOSS ET AL., ENDANGERED ECOSYSTEMS OF THE UNITED STATES: A PRELIMINARY ASSESSMENT OF LOSS AND DEGRADATION, app. A (1995), *available at* http://biology.usgs.gov/pubs/ecosys.

[10] VACLAV SMIL, THE EARTH'S BIOSPHERE: EVOLUTION, DYNAMICS AND CHANGE (2002); *See* THE WORLDWATCH INSTITUTE, VITAL SIGNS 2002, at 106 (2002).

[11] STEPHEN M. MEYER, THE END OF THE WILD (2006); Boris Worm et al., *Impacts of Biodiversity Loss on Ocean Ecosystem Services*, 314 SCI. 787 (2006); Council on Environmental Quality, *Environmental Quality, 21st Ann. Rep.* 137 (1990); Corneia Dean, *One-Third of U.S. Bird Species Endangered, Survey Finds*, N.Y. TIMES, Mar. 20, 2009, at A15, *available at* http://www.nytimes.com/2009/03/20/science/earth/20bird.html.

[12] James Gustave Speth, *The Bridge at the End of the World: Capitalism, the Environment, and Crossing From Crisis to Sustainability* (2008); FRED PEARCE, WITH SPEED AND VIOLENCE: WHY SCIENTISTS FEAR TIPPING POINTS IN CLIMATE CHANGE (2007); Geoffrey Lean, *A World Dying, But Can We Unite to Save It?*, INDEPENDENT U.K., Nov. 18, 2007, *available at* http://www.independent.co.uk/environment/climate_change/a-world-dying-but-can-we -unite-to-save-it-400847.html.

[13] Michael Shellenberger & Ted Nordhaus, *The Death of Environmentalism: Global Warming Politics in a Post-Environmental World* (2004).

[14] *See supra* Chapter 6, section B.

[15] *See, e.g.*, Summers v. Earth Island Inst., 129 S. Ct. 1142, 1148–49 (2009) ("Anglo-American courts . . . [are restricted] to redress or prevent actual or imminently threatened injury to persons . . . ."); Friends of the Earth, Inc. v. Laidlaw Envtl. Servs., Inc., 528 U.S. 167, 181 (2000) ("[It] is not injury to the environment but injury to the plaintiff [that matters]."). *See also* Heather Elliott, *The Functions of Standing*, 61 STAN. L. REV. 459, 485–86 n.126 (2008) (it is difficult "to sue to vindicate environmental interests . . . [because the relevant] harm . . . [is not] to the environment . . . [but] harm to the plaintiff").

This human-centered view reflected in Era IV laws was, and is, consistent with one of the central tenets of welfare economics: Nature is valuable only as a means to the end of individual well-being, defined as the satisfaction of preferences. The goal of social policy, as reflected in laws, has therefore been to raise the level of human welfare—or to maximize the social aggregate of utility—as much as natural resources allow.[16] Legal resource policies are to be assessed exclusively in terms of their effects on individuals; conversely, a law or policy that is unrelated to individual well-being is largely irrelevant.[17] Moreover, welfare economists argue that the satisfaction of individual preferences—and its collective product, social welfare—is best tested by willingness to pay for environmental benefits such as nonuse values.[18] For example, the reduction of pollution from public environmental goods is a preference reflected in environmental quality policies because humans are willing to pay for the enforcement of laws that protect the nonuse benefits of uncontaminated air, water, and soil.[19] And the existence value of unused wild lands is a preference incorporated in laws authorizing conservation easements, because humans are willing to pay to have some lands go undeveloped.[20]

These human-based laws are meant to legitimize resource nonusers so that nonusers can act as a countervailing force to user interests. But there is another stakeholder in natural resources conflicts that is usually not legally legitimated by Era IV laws—the resource itself. User-versus-nonuser conflicts are typically clashes between two classes of humans who are driven by individual self-interest where the central question for each class is: What is the outcome that is good for me? A question that is rarely asked during conflicts between users and nonusers is: What is the outcome that is good for the resource itself?

Gradually, commentators are beginning to take recognition of the anthropocentrism inherent in traditional responses to environmental calamities and the tensions that may arise when nonuse protections are framed in human, but not necessarily environmental terms.[21] These commentators challenge human-centered value systems, and instead embrace the intrinsic worth of plants, animals, habitat, ecosystem, and natural

---

16 Mark Sagoff, Price, Principle, and the Environment 8–9 (2004).

17 *See* Louis Kaplow & Steven Shavell, Fairness versus Welfare 16 (2002); Edith Stokey & Richard Zeckhauser, A Primer for Policy Analysis 275 (1978) ("individual welfare is all that counts in making policy choices"); Kenneth Arrow et al., *Is There a Rule for Benefit-Cost Analysis in Environmental, Health, and Safety Regulation?*, 272 Sci. 221, 221–22 (1996) ("[V]alues to be assigned to program effects . . . should be those of the affected individuals . . . .").

18 James R. Kahn, The Economic Approach to Environmental and Natural Resources (1998).

19 *See, e.g.*, Anne R. Carey & Karl Gelles, *Environmental Concerns*, USA Today, Apr. 28, 2009, at 1A (most adults worry a "great deal" about pollution of drinking water, river and lake pollution, and soil contamination by toxic waste).

20 Margaret Jackson, *Ruling Puts Value on Land Contribution*, Denv. Post, May 12, 2009, at 7B (U.S. Tax Court upholds conservation easement program allowing landowners to receive tax deductions in exchange for restricting use development on their land).

21 *See, e.g.*, Günther Handl, *Human Rights and Protection of the Environment*, *in* Economic, Social and Cultural Rights 303–05 (Asbjørn Eide, Catarina Krause & Allan Rosas eds., 2001); Dinah Shelton, Environmental Rights, People's Rights (Philip Alsten ed., 2001).

resources irrespective of instrumental or economic worth.[22] They also realize protection of nonuse benefits primarily for human ends will likely fall short of meeting global environmental goals.[23] Acknowledgement of ecocentric values suggests that legal norms should not be defined in purely anthropocentric terms, but must also acknowledge the ecocentric worth and benefit of natural resources when they are left alone by humans.

Unfortunately, antipollution and preservation legislation continues to be framed in light of human benefits that derive from nonuse benefits,[24] and environmental protection measures found in international law are also typically couched in human rights terms.[25] Although several state constitutions provide a legal right to a healthful environment, reviewing courts have ruled that these provisions refer only to human health, and not to nonhuman elements of the environment.[26] These decisions are consistent with the prevailing view that conceives of the natural environment and its resources as a mere good that serves to satisfy human needs while possessing no intrinsic value.

This anthropocentric perspective has not been able to halt the four harbingers of planetary collapse noted above in part A.[27] What seems needed is an ecocentric view that begins with the assumption that the nonuse component of resources is a condition to all life on the planet, including but not limited to human health. It would follow then that legal institutions should do more than impose limitations on individual human freedom to exploit the use component of resources and allow individuals to assert the human benefits that arise from resource nonuse. Laws and legal norms should also recognize that natural resources are a good in their own right. Such laws would not have the protection of humans as the central focus, but instead would acknowledge the right to have the natural environment itself protected.

C. A Right of Nonuse and the Rise of a Third Player in the Resource Game

The idea of affording legal rights to natural resources has not escaped the attention of courts or commentators. In *Georgia v. Tennessee Copper Co.*,[28] the U.S. Supreme

---

[22] *See, e.g.*, Christopher J. Preston, Saving Creation: Nature and Faith in the Life of Holmes Rolston III (2009); David Takacs, The Idea of Biodiversity 249–54 (1996). In one survey, 87% of the public agreed with the statement "Our obligation to preserve nature is not just a responsibility to other people but the environment itself." Willett Kempton, James S. Bosten & Jennifer A. Hartley, Environmental Values in American Culture 113 (1997).

[23] Michael R. Anderson, *Human Rights Approaches to Environmental Protection: An Overview*, *in* Human Rights Approaches to Environmental Protection (Alan E. Boyle & Michael R. Anderson eds., 1996).

[24] *See supra* Chapter 6, section B.

[25] Luis E. Rodriguez-Rivera, *Is the Human Right to Environment Recognized Under International Law? It Depends on the Source*, 12 Colo. J. Int'l Envtl. L. & Pol'y 1, 4 (2001).

[26] Glisson v. City of Marion, 720 N.E. 2d 1034, 1044 (Ill. 1999); *see also* Sunburst School Dist. No. Two v. Texaco, Inc., 2007 MT 183, 165 P.3d 1079, 1088 (Mont. 2007).

[27] *See supra* notes 8–11.

[28] 206 U.S. 230, 238–39 (1907).

Court in 1907 expanded the scope of quasi-sovereign interests protected by state *parens patriae* suits from protecting not only the health of their citizens from public nuisances, but also to safeguarding land, air, and natural resources.[29] In 1972, Professor Christopher Stone argued that states should not be the only advocates for natural resources. Stone proposed that natural objects should have the ability to raise their own unique interest in nonuse values and environmental quality.[30] A landmark federal energy bill, the Clean Energy Act of 2009, designed to reduce greenhouse gases contributing to climate change, would encourage resource nonuse actions that have reverse global-warming effects by absorbing carbon dioxide.[31] This bill would permit such resource nonuse decisions—for example, a forest company not cutting trees it would otherwise harvest—to be marketed to resource users and polluters as offsets.[32] Another ecocentric approach is reflected in Ecuador's new constitution, which gives "[n]atural communities and ecosystems . . . the unalienable right to exist, flourish[,] and evolve"[33] The Ecuadorian law explicitly measures environmental injury not to a person or people, but to the ecosystem; it creates a non-anthropocentric right of nonuse in natural resources.

These ecocentric measures are slowly moving us toward a paradigm that sees a natural resource as a good in its own right, rather than only as an instrument of human preference. Such a paradigm would value resources for the worth and benefit they provide the biosphere when they are left alone. But in order to resist human desires to use resources, one cannot rely only on humans raising their own interest in nonuse values by asserting an array of Era IV species-chauvinistic laws. These laws have resulted in noncooperative resource games between users and nonusers, and they have not deterred climate change, natural systems destruction, biomass depletion, or species extinction. Instead, one should also create a legal right in the resource itself: a right of nonuse that acknowledges and empowers a third player in the natural resources game, the natural resource.

A natural resource empowered by a legally cognizable "right of nonuse" would be able to affect and perhaps prevent human development, exploitation, and use of that resource when such use would substantially interfere with the nonuse qualities that are essential to natural ecocentric processes. These processes include the creation and perpetuation of clean air, water, and land capable of sustaining the biosphere. Natural processes also encompass the indirect uses that follow from human nonuse of resources listed in Table 2.1 above, such as carbon sequestration, uncontaminated fertile soils,

[29] *Id.* at 237 ("[T]he state has an interest independent of . . . its citizens, in all the earth and air within its domain."); *see also* Massachusetts v. EPA, 549 U.S. 497, 499 (2007). *See also* American Electric Power v. Connecticut, 131 S. Ct. 2527 (2011).

[30] Christopher D. Stone, *Should Trees Have Standing? Toward Legal Rights for Natural Objects*, 45 S. Cal. L. Rev. 450, 456 (1972).

[31] H.R. 2454, 111th Cong. (2010).

[32] Michael Riley, *Windfall For, or Waste of, Energy?*, Denv. Post, June 27, 2009, at 20A, *available at* http://www.denverpost.com/politics/ci_12701102?source = pkg.

[33] Clare Kendall, *A New Law of Nature*, Guardian, Sept. 24, 2008, *available at* http://www.guardian.co.uk/environment/2008/sep/24/equador.conservation.

contiguous parcels of undeveloped land for natural ecosystems, and moderated climate, weather, temperature, and precipitation. The planet itself benefits from these resource nonuse qualities, not just the one species on this planet that has been so intent on either aggressively using resources for purely anthropocentric ends, or conversely, preventing such uses for human health and existence values. A right of nonuse would permit the nonuse qualities for resources to be asserted for ecocentric purposes.

A right of nonuse would establish an Era V game that now has three players: the user who relies on Era III laws permitting resource use, the nonuser who relies on Era IV laws protecting anthropocentric anti-pollution and resource preservation values, and the resource that can raise its Era V right of nonuse to sustain long-term ecocentric benefits that are of worth to the entire biosphere. Because the resource has become a credible player, the dynamics of the Era IV two-player game between users and nonusers have changed. These two players have traditionally been locked in a noncooperative game where the best that can be expected is an uneasy Nash equilibrium, where neither can improve its condition without ending up in a less desirable situation. But as noted in Chapter 5 in Figure 5.1, when competing resource users clashed, or in Chapter 6, in Figure 6.1, when competing users and nonusers conflicted, this eventual Nash equilibrium outcome has not yielded a satisfactory, socially optimal result. The introduction of a third player—the resource—now able to raise its own interests, provides a critical incentive for coordination between users and nonusers. Coordination can bring about cooperation between these two human players that results in a Pareto optimal solution where everyone, and everything, is made better off.[34]

The three players each have two choices. First, they may contribute to nonuse values, and this contribution in turn both benefits the viability of the biosphere and provides indirect uses consistent with human survival. Second, they may not contribute to nonuse values, which occurs when their choices either interfere with or are neutral toward the nonuse component of resources. The choice to contribute or not refers to whether the choice will provide or deny a payoff to the resource's nonuse potential. In the case of a user or nonuser, the motive behind the choice may be anthropocentric, but the effect of this human choice is experienced by the resource. For example, a user may choose to not contribute by polluting, removing, or otherwise using the resource in a way that prevents the resource's nonuse qualities from being realized. A nonuser may choose to contribute by financially supporting nonuse values—for example, for option value, in order to recreate there in the future—or for existence value, knowing that a landscape will be preserved, or simply by the act of leaving the resource alone.

The third player in this game, the resource, obviously has no opinions or volitional choices. The resource simply exists in one of two states: where humans leave it alone, so it can produce its nonuse benefits, or where humans use it, exploit it, and degrade it, in which case it is more difficult for it to yield nonuse value. In Eras II and III, the resource was used in different ways by the user. In Era IV, nonusers became players and

---

[34] *See generally* Richard H. McAdams, *Beyond the Prisoners' Dilemma: Coordination, Game Theory, and Laws*, 82 S. CAL. L. REV. 209 (2009). *See also* Chapter 15.

were able to slow, deter, or halt resource use by asserting their human-centric interests in resource nonuse. In Era V, where the resource has been conferred a right of nonuse, the resource is no longer a passive reflection of user and nonuser interests; the resource now has the legal ability to protect its ecocentric nonuse capabilities. The choice for the Era V resource is to contribute toward the furtherance of nonuse values by affirmatively asserting its right of nonuse, or to not contribute by existing without imposing the nonuse right.

The exercise of this choice to either assert or not assert the right of nonuse hinges on whether the user and nonuser, in a two-player game, decide to contribute to maintaining the resource and its nonuse benefits. Without the resource's ability to raise its own right of nonuse, users and nonusers typically engaged in two-player noncooperative games of brinkmanship, previously diagrammed in Chapters 5 and 6, in Figures 5.1 and 6.1. These games produced equlibria that were typically neither optimal from the perspective of the parties nor that of the larger society. When a third player is introduced into such a game, and where this third player has a legal voice in the outcome, the dynamics of the normal two-player game change. The fact that the resource can play its "right of nonuse card" alters the behavior of the users and nonusers when they engage in their two-player game.

The right of nonuse does not necessarily need to be asserted by the resource in a three-player game; if the user and nonuser can coordinate their choices in light of an incipient future resource nonuse right, those two human players may engage in a cooperative game that yields a Pareto optimal solution. The role of a right of nonuse by the resource, then, is not to bludgeon users and nonusers into accepting ecocentric nonuse values. It is to provide a mechanism that promotes the alteration of a noncooperative two-player, user-nonuser game into a cooperative game.[35]

The three-player game is in fact a two-stage game.[36] During the first stage, the users and nonusers simultaneously decide whether to contribute to maintaining the resource's nonuse values and its concomitant indirect use benefits that humans thereby enjoy. During this first stage, both players know that the third player, the resource, holds a right of nonuse. Both players also know that the resource would prefer that each player contribute to nonuse values and indirect use benefits. Furthermore, both players know during this stage that the resource would rather not engage in an expensive legal action raising and defending the resource's right of nonuse; the resource would prefer to be left alone, without imposing its legal nonuse right. This knowledge, along with the knowledge of the resource's latent potential to assert its own nonuse interests, should serve as a catalyst during stage one to change what would have been noncooperative strategies into a cooperative solution between users and nonusers.

If nonuse values remain threatened, and if stage one has not produced a cooperative game, the resource may step in and effectively act as a third player in the second stage of the game. By affirmatively asserting its Era V right of nonuse, the resource is now able to contribute to its continued existence. But it will formally trigger the

[35] Robert Sugden, *A Theory of Focal Points*, 105 ECON. J. 533 (1995); McAdams, *supra* note 34, at 231.

[36] *See* the appendix that follows for a more detailed description of this three-player game.

right of nonuse only when the other two human players, the user and nonuser, are not willing to contribute. The resource will sequentially join in the game to maintain its self-interest only if the other two human players do not cooperatively protect ecocentric nonuse values and resulting anthropocentric indirect use values. It is the ability of the resource to effectively trump during stage two the noncooperating human players' actions during stage one that makes this a three-player, two-stage game. And it is the acknowledgement of the resource as an independent player with intrinsic qualities—providing planet-wide nonuse benefits that are not just defined by human utility—that permits this particular game to result in a socially optimal result.

APPENDIX

Economic Model of the Era V "Right of Nonuse" Game

In this game, it is known to all players that Player 3, the resource, now has the right to exist. Nonusers and users understand that the resource will prevail if one of the other players does not contribute to supporting the indirect use values. However, the sub-game requiring a different sequence of decisions between Player 1 and Player 2 is imperfect because it is not known whether either of these two players will take the strategy of contributing to indirect uses. This results in a simultaneous sub-game between users and nonusers, followed by a sequential game where the resource will contribute if the non-users will not contribute.

Figures 7.1 and 7.2 reflect a two-stage, three-by-three game, presented in a two-by-four matrix rather than a three-dimensional matrix. There are three payoffs that reflect indirect use values to each player based upon each player's choices. The left-most payoff is that of Player 1, the user. The middle payoff reflects Player 2, the nonuser. The payoff furthest to the right is that of Player 3, the resource. The best payoff for each player, given the actions of the other players, is italicized. The payoff values can be explained as follows:

- The resource receives the most benefit when both of the other players contribute (4) because indirect use benefits are least threatened.
- The resource receives the second highest level of benefit (3) when one other player contributes and the resource does not need to contribute.
- Players receive a benefit of 2 when one other player contributes to the resource and they do not, because these players are able to receive benefits from free riding on that player's contribution. Users and nonusers also receive a benefit of 2 when

		Player 3: The Resource	Contribute			Not Contribute	
	Player 2: Nonuser		Contribute	Not Contribute		Contribute	Not Contribute
	Contribute		(2, 2, 4)	(1, 2, 2)		(2, 2, 4)	(1, 2, 3)
Player 1: User							
	Not Contribute		(2, 1, 2)	(1, 1, 1)		(2, 1, 3)	(–1, –1, –1)

FIGURE 7.1 Stage 1 in the three-player game of chicken.

both contribute, to reflect the cooperation and shared costs and benefits of maintaining indirect use benefits.

- Players receive a benefit of 1 when they must contribute to the resource and other players do not do so.
- Players receive a payoff of -1 when no one contributes, because the indirect use benefits of the parcel are destroyed.

In the first stage, a sub-game between Player 1 (user) and Player 2 (nonuser), should the user decide to contribute, the payoff to the nonuser is equal to 2, as the nonuser is able to free ride to some extent. Should Player 1 (user) not contribute, the best that the nonuser can do is a payoff of 1, because the nonuser is forced to contribute. This yields a payoff of 2 to the user, who is able to free ride when the nonuser is forced to contribute.

If Player 2 (the nonuser) decides to contribute, the best that Player 1 (the user) can do is contribute, resulting in a payoff of 2. However, if the nonuser decides to not contribute,

		Player 3: The Resource	Contribute			Not Contribute	
	Player 2: Nonuser		Contribute	Not Contribute		Contribute	Not Contribute
	Contribute		(2, 2, 4)	(1, 2, 2)		(2, 2, 4)	(1, 2, 3)
Player 1: User							
	Not Contribute		(2, 1, 2)	(1, 1, 1)		(2, 1, 3)	(–1, –1, –1)

FIGURE 7.2 Stage 2 in the three-player game of chicken.

then the best that the user can do is to contribute, which results in a payoff of 1 to the user. In this case, the nonuser becomes the free rider and receives a payoff of 2.

The payoffs are expressed in this order: Player 1 (user), Player 2 (nonuser), Player 3 (resource).

After the first stage of this game, there are some interesting results. One result is that there are seven potential Nash equilibria. This will be resolved once the resource plays during the second stage. The second interesting result is that this game of chicken forces at least one player (either the user or the nonuser) to contribute to providing indirect use values. The box at the lower right (-1,-1,-1) is not in consideration for the Nash equilibrium.

The results of the second stage, the resource's play, are presented in Figure 7.2. The resource knows the results of the first stage, the sub-game between the users and nonusers. Because the resource knows that others are willing to contribute and the resource prefers not to contribute, it will simply not play its first column (which encompasses the nonusers' first two columns). This leaves the second column, Not Contribute, encompassing the nonusers' second two columns for its actions. Therefore, the resource will choose the path that provides it the highest payoff, given the actions of the other players.

The resource will receive the highest payoff if both Players 1 and 2 contribute, and the resource itself does not contribute. This is also a Pareto optimal solution, and transaction costs may be minimized. While there are two other Nash equilibria, as Player 3 plays a sub-game with each of the players, its payoff of 4 each selected twice (hence, the value is shaded). The effect of giving the resource a right of nonuse means that the best action for both users and nonusers to take is to contribute to the indirect uses maintained by the resource. The right of nonuse effectively creates a quasi-cooperative game.

PART III

A Legal History of Resource Use and Nonuse

PART II OFFERED an economic and social history of resource use and nonuse on this planet. Another history that reveals a similar ignorance of the nonanthropocentric nonuse dimensions of natural resources is one that considers how laws and legal institutions have evolved over time. As part of this evolution, laws first encouraged human use of resources, and then protected human nonuse desires regarding resources, as humans began to realize that they benefitted when natural resources were left alone and not actively used. Both sets of laws, first-generation "use" laws and second-generation "nonuse" laws, were designed to benefit humans. The issue that is the topic of the chapters in Part III is whether, and when, laws might be adopted that protect natural resources for their own intrinsic value, not because of their derivative anthropocentric value. The failure of law adequately to protect natural resources when legal rules are designed only for human purposes suggests that the time has come for a third generation of laws, nonanthropocentric in nature, that reflects the value to this planet of the nonuse component of natural resources.

8 An Introduction to the History of Law and Natural Resources

OUR RELATIONSHIP WITH the earth's natural resources has changed over time. For centuries, humans used resources for their own personal and economic interests. They extracted "stock" resources, such as minerals and energy fuels, to become better off economically. "Renewable commodity" goods, such as timber and rangeland and fisheries, were harvested to further economic growth. And "public environmental" goods, such as the air, waters, land, and underground resources, were used as convenient and free locations to dump emissions, effluent, and waste.

Humanity prospered by controlling, depleting, and polluting nature's resources. Welfare was served when forests were turned into farms, wetlands into cities, mountains into mines. Developing countries were deemed successful if their natural landscapes had been transformed from wild lands to utilitarian places where we could live, work, and create individual wealth. It seemed that three types of natural resources (stock, renewable commodity, and public environmental) had one primary purpose: to be used and exploited by one special planetary species—us.[1]

Initially, laws, and particularly the common law of contract and property, encouraged and protected this resource use. The use value of resources was benefitted first by contract law. This law permitted one user to make enforceable, credible marketplace deals with other potential users of resources, particularly stock resources, so that the resource would wind up with the user most willing to pay for it (and who,

[1] MARK SAGOFF, PRICE, PRINCIPLE, AND THE ENVIRONMENT 15 (2004).

in theory, would put it to the most efficient use).[2] Resource use was next furthered by the invention of property law. This law allowed users to own the resource, and to exercise the right to control, develop, and exploit it to enhance the owner's selfish interests.[3]

These "first generation" resource-use laws, prevalent throughout much of the 19th and early 20th centuries, reflected a judgment that endured for multiple centuries: Stock and renewable commodity resources should first be owned and then utilized by individuals. These owner-individuals would, in pursuit of selfish interests, transform, extract, use, or exchange them in the relevant market. The working assumption was that laws furthering the operation of the economic market would then ensure that what was best for the individual resource owner would ultimately also be best for the overall society in which that owner lived.[4]

Eventually, however, excessive use depleted stock and renewable commodity resources. Reliance on the economic market as a resource-regulating mechanism had failed, in large part because owners of private property had little incentive to not use their resource wealth.[5] Indeed, if they did not use their resources, they were often by operation of law deemed to have abandoned or forfeited their rights to their property.[6] Gradual resource exhaustion and depletion caused lawmakers to adopt another category of "first generation" resource use laws, designed to slow unchecked resource extraction, and create a more sustainable resource base for future generations of resource use.[7]

These conservation laws still had as their primary purpose the long-term use of resources, albeit use that was now somewhat regulated to moderate the unchecked exploitation that had threatened the long-term viability of both exhaustible and renewable resources. But by the middle of the 20th century, both categories of resource use laws (those encouraging present use and those conserving for future use) had not prevented the depletion of the stock and renewable resource base. Moreover, such use had begun to pollute public environmental foods, such as the air, the water, and the soils. The heretofore dominant "use" component of natural uses was now threatening another facet of resources—the critical "nonuse" component.

---

[2] KARL POLANYI, THE GREAT TRANSFORMATION: THE POLITICAL AND ECONOMIC ORIGINS OF OUR TIME (1957); ADAM SMITH, AN INQUIRY INTO THE NATURE AND CAUSES OF THE WEALTH OF NATIONS (1776).

[3] DAVID FEENY, THE DEVELOPMENT OF PROPERTY RIGHTS IN LAND: A COMPARATIVE STUDY, IN TOWARD A POLITICAL ECONOMY OF DEVELOPMENT: A RATIONAL CHOICE PERSPECTIVE 272 (Robert Bates ed. 1988); Harold Demsetz, *Toward a Theory of Property Rights*, 57 AM. ECON. REV. 347 (1967).

[4] *Ronald Findlay, The Roots of Divergence: Western Economic History in Comparative Perspective*, 82 AM. ECON. REV. 158 (1992); DOUGLAS C. NORTH & ROBERT B. THOMAS, THE RISE OF THE WESTERN WORLD: A NEW ECONOMIC HISTORY (1973).

[5] A.V. KNEESE AND BLAIR T. BOWER, ENVIRONMENTAL QUALITY ANALYSIS: THEORY AND METHOD IN THE SOCIAL SCENES 1–6 (1972).

[6] General Mining Law of 1872, 30 U.S.C. § 328, requiring mining claimants on public lands to perform annually $100 of "assessment work" to maintain a mining claim.

[7] *See, e.g.,* the Taylor Grazing Act of 1934, 43 U.S.C. § 315 et seq., restricting the use of public lands for open grazing purposes, which lands were previously opened up for unrestricted use by Buford v. Houtz, 133 U.S. 320 (1890).

Nonuse values prevail when resources are *not* used by humans, and when the resource is left alone in its natural state. Humans benefit in three ways from resources in a nonuse state. First, certain natural resources, especially public environmental goods such as air and water, are preconditions to human survival and existence when they are not used as pollution sinks.[8] Second, undeveloped natural lands and locations have recreational value for those wishing to engage in low-impact play. Also, certain natural objects, such as wild lands or wildlife species, have high "existence" value for humans in that their mere existence in an unused condition is important to us; we place a value on their place in nature, even though we do not intend to consume or own them, as we do stock or renewable commodity resources.[9] Third, some resources, such as wetlands, rain forests, and estuaries, have economic value for humans in their natural condition because they provide crucial ecological services to humans that markets fail to price. Unspoiled nature serves as "natural capital," providing long-term economic benefits that more than offset the short-term disadvantages involved in forgoing human development.[10]

Mid-20th century resource depletion and pollution adversely affected these nonuse components of resources. This alarmed humans who had, for eons, been able to personally thrive and economically prosper due to resource nonuse qualities.[11] Our response to this threat to nonuse benefits was (once again) to turn toward the law and legal institutions. Throughout the Western world, and especially in the United States, a series of statutes was enacted, and government policies adopted, that were designed to curb resource use, not because we wanted to conserve the resource for more future use, but to protect our very human need for resource *nonuse* benefits.[12]

These second-generation legal initiatives served four purposes: (1) to *protect human health* with regard to pollution; (2) to *preserve natural objects* (such as wild lands and wildlife) that humans deemed valuable for either recreational or preservationist benefits; (3) to employ non-command structures that instead relied on *market-based approaches* to environmental quality; and (4) to *prevent destruction of natural systems* deemed economically important to human welfare (such as wetlands).

---

[8] When it is unowned, land is also a public environmental good necessary for human life.

[9] John K. Krutilla, *Conservation Reconsidered*, 57 AM. ECON. REV. 787 (1967).

[10] *See* NATURE'S SERVICES: SOCIETAL DEPENDENCE ON NATURAL ECOSYSTEMS (Gretchen C. Daily, ed. 1997).

[11] Gretchen C. Daily, Susan Alexander, Paul R. Ehrlich et al., *Ecosystem Services: Benefits Supplied to Human Societies by Natural Ecosystems*, ISSUES IN ECOLOGY 2 (Spring 1997); Graciela Chichilnisky & Geoffrey Heal, *Economic Returns From the Biosphere*, 391 NATURE 629 (Feb. 1998).

[12] *See, e.g.*, RICHARD J. LAZARUS, THE MAKING OF ENVIRONMENTAL LAW (2004). Some of these statutes were designed to permit and encourage a resource use that did not entail removal, extraction, or development of the land: recreation. *See* National Park Service Organic Act, 16 U.S.C. § 22; Multiple Use Sustained Act, 16 U.S.C. §§ 528–531; Federal Lands Policy Management Act, 43 U.S.C. § 1701. However, some recreational uses of lands, especially public lands, produced environmental impacts as harmful as traditional extractive uses. Jan G. Laitos & Rachael B. Reiss, *Recreation Wars for Our Natural Resources*, 34 ENVTL. L. 1091 (2004); Southern Utah Wilderness Alliance v. Norton, 542 U.S. 55 (2004). Other laws were designed to provide aesthetic and health benefits when use prohibitions were imposed. *See* Hoffman v. Deschutes County, 240 P.3d 79 (Or. App. 2010) (upholding setback requirements from structures near surface mine operations).

Antipollution laws used command-and-control rules to constrain the risks that one person can impose on another during the course of resource use (particularly when public environmental goods were being overexploited as receptacles for our garbage). Preservation laws protected forests, landscapes, wild lands, and wildlife from resource extraction and development.[13] Laws that attempted to stimulate private markets to protect the environment were seeking economic efficiency.[14] Proposed laws that focused on restoration of natural capital and ecosystem goods sought to protect the capacity of nature to deliver environmental services to humans.[15]

Laws furthering these goals of protection, preservation, efficiency, and restoration were constructed around limiting human "use" intrusions of nature. The assumption behind second-generation antipollution laws was that if use were restricted, there would be less human contamination of the necessary "nonuse" qualities of public environmental goods (e.g., a clean and healthful atmosphere). The assumption behind second-generation preservation laws was that use limits would protect natural objects such as wild places and living organisms for low-level recreation and existence value. The assumption behind market-based solutions was that these would be more effective and less administratively expensive than command-and-control rules. The assumption behind second-generation ecosystem services initiatives was that excessive human use had degraded the ability of natural systems to provide humans with economically essential, but largely undervalued, nature-based goods. These laws and regulations had the effect of constraining and conditioning, and making more expensive and problematic, the use and development of natural resources.

This legal intervention represented an important shift in judgment about the role of law with respect to natural resource development. Previously, first-generation contract and property law sought to bring about what was good for the individual, such as the resource owner. First-generation conservation statutes similarly sought to temporarily limit short-term resource use to ensure that there could be long-term resource use. But once owner-users so overexploited resources that nonuse values became impaired, second-generation laws sought to rein in individual resource use to bring about what was best from the perspective of the larger community.[16]

Such laws also shared a common feature: They focused on the harmful effect resource use had on humans, rather than the effect on the resource itself and its surrounding environment. These laws represented, and still represent, an *anthropocentric* perspective. They conceive nature, nature's resources, and the environment as a mere good that serves to satisfy human needs while possessing no intrinsic value

---

[13] SAGOFF, *supra* note 1, at 12; Endangered Species Act, 16 U.S.C. § 1531 (b): "to provide a means whereby the ecosystems upon which endangered species. . .depend may be conserved,". . .[and to] provide a program for conservation of such. . .species."

[14] David Driesen, *The Economic Dynamics of Environmental Law: Cost Benefit Analysis, Emissions Trading, and Priority Setting*, 31 B.C. ENVTL. AFF. L. REV. 501 (2004).

[15] ERIC S. HIGGS, NATURE BY DESIGN: PEOPLE, NATURAL PROCESSES, ECOLOGICAL RESTORATION (2003).

[16] Leonard Zobler, *An Economic-Historical View of Natural Resource Use and Conservation*, 38 ECON. GEOGRAPHY 190 (1962).

in itself. Most of the statutes and laws that today protect resources from human use still have as their core purposes (1) the protection of human health and safety; (2) the shielding of anthropocentric resource nonuse values—that is, low-impact, recreational play and existence value—from human excesses; (3) the reliance on market-based mechanisms to replace certain traditional regulatory means of protecting human health and welfare; and (4) the restoration and valuing of economically important ecological services and natural capital for current and future generations of humans.[17]

For decades, throughout the latter half of the 20th century and the beginning of the 21st, resource owners, developers, and users battled these second-generation "species chauvinistic" nonuse laws[18] that viewed virtually all harms to resources and the environment through an anthropocentric rights focus.[19] When these harms seemed to continue, or even escalate,[20] attention turned to yet another anthropocentric approach to environmental degradation and natural resources exhaustion. This proposal, still reflecting second-generation values, advocated future legal systems that would create "public" rights to environmental quality while continuing to adopt human-centric goals.

Such arguments in favor of extending human rights principles into the environmental realm posited the creation of a right, found in both international and constitutional norms, that could provide a substantive claim for all people to a clean, healthy, and sustainable environment. This kind of legally acknowledged right could be collectively or individually held, and it would afford humans a priority to environmental nonuse values when resource use demands are being asserted.[21] The central idea behind such a public right to environmental quality was grounded in part in the same premise that held that certain rights held by individuals, such as liberty from

---

[17] *See generally* Mark T. Brown & Mary Jane Angelo, *Valuing Nature*, *in* BEYOND ENVIRONMENTAL LAW: POLICY PROPOSALS FOR A BETTER ENVIRONMENTAL FUTURE 81–109 (A. Flournoy & D. Driessen eds. 2010); J.B. Ruhl, *Valuing Nature's Services—The Future of Environmental Law?*, 13 NATURAL RES, & ENV'T 359–60 (1998); KLAUS BOSSELMANN, HUMAN RIGHTS AND THE ENVIRONMENT: REDEFINING FUNDAMENTAL PRINCIPLES, IN GOVERNING FOR THE ENVIRONMENT: GLOBAL PROBLEMS, ETHICS, AND DEMOCRACY 118–34 (Brendon Gleeson & Nicholas Lowe eds. 2001).

[18] *See, e.g.*, the National Environmental Policy Act, 42 U.S.C. § 4331 (a): ". . .the continuing policy of the Federal Government [is] to use all practicable means and measures. . .in a manner calculated to. . .maintain conditions under which *man* and nature exist in productive harmony, and fulfill the. . .requirement of *future generations of Americans*." [emphasis added].

[19] GUNTHER HANDL, HUMAN RIGHTS AND PROTECTION OF THE ENVIRONMENT: A MILDLY "REVISIONIST" VIEW, IN HUMAN RIGHTS, SUSTAINABLE DEVELOPMENT AND THE ENVIRONMENT 117 (Antonio Trindade ed. 1992).

[20] Steve Newman, *Nearly the Hottest*, BOULDER DAILY CAMERA, Dec. 24, 2010, at 4B; Neela Banerjee, *Climate Scientists Go Public*, DENV. POST, Nov.8, 2010, at 5A; Hagit Affek, *What We Know About the Climate*, YALE ALUMNI MAG. 28 (July/August 2010) ("Anthropogenic climate change is real"); Mark Lynas, SIX DEGREES: OUR FUTURE ON A HOTTER PLANET (2007).

[21] GUNTHER HANDL, HUMAN RIGHTS AND THE PROTECTION OF THE ENVIRONMENT, IN ECONOMIC, SOCIAL AND CULTURAL RIGHTS: A TEXTBOOK (A. Eide, C. Krause & A. Roseas eds. 2001); Neil A. Popovic, *Pursuing Environmental Justice with International Human Rights and State Constitutions*, 15 STANFORD ENVTL. L.J. 338 (1996).

oppression, could be asserted when that right was threatened by government. Similarly when private or government choices adversely affect environmental goods necessary to human survival, humans should have the right to mount a legal challenge to these destructive actions.[22]

Another variety of this kind of human rights approach calls for recognition of the public's overriding interest in private uses of land and resources. Such a public overlay on private resource choices could take one of two forms: (1) private property could be encumbered with the public's interest in ecological conservation,[23] or (2) government management of natural resources could be conditioned by a new duty to protect those resources consistent with a public trust obligation, where the government would serve as a trustee of nature for present and future generations.[24] Either approach would require private and government actions to give formal legal consideration of broader, future, multigenerational ecological values other than near-term private consumptive and extractive use interests.[25]

The question then, of course, is whether first- and second-generation laws now in place, or even the addition of a new round of anthropomorphic second-generation human rights laws being contemplated, can prevent the environmental catastrophes that seem to characterize the 21st century.[26] First-generation, use-regulating conservation laws simply slowed the inexorable exhaustion of stock and renewable resources. A case can be made that second-generation nonuse laws, designed to protect humans from pollution and to preserve natural objects, have not been able to halt, and will not succeed in reversing, a natural planet-wide collapse.[27] Criticism has also been leveled at second-generation laws ostensibly guided by (1) a desire for economic efficiency, and (2) greater reliance on cost-benefit analysis and market-reliant systems as methods of achieving efficiency goals.[28] One can be similarly pessimistic about a new wave of second-generation laws that presume unspoiled nature provides long-term economic benefits from ecosystem services that offset the short-term disadvantages involved in forgoing development. Such skepticism is fueled by economists who question whether the economic growth values measured by ecosystem services are correlated to human development and welfare.[29] Another proposed second-generation law—a substantive human right to a clean environment—is not

---

[22] *See, e.g.*, the Rio Declaration, U.N. Doc. A/CONF. 151/26; 31 I.L.M. 874 (1992)—Principle #1—"Human beings. . .are entitled to a healthy and productive life in harmony with nature."

[23] *See, e.g.*, Eric T. Freyfogle, The Land We Share: Private Property and the Public Good (2003).

[24] Mary Christina Wood, *Advancing the Sovereign Trust of Government to Safeguard the Environment for Present and Future Generations (Part I): Ecological Realism and the Need for a Paradigm Shift*, 39 Envt'l L. 43 (2009).

[25] Alyson C. Flournoy, *The Case for the National Environmental Legacy Act 3-25*, *in* Beyond Environmental Law (A. Flournoy & D. Driesen eds. 2010); Richard P. Hiskes, The Human Right to a Green Future: Environmental Rights and Intergenerational Justice (2009).

[26] Tyler Volk, CO2 Rising: The World's Greatest Environmental Challenge (2008).

[27] James Gustove Speth, The Bridge at the End of the World: Capitalism, the Environment, and Crossing From Crisis to Sustainability (2008).

[28] Frank Ackerman & Lisa Heinzerling, Priceless: On Knowing the Price of Everything and the Value of Nothing (2004).

[29] Nancy E. Bockstael et al., *On Measuring Economic Values for Nature*, 34 Envtl. Sci. & Tech. 1384–89 (2000).

in itself capable of determining priorities among competing goals.[30] A suggested parallel second-generation law—an assertion of a collective right limiting private property choices—has had a mixed record of effectiveness when it has been deployed.[31]

It is the central thesis of this book that there is another, more fundamental explanation for the inability of past and proposed legal norms and institutions to protect resource nonuse values. Each generation of actual legal response, including each proposed second-generation law, has been *anthropocentric*. Each has focused on harmful impacts on individual humans rather than on natural resources themselves. What has been missing in virtually all institutionalized legal responses to resource stress and environmental damage is a perspective that sees resources in nature as a good in their own right, and not just an instrumentality to satisfying human preferences. Such a view would reflect the intrinsic worth of natural resources, not only to humans, but to the survival and continuation of all life on this planet. It would also subsume this assumption: When resources are not overused, and when they are *left alone by humans*, they provide long-term health to ecosystems, to the earth's biosphere, to biodiversity, and therefore (but only incidentally) to humans.

First- and second-generation resource management laws assume that the protection of humans should be the central focus. Such a human-centric approach gave birth to first-generation laws designed to encourage near-term use, and later conserve resources for future use. Second-generation homocentric laws are a reaction to the consequences of first- generation resource use laws; these second generation laws are meant to protect humans from pollution, preserve natural objects for human economic, recreational, existence value, and in some ways, grant legal status to ecosystem services. Proposed second-generation laws seek to acknowledge environmental human rights and impose public considerations on private use choices. Such laws would conform to the traditional view, which has always had humans as the prime beneficiaries of use reduction or use prevention schemes. But this approach has not adequately maintained resource nonuse values. As a result, we now face a combination of global climate change, natural systems destruction, species extinctions, and biomass depletion, which could compromise the integrity and survival of the earth's biosphere.[32]

What seems needed now is a completely new, third-generation response to the age-old problem of resource overuse, which has not only exhausted the resource base,

---

[30] Michael R. Anderson, Human Rights Approaches to Environmental Protection: An Overview, in Human Rights Approaches to Environmental Protection 22–23 (Alan Boyd & Michael R. Anderson eds. 1996).

[31] Craig Anthony Arnold & Leigh A. Jewel, *Litigation's Bounded Effectiveness and the Real Public Trust Doctrine: The Aftermath of the Mono Lake Case*, 14 Hastings W.-N.W.J. Envtl. L. & Pol'y 1177 (2008).

[32] Ann Gibbons, *Are We in the Middle of a Sixth Mass Extinction?*, ScienceNow (March 2, 2011); Robert Barr, *Carbon Output Forecast to Rise*, Denv. Post, Jan. 20, 2011, at 7B; Juliet Eilperin, *Study: Extinction Crisis Looms*, Denv. Post, Oct. 27, 2010, at 13A; Jonathan Leake, *Fish Stocks Eaten to Extinction by 2050*, London Times, July 11, 2010, at 9; Justin Gillis, *Is It Global Warming? Probably, Scientists Say*, N.Y. Times, Aug. 15, 2010, at 19A; Vaclav Smil, The Earth's Biosphere: Evolution, Dynamics, and Change (2003); Noaki Schwartz, *60 Percent in Nation Live in Dirty Air*, Denv. Post, Apr. 24, 2009; Lindsey Tanner, *Pre-Birth Air Pollution May Damage Kids' IQ's*, Denv. Post, July 20, 2009, at 6A.

but impaired resource nonuse values.[33] A paradigm shift is necessary that does not just think about nature and the environment within the existing framework of resource use law, and resource economics, in which the protection of humans and the welfare of people are the primary goals. Instead, one should also reconsider the role of purely environmental rights, where what should be legally recognized is the intrinsic worth of nature and natural resources, irrespective of humans. Specifically, an ecocentric, rather than an anthropocentric, legal right would reflect the value to the entire planet of resource nonuse. Such a third-generation legal right, *held by the resource*, would legitimate the resource's power not to be directly used and exploited by humans. This right would be the resource's right of nonuse, a counterweight to the embedded traditional human right of use.

Part III reviews how, over time, laws have been used by people to establish a formal relationship between human needs and the natural resources that comprise the surrounding environment. During each iteration, legal doctrine emerged that was meant to permit people to maximize their own human-centric values and needs with respect to natural resources. Chapter 9 will discuss how resource use initially dominated the creation of first-generation legal rights, including laws that were eventually adopted to curb resource use in order to conserve natural resources for future use. Chapter 10 will review second-generation laws that (1) protect the nonuse health benefits that humans experience when public environmental goods are not employed as a pollution sink, (2) preserve natural objects from extractive developmental use to maximize recreational and existence value, (3) seek to carry out regulatory reforms guided by a desire for economic efficiency and market-based approaches to environmental quality, and (4) incorporate into decision making a system that would account for the economic services provided humans when ecosystems are left alone. Chapter 11 will consider an emerging second generation of resource-regulating laws, still anthropomorphic, which would benefit humans by (1) recognizing a substantive human right to an unpolluted and nondepleted natural environment, and (2) requiring that public ecological values be a check on private resource use decisions.

Chapter 12 will argue that all these prior approaches are self-limiting because they conceive of nature and natural resources as goods that have no inherent value, and instead deserve legal protection only to satisfy human use preferences and nonuse needs. Chapter 12 will suggest that an entirely new, third-generation perspective may now be in order that does not simply view looming environmental crises through a traditional human rights focus. A nonanthropocentric right of nonuse, held by the resource, gives legal credibility to the notion that natural resources left in a natural state are a condition to all life on earth, not just human life. With planetary ecological bankruptcy now a real threat, the creation of an entirely different, ecocentric relationship between law and natural resources may now be in order.

---

[33] Ted Nordhaus & Michael Shellenberger, Break Through: Why We Can't Leave Saving the Planet to Environmentalists (2009).

9 First-Generation Laws

CREATING USE INTERESTS IN NATURAL RESOURCES

RESOURCE USE VALUES have long enjoyed legal legitimacy. Initially, use values were protected by first-generation laws acknowledging and providing security to resource user interests. The advent of property law, in particular, established ownership interests that permitted owner-users to resist the advances of competing users and to exploit the economic use potential of resources. Later, federal and state statutes provided further legal stature to resource owners while imposing sanctions for failure to use owned commodities. Some of these statutes also authorized government ownership of resources so that administrative managers could allocate publicly owned resources to deserving private parties. Common law and constitutional law also rewarded resource use.

The general theme behind these laws was that humans should have a virtually unlimited right to exploit natural resources. These legal assertions of an unfettered right to exploit nature were in keeping with the utilitarian rationale that wealth maximization (through resource use) works as the motor for human welfare production. Such utilitarian rationales consciously subjugated nature in the superficially calculated interest of humanity.[1]

The legal protection of resource use interests not only provided owner-users with security with respect to rivalrous nonowners, it also, and not surprisingly, encouraged

[1] RICHARD POSNER, THE ECONOMICS OF JUSTICE 74–76 (1983); Indira H. Carr, *Saving the Environment—Does Utilitarianism Provide a Justification?*, 12 LEGAL STUDIES 92, 94–101 (1992); Peter A.Y. Gunter, *The Big Thicket*, *in* PHILOSOPHY AND ENVIRONMENTAL CRISIS 117–136 (W.T. Blackstone ed. 1974).

owners to use their resources. And they did. During the 20th century, the world's total urban population grew by 13-fold, and its industrial output increased by roughly 40-fold. The world's population and its industrial base needed natural resources: food, fiber, oil, gas, coal, minerals, water, rangeland, timber, etc. These resources were extracted, developed, depleted, and otherwise used at an unprecedented rate. The resulting accelerated exploitation of natural resources began to exhaust, or make unsustainable, stock and renewable commodity resources.

Nonrenewable stock resources such as minerals and energy fuels were removed with little concern about the inevitable fact that once exhausted, these resources would be gone forever.[2] Renewable commodity resources, such as forests, woodlands, fisheries, water supplies, and rangeland, were similarly exploited by humans, often at or above sustainable levels.[3]

When humans realized that stock and even renewable resources necessary for 20th-century human societies were being exhausted, with no easy substitutes available, another variety of first-generation laws was enacted. These so-called "conservation laws" restricted otherwise unlimited use in order to perpetrate future use. In other words, we sought to address the first consequence of overuse by adopting laws requiring some conservation of the resource base so that future use was not impaired. Restraint was exercised out of recognition that excessive use could hurt our long-term economic interest to overexploit natural resources.

A. Immediate Use Laws

1. PROPERTY INTERESTS CREATED

For humans to fully exploit the use component of natural resources, it was first necessary to halt the rapid depletion of resources that comes with open access conditions. When resources are unowned, stock resources such as minerals are too quickly extracted,[4] and renewable commodity resources such as timber are removed at a non-sustainable rate.[5] Such resource exhaustion leads to the excessive dissipation

[2] John R. McNeill, *Resource Exploitation and Over-Exploitation: A Look at the 20th Century*, *in* EXPLOITATION AND OVEREXPLOITATION IN SOCIETIES PAST AND PRESENT 52–53 (Brigitta Benzing & Bernard Hermann eds. 2003); KENNETH S. DEFFEYES, HUBBERT'S PEAL: THE IMPENDING WORLD OIL SHORTAGE (2001); VACLAV SMIL, ENERGIES: AN ILLUSTRATED GUIDE TO THE BIOSPHERE AND CIVILIZATION (1999).

[3] Jeremy B. Jackson et al., *Historical Overfishing and the Recent Collapse of Coastal Ecosystems*, 293 SCI. 629 (2001); SING S. CHEW, WORLD ECOLOGICAL DEGRADATION: ACCUMULATION, URBANIZATION, AND DEFORESTATION, 3000 B.C.—A.D. 2000 (2001); Antonio D'Amato & Sudhir K. Chopra, *Whales: Their Emerging Right to Life*, 85 AM. J. INT'L L. 21, 30 (1991). By the 21st century, renewable resources were being overexploited and degraded not only by extractive commodity uses, but by recreational uses, especially motorized recreation. *See* Byron Kahr, *The Right to Exclude Meets the Right to Ride: Private Property, Public Recreation, and the Rise of Off-Road Vehicles*, 28 STAN. ENVTL. LAW REV. 51 (2009).

[4] EDWARD B. BARBIER, NATURAL RESOURCES AND ECONOMIC DEVELOPMENT 130 (2005).

[5] James A. Brander & M. Scott Taylor, *Open-Access Renewable Resources: Trade and Trade Policy in a Two-Country Model*, 44 J. INT'L ECON. 181 (1998).

of resource rents[6] and the eventual collapse of resource-dependent economies.[7] Nonexistent or poorly developed property rights also require resource users to incur high costs, first in claiming the resource and then in excluding others from it. The time, effort, and expense of warding off competing users often results in either premature development (i.e., extract the resource before a rival does) or dissipation of net capitalized rents.[8]

The obvious solution to these negative consequences of open access conditions was to "privatize" both stock and renewable commodity resources. The ability to establish private property rights over these resources meant that they could be removed and developed only by those users with an ownership interest in them. Owner-users could exclude other would-be users and enjoy the fruits of the resource's use component.[9] Applicable property law protected owner-users when nonowner would-be users sought to invade or assert control over the resource interest. Secure legal rights over natural resources also provided owner-users with incentives for increased investments in resource improvements and productivity.[10] In the case of minerals, security of legal title to the resource may have even brought substantial "knowledge" spillovers, which helped to encourage knowledge-based economic growth.[11]

Property law permitted resource users the ability to (1) acquire an ownership interest in resources, (2) assert a right of use and disposition regarding the owned resource, and (3) exclude other claimants who wished to assert a competing use interest.[12] The right to have a legal property interest in a natural resource grants the owner dominion over it, which in effect removes the privately owned resource from the realm of nature while transferring its potential utility to the human owner.[13]

---

[6] Louis Hotte, Ngo Van Long, & Huilan Tian, *International Trade with Endogenous Enforcement of Property Rights*, 62 J. DEV. ECON. 25 (2000).

[7] Linda Cordell, *Aftermath of Chaos in the Pueblo Southwest*, *in* ENVIRONMENTAL DISASTER AND THE ARCHAEOLOGY OF HUMAN RESPONSE 179, 189 (Garth Bawden & Richard Martin Reycraft eds. 2000).

[8] Terry L. Anderson & Peter J. Hill, *The Race for Property Rights*, 33 J.L. & ECON. 177 (1990); C. Southey, *The Staples Thesis, Common Property and Homesteading*, 11 CAN. J. ECON. 547, 557 (1978).

[9] JAMES WILLARD HURST, LAW AND CONDITIONS OF FREEDOM IN THE NINETEENTH CENTURY UNITED STATES 7 (1956).

[10] Henning Bohn & Robert T. Deacon, *Ownership Risk, Investment, and the Use of Natural Resources*, 90 AM. ECON. REV. 526 (2000); Gershon Feder & David Feeny, *Land Tenure and Property Rights: Theory and Implications for Development Policy*, 5 WORLD BANK ECON. REV. 135 (1991).

[11] Paul A. David & Gavin Wright, *Increasing Returns and the Genesis of American Resource Abundance*, 6 INDUS. & CORPORATE CHANGE 203, 240–01 (1997) ("the [American] minerals economy was an integral part of the emerging knowledge-based economy of the twentieth century. . ..").

[12] 1 WILLIAM BLACKSTONE, COMMENTARIES 138; United States v. Gen. Motors Corp., 323 U.S. 373, 378 (1945); John R. Sand & Gravel Co. v. United States, 60 Fed. Cl. 230, 236–07 (2004) (property is a group of rights, such as the right to process, use, and dispose of it).

[13] Without private ownership, and dominion over the resource, stock, renewable, and public environmental natural resources remain open to use by everyone, and therefore subject to the "tragedy of open access"—overuse, depletion, and pollution. DANIEL H. COLE, POLLUTION AND PROPERTY 5–7 (2002); Garrett Hardin, *The Tragedy of the Commons*, 162 SCI. 1243 (1968).

The right of use protects the owner's privilege to utilize this ownership interest in the owner's discretion. This utilitarian function of property law has been characterized as one of the most important rights in the bundle of sticks provided by property ownership.[14] The right to exclude protects the interest holder and resource user from harm by competing nonowners.[15] All these elements of property encouraged and legitimated use and exploitation of natural resources. Traditional property law neither promoted resource conservation nor protected resource nonuse benefits from excessive use.

2. STATUTORY LAW ENCOURAGING USE

The advent of property law gave owners the exclusive right to use certain resources and the ability to prevent competitors from enjoying the same use benefit. This consequence of resource ownership created two classes of users: those who own it and those who do not. For centuries, resource conflicts tended to involve just these two user interests, where one party sought to perfect an exclusive right to resource use, while another party sought to either establish a countervailing ownership interest (permitting that party to use it instead), or collaterally attack an ownership right that was not being used. Federal and state statutes helped resolve such conflicts between competing use interests. These laws both defined how users could acquire an ownership interest in natural resources and established rules allowing owner-users to defeat the claims of nonowner would-be users. Statutes reflected a generally accepted policy judgment about natural resources: Once they are owned, they should be *used* by the owners. Indeed, failure to use often meant the loss of ownership.

Federal laws allowed private parties to exploit natural resources located on public lands. These statutes created the possibility of ownership interests for the purpose of promoting the discovery, extraction, development, and use of resources.[16] Rights were

[14] Trotzer v. Vig, 203 P. 3d 1056 (Wash. App. 2009) (landowner action against neighbor for trespass to timber interest); Hillsmere Shores Improvement Ass'n v. Singleton, 959 A. 2d 130, 144 (Md. App. 2008) (adverse possession grounded in the view that property should be used); United States v. Craft, 535 U.S. 274, 283 (2002) (stating that state law "grants a tenant. . .one of the most essential property rights: the right to use the property. . . .").

[15] Nollan v. Cal. Coastal Comm'n, 483 U.S. 825, 831 (1987) ("We have repeatedly held that, as to property reserved by its owner for private use, "the right to exclude is one of the most essential sticks in the bundle of rights that are commonly characterized as property").

[16] General Mining Act of 1872, 30 U.S.C. § 22 (providing for private development and use of the mineral resources on federal lands); Organic Act of 1897, 16 U.S.C. § 472–482 (opening up for private use timber reserves on federal land); National Forest Management Act, 36 U.S.C. § 1600 (opening up timber resource to private harvest and sale); Taylor Grazing Act of 1934 (regulating grazing uses of federal lands), 43 U.S.C. § 315–315r; Multiple Use Sustained Yield Act of 1960, 16 U.S.C. § 528–531 (opening up national forests to the uses of outdoor recreation, timber, watershed, and wildlife and fish purposes); Federal Land Policy Management Act, 43 U.S.C. § 1701–1784 (directing the BLM to regulate the use of federal lands, including for resource and grazing uses); Reclamation Act, 43 U.S.C. § 373 (providing a mechanism for private parties to exploit the water resources on federal lands); Warren Act, 43 U.S.C. §§ 485, 523 (allowing the government to enter into private contracts for the impoundment, storage, and carriage of water located on federal lands). See generally United States v. Minard Run Oil Co., 1980 U.S. Dist. Ct. Lexis 9570 (W.D. Pa. 1980) (under 1911 Weeks Act, owner of mineral rights had "an unquestionable right" to enter and extract minerals).

granted to the parties best able to use and exploit resources while, conversely, nonuse was discouraged.[17] Two classes of conflicts emerged among users: (1) owner-users and competing would-be users who wished to become owners,[18] and (2) owners of two different resource interests whose different use interests clashed.[19]

When two resource users in the federal scheme came into conflict, the class that intended to put the property to the most valued use often prevailed.[20] As a result, courts tended to favor the active mineral estate over the surface estate, even when use of the mineral estate caused damage to the surface estate.[21] However, when the mineral estate was not actually used, the claims of the putative mineral estate owner could be lost.[22] Similarly, if a user wished to secure a patentable ownership interest in a resource, especially a mineral resource, the critical test was acceptance by the commercial market. In order for the United States to lose its interest in a resource to a private developer, that resource needed to be sufficiently valuable so as to be used and sold in the relevant market.[23]

State statutory law has also provided a mechanism for private property interests in resources to be acquired in state-owned public lands.[24] Like federal resource statutes,

---

[17] United States v. Locke, 471 U.S. 84 (1985) (finding constitutional a provision of FLPMA providing for abandonment and forfeiture of mining claim for failure to comply with mining claim filing requirements).

[18] Bedroc Ltd. v. United States, 541 U.S. 176 (2004) (where patentee sought to quiet title to sand and gravel on its property, finding such sand and gravel not "mineral" in nature and therefore not reserved by the United States for purposes of the Pittman Underground Water Act of 1919); Watt v. W. Nuclear, 462 U.S. 36 (1983) (where mining company removed gravel from lands patented under the Stock-Raising Homestead Act, finding gravel a "mineral" reserved to the United States); Rosette, Inc. v. United States, 277 F. 3d 1222 (10th Cir. 2002) (where landowner sought to quiet title to land's geothermal resources, finding those resources qualified as "minerals" reserved by the United States under the Stock-Raising Homestead Act).

[19] TransWestern Pipeline Co. v. Kerr-McGee Corp., 492 F. 2d 878 (10th Cir. 1974) (mineral lessee allowed to cause surface subsidence).

[20] *See, e.g.*, Kinney-Coastal Oil Co. v. Kieffer, 277 U.S. 488 (1928) (where the surface and mineral estate had been severed, interpreting federal law to require that a homesteaded surface owner yield its residential real estate development to the extent that it interfered with a later-acquired oil and gas lease); Bill Barrett Corp. v. U.S. Dep't of Interior, 601 F. Supp. 2d 331 (D.D.C. 2009) (coal bed methane gas company denied injunction that would have prevented coal exploration by a different company under federal lease from proceeding).

[21] *See, e.g.*, Keystone Bituminous Coal Ass'n v. DeBenedictus, 480 U.S. 470 (1987) (finding no unconstitutional taking of surface estate under law regulating coal mining); *TransWestern Pipeline*, 492 F.2d 878 (allowing the mineral lessee to cause surface subsidence without liability).

[22] United States v. Begwell, 961 F.2d 1450 (9th Cir. 1992) (finding the doctrine of *pedis possessio* protected prior claims from subsequent rival claimants only where the claimant actually explores for a valuable mineral diligently and in good faith).

[23] United States v. Coleman, 390 U.S. 599 (1968) (the resource must be extracted and marketed at a profit); United States v. Etcheverry, 230 F.2d 193 (10th Cir 1956) (holding that discovery of a valuable mineral is required to perfect the miner's unpatented mining claim under the General Mining Act of 1872); Ernest K. Lehmann & Assoc. of Montana, Inc. v. Salazar, 602 F. Supp. 2d 146 (D.D.C. 2009) (finding "discovery" not made where claimant did not establish probable profitability of claims).

[24] NEB. REV. STAT. § 72–306 (1929) (directing the regulation of mineral substances on state lands); ALASKA STAT. § 44.99.110 (1988) (providing for the mineral policy of the state); N.M. STAT. § 69-10-4 (1978) (directing the private development of mineral resources); 32 PA. STAT 141 (1961) (providing for the development of minerals on state forest land); ARIZ. REV. STAT. 27–102 (2003) (directing the private development of mineral

these state laws served to encourage the discovery, use, and development of natural resources on state lands.[25] The policy reflected in these laws was that there was an important public interest in using natural resources.[26] Indeed, states imposed sanctions when use was delayed, or when certain development standards were not met.[27] Use was preferred over nonuse. When either the timing or the intensity of resource use did not fulfill the full potential for exploitation, these laws provided for forfeiture of the interest.[28] Alternatively, state forfeiture laws could be suspended only if doing so served to encourage future mineral production.[29]

3. THE COMMON LAW AND CONSTITUTIONAL LAW

The common law set out the conditions of ownership, and constitutional law resolved conflicts that arose between government and potential owner users. The common law of contracts helped ensure that where disputes were between owner-users and nonowner would-be users, owners would prevail where the nonowner sought to invade or assert control over the resource interest.[30] Disputes between owner-users and nonowner would-be users were also resolved with reference to the state-specific common law of property. Property law was inclined toward resource exploitation, favoring the party whose intention best furthered the use interest. For instance, the Kansas Supreme Court in one case considered a deed granting all coal but reserving "all rights, surface, mineral or otherwise not specifically granted."[31] The Court found this deed to have conveyed coal bed methane gas, relying heavily on the fact that the grantee had drilled and obtained production, whereas the grantor had "[n]ever exercised the right to mine and remove coal from any of the tracts . . . [and] never

---

resources of the state); 7 Del. C. 6001 (1973) (directing the development of mineral production and mineral products from state lands).

[25] *See, e.g.*, Pono v. Molokai Ranch, Ltd., 194 P. 3d 1126 (Haw. 2008) (reviewing state law encouraging that "land resources" be "utilized" for "the needs of the economy.").

[26] Am. Aggregates Corp. v. Highland TWP, 390 N.W. 2d 192 (Mich. App. 1986); R. Norton & M. Wyckoff, *Term-Limited Legislature Restores Mining's Exemption from Local Zoning*, 64 Planning & Envtl. L. 3 (Jan. 2012).

[27] Tex. Natural Res. Code 52.174 (providing for forfeiture of the mineral estate lease interest where there is failure to drill within the prescribed time period).

[28] *See, e.g.*, Neb. Rev. Stat. 72–306 (1929) (allowing the Nebraska Board of Educational Lands and Funds to demand more rapid development from a lessee, or alternatively lease cancellation, when an unreasonable delay is found between the discovery and development of mineral substances); Nelson v. Kansas Dep't of Agriculture, 242 P. 3d 1259 (Kan. App. 2010) (nonuse of a water right may be considered an abandonment of the right).

[29] Idaho Code Ann. § 42–223(11) (2008) (suspending forfeiture of water rights with a beneficial use related to mining where water right owner has maintained the property and the property has potential for future mineral production).

[30] Am. Silver Mining Co. v. Coeur D'Arlene Mines Corp., 480 P.2d 900 (ID 1971) (contract for exploration work was not abandoned where the contract did not require all levels to be explored and where silver veins were actually discovered in the levels that were explored); M.J.S. Res. v. Circle G. Coal Co., 506 F. Supp. 341 (E.D. Miss. 1980) (coal mining agreement invalid and unenforceable where it did not obligate the mining of coal unless specifically requested to do so, but contained no similar obligation for the opposing party to make such a request).

[31] Cent. Natural Res. v. Davis Operating Co., 201 P.3d 680 (Kan. 2009).

attempted to explore or produce the natural gas."[32] The Court's message: The law tends to favor use over nonuse.

The common law doctrines of adverse possession and prior appropriation of water similarly advocated a "use it or lose it" approach to property and resource ownership. Under the doctrine of adverse possession, the owner must assert an ownership right in the property through use, or risk forfeiting this interest altogether to a competing nonowner would-be user.[33] The doctrine of prior appropriation favors the water user that establishes use, and that does not abandon the use.[34] If there is evidence of nonuse, the owner's water right may be lost so that the resource may be put to use by some other appropriator.[35]

Although common law doctrine favored resource use over nonuse when property owners confronted competing private user interests, the takings clause of the U.S. Constitution recognized the significance of an owner's right to use and enjoy property when owners confronted government action designed to prevent such use. Takings jurisprudence from the courts established the rule that land use regulations could become unconstitutional takings if they "go too far" by greatly diminishing the economic use value of property rights,[36] if they "unreasonably interfere" with the owner's right to use the property,[37] or if they deprive an owner of "all economically beneficial use" of the property.[38] Central to these takings tests is the issue of whether use values remain for resource owners after regulations have been imposed; if few or no remaining uses are available to affected property owners, there is more likelihood that the regulation becomes a taking.[39] The Takings Clause thereby reinforced the notion that resource use was not just a preferred value under common law and statutory law, but in some cases, also under constitutional law.

---

[32] *Id.* at 682–83.

[33] Thomas v. Rex A. Wilcox Trust, 463 N.W.2d 190 (Mich. App. 1990) (oil and gas lease interests capable of adverse possession); Pickens v. Adams, 131 N.E.2d 38 (Ill. 1956) (to establish adverse possession, minerals had to actually be removed from the ground or oil and gas actually produced); Otter Creek Reservoir Co. v. New Escalante Irrigation Co., 203 P.3d 1015 (Utah 2009) (applying the doctrine of adverse possession to determine the proper owner of water right).

[34] *See, e.g.*, *In re* Clark Fork River Drainage Area, 833 P.2d 1120 (Mont. 1992) (finding rebuttable presumption of abandonment where nonuse of water right for 23 years was established).

[35] Okanogan Wilderness League, Inc. v. Town of Twisp, 947 P.2d 732 (Wash. 1997) (abandonment of water right where would-be owner failed to use the water right for a continuous, prolonged period of time).

[36] Pennsylvania Coal Co. v. Mahon, 260 U.S. 393 (1922).

[37] Vulcan Materials Co. v. Tehuacana, 369 F. 3d 882 (5th Cir. 2004); Palm Beach Isles Assoc. v. United States, 231 F. 3d 1354, 1359 (Fed. Cir. 2000).

[38] Lingle v. Chevron U.S.A., Inc., 544 U.S. 538 (2005); Lucas v. South Carolina Coastal Council, 505 U.S. 1003, 1019 (1992) ("by requiring land to be left substantially in its natural state... to sacrifice all economically beneficial uses... to leave his property economically idle... [is a taking].").

[39] Alabama Dep't of Transportation v. Land Energy, Ltd., 886 So. 2d 787 (Ala. 2004); Friedenburg v. New York Dep't of Environ. Conservation, 767 N.Y.S. 2d 451 (N.Y. App. 2005).

B. Future Use Laws: Conservation of Natural Resources

When both market forces and legal doctrine emphasized and encouraged resource use, the inevitable consequence was that stock and renewable commodity resources were indeed used by humans at escalating rates. At first, it seemed as though there was a never-ending supply of stock resources—if one gold deposit was exhausted, another was discovered. Renewable commodities, such as timber, rangeland, and water, seemed to be able to replenish themselves despite increasing exploitation of their use value. Eventually, however, excessive resource use began to inexorably deplete stock resources and make unsustainable renewable commodity resources.

Initially, what caught the attention of policy makers was the decrease in resources that had the highest *use* potential (i.e., those such as oil and gas, or timber that seemed to benefit humans economically when they were used in a market setting). Because most laws encouraged resource use, a diminution of resources valuable for their use potential required some immediate legal action. Lawmakers responded to this very real economic threat by adopting legislation designed to regulate and restrict private resource use, even by resource owners. The driving realization behind these first-generation laws was that the viability of resources should not be left to the market. Such use-regulating and resource conservation laws were meant to ensure the long-term sustainability of the use component of many economically valuable natural resources.[40]

An early example of awareness of the exhaustibility of natural resources came in 1920 with the enactment of the Mineral Leasing Act.[41] Prior to this statute, energy minerals on public lands were being lost to private ownership under the General Mining Act of 1872.[42] The Mineral Leasing Act withdrew oil, gas, coal, and oil shale from the giveaway provisions of the 1872 Mining Act and placed these stock energy resources under a federal leasing system, where their use could be more easily regulated. State well-spacing, pooling, and unitization regulations also sought to conserve underground oil and gas deposits, which otherwise would have been depleted too quickly by competing surface owners.[43]

Lawmakers next turned their attention to renewable commodity resources, such as timber, rangeland, water, and aquatic life. The Multiple Use Sustained Yield Act of 1960[44] declared that national forests be administered to produce "sustained yield."[45] A sustained yield was one that did not exhaust the timber resource. Later, the National Forest Management Act of 1976[46] attempted to slow the harvesting of timber by requiring extensive planning before cutting. Of course, planning does not

---

[40] Adrian Parr, Hijacking Sustainability (2009).

[41] 30 U.S.C. § 181.

[42] 30 U.S.C. § 22.

[43] John S. Lowe, Oil and Gas Law 18–26 (1995).

[44] 16 U.S.C. §§ 528–531.

[45] *Id.* § 529.

[46] 16 U.S.C §§ 1600–1614.

halt deforestation if the plan both contemplates and provides for timber cutting. The unregulated use of federal rangeland for grazing was addressed by the Taylor Grazing Act of 1934;[47] this federal statute attempted (with mixed results) to impose controls on what would have become an unsustainable and nonrenewable grassland resource if unchecked overgrazing had continued.[48]

The fate of two other overused renewable commodities—water and aquatic life—was in large part determined, and doomed, by state law and loosely regulated international agreements. The conservation of surface water was thwarted by state "use-it-or-lose-it" prior appropriation rules prevalent in the West,[49] while groundwater still suffers from an underground "tragedy of the commons" that encourages excessive pumping.[50] Overfishing, especially in the oceans, has proven maddeningly difficult to control. Fish tend to exist in a classic open access setting, out of the reach of normal regulatory systems. International understandings have been largely unenforceable. Curbing the exploitation of fisheries, especially in oceans, will likely require some bottom-up property rights approach among users, secured by international treaty.[51]

---

[47] 43 U.S.C. §315–315r.

[48] W. GARD, FRONTIER JUSTICE 81–149 (1949).

[49] *See* Melinda Kassen, *A Critical Analysis of Colorado's Water Right Determination and Administration Act of 1969*, 3 U. DENV. WATER L. REV. 58 (1999).

[50] ROBERT GLENNON, WATER FOLLIES: GROUNDWATER PUMPING AND THE FATE OF AMERICA'S FRESH WATERS (2002).

[51] *See, e.g.*, Katrina Miriam Wyman, *From Fur to Fish: Reconsidering the Evolution of Private Property*, 80 N.Y. U. L. REV. 117 (2005); Carrie A. Tipton, *Protecting Tomorrow's Harvest: Developing a System of Individual Transferable Quotas to Conserve Ocean Resources*, 14 VA. ENVTL. L.J. 381 (1995). The federal government's primary response to overuse of animals that inhabit the marine environment was the Marine Mammal Protection Act of 1972, 16 U.S.C. §§ 1361–1407, which sought to maintain the "optimum sustainable population" of seals, whales, porpoises, walruses, and other marine mammals.

10 Second-Generation Laws

PROTECTING HUMAN NONUSE INTERESTS

FIRST-GENERATION LAWS encouraged the use and exploitation of natural resources for both near-term and future human benefit. Ironically, these laws and the resource exhaustion and contamination they furthered eventually produced environmental and ecological damage that harmed, or threatened to harm, humans. But the harm was not just to humans; it was also to the "nonuse" component of the natural resources themselves. One feature of this nonuse quality is that humans are benefitted when they leave resources alone. When they do not use resources, but instead leave them in a natural state, the resource's nonuse component is able to provide humans with clean air and water, as well as a naturally sustainable resource base. These nonuse values provide competing benefits that are as important as the economic gains that flow to users when resources are extracted and developed for market advantage. Conversely, when excessive human use destroys or impairs this inherent nonuse dimension of resources, humans bear the cost when their health, welfare, and economic well-being become impaired.

First-generation laws, even conservation laws, still stimulated resource use. They had little effect on the overexploitation of public environmental goods such as the atmosphere, the water cycle, and the earth's surface and subsurface. These goods are necessary for human existence. They also serve as "sinks" for the wastes and poisonous emissions from human society; up to a point they have the capacity to absorb, break down, or recycle certain amounts of various pollutants. Overexploitation occurs when pollutants accumulate faster than they can be dissipated. By the mid-20th century, it was becoming apparent that human use activities had so overloaded these sinks that they could not absorb and retransform these human wastes and emissions sufficiently for a healthy human livelihood. "Second-generation" antipollution laws were enacted to protect us from our own pollution, and to restore this vital anthropocentric nonuse role of public environmental goods. Many of these laws were designed to protect humans from the health hazards of human resource use activities without making such protection conditional upon utility calculations.[1]

Second-generation antipollution laws could not prevent the harm that resource use activities were inflicting on certain natural places, such as wild lands, and on natural objects, such as wildlife species. These resources have value to humans because people either want to play and recreate in undisturbed forests and landscapes or enjoy the knowledge that living things still exist in an unused natural state.[2] When it was realized that some people place a value on resources for future recreational activities that do not consume or exploit the resource, and some people place a value on the mere existence of natural resources simply because they are natural, it became necessary for yet another category of second-generation nonuse laws to be enacted. These laws were *preservation* laws; they preserved natural objects such as forests, wilderness, wildlife, and historical sites so that humans could benefit from the nonuse values that emerge when humans are prevented from engaging in resource use practices that affect natural objects.

When the extraordinarily complex system of environmental laws proved more difficult to implement than anticipated, a wave of regulatory reforms were instituted to achieve better economic efficiency. These reforms sought to simulate private markets by creating a capped system of transferable pollution "rights" to protect the environment; at times these reforms also relied on cost-benefit analysis to choose the goals of environmental law.[3] These second-generation laws were designed to make environmental regulations less costly and more efficient while mimicking market-based mechanisms as methods of achieving anthropocentric resource nonuse objectives. A final class of second-generation laws was premised on the belief that when certain natural resources were not used, they would then provide for humans various "ecosystem services" that benefitted human welfare. A series of legal mandates slowed the destruction of wetlands, estuaries, and other similar resources that perform services maximizing homocentric welfare when these resources are left alone.

---

[1] Marian Fischer-Kowalski, *Modes of Colonizing Nature, in* EXPLOITATION AND OVEREXPLOITATION IN SOCIETIES PAST AND PRESENT (Brigitta Benzing & Bernard Hermann eds. 2003); 42 U.S.C. § 7409(b)(1) ("National ambient air quality standards . . . shall be . . . based on such criteria . . . to protect the public health."); Whitman v. Am. Trucking Ass'n, 531 U.S. 457 (2001) (cost considerations not permitted when setting national ambient air quality standards).

[2] *See, e.g.*, E.B. Barbier et al., *Economic Value of Biodiversity, in* GLOBAL BIODIVERSITY ASSESSMENT 823, 829 (V.H. Hegwood et al. eds. 1995); John K. Krutilla, *Conservation Reconsidered,* 57 AM. ECON. REV. 787 (1967).

[3] Daniel H. Cole, *Pollution and Property* 45–66 (2002).

A. Antipollution Laws: Protecting Human Health

Throughout the latter half of the 20th century, and certainly by the beginning of the 21st century, there was accumulating evidence of human harm caused by toxic pollution, deforestation, wetlands destruction, over-appropriation and pollution of water, and loss of fisheries.[4] Human health seemed threatened by the pollutants that people were breathing and ingesting.[5] Our ability to experience the ecological and atmosphere-cleaning benefits of forests had been jeopardized by the removal of nearly 90 percent of the nation's old-growth forest lands.[6] The collapse of sea fisheries, caused by pollution and overfishing, portended a loss of wild seafood in the future.[7] The amount of urban land development quadrupled between 1954 and 2000,[8] bringing about a concomitant reduction of ecosystem services vital to human welfare, wild lands, and native grasslands.[9] Species extinction rates accelerated to the point that by the 21st century, they were a thousand times faster than normal.[10]

These threats to and assaults on life-sustaining and life-enhancing natural resources brought about a realization that there should be a profound paradigm shift toward resources management. Instead of encouraging, or regulating the sustainability of, resource *use*, it was thought that legal regimes should now help individuals to experience the benefits that arise from resource *nonuse*. The first wave of second-generation regulations appeared. These second-generation laws served a primary anthropocentric purpose: the protection of personal health, especially with regard to pollution.[11]

---

[4] Benjamin Toss & Steven Amter, The Polluters: The Making of Our Chemically Altered Environment (2010); James Gustave Speth, The Bridge at the End of the World: Capitalism, The Environment, and Crossing from Crisis to Sustainability, ch. 1 (2008).

[5] John Wargo, Creating Environments That Protect Human Health (2009); General Accountability Office, Doc. No. GAO-06-669, Rep. to Congressional Requestors, Clean Air Act: EPA Should Improve the Management of its Air Toxics Program 1 (June, 2006); Thomas H. Maugh II, *Study: Long-Term Ozone Exposure Boosts Deaths*, Denv. Post, Mar. 12, 2009, at 4A; *Lindsey Tanner, Pre-Birth Air Pollution May Damage Kids' IQs*, Denv. Post, July 20, 2009, at 6A.

[6] Reed Noss et al., *Endangered Ecosystems of the United States: A Preliminary Assessment of Loss and Degradation*, app. A, *available at* http://biology. usgs.gov/pubs/ecosys.htm.

[7] Robert F. Service, *Out of the Frying Pan?*, 334 Sci. 890 (Nov. 18, 2011) (climate change and ocean acidification threaten to wipe out many salmon runs by the end of this century); Boris Worm et al., *Impacts of Biodiversity Loss on Ocean Ecosystem Services*, 314 Sci. 787 (Nov. 3, 2006); Jonathan Leake, *Fish Stocks Eaten to Extinction by 2050*, The London Times 9 (July 11, 2010).

[8] U.S. Environmental Protection Agency, Doc. No. EPA-231-R-01-002, Our Built and Natural Environments: A Technical Review of the Interaction between Land Use, Transportation, and Environmental Quality 4 (2001).

[9] Ross W. Gorte, Wilderness: Overview and Statistics (Cong. Research Service, CRS Report for Congress Order Code RL 31447, June 11, 2002); *Noss*, *supra* note 6.

[10] E. O. Wilson, The Diversity of Life 280 (1992); World Conservation Union (IUCN), 2006 IUCN Red List of Threatened Species, Summary Statistics, Table 1 (2006); *Speth*, *supra* note 4 at 1; Juliet Eilperin, *Study: Extinction Crisis Looms*, Denv. Post, Oct. 27, 2010, at 13A.

[11] *See, e.g.*, Juliet Eilperin, *Stricter Chemical Release Law Ok'd*, Denv. Post, Mar. 12, 2009, at 9A (companies must provide detailed disclosure of toxic chemicals released into the air).

Second-generation antipollution laws, such as the Federal Clean Air Act[12] and Clean Water Act,[13] and state environmental protection laws,[14] were grounded in resource nonuse. The central premise of these second-generation laws was (and still is) that when public environmental goods are not used as a garbage dump for our wastes, these resources provide critical health benefits that humans enjoy when they breathe clean air, use uncontaminated water, and inhabit land not made toxic by human-created hazardous substances.[15]

1. FEDERAL ENVIRONMENTAL LAWS

During the latter half of the 20th century, it became apparent to federal policy makers that personal health was being adversely affected by pollution of air and water, as well as from the improper disposal of hazardous wastes. Scientific advances led to an awareness of the human health hazards of certain poisonous and toxic pollutants, resulting in the enactment of environmental laws. This new knowledge enabled a science and policy partnership, creating a legal framework that incorporated minimum quality thresholds for life-sustaining public environmental goods and standards for land-based hazardous waste disposal.

Federal environmental laws reflected personal health concerns that followed from the harmful effects from using resources as waste-dumping grounds.[16] Nonuse was advanced based on the degree of the danger to human health when using the air or water as pollution sinks.[17] Rather than advocating a complete use bar, the goal of these second-generation federal environmental laws was to reduce use intensity to the point necessary to protect the nonuse component of the resource so that human health was furthered. For instance, the Clean Air Act developed limitations on lung-harmful particulate emissions.[18] The Clean Water Act similarly required standards

---

[12] 42 U.S.C. § 7401 et seq.

[13] 33 U.S.C. § 1251 et seq.

[14] *See, e.g.*, Mississippi Department of Environmental Quality, MI CODE ANN. § 49-2-1; New Mexico Environmental Improvement Act, N.M.S. § 74-1-2.

[15] Economists label as "indirect use values" the health benefits that follow from not using public environmental goods as pollution dumps.

[16] The Clean Air Act of 1970, 42 U.S.C. § 7401 (providing that "the purposes of this subchapter are . . . to protect and enhance the quality of the Nation's air resources so as to promote the public health and welfare and the productive capacity of its population); the Clean Water Act of 1972, 33 U.S.C. § 1251(a) (stating that "[t]he objective of this chapter is to restore and maintain the chemical, physical, and biological integrity of the Nation's waters."); Ocean Dumping Act of 1988, 33 U.S.C. § 1401 (finding that "unregulated dumping of material into ocean waters endangers human health, welfare, and amenities. . . ."); Resource Conservation and Recovery Act of 1976, 42 U.S.C. § 6901(b) (providing that "[d]isposal of solid waste and hazardous waste in or on the land without careful planning and management can present a danger to human health and the environment."); Safe Drinking Water Act of 1974, 42 U.S.C. § 9611(b) (regulating "contaminants which, in the judgment of the Administrator, may have any adverse effect on the health of persons.").

[17] WILLIAM T. BLACKSTONE, ETHICS AND ECOLOGY IN PHILOSOPHY AND ENVIRONMENTAL CRISIS 16–42 (W. Blackstone ed. 1974).

[18] The Clean Air Act of 1970, 42 U.S.C. § 7408 (developing particulate air quality criteria).

for water based on use limitations allowed for specific pollutants.[19] These second-generation environmental laws also provided minimum health quality thresholds for the disposal of hazardous wastes and their cleanup.[20]

The judicial system resolved conflicts between use and nonuse interests that emerged regarding the standards imposed by these environmental laws. Such disputes often arose when private industry was unable or unwilling to meet the quality standards required by these laws.[21] Conflicts also arose when citizen groups argued that the standards provided in these second-generation laws were inadequate, or were not being properly enforced by the relevant federal agencies.[22] Conflicts were equally likely when private industry interests found these standards too burdensome, and when utilitarian concerns, such as a cost-benefit analysis, seemed an efficient condition precedent to standard setting.[23]

2. STATE ENVIRONMENTAL LAWS

State law followed the example of federal law, which meant that lawmakers began enacting legislation to reflect the return of nonuse values for otherwise polluted public environmental goods.[24] Second-generation state legislation, like that of the federal legislation, focused on the protection of human health and on the indirect use benefits that occur when humans live in an unpolluted environment. The use of public environmental goods as waste sinks was deemed inconsistent with the nonuse benefits that arise with respect to individual health and welfare when these goods are

[19] The Clean Water Act of 1972, 33 U.S.C. § 1311 (developing strict effluent limitations for specified toxic pollutants and providing a time line for achievement of those objectives.).

[20] Resource Conservation and Recovery Act of 1976, 42 U.S.C. § 6901 et seq. (giving the Environmental Protection Agency the authority to control specified hazardous wastes from the "cradle-to-grave."); the Comprehensive Environmental Response, Compensation, and Liability Act, 42 U.S.C. § 9601 et seq. (safeguarding human health from the toxic consequences of irresponsible waste disposal).

[21] United States v. Alcoa, 533 F. 3d 278 (5th Cir. 2008) (federal government sued operator of aluminum smelting plant, alleging that owner modified three lignite-fired boilers in violation of the Clean Air Act).

[22] Center for Biological Diversity v. U.S. Dep't of Interior, 563 F. 3d 466 (D.C. Cir. 2009) (challenge to Interior Department decision to expand leasing areas within outer continental shelf off coast of Alaska for oil and gas development on grounds that oil spills might harm humans living near coastal shorelines); Nat'l Res. Defense Council v. EPA, 559 F. 3d 561 (D.C. Cir. 2009) (challenging regulation governing an exclusion of emissions data during "exceptional events" under the Clean Air Act); Southern Utah Wilderness Alliance v. Allred, 2009 WL 765882 (D.C. App. 2009) (finding BLM's air quality analysis relied upon to issue leases located near the Arches and Canyonlands national parks deficient due to a failure to conduct quantitative ozone dispersion modeling required by the National Environmental Policy Act); Ohio Valley Envtl. Coalition v. Hurst, 604 F. Supp. 2d 860 (S.D. W. Va. 2009) (Clean Water Act violated by discharge of dredged and fill material associated with surface coal mining mountain top removal, because such use threatens water supplies for humans living there).

[23] Entergy Corp. v. Riverkeeper, 129 S. Ct. 1498 (2009) (Clean Water Act authorizes the EPA to compare costs with benefits in determining the "best technology available for minimizing adverse environmental impact" at cooling water intake structures).

[24] This second-generation legislation usually encompassed the creation of state environmental protection agencies, charged with abating pollution. *See, e.g.*, Ohio Environmental Protection Act, OHIO REV. CODE § 3745.011; Oklahoma Conservation District Act, OKLA. STAT. § 3-1-102; Maine Environmental Protection Board, 38 MAINE REV. STAT. § 481.

not exploited by humans. Many states therefore enacted laws declaring pollution abatement a public policy of the state.[25] Some states went so far as to amend their constitution to provide their citizens with an inalienable right to a clean and healthful environment.[26] Most of the legislation was more focused, addressing the quality of the state's air[27] and water[28] resources. Conflicts arose under these statutes when private industry was unable or unwilling to meet the environmental quality standards required by these laws,[29] and when public interest groups believed that such standards were not being properly enforced.[30]

State common law also enabled courts to protect human health when uses constituted an unreasonable interference with the well-being of humans adversely affected by the use. Often this interference was in the form of an environmental harm to adjacent human dwellings or residences. Relief was sought for such harm to indirect use value (the value of an environment that is not contaminated) under theories of nuisance,[31] negligence,[32] and trespass.[33]

---

[25] IDAHO CODE § 39–101, 39–202 (declaring that "it is . . . the policy of the state to provide for the protection of the environment and the promotion of personal health and to thereby protect and promote the health, safety and general welfare of the people of this state."); 7 DEL. CODE § 6001(a)(1)(5) (stating that "[t]he land, water, underwater and air resources of the State must be protected from pollution in the interest of the health and safety of the public. . . ."); FLA. STAT. § 403.021(5) (declaring that "the prevention, abatement, and control of the pollution of the air and waters of this state are affected with a public interest. . . ."); 38 ME. REV. STAT. § 341A (directing the state Department of Environmental Protection to "prevent, abate, and control the pollution of the air, water and land and preserve, improve, and prevent diminution of the natural environment of the State."); 415 ILL. COMP. STAT. 5/2(a) (finding that "environmental damage seriously endangers the public health and welfare. . . ."); ALASKA REV. STAT. § 46.03.10(a) (finding it a policy of the state to control water, land and air pollution for the welfare of the people of the state and their overall well-being).

[26] *See, e.g.*, MONT. CONST. art. 2, § 3; HAW. CONST. art. 11, § 9; PENN. CONST. art. 1, § 27; MICH. CONST. art. IV, § 52.

[27] Indiana Air Pollution Control Act, IND. CODE § 13–17-1-1; Tennessee Air Quality Act, TENN. CODE ANN. § 68-201-103; North Dakota Air Pollution Control, N.D.C.C. § 23–25-01.1; Rhode Island Clean Air Act, R.I. GEN. LAWS § 23-23-2; Utah Air Conservation Act, UTAH CODE ANN. § 19-2-101; Washington Clean Air Act, WASH. REV. CODE § 70.94.011.

[28] South Dakota Water Pollution Control Act, S.D. CODIFIED LAWS § 34A-01-01; California Water Quality Control Act, CAL. WATER CODE § 13000.

[29] *See, e.g.*, Gray v. County of Madera, 85 Cal. Rptr. 3d 50 (Cal. Ct. App. 2008) (finding mitigation measures related to water at proposed hard rock quarry inadequate to meet California Environmental Quality Act).

[30] Friends & Fishers of Edgartown Great Pond, Inc. v. Dep't of Envtl. Protection, 848 N.E.2d 393 (Mass. 2006) (challenging grant of a groundwater discharge permit for discharge into pond as violating the state Clean Water Act).

[31] *See, e.g.*, North Carolina v. Tennessee Valley Auth., 615 F. 3d 291 (4th Cir. 2010) (state bringing public nuisance action against the Tennessee Valley Authority, seeking injunction halting hazardous emissions from coal-fired power plants); Ayers v. Township of Jackson, 493 A. 2d 1314 (NJ 1987) (enjoining landfill operation as constituting a nuisance by contaminating municipal water supply).

[32] *See, e.g.*, Anderson v. W.R. Grace & Co., 628 F. Supp 1219 (D. Mass. 1986) (allowing negligence suit for physical injuries from disease contracted through ingestion of well water contaminated by operations of chemical manufacturing company).

[33] *See, e.g.*, Bradley v. Am. Smelting & Refining Co., 709 P.2d 782 (Wash. 1985) (finding that invisible particles from copper smelting pass could constitute a trespassory invasion).

B. Resource Nonuse to Preserve Natural Places and Objects

Some second-generation laws served to preserve from use pristine places, endangered species, wild rivers, and other natural objects. Second-generation statutes preserved *places*, such as national forests,[34] landscapes,[35] wilderness study areas,[36] wild lands,[37] wild rivers,[38] and wetlands.[39] These laws also preserved *natural objects*, such as bald eagles,[40] migratory birds,[41] marine mammals,[42] and endangered species.[43] The premise behind second-generation laws preserving these places and objects was that people value certain nonused natural resources simply because they are natural, which can only occur when they are not used, destroyed, degraded, or altered by humans. If these natural objects are used, this nonuse natural value is lost and technological advances can never provide substitutes.[44]

Some laws combined an interest in furthering both the health and preservationist benefits that followed from not actively using natural resources. At the federal level, the National Environmental Policy Act (NEPA)[45] required federal agencies to consider, before they acted, whether proposed federal actions might trigger human health concerns or impair preservation values.[46] At the state level, some statutes prohibit or limit certain resource use activities if the proposed use will either adversely affect human health or threaten natural objects. For example, Colorado empowered the State Oil and Gas Conservation Commission to promulgate rules for oil and gas drilling in order to protect (1) public health, and (2) "the environment and wildlife resources."[47]

These preservationist laws reflect twin assumptions about people's desires. First, we want some places preserved from excessive economic use (i.e., use that extracts

---

[34] 43 U.S.C. § 1782 (lands subject to the Forest Service's "roadless rule").

[35] *E.g.*, the National Landscape Conservation System within the U.S. Bureau of Land Management. *See* John D. Leshy, *The Babbitt Legacy at the Department of Interior: A Preliminary View*, 31 ENVTL. L. 199, 219 (2001).

[36] 43 U.S.C. § 1782 (c).

[37] The Wilderness Act of 1964, 16 U.S.C. § 1131. *See also* the Ommbus Public Land Management Act of 2009, S. 22, 111th Cong. (2009) (setting aside over two million acres in nine states as protected wilderness).

[38] The Wild and Scenic Rivers Act of 1968, 16 U.S.C. § 1271.

[39] 33 U.S.C. § 1344.

[40] 16 U.S.C. § 668.

[41] The Migratory Bird Treaty Act of 1918, 16 U.S.C. § 703.

[42] 16 U.S.C. § 1361.

[43] The Endangered Species Act of 1973, 16 U.S.C. § 1531.

[44] *Krutilla, supra* note 2 at 783.

[45] 42 U.S.C. § 4321.

[46] 40 C.F.R. § 1508.27(b)(2) (does the proposed action affect public health?); § 1508.27 (b)(3) (does the proposed action affect unique characteristics of the geographic area?); § 1508.27 (b) (9) (does the proposal affect endangered or threatened species?); Theodore Roosevelt Conservation Partnership v. Salazar, 605 F. Supp. 2d 263 (D.D.C. 2009) (NEPA challenge to federal government decision to grant gas drilling permits, on the ground that the agency failed to take a hard look at air quality effects and impacts on sage grouse).

[47] Colo. Rev. Stat. §34-60-102.

resources from natural settings as those resources are commodities, like minerals) because people would prefer to play there. Some places that are preserved in a nonused state are attractive to many individuals primarily because these locations may then be available for recreational purposes.[48] Second, many people place value on certain natural objects, such as wild lands, archaeological sites, and species, because of their mere existence.[49] These individuals want to preserve this "existence," "option," or "nonuse" value of natural objects not because they want to experience them, or because they want to use or consume them, but because they want them to exist in a state unaffected by humans.[50]

Federal, state, and even constitutional law contain elements implementing or administering a system of nonuse for the sake of natural object preservation. Examples of such federal laws include the Wilderness Act, implementing a system promoting the preservation of the wilderness resource.[51] State law has followed suit with its own regulations, often supplementing or strengthening standards developed by the federal regulations.[52] Constitutional law promotes nonuse values by upholding police power exercises that restrict property use to the point that little use value remains, but where recreation or existence value is preserved.[53]

1. FEDERAL PRESERVATION LAWS

Federal law reflected a growing concern for the preservation of unique places and natural objects.[54] The preservation of pristine places through this legislation serves dual purposes. First, these laws advance the anthropocentric purpose of safeguarding these lands from extractive and development use, to preserve them for present and future low-impact, nonconsumptive recreational use, such as hiking, fishing,

---

[48] However, some recreational uses, such as motorized recreation, can be just as damaging to nonuse values as resource extractive uses. Jan G. Laitos & Rachael B. Reiss, *Recreation Wars for Our Natural Resources*, 34 ENVTL. L 1091 (2004).

[49] *Krutilla*, *supra* note 2 at 787.

[50] Moreover, many people are willing to pay to preserve these natural objects because they believe nature undisturbed is economically worth more than nature domesticated. Mark Sagoff, *Price, Principle, and the Environment* 37, 137 (2004), 137. They may also derive spiritual pleasure from the nonuse of these natural objects. John Copeland Nagle, *The Spiritual Values of Wilderness*, 35 ENVTL. L. 955 (2005); Sigurd F. Olson, *The Spiritual Need*, *in* WILDERNESS IN A CHANGING WORLD 215 (Bruce M. Kilgore ed. 1965).

The value that humans place on an opportunity to enjoy, or benefit from, some activity in the future is called an "option value." *See generally* Katherine K. Baker, *Consorting with Forests: Rethinking Our Relationship to Natural Resources and How We Should Value Their Loss*, 22 ECOLOGY L.Q. 577 (1995). Humans are presumed to place a measurable option value on the future recreational benefits that follow from preventing lands, otherwise available to play in, from being used by extractive industries or renewable commodity purposes.

[51] The Wilderness Act of 1964, 16 U.S.C. § 1131 (providing that the goal of the Act is to "establish a National Wilderness Preservation System for the permanent good of the whole people....").

[52] *See, e.g.*, Colorado Natural Areas Act, COLO. REV. STAT. § 33-33-102 (protecting certain identified areas and other natural features not otherwise protected by federal law for the purpose of their preservation).

[53] *See, e.g.*, Palazzolo v. Rhode Island, 533 U.S. 606 (2001).

[54] CHAD P. DAWSON & JOHN C. HENDEE, WILDERNESS MANAGEMENT: STEWARDSHIP AND PROTECTION OF RESOURCES AND VALUES (4th ed. 2009).

and camping.[55] Second, because certain wild lands and landscapes have value in and of themselves, these laws preserve unique natural lands and features for the purpose of promoting their continued existence, irrespective of whether humans actually ever visit these places.[56] For example, the National Landscape Conservation System was explicitly created to protect and restore nationally significant landscapes.[57]

Also evident in these federal laws is a concern for the preservation of natural objects, such as wildlife and archaeological resources, and even scenic vistas.[58] For instance, the Fish and Wildlife Conservation Act of 1980 promotes the protection

---

[55] National Trails System Act of 1968, 16 U.S.C. §§ 1241–1251 (the stated purpose of which is "to provide for the ever increasing outdoor recreation needs . . . enjoyment and appreciation of the open-air, outdoor areas and historic resources of the Nation."); Federal Lands Policy Management Act, 43 U.S.C. § 1701 (finding that one purpose of the act is to "provide for outdoor recreation and human occupancy and use. . . ."); National Parks & Recreation Act of 1978, 16 U.S.C. § 1(a)-1 (establishing one unified national park system to be "managed for the benefit and inspiration of all the people of the United States").

[56] Wilderness Act of 1964, 16 U.S.C. § 1131 (securing the benefit of lasting wilderness for the American people); 43 U.S.C. § 1782(c) (creating "wilderness study areas within Bureau of Land Management property"); Roadless Area Conservation Rule 36 C.F.R. § 294 et seq. (providing lasting protection for roadless areas within the National Forest System); Coastal Zone Management Act, 33 U.S.C. § 1451(a)–(c) (providing protection for the coastal zone as a resource "rich in a variety of natural, commercial, recreational, ecological, industrial, and esthetic resources of immediate and potential value to the present and future well-being of the Nation."); Wild & Scenic Rivers Act of 1968, 16 U.S.C. §§ 1271–1287 (preserving certain selected rivers "in free-flowing condition . . . for the benefit and enjoyment of present and future generations.").

[57] *See* the Omnibus Public Land Management Act of 2009, H.R. 146, section 2002; *Salazar Orders Conservation Focus for 27 Million Acres of BLM Land across West*, DENV. POST, Nov. 16, 2010, at 7A; Andy Kerr & Mark Salvo, BUREAU OF LAND MANAGEMENT NATIONAL CONSERVATION AREAS: LEGITIMATE CONSERVATION OR SATAN'S SPAWN?, 20 UCLA J. ENVTL. L. & POLICY 67 (2001); Kristen Wyatt, *Obama to Reverse Policy on Fed Land*, BOULDER DAILY CAMERA, Dec. 24, 2010, at 1A. (Department of Interior to review 220 million acres not under wilderness protection as candidates for "wild lands" designations).

[58] National Wildlife Refuge Administration Act of 1966, 16 U.S.C. § 668dd(2) (providing for the "protection and conservation of fish and wildlife that are threatened with extinction, wildlife ranges, game ranges, wildlife management areas, or waterfowl production areas."); Kim Murphy, *Effort Aims to Block Oil Drilling in Refuge*, L.A. TIMES, Nov. 20, 2010, at A19 (plans to make the Arctic National Wildlife Refuge a national monument); Archeological Resources Protection Act 16 U.S.C. § 470ee (providing protection from excavation, alternation, or defacement of archaeological resources on public or Indian lands); Marine Mammal Protection Act, 16 U.S.C. § 31 (1972) (finding that "certain species . . . should not be permitted to diminish below their optimum sustainable level."); Endangered Species Act of 1973, 16 U.S.C. § 1531 (providing protection for certain species of "esthetic, ecological, educational, historical, recreational, and scientific value to the nation."); Fish and Wildlife Conservation Act of 1980, 16 U.S.C. §§ 2901–2911 (finding that "the improved conservation and management of fish and wildlife . . . will assist in restoring and maintaining fish and wildlife and in assuring a productive and more esthetically pleasing environment for all citizens."); Refuge Improvement Act of 1997, 16 U.S.C. § 668(a)(2) (declaring a mission of the Refuge System "to administer a national network of lands and waters . . . for the benefit of present and future generations"); Fish & Game Sanctuary Act, 16 U.S.C. § 694 (establishing the Act "for the purpose of providing breeding places for game birds, game animals, and fish on lands and waters in the national forest.").

The federal Wilderness Act permits humans to hike in wilderness lands, but prevents mountain biking and motorized recreation. 16 U.S.C. § 1133(c); 36 C.F.R. § 261.18 (2006). However, even hiking has become a resource "use" producing enormous environmental damage. *See* Jan G. Laitos & Rachael B. Gamble, *The Problem with Wilderness*, 32 HARV. ENVTL. L. REV. 503 (2008).

of nongame fish and wildlife through the implementation of conservation plans.[59] The Archaeological Resource Protection Act protects archaeological sites through strict law enforcement regulation, and recordkeeping requirements, all for the sake of preserving such sites and their contents.[60] The Wild and Scenic Rivers Act blocks resource use proposals that might either interfere with the scenic qualities of certain rivers or have a negative visual impact for viewers of these rivers.[61] These laws favor nonuse of certain natural objects where their intrinsic existence value outweighs the benefits of a use that threatens their natural, nonused condition.

When conflicts arose from this preservation legislation, they too were resolved by the court system. For instance, judicial disputes between resource use and nonuse interests occurred when the federal government chose to withdraw lands from resource extractive uses for conservation preservation purposes,[62] or attempted to limit recreational use in such areas.[63] There also were judicial conflicts when citizen groups regarded decisions or standards developed by the agency responsible for administering the legislation to be inconsistent with or inadequate to meet the legislation's nonuse objectives.[64] Such citizen groups were granted standing to sue these

---

[59] Fish and Wildlife Conservation Act of 1980, 16 U.S.C. §§ 2901-2911 (establishing a conservation program for such resources due to their "ecological, education, esthetic, cultural, recreational, economic, and scientific value of the Nation.").

[60] Archeological Resources Protection Act 16 U.S.C. § 470ee (providing that "[n]o person may excavate, remove, damage, or otherwise alter or deface any archaeological resources located on public lands or Indian lands. . . .").

[61] 16 U.S.C. §§ 1271, 1281(a); Sierra Club N. Star Chapter v. LaHood, 693 F. Supp. 2d 958 (D. Minn. 2010).

[62] Mount Royal Joint Venture v. Kempthorne, 477 F. 3d 745 (D.C. Cir. 2006) (upholding withdrawal from mineral location and entry lands that are habitat to wildlife species and that provide potable water in the area); Wind River Multiple-Use Advocates v. Espy, 835 F. Supp. 1362 (Wyo. 1993) (finding Forest Service Resource Management Plan not arbitrary and capricious when it halted use activities); Pathfinder Mines Corp. v. Hodel, 811 F.2d 1288 (9th Cir. 1986) (BLM decision voiding mining claims within the boundaries of the Grand Canyon National Game Preserve); Sagebrush Rebellion v. Hodel, 790 F.2d 760 (9th Cir. 1986) (creation of a "birds of prey" conservation area by the Secretary of the Interior).

[63] White Tanks Concerned Citizens, Inc. v. Strock, 563 F. 3d 1033 (9th Cir. 2009) (challenging decision allowing land developers to fill 27 acres of desert washes as violation of NEPA, because citizen group members rode horses there and had "aesthetic interest in preserving undeveloped nature of area"); Stupak-Thrall v. United States, 89 F. 3d 1269 (6th Cir. 1996) (challenging the authority of the Forest Service to ban the use of Crooked Lake by sailboats and houseboats); Blue Water Network v. Salazar, 721 F. Supp. 7 (D.D.C. 2010) (challenging Park Service's decision to permit Jet Skis back into two national parks).

[64] Alliance for Wild Rockies v. Cottrell, 622 F. 3d 1045, 1056 (9th Cir. 2010) (public interest in "preserving nature" outweighs the public interest asserted by the Forest Service in approving the logging of a forest—aiding a struggling local economy and preventing job losses); Meister v. U.S. Dep't of Agriculture, 623 F. 3d 363 (6th Cir. 2010) (Forest Service had improperly favored "gun hunters and snowmobile users" in national forest over "other persons—for example hikers and birdwatchers—who use the Forests for quiet solitary activities."); S. Utah Wilderness Alliance v. Allred, 2009 WL 765882 (D.D.C. 2009) (challenging BLM issuance of leases near the Arches and Canyonlands national parks as a violation of the National Environmental Policy Act, National Historic Preservation Act, and the Federal Land Policy and Management Act); Rock Creek Alliance v. U.S. Fish & Wildlife Service, 390 F.Supp. 2d 993 (Mont. 2005) (challenging issuance of biological opinion allowing construction of copper and silver mine in national forest as violative of Endangered Species Act); Wilderness Society v. Salazar, 603 F. Supp. 2d 52 (D.D.C. 2009) (challenging BLM and Fish and Wildlife Service decision to allow oil and gas leasing in national petroleum reserve as a violation of the National Environmental Policy Act and Endangered

agencies if the primary injury experienced by their members was harm to aesthetic or recreational interests.[65]

2. STATE PRESERVATION LAWS

State laws also reflected a growing concern for the preservation of unique places and land features of the state that were not otherwise protected under federal laws. A major focus of these laws was on the preservation of places, either for their intrinsic value,[66] or for the nonconsumptive recreational uses the place provided.[67] These laws also functioned to protect and preserve nonuse values associated with the state's wildlife resource.[68]

State courts were one forum for nonuse interests to raise the protections afforded by this state legislation when resource use activities seemed threatening.[69] Often these courts provided protection to recreational values, explicitly reasoning that such values were preferred when natural resources such as forests were not used for extractive use purposes (such as timber harvesting or wood milling), and instead were left alone so humans could play there.[70] Conflicts between use and nonuse interests sometimes may not reach the courtroom; instead they are resolved by local lawmakers.

Species Act); League of Wilderness Defenders-Blue Mountains Biodiversity Project v. U.S. Forest Serv., 549 F. 3d 1211 (9th Cir. 2008) (challenging the allowance of commercial logging of 6,281 acres of forest as a violation of the National Environmental Policy Act and the Ochoco National Forest Land Resource and Management Plan); Center for Biological Diversity v. U.S. Fish & Wildlife Serv., 450 F. 3d 930 (9th Cir. 2005) (challenging failure to designate habitat of endangered stickleback fish species as "critical habitat" under the Endangered Species Act).

[65] Summers v. Earth Island Inst., 129 S. Ct. 1141, 1149 (2009); Animal Welfare Inst. v. Martin, 623 F. 3d 19, 25 (1st Cir. 2010) (a desire to observe an animal species is a legally cognizable interest for purposes of standing); Sierra Club v. Kimbell, 623 F. 3d 549, 557 (8th Cir. 2010) (agency action had diminished opportunities for nonmotorized recreation).

[66] New Hampshire Rivers Management and Protection Program, N.H. Rev. Stat. § 483:1; Alaska Environmental Conservation Act, Alaska Rev. Stat. § 46.03.10(a); California Wildlife, Coastal & Park Land Conservation Act, Cal. Pub. Res. Code § 5901; Kentucky Wild Rivers Act, Ky. Rev. Stat. § 146.220; Tennessee Scenic Rivers Act, Tenn. Code Ann. § 11-13-101.

[67] *See, e.g.*, Colorado Parks and Outdoor Recreation, Colo. Rev. Stat. § 33-10-101 (declaring it a policy of the state that "outdoor recreation areas of this state are to be protected, preserved, enhanced, and managed for the use, benefit, and enjoyment of the people of this state and visitors of this state. . . .").

[68] New Hampshire Healthy Tidal Waters and Shellfish Protection Program, N.H. Rev. Stat. § 487:35; Maryland Endangered Species Act, Md. Code Rev. § 08.03.08; Mississippi Non-Game & Endangered Species Conservation Act, Miss. Code Ann. § 49-5-103; South Dakota Environmental Protection Act, S.D. Codified Laws § 34A-8-2; New Jersey Endangered and Non-Game Species Conservation Act; N.J. Stat. § 23:2A-2; California Non-Game, Endangered or Threatened Species Conservation Act, Cal. Rev. Stat. § 33-2-102.

[69] *See, e.g.*, Envtl. Prot. & Info. Ctr. v. California Dep't of Forestry & Fire Prot., 187 P.3d (Cal. 2008) (finding state-approved logging plan inadequate under California Sustained Yield Plan and California Environmental Quality Act); Ctr. for Biological Diversity, Inc. v. FPL Group, 83 Cal. Rptr. 588 (Cal. App. 2008) (state public trust doctrine protects wildlife from proposed wind turbines because "they are natural resources of inestimable value to the community"); Zarock v. Bd. of Supervisors, 2008 WL 5101327 (Pa. App. 2008) (zoning law can prohibit mining to protect "natural and historic resources").

[70] *See* Friends of Columbia Gorge Comm. v. Columbia River Gorge, 238 P. 3d 378 (Or. App. 2010); Chuckanut Conservancy v. Washington State DNR, 232 P. 3d 1154 (Wash. App. Div. 1 (2010).

For example, county commissioners turned down a proposal to build a disposal facility for oil and gas drilling waste near the Canyons of the Ancients National Monument, containing the country's greatest concentration of archaeological sites.[71] The community had to choose between furthering use values—local industry interests and economic development—and preserving unique nonuse features of their historic environment, or risk having the court system decide for them.

Local governments have enacted zoning regulations that promote nonuse values by restricting land uses, by requiring exactions as a condition of development, and by encouraging the use of conservation easements. Low-density zoning regulations prohibit intensive development while ensuring the preservation of natural landscapes.[72] Cities, counties, and municipalities may also adopt land use ordinances and zoning regulations that require nonuse exactions from potential land users,[73] or that devote lands to an exclusive purpose that prohibits use development while mandating nonuse, such as for land preservation or open space purposes.[74] State law may authorize conservation easements, which enable persons or entities to donate lands to government entities or charitable organizations on the condition that the lands stay in their nonused natural state.[75] Such easements ensure the preservation of nonuse values for these lands not only in the present, but into perpetuity.[76] Federal, state, and local governments may provide further inducement for conservation easements in the form of tax incentives.[77]

3. CONSTITUTIONAL LAW

A growing trend in state constitutional law is to expressly provide each citizen a right to a clean and healthful environment, necessarily implying that humans have a constitutional right to resource nonuse when conservation and preservation promotes

---

[71] Nancy Lofholm, *Modern-Day Clash near Ancient Site*, DENV. POST, May 24, 2009, at 1A; Nancy Lofholm, *Montezuma County Turns Down Disposal Site for Drilling Waste*, DENV. POST, June 2, 2009, at 1B. *See also* Jim Mimiaga, *Mining Past Meets Present*, DENV. POST, June 13, 2009, at 4B (county commissioners reject plan to mine molybdenum deposit in Colorado, despite owner asking commissioners "to recognize mining as a use by right").

[72] Note, *New Reactions to Old Growth: Land Use Law Reform in Florida*, 34 COLUM. J. ENVTL. L. 191 (2009).

[73] An exaction is the practice by which local governments require developers to provide public goods, such as an easement for viewing a natural object. *See, e.g.*, Nollan v. California Coastal Comm'n, 483 U.S. 825 (1987).

[74] *In re* Rattee, 761 A.2d 1076 (N.H. 2000) (affirming denial of an application to construct a home on land subject to an agricultural preservation restriction); Open Space Regulations, City of Holly Springs, N.C. Unified Development Ordinance § 7.10.

[75] Anna Vinson, *Re-Allocating the Conservation Landscape: Conservation Easements and Regulation Working in Concert*, 18 FORDHAM ENVTL. L. REV. 273 (2007).

[76] Nancy A. McLaughlin & W. William Weeks, *In Defense of Conservation Easements: A Response to the End of Perpetuity*, 9 WYO. L. REV. 1 (2009).

[77] *See, e.g.*, 26 C.F.R. § 1.170A-14(a) (providing tax advantages for the contribution of real property interests for conservation purposes); Margaret Jackson, *Ruling Puts Value on Land Contribution*, DENV. POST, May 12, 2009, at 7B (U.S. Tax Court overrules IRS determination that conservation easements are worth zero, concluding that such easements can form the basis for charitable-contribution deduction.).

human health and welfare.[78] Federal and state constitutional law further promote nonuse preservation and conservation values by upholding, as against constitutional takings claims, regulations that severely restrict or limit certain resource uses.[79] State courts have also recognized that significant value still remains in land in an undeveloped state, thereby sanctioning state regulation that may completely ban most land use, especially extractive uses, if the ban supports nonuse values.[80]

C. Economic Efficiency as the Goal

Another hallmark of second-generation laws was the desire to achieve environmental goals in ways that were more economically efficient.[81] Regulatory reforms were adopted that were thought to lower costs, especially those incurred by regulated firms seeking to comply with pollution reduction and resource conservation targets. These reforms included (1) market-based mechanisms as methods for achieving regulatory environmental standards, (2) greater reliance on cost-benefit analysis (CBA) to choose environmental goals, and (3) taxation of pollution as an efficient environmental protection instrument.[82] Such approaches were seen as being less costly than traditional command-and-control rules. They were thought also to be inherently efficient, especially when contrasted with the essentially inefficient alternative system of statute + accompanying standard + requirement that firms comply with standard.

Second-generation pollution control regulations were imposed as a means of addressing the harmful effects of using "commons resources" such as air, water, and underground as waste sinks. These initial regulatory approaches were usually technology-based command-and-control rules.[83] Economists argued instead that a better system (because it was more efficient) would be one that allocated limited but transferable private property rights in pollution emissions. The transferability of pollution rights was seen as ensuring that the required reduction in waste discharge would

---

[78] *See, e.g.*, MONT. CONST. art. 2, § 3; HAW. CONST. art. 11, § 9; PENN. CONST. art. 1, § 27; MICH. CONST. art. IV, § 52.

[79] *See, e.g.*, Plmyra Pacific Seafoods v. United States, 561 F. 3d 1361 (Fed. Cir. 2009) (upholding regulation prohibiting commercial fishing in wildlife refuge).

[80] Kyser v. Kasson Twp., 2010 WL 2787954 (Mich. 2010) (state's-long standing judicial doctrine that a zoning ordinance is unreasonable if the person challenging the ordinance can show that there are natural resources on the property capable of being extracted is no longer constitutionally required—mineral extraction is no longer a specially protected land use); Gove v. Zoning Bd. of Appeals, 831 N.E. 2d 865 (Mass. 2005) (upholding a state regulation banning all new residential construction located within a 100-year floodplain).

[81] Alyson C. Flournoy, *The Case for the National Environmental Legacy Act xix, in* BEYOND ENVIRONMENTAL LAW (A. Flournoy & D. Driesen eds. 2010); Daniel H. Cole & Peter Z. Grossman, *When is Command-and-Control Efficient? Institutions, Technology, and the Comparative Efficiency of Alternative Regulatory Regimes for Environmental Protection,* 1999 WIS. L. REV. 887.

[82] David Schoenbrod, Richard B. Stewart, Katrina M. Wyman, *Breaking the Logjam: Environmental Protection That Will Work* (2010); Richard B. Stewart, *The Future of Environmental Regulation: United States Environmental Regulation: A Failing Paradigm,* 15 J.L. & COM. 585, 587 (1996).

[83] *Cole, supra* note 3 at 46.

be achieved at the smallest possible aggregate compliance and abatement cost.[84] Transferability helps ensure lower costs by creating markets that efficiently allocate these costs of pollution control among regulated firms. When pollution exchanges occur, regulated firms with the lowest costs of control would theoretically wind up taking on the largest emissions reduction burden.

A prominent example of such a trading system is Title IV of the 1990 Clean Air Act Amendment, which sought to reduce SO_2 emissions, because SO_2 contributed to acid rain.[85] The goal of Title IV was to minimize total costs of achieving the legislatively ordered reductions in SO_2 emissions, in part by developing a well-functioning emissions market made up of coal-burning power plants issued tradable emissions allowances. Several states are also contemplating the creation of a similar "cap-and-trade" market in greenhouse gases.[86]

Although this model has efficiency advantages, it also comes with several endemic problems. Any emissions trading program requires government officials to set limits on the total amount of pollution permitted. If these officials are too timid to set stringent emission limits, then firms need not develop the basic technological changes in operation that will then be necessary to meet such limits. Moreover, for a robust emissions market to develop, the owner of the tradable pollution allowance would need to feel secure in the property right inherent in the allowance.[87] Also, a national market cap in overall emissions may overlook the distributional consequences of one geographic sector with lowered emissions being invaded by the emissions of a sector that failed to reduce its pollution.

If market-based mechanisms were deemed preferable to command-and control as methods of achieving environmental goals, CBA was perceived as a more systematic and efficient way to choose these goals. Under the Regulatory Right-to-Know Act of 2001,[88] the Office of Management and Budget must prepare an annual report estimating the total costs and benefits of mayor federal rules imposed by specified federal departments and agencies. Several federal natural resources agencies engaged in a weighing of costs and benefits of alternative policies as a standard statutorily required decision-making mode.[89] However, CBA, which was originally sold as a way to rationalize environmental law, too often simply provided cover that permitted regulated firms (and those in power who protected them) to thwart effective

---

[84] *See* J.H. Dales, Pollution, Property and Taxes: An Essay in Policy-Making and Economics 107 (1968).

[85] 42 U.S.C. § 7651.

[86] Jason Dearen, *California on Verge of Greenhouse Gas Rules*, Boulder Daily Camera, Dec. 17, 2010, at 6B.

[87] *See, e.g.*, Arkema, Inc. v. EPA, 618 F. 3d 1 (D.C. Cir. 2010) (challenge to EPA rule honoring only intercompany transfers of baseline allowance for hydrochlorofluorocarbons as being an impermissible retroactive rule impairing vested rights in the allowance).

[88] Pub. L. No. 106-554.

[89] Otay Mesa Property L.P. v. U.S. Dep't of Interior, 714 F. Supp. 73, 87 (D.D.C. 2010) (U.S. Fish and Wildlife Service CBA analysis under the Endangered Species Act); Sierra Club v. Kimbell, 623 F. 3d 549, 559 (8th Cir. 2010) (U.S. Forest Service CBA analysis under the National Environmental Policy Act); Home Builders Ass'n. of N. Cal. v. U.S. Fish & Wildlife Serv., 616 F. 3d 983, 987 (9th Cir. 2010) (Fish and Wildlife Service CBA analysis under the Endangered Species Act).

pollution control.[90] The natural resource commons, such as the atmosphere and waters, continued to be used as a pollution sink.

Similarly, although economists have traditionally supported pollution taxes as an efficient instrument for achieving protection of the nonuse component of air, water, and underground resources,[91] the reality is that reliance on such "economic" instruments as taxes are not necessarily more efficient than command-and-control regulations.[92] Moreover, a tax system would provide a continuous incentive to reduce pollution, but only for a limited class of innovative technologies—those with marginal costs less than the marginal tax rate. Taxes would not be an incentive for firms to develop advanced technologies that would entail significant start-up investments whose marginal costs exceeded the marginal tax rates.[93]

D. Legal Protection of Ecosystem Services

A final class of second-generation laws urge resource users and policy decision makers to account for the benefits of the "ecosystem services" that unused natural resources provide humans when they are not directly used or altered by humans. These services, which maintain air and water quality, suppress floods, enhance habitat, and supply renewable commodity goods, include wetlands, watersheds, riparian habitat, estuaries, floodplains, undisturbed forested lands, and natural grasslands.[94] But resource developers continually threaten, or damage, the nonuse components of ecosystems, thereby depriving humans of the benefits provided by the ecosystem functions.[95] As "free" ecosystem services are neither explicitly valued by, nor integrated into, market economies,[96] some have argued that legal and regulatory

---

[90] *Flournoy, supra* note 81 at xix; RICHARD REVESZ & MICHAEL A. LIVERMORE, RETAKING RATIONALITY: HOW COST-BENEFIT ANALYSIS CAN BETTER PROTECT THE ENVIRONMENT AND OUR HEALTH (2011) (industry groups have captured cost-benefit analysis and used it to further their antiregulatory ends); DOUGLAS A. KYSAR, REGULATING FROM NOWHERE: ENVIRONMENTAL LAW AND THE SEARCH FOR OBJECTIVITY (2010) (climate change is the "poster child for the limitation of [CBA]"). *See also* Dan Farber, *Taking Responsibility for the Planet*, 89 TEX L. REV. 149 (2010); Daniel H. Cole, *"Best Practice" Standards for Regulatory Benefit-Cost Analysis*, 23 RES. L. & ECON. 1 (2007).

[91] Shi-Ling Hsu, *The Case For a Carbon Tax* (2011); T.H. TIETENBERG, *Economic Instruments for Environmental Protection, in* ECONOMIC POLICY TOWARD THE ENVIRONMENT (Dieter Helm ed. 1991).

[92] Daniel H. Cole & Peter Z. Grossman, *When is Command-and-Control Efficient? Institutions, Technology, and the Comparative Efficiency of Alternative Regulatory Regimes for Environmental Protection*, 1999 WIS. L. REV. 887.

[93] *Flournoy, supra* note 81 at 177.

[94] GRETCHEN C. DAILY, NATURE'S SERVICES: SOCIETAL DEPENDENCE ON NATURAL ECOSYSTEMS (1997).

[95] David Dana, *Natural Preservation and the Race to Develop*, 143 U. PENN. L. REV. 655 (1995).

[96] GEOFFREY HEAL, NATURE AND THE MARKETPLACE (2000); Curtis H. Marshall et al., *Crop Freezes and Land Use Change in Florida*, 426 NATURE 29 (2003); John Moir, *An Economist for Nature Calculates the Need for More Protection*, N.Y. TIMES, Aug. 9, 2011, at D3.

frameworks should be modified so that resource use decisions no longer ignore the tremendous nonuse value of natural systems.[97]

The rationale for ecosystem preservation in an unused, natural condition is not based on traditional justifications for resource nonuse—human health, nonconsumptive recreation, or anthropocentric existence value. Rather, the case for ecosystem services is built on human-centric *economic* values. The argument is that undeveloped, unused, and unspoiled nature provides measurable long-term economic benefits to humans; these benefits are thought to offset the short-term disadvantages of forgoing development. The economic basis for laws requiring ecosystem protection is that wild and natural ecosystems supply (for free) services to humans that provide directly for our needs. Because ecosystem services are not fully "captured" in commercial markets or adequately quantified in terms comparable with economic services and manufactured capital, they play little role in policy decisions.[98] Polices therefore should be adopted that require humans to leave nature alone. Indeed, if nature undisturbed is worth more economically than nature domesticated, laws protecting the nonuse component of nature will help ensure that natural resources can continue to benefit us.[99]

Existing regulatory regimes provide a mixed array of ecosystem protections.[100] Ecosystems important for the services they provide humans may be preserved by (1) the National Environmental Policy Act (NEPA),[101] which requires that federal actions that impact sensitive ecosystems be adequately identified;[102] (2) the Endangered Species Act (ESA),[103] which imposes a duty on federal agencies to "insure that any [agency action] is not likely to . . . result in the destruction or adverse modification of habitat . . .,";[104] (3) the Federal Lands Policy Management Act (FLPMA),[105] which requires that certain federal lands potentially suitable as wilderness be managed "so as not to impair" their wilderness qualities;[106] and (4) the National Forest

---

[97] J. B. Ruhl, *Valuing Nature's Services—The Future of Environmental Law*, 13 Natural Res. & Env't 359 (1998); James Salzman & J.B. Ruhl, *Currencies and the Commodification of Environmental Law*, 53 Stan. L. Rev. 607 (2000); J.B. Ruhl, Steven E. Kraft & Christopher L. Lant, The Law and Policy of Ecosystem Services (2007).

[98] Robert Coztanza et al., *The Value of the World's Ecosystem Services and Natural Capital*, 387 Native 253–60 (May 15, 1987).

[99] *Sagoff, supra* note 50 at 127–28, 137; Gretchen Daily et al., *The Value of Nature and the Nature of Value*, 289 Sci. 395 (2000).

[100] Michael C. Blum & J.B. Ruhl, *Background Principles, Takings, and Libertarian Property: A Reply to Professor Huffman*, 37 Ecology L.Q. 805, 820 (2010); J.B. Ruhl & James Salzman, *The Law and Policy Beginnings of Ecosystem Services*, 22 J. Land Use & Envtl. L. 157, 158–61 (2007).

[101] 42 U.S.C. § 4332(2)(C).

[102] New Mexico *ex rel.* Richardson v. BLM, 565 F. 3d 683, 688–89 (10th Cir. 2009).

[103] 16 U.S.C. § 1536(a)(2).

[104] Natural Res. Defense Council v. Houston, 146 F. 3d 1118 (9th Cir. 1998); Pacific Coast Fed'n of Fishermen's Ass'ns v. Gutierrez, 606 F. Supp. 2d 1122 (E.D. Cal. 2008) (endangered species protected when river ecosystems restored); Alliance for the Wild Rockies v. Bradford, 720 F. Supp. 2d 1193, 1207 (D. Mont. 2010).

[105] 43 U.S.C. § 1782(a), (c).

[106] Utah v. U.S. Dep't of Interior, 535 F. 3d 1184 (10th Cir. 2008).

Management Act (NFMA),[107] which calls for a management plan for each national forest, and which may, given the appropriate circumstances, prevent surface disturbances that could harm ecosystems.[108] These federal laws do not explicitly target actions that might adversely affect ecosystems, and their focus is usually federal public lands, not state or private holdings.[109] They also do not mandate that resource use decisions consider the value to humans if nonuse was preferred, so that otherwise free ecosystem services remain undisturbed.

Legal protection of ecosystem services seems most pronounced in the case of federal wetlands regulations. The statutory protection for wetlands provided by Section 404 of the Clean Water Act[110] and accompanying Army Corps of Engineers Wetlands Regulations[111] require the Corps to determine the nature and effect that any proposed discharge will have on the function of the wetlands' "aquatic ecosystem"[112] Reviewing courts have concluded that these rules obligate the Corps to make a best professional judgment about "all ecological functions" that might be impacted by the granting of a Section 404 permit.[113] Federal regulations acknowledge the potential ecosystem service that wetlands perform in reducing greenhouse gases and alleviating water pollution.[114] Academic commentators have also urged that the common law should be enlisted to recognize human interferences with wetlands ecosystem systems as the kind of harms for which nuisance law should provide a remedy.[115]

This second-generation regulatory framework for managing ecosystem services for its nonuse is grounded in the economic benefits that accrue *to humans* by maintaining certain environmental systems in a natural condition.[116] The legal response supporting ecosystem values is human-centric, where the preservation values are not for ecocentric or nature-based reasons, but for very human instrumental and economic ones. Those advocating legal recognition of ecosystem services are consistent

[107] 16 U.S.C. § 1604(a).

[108] Siskiyov Reg'l Educ. Project v. U.S. Forest Serv., 565 F. 3d 545 (9th Cir. 2009).

[109] *See, e.g.*, J.B. Ruhl, *Ecosystem Services and Federal Public Lands: Start-Up Policy Questions and Research Needs*, 20 Duke Envtl. L. & Pol'y F. 275 (2010).

[110] 33 U.S.C. § 1344.

[111] 40 C.F.R. § 230.11(e).

[112] Ohio Valley Envtl. Coal. v. Aracoma Coal Co., 556 F. 3d 177, 198 (4th Cir. 2009).

[113] *Id.* at 199; Butte Envtl. v. U.S. Army Corps of Eng'rs, 607 F. 3d 570, 574–75 (9th Cir. 2010); Sierra Club v. Van Antwerp, 719 F. Supp. 2d 58, 66 (D.D.C. 2010); Sierra Club v. Van Antwerp, 709 F.Supp. 2d, 1254, 1269 (S.D. Fla. 2009).

[114] 73 Fed. Reg. 19594, 19673–19676 (2008); USA EPA, Mitigation Banking Factsheet, *available at* http://ww.epa.gov/owow/wetlands/facts/fact16.html; Fred Bosselman, *Planning for a Bull Market for Wetlands*, 61 Plan. & Envtl. L. 3 (Feb. 2009); J.B. Ruhl, *Ecosystem Services and the Clean Water Act: Strategies for Fitting New Science into Old Law*, 40 Envtl. L. 1381 (2010).

[115] *See* J.B. Ruhl, *Making Nuisance Ecological*, 58 Case W. Res. L. Rev. 753 (2008); John Copland Nagle, *From Swamp Damage to Wetlands Regulation to Ecological Nuisances to Environmental Ethics*, 58 Case W. Res. L. Rev. 787 (2008).

[116] Ruhl et al., *supra* note 97, at 7, 63 ("immense economic benefits accrue to humans by maintaining [ecosystems] under natural flow regime conditions"; "Natural capital resources are capable of providing . . . economically valuable services to humans").

in their assertion that ecological resources producing such service values, such as forests, riparian habitat, and wetlands, "are economically valuable *to humans.*"[117] Laws designed to protect ecosystem services are linked directly primarily to human well-being, to ensure that humans will be provided with essential services from nature.[118]

Any future laws giving special recognition to ecosystem services and natural capital would likely also have an anthropocentric focus. Emphasis would not be on ecological benefits resulting to nature when natural resources are preserved, but to human economic welfare.[119] Second-generation laws protecting ecosystem services for human-centric reasons, both present and contemplated, de-emphasize the purely ecocentric functions supplied by natural resources left alone by humans. As such, they inevitably encounter many of the criticisms that have been made of a policy based on the economic value of wild ecosystems.

First, although nature's services certainly provide benefits to humans, nature also imposes costs and damage to humanity. Such disservices, such as landscape-destroying storms, human-killing viruses, excessive hear or cold, drought, floods, and pests, should be subtracted from the positive value associated with nature.[120] Second, after one so reduces the economic value of an ecosystem service, one should not then simply measure the net contribution of the service to human welfare or well-being, because the true worth of a good is not just its value to humanity. Economic value is really a measure of the scarcity of a good (or ecosystem service) relative to demand. However, because nature provides ecosystem services and natural capital for free, these attributes of nature are not scarce relative to effective demand. As a result, the true economic services would be, relative to demand, negligible.[121]

Third, and finally, although attempts have been made to calculate an economic valuation of ecosystems,[122] these values are problematic. Both the U.S. Supreme Court and the U.S. Environmental Protection Agency have found it impossible, or "indeterminate," to place a value on the "non-use [ecosystem] benefits" associated with protecting fish and aquatic systems from cooling water-intake structures in power plants.[123] Commentators have also criticized those estimating the economic

---

[117] J.B. Ruhl, *Agriculture and Ecosystem Services: Strategies for State and Land Government*, 17 N.Y.U. ENVTL. L.J. 424, 426 n.10 (2008) (emphasis added).

[118] Barton H. Thompson, Jr., *Ecosystem Services & Natural Capital: Reconceiving Environmental Management*, 17 N.Y.U. ENVTL. L.J. 460, 461–63 (2008) (environmental policy should be improved to more fully account for the impacts of ecosystem services "on humans").

[119] *See* James Salzman, Barton H. Thompson, Jr. & Gretchen C. Daily, *Protecting Ecosystem Services: Science, Economics, and Law*, 20 STAN. ENVTL. L.J. 309, 312 (2001); Graciela Chichilnisky & Geoffrey Heal, *Economic Returns from the Biosphere*, 391 NATURE 629 (1998).

[120] *Sagoff, supra* note 50 at 144–45.

[121] *Id.* at 148–49.

[122] Robert Costanza et al., *The Value of the World's Ecosystem Services and Natural Capital*, 387 NATURE 253–60 (May 15, 1987).

[123] Entergy Corp. v. Riverkeeper, Inc., 129 S. Ct. 1498, 1509 (2009). *See also* Mark Sherman, *Court Takes Power Plants' Side over Fish*, DENV. POST, Apr. 2, 2009, at 8A ("'Trying to put a dollar figure on fish and aquatic sys-

value of ecosystems services for confusing the "value in use" for such services with their "value in exchange." Although ecosystem services contribute to the former value, which measures overall enhancement of human well-being and contentment, these services have an ambiguous connection to the latter, which measure true economic growth (i.e., the total market value of goods and services produced and consumed).[124]

An inability to overcome these criticisms may be one reason there has been a "systematic failure of the legal framework of natural resource decision making to account for ecosystem benefits."[125] One should therefore consider other categories of second-generation laws that are not yet in place, but which have been proposed, as yet another example of anthropocentric regulatory and legal reforms that seek to protect resource nonuse values.

---

tems gets very difficult and contentious,' said Amy Sinden, a Temple University law professor who wrote a brief in the case for the environmental groups."). *See also* FRANK ACKERMAN & LISA HEINZERLING, PRICELESS: ON KNOWING THE PRICE OF EVERYTHING AND THE VALUE OF NOTHING (2001).

[124] *Sagoff, supra* note 50 at 152. *See also* Dale D. Goble, *What Are Slugs Good For? Ecosystem Services and the Conservation of Biodiversity*, J. LAND USE & ENVTL. L. 411, 435–39 (2007).

[125] RUHL ET AL., *supra* note 97, at 7.

11 Proposed Second-Generation Laws

PROTECTING HUMAN NONUSE INTERESTS BY ACKNOWLEDGING THE PUBLIC INTEREST IN NATURAL RESOURCES

SECOND-GENERATION LAWS—antipollution mandates, preservation regimes, market-based approaches, and those protecting ecosystem services—all had two common themes. First, they presumed, consistent with standard welfare economics, that their success or failure should be judged exclusively in terms of their effects on the *well-being of humans*.[1] Second, as the world moved into the 21st century, second-generation laws proved incapable of halting, or even slowing, our overpowering desire to exploit natural resources, regardless of consequences.[2]

In fact, even when the planetary consequences of use and overuse of resources became visible and alarming, too often the institutional reaction was either denial[3] or paralysis.[4] Commentators and environmental advocates have stepped into this legal hiatus, and have proposed consideration of two types of legal responses that take a different approach than existing laws. One advocates that natural resource nonuse can be brought about by a "human rights" perspective. The other believes

---

[1] ECONOMIC INSTITUTIONS AND BEHAVORIAL ECONOMICS (Peter Diamond & Hannu Vartiainen eds. 2007); Mark Sagoff, *Price, Principle, and the Environment* 3–9 (2004).

[2] *Oceans Heading for Mass Extinctions, Experts Warn,* MSNBC (June 21, 2011), *available at* http://www.msnbc.msn.com/id/43479398/ns/world_news-world (extinctions of species in oceans inevitable if trends of overfishing, habitat loss, global warming and pollution continue); CARL SAFINA, THE VIEW FROM LAZY POINT: A NATURAL YEAR IN AN UNNATURAL WORLD (2010).

[3] KARI MARIE NORGAAR, LIVING IN DENIAL: CLIMATE CHANGE, EMOTIONS AND EVERYDAY LIFE (2011).

[4] ECONOMIC THOUGHT AND U.S. CLIMATE CHANGE POLICY (D.M. Driesen ed. 2010).

that traditional legal norms should reflect public ecological values. Although both are still based on second-generation anthropocentric measures, they at least represent another pragmatic try at limiting the human penchant for using and abusing the planet's remaining supply of natural resources.

A. Legal Recognition of Environmental Human Rights

If one views resource nonuse from a "human rights" perspective, then the harm caused to individuals and communities by resource exploitation and overuse, as well as degradation of resource nonuse values, become threats to an inchoate *right* held by all humans. This is a right to a healthy environment, which is a recasting of human rights guarantees, where this one seeks to ensure that the natural environment does not deteriorate to the point where the human right to life, the right to health, or other human rights are seriously impaired.[5] Although such a right to a clean and healthful environment may be present within existing human rights, it is increasingly argued that what needs to be adopted is a new set of human rights relating directly to environmental goods.[6]

A human right to a healthy environment is an emerging international right.[7] It can sometimes be inferred from explicitly stated international human rights because the goal of environmental quality and protection from pollution is to enhance the quality and dignity of human life.[8] Such a right might permit individuals or groups to file legal actions to protect the environment or fight against pollution.[9] The right also typically carries with it the "responsibility to protect and improve the environment for present and future generations."[10]

Environmental human rights of one kind or another have been adopted in the national constitutions of more than one hundred countries, as well as in the constitutions of several states in the United States.[11] These strongly anthropocentric

---

[5] Dinah Shelton, *Environmental Rights*, in People's Rights (Philip Alston ed. 2001).

[6] Symposium, *The Confluence of Human Rights and the Environment*, 11 Or. Rev. Int'l L. 225 (2009); Michael R. Anderson, *Human Rights Approaches to Environmental Protection: An Overview, in* Human Rights Approaches to Environmental Protection (A. Boyle & M. Anderson eds. 1996).

[7] Dinah Shelton, *Human Rights, Environmental Rights, and the Right to Environment*, 28 Stan. J. Int'l L. 103, 104 (1991).

[8] W. Paul Gormley, *The Legal Obligation of the International Community to Guarantee a Pure and Decent Environment: The Expansion of Human Rights Norms*, 3 Geo. Int'l. Env't. L. Rev. 85, 97, 105 (1990).

[9] U.N. High Commissioner for Human Rights, Conclusions, Meeting of Experts on Human Rights and the Environment 14–15 (Jan. 2002).

[10] Stockholm Declaration, Principle I, United Nations Conference on the Human Environment (June 16, 1972); Richard P. Hiskes, The Human Right to a Green Future: Environmental Rights and Intergenerational Justice (2009).

[11] Gunther Handle, *Human Rights and the Protection of the Environment* (A. Eide, C. Krause & A. Rosas, eds. 2d ed., 2001); Luis E. Rodriguez-Rivera, *Is the Human Right to Environment Recognized under International Law? It Depends on the Source*, 12 Colo. J. Int'l Env't L. & Policy 1, 20–37 (2001); Barry E. Hill, Steve Wolfson & Nicholas Targ, *Human Rights and the Environment: A Synopsis and Some Predictions*, 16 Geo. Int'l Envtl. L. Rev. 359 (2004).

environmental rights can be found in the constitutions of Columbia ("every individual has the right to enjoy a healthy environment")[12] and Chile ("the right to live in an environment free from contamination")[13] The Indian Supreme Court has found a right to a healthy environment by interweaving constitutional directives on environmental policy with the right to life.[14] The Philippine constitution imposes on the "State" an affirmative duty to "protect and advance the right of the people to a balanced and healthful ecology in accord with the rhythm and harmony of nature.[15]

However, despite its growing popularity, a human rights approach to a clean and healthful environment has been criticized on several grounds. First and foremost, such a "right" held by humans is deficient because it generally does not address threats to nonhuman species, and natural resources in general. This anthropocentrism inherent in a human rights model to environmental protection necessarily focuses on an environment that is safe only for humans, but not one that is ecologically balanced and sustainable in the long run.[16] Second, such a human right is not capable of determining priorities among competing societal goals.[17] Third, implementation of a universal human right could bring about incursions into natural sovereignty, requiring human rights bodies to impose their will on the other nations—a dubious prospect. This reality is why most environmental rights for humans found in constitutions are typically only statements of broad aspirations, but not yet enforceable laws.[18]

An environmental human right would seek to ensure that nature never deteriorates to the point where a human right to life, to health, and to nonuse ecological benefits would be seriously impaired. Legal acknowledgement of such an enforceable human right to resource nonuse benefits would have a corresponding depressing effort on the right of firms and individuals to *use* resources. If resource nonuse were to be recognized as not just an economic benefit, but also a legal or constitutional right, use interests could find themselves overpowered by those wishing to prevent resource development.[19]

---

[12] 4 CONSTITUTIONS OF THE COUNTRIES OF THE WORLD 20 [art. 79 of the Columbia Constitution] (Rudiger Wolfrum & Rainer Grote eds. 2005).

[13] 4 CONSTITUTIONS OF THE COUNTRIES OF THE WORLD 42 [art. 19(8) of the Constitution of the Republic of Chile] (Albert P. Blaustein & Gisbertlt Flanz eds. 1991).

[14] Charon Lal v. Union of India, A.I.R. 1990 S.C. 1480, 1509, (1989) ("The right of life and liberty also includes the right to a healthy environment free from hazardous pollutants.").

[15] CONST. (1987), art. II, 16 (Phil.).

[16] Shelton, *supra* note 5; Anderson, *supra* note 6.

[17] Handle, *supra* note 11.

[18] *See, e.g.*, Elaine Kurtenbach, *Pelosi, U.S. Delegation Tours China's Financial Hub: Human Rights Take Back Seat to Environment*, USA TODAY, May 26, 2009, at 2A (U.S. House Speaker Nancy Pelosi stating: "I will continue to speak out for human rights. . . ..Indeed, protecting the environment is a human rights issue."). *But see* Sunburst v. Texaco, Inc., 165 P. 3d 1079 (Mont. 2007); Montana Envtl. Info. Ctr. v. Dep't of Envtl. Quality, 988 P. 2d 1236, 1244 (Mont. 1999) (empowering parties to challenge resource use actions in light of Montana's constitution grating all persons fight to a "clean and healthful environment").

[19] *Shelton, supra* note 5.

B. Legitimating the Public's Interest in Moderating Private Resource Use and Development

The pervasiveness of first-generation laws—those that create private use interests in natural resources[20]—has led to a call to create or expand a countervailing legal doctrine that would permit individuals valuing resource nonuse to curb use and development rights. Three preexisting legal principals hold some promise to serve this role as a nonuse advocate: the public trust doctrine, the "common good" conception of private property, and the "public interest" inquiry that courts consider when they are asked to issue injunctions halting resource use activities. Each holds the potential to raise the legal stature of the general public's needs regarding resource nonuse to the point where use decisions might be halted, even use decisions backed by first-generation laws.

Public Trust Doctrine—Although the original public trust doctrine focused primarily on navigable waters of a state and the lands underlying those waters,[21] commentators and some courts have argued that the doctrine should be expanded to include as "trust resources" many property interests in natural resources beyond water.[22] The effect of a resource deemed to be a trust resource varies by jurisdiction, ranging from limiting the private right by the public's *jus publicum* rights,[23] to transforming a fee simple absolute into a defeasible fee, to ensuring that the owner's property was used for truly public purposes,[24] to imposing a public easement on private property.[25] Whatever the effect though, the public trust doctrine holds the potential to alter resource development and use, based on an acknowledgement of the public's overriding interest in various nonuse qualities of natural resources.[26]

Public Obligations of Private Owners—A parallel school of thought has suggested that the entire concept of private property in land and resources should be reexamined, so that instead of focusing on the private *use rights* accompanying ownership, the private owner should also have *public obligations* associated with that right.[27]

---

[20] *See*, Chapter 9, *supra*.

[21] *See, e.g.*, Nat'l. Audubon Soc'y v. Super. Ct., 658 P. 2d 709 (Cal. 1983).

[22] Michael C. Blumm, *The Public Trust Doctrine—A Twenty First Century Concept*, 16 W. & Nw. J. Envtl. L. & Pol'y 105 (2010); Carol Rose, *The Comedy of the Commons: Custom, Commerce, and Inherently Public Property*, 53 U. Chi. L. Rev. 711 (1986); Raleigh Ave. Beach Ass'n. v. Atlantis Beach Club, 879 A. 2d (N.J. 2005).

[23] Marks v. Whitney, 491 P. 2d 374 (Cal. 1971).

[24] Vermont v. Cent. Vt. Ry., 571 A. 2d 1128 (Vt. 1989).

[25] Nat'l Home Ass'n. Builders v. New Jersey Dep't of Envtl. Prot., 64 F. Supp. 2d 354 (D.N.J. 1999).

[26] Michael C. Blumm, *The Public Trust Doctrine and Private Property: The Accommodation Principle*, 27 Pace Envtl. L. Rev. 649 (2010); Mary Christina Wood, *Advancing the Sovereign Trust of Government to Safeguard the Environment for Present and Future Generations (Part I): Ecological Realisms and the Need for a Paradigm Shift*, 39 Envtl. L. 43 (2009).

[27] Joseph W. Singer, *The Ownership Society and Takings of Property: Castles, Investments and Just Obligations*, 30 Harv. L. Rev. 309 (2006); Myrl L. Duncan, *Reconceiving the Bundle of Sticks: Land as a Community Based Resource*, 32 Envtl. L. 773 (2002); Gregory S. Alexander & Eduardo M. Penalver, Property and Community (2010).

In other words, ownership of a natural resource might entail public responsibilities, tempering and even checking private use desires if the resource's nonuse potential would otherwise be jeopardized.[28] This radical rethinking of the concept of private property would, in order to benefit the anthropomorphic interests of the larger human community, imprint on resources subject to private ownership an obligation to not over-use and exploit land and natural resources.

The Public Interest and Injunctive Relief—When environmental advocates seek to enjoin government actions that might adversely affect the survival and health of natural resources, the courts must engage in an exercise involving a balancing of competing public interests. One such interest is the benefit enjoyed by the public when the resource is used by someone (e.g., for employment possibilities, job creation, or an invigorated local economy).[29] A countervailing interest is the public's enjoyment when nature is *not* used, when it is preserved and protected from use activities that might injure the resource.[30] Increasingly, courts are taking seriously, and could take even more seriously, the public's interest in the nonuse component of resources in the context of deciding whether injunctive relief should be granted.[31]

---

[28] Eric T. Freyfogel, On Private Property: Finding Common Ground on the Ownership of Land (2007); Eric T. Freyfogel, The Land We Share: Private Property and the Common Good (2003).

[29] *See, e.g.*, Alliance for the Wild Rockies v. Cottrell, 632 F.3d 1127 (9th Cir. 2011).

[30] The Consolidated Salmonid Cases, 713 F. Supp. 2d 1116 (E.D. Cal. 2010).

[31] The Lands Council v. McNair, 537 F.3d 981, 1005 (9th Cir. 2005).

12 Toward a Third Generation of Nonanthropocentric Resource Nonuse Laws

The first generation of resource laws emphasized use, so that humans could enjoy the benefits of developing the use potential of the earth's natural resources. The second generation, both adopted and contemplated, focused more on nonuse. But the assumption behind all the second generation laws was the same: Humans would benefit if resources were not directly used by humans. However, neither the first- nor second-generation laws seem to have protected the earth's resources, which continue to be polluted, depleted, and adversely altered.[1] This persistent failure to preserve resource nonuse values suggests that an entirely new approach may be necessary. Perhaps a *third* generation of resource laws is now in order, one where the benefits are not purely anthropocentric, but instead ecocentric, and where the rights are not held by humans, but by nature.[2]

---

[1] *See* Ted Nordhaus & Michael Shellenberger, *Break Through: Why We Can't Leave Saving the Planet to the Environmentalists* (2009); Anthony DePalma, *Mercury's Harmful Reach Has Grown, Study Suggests,* NY TIMES D3 (Jan. 24, 2012); *Climate Change Summit: A Deal in Durban,* The Economist (Dec. 17, 2011) (the United Nations Durban agreement acknowledges that there is a widening gap between mitigation efforts currently promised and those needed to keep global warming within safety limits); *Oceans Heading for Mass Extinctions, Experts Warn,* MSNBC (June 21, 2011), *available at* http://www.msnbc.msn.com/id/43479398/ns/world_news-world.

[2] Susan Emmenegger & Alex Tschentscher, *Taking Nature's Right's Seriously: The Long Way to Biocentrism in Environmental Law,* 6 GEO. INT'L ENVTL. L. REV. 545 (1994).

A. The Limits of a Purely Anthropocentric Perspective in First- and Second-Generation Resource Laws

Virtually all natural resources and environmental laws are *anthropocentric*. They either focus on exploiting the use component of natural resources and environmental goods when humans wish to maximize their well-being and economic welfare (first-generation laws), or remedying the environmental problems that follow when humans so overuse resources that there are pollution and health issues that adversely affect us (second-generation laws). Second-generation laws may also seek to protect the nonuse value of certain resources, because humans have discovered that nature and natural processes have benefit to us when lands, landscapes, and environmental goods remain unused by humans. Whether nature is thought most valuable to humans when it is used, or when it is not used, the rationale for the legal intervention has primarily been anthropocentric—to enhance immediate human self-interest, or to prevent harm to humans.[3]

This human-centric emphasis should not be surprising. Human beings have so altered and dominated the planet in just the past century or two that some stratigraphers believe we have ushered in a new, post-Holocene epoch: the Anthropocene.[4] Humans have transformed the prehominid world in several obvious ways. They have occupied much of the land with their cities and agricultural practices. Conversely, they have denuded natural landscapes by leveling forests, which has destroyed habitat for species and helped accelerate extinctions. They have removed much aquatic life from the oceans through extensive industrial fishing techniques. They have added enormous quantities of chemicals to the atmosphere, which likely have triggered climate changes. And humans have completely populated the earth, making their biomass already a hundred times larger than that of any other animal species that ever inhabited the planet.[5]

Moreover, consistent with standard welfare economics theory, legal policies should "depend solely on concerns for *human* welfare."[6] And human welfare is presumed to be a function of individuals' well-being and existing preferences; it follows then that human welfare is not dependent on the welfare of any nonhuman, natural systems. "The hallmark of welfare economics is that [legal] policies are assessed exclusively in terms of their effects on the well-being of individuals. . . . [W]hatever is unrelated to individuals' well-being is excluded from consideration under welfare economics."[7]

---

[3] Note, *Giving Nature Constitutional Protection: A Less Anthropocentric Interpretation of Environmental Rights*, 86 Tex. L. Rev. 615, 618 (2008); Emmenegger & Tschentscher, *supra* note 2, at 550.

[4] Elizabeth Kolbert, *Seven Billion*, Nat'l Geographic 69–70 (Mar. 2011); *The Anthropocene: A Man-Made World*, Economist, May 26, 2011 (the term *anthropocene* originated with Paul Crutzen, an atmospheric chemist, in 2000).

[5] Kolbert, *supra* note 4, at 72–75.

[6] Louis Kaplow & Steven Shavall, Fairness versus Welfare 23 (2002).

[7] *Id.* at 16.

If the goal of social and legal policy is to raise the overall level of human welfare, and to maximize the social aggregate of utility as much as natural resources allow, then, of course, the laws that seek to bring about this goal will be anthropocentric. Indeed, anthropocentrism is the basis for a societal goal that strives to satisfy the preferences of individuals, and its collective product, social welfare. Or, as environmental economists flatly assert, "individual welfare is all that counts in making policy choices."[8]

Such a human-focused metric explains why first- and second-generation natural resource and environmental laws were instruments to advance purely anthropocentric interests, irrespective of any notions that resources had intrinsic value not associated with human welfare. First-generation laws reflected utilitarian rationales, championed by Jeremy Bentham, which presumed that humans should have a virtually unlimited right to exploit nature for purely selfish ends.[9] Those first-generation laws that required resource sustainability and conservation were similarly anthropocentric because the use restraints required by those laws were a result of the recognition that humans might harm their long-term economic interests if they were permitted to overexploit their resources.[10] All these laws were grounded in the principle of *utility*, relying on human self-interest as the primary criterion for policies and laws associated with natural resources.[11]

Second-generation laws that recognized and protected the nonuse value of natural and environmental resources similarly exhibited a fundamentally anthropocentric character. They viewed pollution concerns and preservationist desires through a human welfare focus. So prevalent were the interests of humans that these resource nonuse rules have been termed a form of "species chauvinism."[12] Antipollution laws were not enacted to remove pollutants from the atmosphere and waters so that natural processes would function better; these laws were enacted to protect humans from the health hazards of pollution.[13] Similarly, legal initiatives seeking to preserve nature's services, in the form of ecosystem functions and natural capital, are based on the *economic* value of the function or service to *human* welfare.[14] And, human welfare is obviously measured in terms of each individual's own assessment of that person's well-being when a natural function or service is left alone and not directly used by humans. Human welfare is not defined by the contribution the nonused function or service makes to overall ecosystem health.

---

[8] Edith Stokey & Richard Zeckhausen, A Primer for Policy Analysis 275 (1978).

[9] Alasdair MacIntyre, *Reformers, Utilitarians, Idealists*, *in* A Short History of Ethics 227, 232 (1966); Indira Carr, *Saving the Environment - Does Utilitarianism Provide a Justification?* 12 Legal Studies 92, 94–101 (1992).

[10] Antonio D'Amato & Sudhir K. Chopra, Whales: *Their Emerging Right to Life*, 85 J. Int'l L. 21, 30 (1991).

[11] Carr, *supra* note 9, at 97.

[12] Gunther Handle, *Human Rights and Protection of the Environment: A Mildly "Revionist" View*, *in* Human Rights, Sustainable Development and the Environment 117 (Antonio Trindade ed. 1992); Richard Routley & Val Routley, *Human Chauvinism and Environmental Ethics*, *in* Environmental Philosophy 96, 136 (D. Mannison et al. eds. 1980).

[13] Peter A.Y. Gunter, *The Big Thicket*, *in* Philosophy and Environmental Crisis 117, 129–136 (W.T. Blackstone ed. 1974).

[14] Nancy E. Bockstael, A. Myrick Freeman III, Raymond J. Kopp, Paul R. Portney, & V. Kerry Smith, *On Measuring Economic Values for Nature*, 34 Envtl. Sci. & Tech. 1384, 1385 (2000).

Even second-generation resource preservation laws were grounded in anthropocentrism. Wild lands, parks, open spaces, wilderness areas, endangered species, and historic sites were not set aside because nature benefits from their nonuse by humans; rather, they were preserved because of the high "existence" and "amenity" value that they hold for humans.[15] Preservation laws address the failure of markets to respond to the nonuse value of natural places and objects that humans want to preserve, but may never experience.[16] But, as with first-generation laws, the interest and needs of *humans* drive the policy and the eventual law. If a landscape has potential either for resource extraction (because it contains gold) or for existence value (because it is aesthetically beautiful), then the question of whether to exploit it or preserve it becomes a calculation of countervailing human interests—if the balance tips in favor of humans enjoying nonused nature, then a second-generation law will preserve it; if humans wish to use the land's resources, then a first-generation law will make that preference possible.[17]

Virtually all first- and second-generation laws provide rights to individuals, groups, nongovernmental organizations, business associations, and corporations. These entities are empowered to raise their own interests should they wish to access information, judicial remedies, and political processes. Some commentators have urged that environmental quality and nonuse values should be treated more as a collective right.[18] Under this view, communities of people (rather than individuals) could be given a right to determine how their land, resources, and environment should be managed or protected. Alternatively, individuals could raise the broader "public interest" affected by resource use and nonuse decisions.[19] Laws recognizing individual rights, and proposed laws contemplating collective rights, are still anthropocentric.

In light of the ongoing and endemic resource and environmental problems that continue to plague this planet despite the broad sweep of second-generation laws,[20] it is timely to consider whether a *nonanthropocentric* approach to resource nonuse protection might be in order. Although existing second-generation laws seemingly offer a good deal of global and local environmental and resource protection, there is growing suspicion that they are falling short of meeting desired ends.[21] An approach that relates directly to environmental goods may be required.[22]

---

[15] *See* John K. Krutilla, *Conservation Reconsidered,* 57 AM. ECON. REV. 787 (1967); (people place a value on the mere existence of certain resources, even though they do not intend to consume or own them).

[16] Mark Sagoff, *Price, Principle, and the Environment* 37 (2004).

[17] MILTON FRIEDMAN, CAPITALISM AND FREEDOM 31 (1961).

[18] *See* Chapter 11 *supra.*

[19] Alan Boyle, *Human Rights or Environmental Rights? A Reassessment,* 17 FORDHAM ENVT'L L. REV. 471, 472, 506 (2007).

[20] *See* Chapter 10 *supra.*

[21] *See supra* note 1.

[22] Michael R. Anderson, *Human Rights Approaches to Environmental Protection: An Overview, in* HUMAN RIGHTS APPROACHES TO ENVIRONMENTAL PROTECTION (A. Boyle & M. Anderson eds. 1996).

The prevailing anthropocentric approach is deficient because it does not address threats to natural resources, objects, and processes that are not tied somehow to human welfare. The alternative, the formulation of a right that is not defined in purely anthropocentric terms, will protect resource nonuse that benefits more than humans. When anthropocentrism is supplemental (or is some cases even replaced by) ecocentrism, then resource long-term sustainability and the planet's survivability is more likely.[23] In other words, what seems needed is a recognition that natural resources and environmental values are a good in their own right, where resource nonuse has *intrinsic value,* irrespective of human welfare.[24]

B. Why Resource Nonuse Laws Should Be Less Anthropocentric

Both first-generation resource use laws and second-generation resource nonuse laws were anthropocentric—they addressed issues regarding resource use and nonuse that affected humans. These laws valued nature for the material or physical benefits that it can provide humans, either when it is used or not used. Nonanthropocentric resource laws, especially resource nonuse laws, instead concern themselves with issues affecting nature and the natural world irrespective of humans. Such laws value nature for its own sake, for its intrinsic worth. Whereas first- and second-generation laws saw immediate human self-interest as the primary reason for laws either encouraging resource use or requiring resource nonuse, a third-generation law might transcend such an anthropocentric approach and be based on a recognition of the inherent value of nature, a value not derivative of human interest.[25]

It would be a paradigm shift to cease a long-standing policy in which the protection of humans is the central focus and replace it with one in which the natural environment itself was protected. Such a shift would mean that law and policy makers would not simply ask: What can we do to preserve and maintain something that is good for us? Rather, the question would be: What should we do to protect something that is good because of its intrinsic inherent qualities?[26] This change in perspective is identical to the altered worldview that took place in the 17th century when scientists such as Galileo and Newton realized that humans were not the center of the cosmos, where "the [pre-17th century] world was a play performed for our benefit. . . . In the new picture, man is not the pinnacle of creation, but an afterthought."[27]

[23] Dinah Shelton, *Environmental Rights, in* People's Rights (Philip Alston ed. 2001).

[24] Sagoff, *supra* note 16, at 6l; *Boyle, supra* note 19, at 473 ("Should we transcend the anthropocentric in favor of the eco-centric?").

[25] Myrl L. Duncan, *The Rights of Nature: Triumph of Holism or Pyrrhic Victory?*, 31 Washburn L.J. 62, 70 (1991); Lawrence H. Tribe, *Ways Not to Think about Plastic Trees: New Foundations for Environmental Law*, 83 Yale L.J. 1315, 1343 (1974).

[26] Eccy de Jonge, Spinoza and Deep Ecology: Challenging Traditional Approaches to Environmentalism 9–15 (2004); Sagoff, *supra* note 16, at 2.

[27] Edward Dolnick, The Clockwork Universe: Isaac Newton, the Royal Society and the Birth of the Modern World 94–95 (2011).

The assertion of nature's intrinsic value has already made its way into the lawmaking of international multilateral environmental instruments. In 1982, the General Assembly of the United Nations adopted the World Charter for Nature, which acknowledged that "every form of life is unique, warranting respect regardless of its worth to man."[28] Ten years later, in 1992, the United Nations approved the Convention on Biological Diversity, whose preamble explicitly recognized "the intrinsic value of biological diversity."[29] These pronouncements reflect a growing realization that humankind should no longer be the sole yardstick against which the utility of resource nonuse should be measured. Rather, this new approach recognizes nature, and natural processes, as being entitled to integrity independent of human interest.[30]

Anthropocentrism is too limited a worldview to grasp the inherent value of nature. The interests of humans are not necessarily congruent with the interests of nature.[31] Historic anthropocentric approaches to resource nonuse and environmental protection do not recognize the value of nature itself.[32] As a result, second-generation anthropocentric resource nonuse laws are thought by some to be the true root cause of environmental failures worldwide.[33] For example, because the focus of many second-generation antipollution laws is primarily human health, the reality is that harm to nature can occur before humans are harmed.[34] When the laws are triggered because of human harm, the damage to nature may be irreversible.

Of course, any nonanthropocentric resource nonuse law runs the risk of being nonenforceable. It is difficult to conceptualize how nature's interests can be protected from human use demands without humans also raising human concerns.[35] Indeed, any law focused on nonanthropocentric ends would likely have to be both asserted and enforced by very anthropomorphic humans. Accordingly, many commentators have argued that natural objects should not be accorded their own legal nonuse rights.[36] Others have maintained that an anthropocentric focus can provide

---

[28] World Charter of Nature, G.S. Res. 37/7, U.N. GAOR, 37th Sess., Supp.. No. 51, pmbl., para. 3(a), at 17, U.N. Doc. A/37/51 (1982).

[29] United Nations Environment Programme Convention on Biological Diversity 5 (June 1992), 1760 U.N.T.S. 143–46.

[30] Environmental ethicists term such nonanthropocentric environmentalism as *deep ecology*. Arne Naess, *The Shallow and the Deep, Long-Range Ecology Movement: A Summary*, 16 INQUIRY 95 (1973); Bill Devall, *The Deep Ecology Movement*, *in* KEY CONCEPTS IN CRITICAL THEORY ECOLOGY 125 (C. Merchant ed. 1994).

[31] Suzanne C. Gagnon Thompson & Michelle A. Barton, *Ecocentric and Anthropocentric Attitudes toward the Environment*, 14 J. ENVTL. PSYCHOL. 149 (1994); Tribe, *supra* note 25, at 1331.

[32] Prudence E. Taylor, *From Environmental to Ecological Human Rights: A New Dynamic in International Law?*, 10 GEO. INT'L ENVTL. L. REV. 309, 351–2 (1998).

[33] DE JONGE, *supra* note 26, at 11; Judith I. McGeary, *A Scientific Approach to Protecting Biodiversity*, 14 J. NAT. RES. & ENVTL. L. 85, 92 (1999); DAVE FOREMAN, CONFESSIONS OF AN ECO-WARRIOR 1, 3 (1991).

[34] Elizabeth F Brown, Comment, *In Defense of Environmental Rights in East European Constitutions*, 1933 U. CHI. L. SCH. ROUNDTABLE 191, 212.

[35] J.E. DE STEIGUER, THE AGE OF ENVIRONMENTALISM 143 (1997); Anderson, *supra* note 22, at 14.

[36] J.G. Merrills, *Environmental Protection and Human Rights: Conceptual Aspects*, *in* HUMAN RIGHTS APPROACHES TO ENVIRONMENTAL PROTECTION 25, 31, 34 (Alan E. Boyle & Michael R. Anderson eds. 1996).

the same protection of nature as a purely ecocentric or biocentric approach.[37] However, first-generation resource laws based on anthropocentric values caused natural resources to be overused,[38] while anthropocentric second-generation laws have failed to prevent humans from endangering the planet.[39] We should realize that the interests of humans and nature are not necessarily the same.[40]

C. Nonanthropocentric Protection of Natural Resource Nonuse Values

If we are to enlist the law to facilitate the greater cause of protecting and preserving resource nonuse values, then we must begin by recognizing (1) the intrinsic, non-human-centric worth of nature and natural resources,[41] and (2) the limits of an anthropocentric approach to environmental and resource-protective laws.[42] The alternative to traditional legal responses—nonanthropocentric protection of resource nonuse—raises three issues. First, should such protection be manifested by imposing a *duty* on humans to preserve resources nonuse, or should resources be granted their own *right* of nonuse? Second, which components or manifestations of nature and the natural world should be protected? Third, if natural and environmental resources are to be protected as a matter of law for their own sake[43] and not for their instrumental value to humans,[44] then from what should there be such protection? And to what end? These important issues are examined below, and then again, in more depth, in Chapter 17.

A Duty Toward Nature or a Nature-Held Right of Nonuse?—If nonanthropocentric legal nonuse rights are going to be provided to nature, one threshold inquiry is whether positive law should impose a duty on humans to not use natural resources in some circumstances, or whether nature should be conferred its own right of nonuse. Such a duty or right would have to possess sufficient legal clout to override

---

[37] James L. Huffman, *Do Species and Nature Have Rights?*, 13 PUBLIC LAND L. REV. 51, 75 (1992); P.S. Elder, *Legal Rights for Nature: The Wrong Answer to the Right(s) Question*, 22 OSGOODE HALL L.J. 285, 291 (1984).

[38] *See* Chapter 9 *supra*.

[39] Richard A. Kerr, *Humans Are Driving Extreme Weather: Time to Prepare*, 334 Science 1040 (Nov. 25, 2011) (human activity has driven not just climate change, but also increases in extreme weather and climate events around the world); L.J. GRAY ET AL., SOLAR INFLUENCES ON CLIMATE 1, 43 (2010) ("Despite uncertainties [about the role of solar variability in climate change compared to the importance of human activity], solar radiative forcing [is] nevertheless much smaller than the estimated radiative forcing due to anthropogenic changes. . . ."); GLOBAL WARMING, STANFORD SOLAR CENTER 3 (2008) ("The global increases in carbon dioxide concentration are primarily due to fossil fuel use and land-use change.").

[40] Tribe, *supra* note 25, at 1331.

[41] DE JONGE, *supra* note 26, at 16–21.

[42] FREDRIC L. BENDER, THE CULTURE OF EXTINCTION: TOWARD A PHILOSOPHY OF DEEP ECOLOGY (2003).

[43] DEEP ECOLOGY FOR THE 21ST CENTURY: READINGS ON THE PHILOSOPHY AND PRACTICE OF THE NEW ENVIRONMENTALISM (George Sessions ed. 1995).

[44] TIMOTHY W. LUKE, ECOCRITIQUE: CONTESTING THE POLITICS OF NATURE, ECONOMY, AND CULTURE (1997).

purely utilitarian considerations regarding resources. And, it would likely need to be enforceable without the need to show some harm to human interests.[45]

Environmental ethicists—those who study how humans should act concerning nature—tend to support a rights approach over a duty imposed on humans toward nature. One advantage of a right of nonuse is that it is consistent with and supportive of the notion that natural and environmental resources have intrinsic, inherent value apart from humans. It will be difficult to see or appreciate value in nature's nonuse benefits if nature itself is not provided a right of nonuse.[46] An acknowledgement of a nonuse right held by natural resources would also help ensure that the resource protected by the right was not simply part of a calculus in human considerations in the context of some duty to the resource.[47] A nonuse right held by the resource abandons anthropocentric triggers and concentrates on the purely natural values that flow from leaving the resource alone.[48] Moreover, the creation of a duty to respect resource nonuse interests would not necessarily mean that the resource itself would have any correlative enforceable legal right to enforce nonuse values on humans wishing to indulge their use interests.[49]

Which Components of Nature Should Have Rights?—If policy makers are going to confer on natural resources, environmental goods, or ecological processes a legally enforceable "right" of nonuse, capable of sometimes resisting human use demands, then one important issue that needs to be resolved is this: What exactly in nature should be provided such a right? There appears to be three choices. First, a *biocentric* approach assumes that all living organisms are entitled to equal consideration under law, if not a right to fulfill their existence as evolutionary beings.[50] Second, *deep ecology* transcends biocentrism and encompasses all natural entities and compounds, even nonliving beings.[51] Third, *ecological holism* presumes that all components of a natural system are important, living or not living, and that the relevant natural entity is the interrelationship that emerges between nature's parts when humans do not interfere.[52]

Biocentrism acknowledges all living entities as inherently valuable, and that no living being (i.e., humans) is inherently superior to other living organisms. This notion that all living things have equal intrinsic value means that this branch of environmental ethics has sometimes been dubbed "biocentric egalitarianism."[53] Biocentric perspectives have the advantage of evading the awkwardness that follows

---

[45] Robert Elliott, *Environmental Ethics*, *in* A COMPANION TO ETHICS 112 (Peter Singer ed. 1993).

[46] Christopher D. Stone, *Should Trees Have Standing?—Toward Legal Rights for Natural Objects*, 45 S. CAL. L. REV. 450, 456 (1972).

[47] DE JONGE, *supra* note 26, at 16–19.

[48] George Sessions, *Ecocentrism and the Anthropocentric Detour*, *in* KEY CONCEPTS IN CRITICAL THEORY ECOLOGY 140, 144–45 (C. Merchant ed. 1994); Anderson, *supra* note 22.

[49] Huffman, *supra* note 37, at 55–56; D'Amato & Chopra, *supra* note 10, at 52; Stone, *supra* note 46, at 488–89.

[50] DE JONGE, *supra* note 26, at 21–25.

[51] Devall, *supra* note 30, at 132.

[52] *See, e.g.*, ALDO LEOPOLD, A SAND COUNTY ALMANAC (1949) (arguing for environmental ethics based on the earth as a whole).

[53] Naess, *supra* note 30, at 95–100.

when one confers environmental rights on nonliving inanimate objects, such as mountains, rivers, rocks, and even the earth itself.[54] But a right based on biocentrism leaves out of its protection natural resources and environmental goods, such as the atmosphere and estuaries and even alpine mountain ranges, that are essential to life-forms. A much broader conception of nature seems necessary if one is to protect the nonuse component of natural resources from human use interests.

The idea of deep ecology extends the scope of the relevant natural environment to every natural entity that affects life, even though the object itself may not be alive. The waters of the world's oceans are not themselves living, but they are the home of most of the living organisms that inhabit this planet. The earth's atmosphere is not living, but the gases in the air make life possible, and all terrestrial organisms, and most aquatic ones, require the presence of the gaseous envelope surrounding the earth. Aldo Leopold urged that for humans to survive on this planet for the long term, we must "think like a mountain."[55] This hallmark of deep ecology is directed at selfish humans (and welfare economists) who typically focus exclusively on human needs and wants. "Thinking like a mountain" incorporates in our consciousness an attitude that encompasses all natural things, living and not living, so that it is conceivable to imagine a world where we can answer in the affirmative this otherwise ridiculous question (posed by Roderick Nash): "Do rocks have rights?"[56]

Deep ecology recognizes that it makes no sense to embrace a life-centered ethic (biocentrism) when life itself depends on nonliving beings. However, deep ecology does not necessarily extend to natural systems that exist between, and the interrelationships that form among, *all* natural beings—sentient and non-sentient animals, living trees and plants, nonliving natural objects such as rivers and mountains and air. The hydrologic cycle, photosynthesis, weather, and organic decomposition are all natural systems that permit the earth to harbor life. To protect living and nonliving natural entities, as well as the systems in which they evolve, exist, and thrive, one must recognize that ecosystems as a whole have value, regardless of whether they are considered alive, or even a natural resource. The much broader concept of "ecological holism" captures the entire network of interrelations that exist between entities in nature, living or not, and the earth.[57] When in the future policy makers create a right of nonuse to protect resources from human use choices, perhaps the "right" should be an ecocentric one, transcending the anthropocentric and biocentric, and encompassing the interconnections of all beings.[58]

What Should be the Purpose and Content of the Right? Any right of nonuse afforded natural resources (where the protected natural "resources" would be defined and

[54] J.G. Merrills, *Environmental Protection and Human Rights: Conceptual Aspects, in* HUMAN RIGHTS APPROACHES TO ENVIRONMENTAL PROTECTION 25, 31 (Alan Boyle & Michael Anderson eds. 1996).

[55] Devall, *supra* note 30.

[56] Roderick Nash, Do Rocks Have Rights?, 10 CTR. MAG. 2 (1977).

[57] Bill Devall & George Sessions, *The Development of Natural Resources and the Integrity of Nature*, 6 ENVTL. ETHICS 293, 302–12 (1984).

[58] Boyle, *supra* note 19, at 473.

limited by biocentrism, deep ecology, or ecological holism) would have to set out under what circumstances the right could be triggered. In other words, what would be the nonuse status sought to be achieved or maintained by asserting the right? Or, what nonuse values would have to be threatened by human use desires before the right could be raised? The purpose and content of a right of nonuse would have to be articulated in order for decision-makers, such as courts or special bodies vested with use/nonuse decisionmaking authority, to determine when, and to what extent, the interests of natural resources would prevail over the countervailing rights of humans wishing to use or exploit those resources.[59]

Among the most basic rights that a natural resource might enjoy is the right to exist, especially when confronted with a human desire to destroy it for utilitarian ends.[60] Another right that is biocentric in nature is the right to be able to continue to evolve as a species.[61] A right more consistent with ecological holism would prevent human use actions that either threaten ecosystems and habitat, or endanger natural resources that are "viable components of their ecosystems."[62] An even broader right is one that not only halts human use activities, but that also seeks to preserve and restore "natural values" in an area.[63] Preservationist and restoration goals are prominent in wilderness acts[64] and in stream flow protection laws.[65]

If any of the above rights are triggered, the difficult policy question would then be whether those nonuse rights, held by natural resources, could actually veto a concomitant right, held by humans, to use the resources. In other words, is a right of nonuse an absolute right? It would be politically infeasible, and economically impractical, to provide nature with the means to halt human resource use activities whenever natural values, or ecosystem health, were threatened. Instead, if a right of nonuse is established, the right would need to *considered* as part of the use calculus, along with the consequences for nature and natural systems if the right were ignored.[66]

---

59 Mary Anne Warren, *The Rights of the Non-Human World*, *in* ENVIRONMENTAL PHILOSOPHY 115 (Robert Elliot & Arran Gare eds. 1983); Stone, *supra* note 46 at 457.

60 *See, e.g.*, the Forest Service Organic Administration Act of 1897, 16 U.S.C. § 551, which requires the Forest Service to "preserve the forests from destruction." *See also* Rock Creek Alliance v. U.S. Forest Serv., 703 F. Supp. 2d. 1152, 1164–65 (D. Mont. 2010); Joel Feinberg, *Human Duties and Animal Rights*, in ON THE FIFTH DAY: ANIMAL RIGHTS AND HUMAN ETHICS 45, 56 (Richard Morris & Michael Fox eds. 1978).

61 *See, e.g.*, the Endangered Species Act, 16 U.S.C. § 1532 (16); Trout Unlimited v. Lohn, 559 F. 3d 946, 950 (9th Cir. 2009); S. Yuba River Citizens League v. Nat'l Marine Fisheries Servs., 723 F. Supp. 2d 1247, 1251 (E.D. Cal. 2010).

62 Rock Creek Alliance v. U.S. Fish and Wildlife Service, 663 F. 3d 439 (9th Cir. 2011); Arizona Cattle Growers Ass'n v. Salazar, 606 F. 3d 1160, 1166 (9th Cir. 2010); Siskiyou Reg'l Educ. Project v. U.S. Forest Serv., 565 F. 3d 545, 550–51 (9th Cir. 2009).

63 Pacific Coast Fed'n of Fishermen's Ass'ns v. Gutierrez, 606 F. Supp. 2d 1122 (E.D. 2008).

64 *See, e.g.*, 16 U.S.C. § 1133 (c); Wolf Recovery Found. v. U.S. Forest Serv., 692 F. Supp. 2d 1264, 1267 (D. Idaho 2010).

65 *See, e.g.*, COLO. REV. STAT. § 37-92-102(3); OR. REV. STAT. § 537.348(2).

66 *See, e.g.*, DE JONGE, *supra* note 26, at 21 (when natural entities are thought to have nonanthropocentric value for their own sake, then such entities deserve consideration by humans before humans use them).

D. Countries That Provide for Ecocentric Resource Nonuse Protections

Various countries have already embraced the idea of providing nature and natural resources with a right *not* to be used by humans. In 2008, Ecuador's citizens voted their approval of a new constitution that expressly provides "nature . . . the right to exist, persist, maintain and regenerate its vital cycles, structure, functions and its processes in evolution."[67] This change in its constitution made Ecuador the first country to legislate rights for nature. The new constitution also provided "every person, people, community" the ability "to demand the recognition of rights for nature before public bodies."[68] In Ecuador, therefore, not only does nature now have a right of nonuse, but also anyone, or any group of people, have been granted standing to raise this right "before 'public bodies.'" A nonanthropocentric nonuse right may thereby be enforced by anthropomorphic initiative.

Another South American country, Bolivia, seems likely to pass a law granting all nature equal rights to humans. Nature's rights include the right to life and to exist, the right to continue vital cycles and processes free from human alteration, the right to pure water and clean air, and the right not to be polluted.[69] These are classic nonuse rights. The underlying motive for them is the perceived need for humans to leave natural resources alone. When resources are not used, then not only are they "not polluted" by humans eager to use public environmental goods as waste sinks, but they can also perform natural services ("continue vital cycles and processes") that are necessary for planetary health. Although it is not clear what actual protection such new rights will provide, the Bolivian government is expected to establish a new "ministry of mother earth," and to appoint an earth ombudsman.

Argentina's Congress has adopted legislation forbidding on its glaciers all "activities that may affect their natural condition or their function as a source of water."[70] The enforcement authority is the country's Secretary of Environment and Sustainable Development. These legal protections of glaciers are both nonanthropocentric (forbidding all human use activities that might "affect their natural condition") and human-centric (securing the function of glaciers as "a source of water," presumably for both humans and ecocentric systems).

Two factors have been influential in the adoption of those South American nonuse initiatives. First, in countries such as Ecuador, there has been a perception that major environmental damage has followed from the activities of oil and gas and mining companies. This perception is grounded in the belief that these resource-extractive activities have seemingly poisoned much of the natural landscape. Second, in countries such as Bolivia, resurgent indigenous peoples have demanded that the laws provide nature

---

[67] http://blogs.nature.com/news/thegreatbeyond/2008/09/ecuador.

[68] *Id.*

[69] http://www.guardian.co.uk/environment/2011/apr/10/bolivia.

[70] Leonardo G. Rodriguez & Francisco A. Macias, *New Law on Minimum Standards for Protection of Glaciers, Marval*, O'FARRELL & MAIRAL MONTHLY REP. (Oct. 2010).

and the natural world with the same kind of respect afforded human life. These urgings are consistent with a traditional spiritual view of the South American world that places nature and the environment, but not humans, at the center of all life.

If first- and second-generation resource use and nonuse laws have failed to protect the viability of natural and environmental resources, then the time has come to seriously consider the introduction of a third generation of nonuse laws. These would be nonanthropocentric, recognizing the tautological fallacy of having human welfare be the basis (found in most second-generation laws) for defining the value of the natural world. When natural resources and environmental goods are seen to possess intrinsic value, and when that value is acknowledged by laws and legal institutions, the nonuse component of nature will better have the ability to compete with otherwise overwhelming human resource use desires.

PART IV

Revealing the Nonuse Component of Natural Resources

DO ALL NATURAL resources have both a use and nonuse component, where the former is what humans historically value, wheras the latter is what the planet needs? Part IV applies three separate disciplines to make the argument that natural resources do indeed have a nonuse component and function, which is part of the intrinsic nature of all the environmental features of this earth. Chapter 13 considers how evolutionary biology seems to suggest that living organisms would not have evolved to the point where humans could exist if humans had more of an opportunity to wreak havoc on the natural world by their relentless and systematic *use* of natural resources. Indeed, in Chapter 13 we will see hints that human interference with resource nonuse may be adversely affecting the evolutionary mechanism that had been in place long before humans were here. One response to this uniquely biological harm brought about by human activity is for humans to consider the benefits that might flow if they were to leave nature alone, so that the nonuse features of resources have the opportunity to correct the harms caused by human use demands. Chapter 14 makes the argument that some of the fundamental forces and scientific "laws" of the universe may reveal that natural resources are not just made up of use qualities, but also a parallel, and equal, nonuse dimension. Recognition of resource nonuse, as a symmetrical mirror to resource use, would be consistent with broadly held beliefs about the functioning of nature, and the universe, in other contexts. Chapter 15 uses an outgrowth of economics—game theory—to make the case that a more optimal result might occur if we viewed the natural resources "game" as consisting of more than just humans who wanted to use resources, and humans who wanted (usually for their own anthropomorphic purposes) to not use resources. If we empowered a third player, the natural resource itself, and permitted that new player to join the resources game as an equal member that could assert its own nonuse interest, then we (and the planet) would experience a preferable allocation of resource use and nonuse benefits.

13 The Biology of Resource Nonuse

A. Introduction

Human activities, greed, and carelessness have led to numerous natural resource disasters and declining species around the world. Such interference causes destructive changes to organisms and their environments. There are countless global examples of environmental catastrophes produced by human development that have brought about the eradication of critical species and natural resources, and which, because of their magnitude, continue to plague the surrounding areas years later. Oil seepages, chemical spills, releases of toxic gases, and numerous other human-caused interferences are killing species and destroying natural resources at a devastating rate.[1] This outcome may be unstoppable unless something dramatic is done.

One well-publicized example of a human-caused disaster affecting natural resource is the 2010 oil spill in the Gulf of Mexico. The British Petroleum (BP) oil spill was one of the largest accidental spills into marine waters in history.[2] The oil spill put at risk the thousands of miles of irreplaceable wetlands, beaches, and fisheries that could be damaged for seasons. The result has been parts of a sea floor covered in oil, and the

[1] *See* Stephanie Rogers, *7 Biggest Environmental Disasters—Where Are They Now?*, EcoSalon, *available at* http://www.ecosalon.com/7-biggest-environmental-disasters- percent E2 percent 80 percent 93-where-are-they-now/.

[2] Erin Aigner et al., *Tracking the Oil Spill in the Gulf*, N.Y. Times, Aug. 2, 2010, *available at* http://www.nytimes.com/interactive/2010/05/01/us/20100501-oil-spill-tracker.html.

potential wiping out of fragile species.[3] A senior scientist from Oceana, a nonprofit organization warned, "a lot of animals live in the ocean, and a spill like this becomes bad for marine life as soon as it hits the water . . . we may never fully understand the full impacts on ocean life."[4]

The Gulf oil spill is but one example in an array of environmental harms that follow from human interference in the natural order of life. The ongoing disaster at the Niger Delta includes seven thousand oil spills between 1970 and 2000.[5] This area endures the equivalent of an Exxon Valdez oil spill every year, with some estimating that it has been occurring for as long as 50 years.[6] Nigeria has produced more than two million barrels of oil a day, and thousands of miles of leaking pipes have been laid through the swamp lands encompassing the area. Oil companies claim that much of the oil in these spills is cleaned up, yet experts say these companies attribute much of the problem to sabotage in order to lessen their culpability. The Niger Delta area is slowly being destroyed by unchecked oil spills caused by rusting and aging pipes, ineffective regulation, and deficient maintenance. The swamplands exposed to the oil are largely lifeless. Aquatic areas once teaming with shrimp and crab are now void of life, and environmentalists have deemed the area a "dead environment."

The Black Sea is another example of a natural resource that some Russian environmentalists claim is in danger of "dying."[7] Marine biologists have reported that only five species of fish remain in the Black Sea, which once boasted a highly diverse ecosystem containing at least 26 different species. Between 1985 and 1994 the total fish catch in the Black Sea went from approximately 675,000 to 45,000 kilograms. Only 10 percent of its near surface volume contains enough oxygen to support life. The deoxygenation of the Black Sea is primarily caused by large-scale infusions of hydrogen sulfide, which comes mainly from the Danube, Don, South Bug, and Dnepr Rivers that flow into the sea from the north and the west. Large amounts of military waste and chemical weapons were once discharged into the rivers in Poland and the Baltic Sea republics during the Soviet Era, aiding in the death of the Black Sea. Additionally, other nonnatural, human-introduced substances have been identified in the Black Sea, including mercury, cadmium, arsenic, and oil. Political conflicts have hindered cleanup efforts.

Human-created pollution of the atmosphere poses an additional serious threat to our natural environment. Air pollution, while often invisible, creates smog and acid rain, diminishes the protective ozone layer in the upper atmosphere, and contributes

---

[3] John M. Broder & Tom Zeller, Jr., *Gulf Oil Spill Is Bad, but How Bad?*, N.Y. Times, May 3, 2010, *available at* http://www.nytimes.com/2010/05/04/science/earth/04enviro.html.

[4] *Id. See also* Niles Eldredge, *The Sixth Extinction*, https//www.actionbioscience.org (the Sixth Extinction would be the first global extinction that has a biotic, rather than physical, cause).

[5] *The World's Worst Environmental Disasters Caused by Companies*, N.Y. Times, June 21, 2010, *available at* http://www.businesspundit.com/the-worlds-worst-environmental-disasters-caused-by-companies/.

[6] Cain Burdeau, *Big Questions Linger a Year after Oil Spill*, Denv. Post, Apr. 20, 2011, at 16A; Adam Nossiter, *Far from Gulf, a Spill Scourge 5 Decades Old*, N.Y. Times, June 16, 2010, *available at* http://www.nytimes.com/2010/06/17/world/africa/17nigeria.html.

[7] *Environmental Problems*, http://countrystudies.us/russia/25.htm.

to the possibility of world climate change.[8] Human impact on the world's climate is an issue that is widely accepted among atmospheric and environmental scientists.[9] Although experts have claimed that "no single weather event can be traced to human activity and greenhouse gases . . . natural variation cannot explain the decade-long record. If you don't take the human emission into account you cannot reproduce what you observe."[10] Global warming has been pronounced in Africa, parts of Asia, and the Arctic.[11] In fact, 2010 has been estimated to be the warmest year to date, surpassing both 1998 and 2005.[12] Climate change contributes to worldwide environmental alterations of ecosystems and threats to species survival.

Water pollution caused by human development is also a global problem for natural resources. Some estimate that 40 percent of America's rivers are too polluted for fishing, swimming, or sustaining aquatic life.[13] Untreated sewage, stormwater, and industrial waste are dumped into water sources, causing harmful environmental effects.[14] Furthermore, land pollution caused by fertilizers, insecticides, and herbicides from agricultural and residential areas contribute to water contamination.[15] The concern is that "[f]ertilizer runoff and fossil-fuel use lead to massive areas in the ocean with scant to no oxygen."[16] The resultant pollution of water is a serious hazard to the existence and reproductive capacity of many living organisms.

As exploitation of natural resources outpaces natural regeneration of those natural resources, or completely depletes nonrenewable natural resources, the sustainability and continuation of some resources is put in doubt.[17] An illustrative example is how human-caused depletion of fisheries has radically changed natural ways of life, production, and ecosystems.[18] Within the last hundred years, close to two-thirds

---

[8] Melissa McNamara, *Pollutants Can Injure Health, and Harm the Environment. Find Out More about Them*, CBS News (Jan. 31, 2007), *available at* http://www.cbsnews.com/stories/2006/10/26/fyi/main2126583.shtml.

[9] *See Climate Study "Unequivocally" Shows World Growing Warmer*, Denv. Post, June 29, 2011, at 8A; Renee Hetherington, The Climate Connection (Robert G.B. Reid ed., 2010); *see also* William R. Cotton, Human Impacts on Weather and Climate (Roger A. Pielke, Sr. ed., 2d ed. 2010); Michael D. Mastandrea & Stephen H. Schneider, Preparing for Climate Change (2010).

[10] *Last Decade Warmest on Record, Review Finds*, msnbc.com Staff & News Serv. Reps. (Dec. 2, 2010), *available at* http://www.msnbc.msn.com/id/40474599/ns/us_news-environment. See also Global Warming and Climate Change (2011 Durban Conference), N.Y. Times, Dec. 15, 2011 (global emissions of greenhouse gases, produced by the burning of fossil fuels and forests, jumped by the largest amount on record in 2010).

[11] Justin Gillis, *As Permafrost Warms, Scientists See a Threat*, N.Y. Times (Dec. 17, 2011); Brian Vastag, *Arctic Life Risks Meltdown: Study Says Retreating Ice Could Threaten an Entire Food Chain*, Denv. Post, Mar. 8, 2011, at 8A.

[12] *Vast Ice Sheets Melting Fast, Report Finds*, Denv. Post, Mar. 10, 2011, at 12A.

[13] *Water Pollution Facts*, Grinning Planet, *available at* http://www.grinningplanet.com/2005/07-26/water-pollution-facts-article.htm.

[14] *Id.*

[15] Bernard P. Nelson, *Causes of Land Pollution*, Suite 101 (Dec. 24, 2008), *available at* http://www.suite101.com/content/land-pollution-facts-a86061.

[16] *Id.*

[17] M. Gismondi, Power and the Politics of Sustainability 1 (Les Samuelson & Wayne Antony eds., 2003).

[18] *Id.* at 2; Mark Kurlansky, World without Fish (2011); *Oceans Heading for Mass Extinctions, Experts Warn*, MSNBC (June 21, 2011), *available at* http://www.msnbc.com/id/43479398/ns/world_news.

of the ocean's large predator fish have been caught and consumed by humans.[19] As a result, small fish such as sardines and anchovies are overpopulating, which is creating an ecological imbalance in the ocean. If large predator fish, such as tuna, sword fish, grouper, and cod, continue to be caught at the present rate, the fisheries will be so out of balance that disease among remaining fish may be rampant, and there will be an increased level of algae or bacteria, which take oxygen out of the waters, making them uninhabitable.

A specific example of fishery depletion and its effects is illustrated by the closure of the northern cod fishery in Newfoundland in 1992–1993.[20] The northern cod had been easy to catch with simple and economical technology, and had sustained a local inshore fishery of small boats led by local fishers. The northern cod were considered by the people in the community to be a common property resource. However, the fisheries began to change in the 1960s as large national and foreign ships took enormous amounts of cod from deepwater breeding grounds. This process altered the fish population's capacity to reproduce and the ability of the ecosystem to properly recover. Despite the Canadian government's attempt to intervene, overfishing continued. In order to compete, local fishermen used larger traps and long-liner boats, and began using new technologies such as fish finders. As the fish population declined further, the Canadian government finally had to declare a moratorium in the area.[21] Short-term use pressures proved far more powerful than the nonuse advantages that would have benefitted the fisheries in the long term.

Fisheries are not the only natural resources that may not be sustainable in the face of human greed. Rainforest deforestation is another striking example of human interference disturbing the natural balances of ecosystems.[22] There are approximately three billion people living in the world's tropical areas. Rainforests are disappearing at a rapid rate as they are seen as sources to supply food, provide fuel, and make room for a growing population.[23] Scientists have estimated that rainforests harbor about half of the world's species. Many of the species living in rainforests are unique in that they are only found in small areas of those forests. The specialization of species living in the rainforests creates vulnerabilities because even small changes may cause a species extinction. Species living at the edges of deforested areas are particularly exposed to extreme conditions, such as hot winds, to which they had not previously been exposed or adapted. Destruction of the types of trees, plants, and insects that cannot survive at the edges of the deforested areas reduces the remaining biodiversity in the forest.[24]

All of these organisms, species, and resources have arisen through the natural selection process. The theory of natural selection explains how species adapt to

---

[19] Marc Kaufman, *Extinction Ahead for Predator Fish?*, DENV. POST, Feb. 22, 2011, at 9A.

[20] GISMONDI, *supra* note 17, at 5.

[21] *Id.* at 6.

[22] *Id.*

[23] *The Deforestation and Depletion of the Rainforest* (Aug. 9, 2008), *available at* http://www.articlesbase.com/nature-articles/the-deforestation-and-depletion-of-the-rainforest-515704.html.

[24] Rebecca Lindsey, *Tropical Deforestation*, EARTH OBSERVATORY (March 30, 2007), *available at* http://earthobservatory.nasa.gov/Features/Deforestation/.

changes in the environment such that only those species that can adequately adapt can survive. However, human interference in this natural process creates disturbances so great that a species may not be able to adapt to the changes produced by humans. Such human-created developments as oil drilling, pollution, deforestation, and exhaustion of fisheries may prevent natural selection from occurring. The organic processes governing species and resources are being disturbed by human abuse, and because of that abuse, species and resources may not be able to develop in the way nature intended.[25]

The consequence may be unnatural, human-induced higher rates of extinction. E. O. Wilson has noted that the current extinction rate of .1 percent a year is a thousand times greater than the level of extinction of species before humans arrived on the planet, which was in the range of only .0001 percent per year. Moreover, Wilson contends that the rate of extinction is expected to rise dramatically because of human-caused environmental changes, such as global warming, deforestation, and growing number of human-introduced species in nonnatural habitats. Humans seem to have altered natural selection.[26]

Because human beings have interfered to such a high degree in the natural selection process, one should consider some affirmative action that, if taken, might regenerate natural processes. The perpetuation of natural resources, particularly resources that humans depend on for survival, may require that humans back off from their endless need to use and exploit them. To alleviate such human-induced pressure, natural resources could be given certain levels of autonomy so that they may prosper unaffected by human demands. If living organisms are given a chance to live relatively free from destructive human interference, and if resources are even conferred a legal right entitling them to demand noninterference, then natural resources might acquire a sustainable level of protection against the human activities that seem bent on destroying them.[27]

B. Natural Selection

Charles Darwin's theory of evolution describes the process by which only the strongest and most adaptable organisms remain for reproduction; it also helps explain the natural processes in play for species' environmental existence.[28] The theory of natural selection explains how evolution occurred, and illustrates how environmental forces functioned prior to human interference. Natural selection is a process spanning the entire existence of organisms, and in its most unaffected form, it is a system

[25] Loss of Biodiversity and Extinctions, Global Issues (April 6, 2011) (the current extinction rate caused by human activity is now approaching 1000 times the normal background rate) http://www.globalissues.org; DAVID J. DEPEW & BRUCE H. WEBER, DARWINISM EVOLVING: SYSTEMS DYNAMICS AND THE GENEALOGY OF NATURAL SELECTION (2d ed. 1997); BJORN LOMBERG, THE SKEPTICAL ENVIRONMENTALIST (2001).

[26] PAUL WAPNER, LIVING THROUGH THE END OF NATURE (2010).

[27] Daniel R. Ortiz, *Privacy, Autonomy, and Consent*, 12 HARV. J.L. & POL'Y 91 (1988).

[28] Laurence Moran, *The Modern Synthesis of Genetics and Evolution*, THE TALKORIGINS ARCHIVE (Jan. 22, 1993), *available at* http://www.talkorigins.org/faqs/modern-synthesis.html.

by which nature selects out the organisms who should not continue to pass on their DNA, while promoting the existence and survival of others that should. Darwin himself said that in a natural world (i.e., a prehuman one), it "is daily and hourly scrutinizing, throughout the world, every variation, even the slightest,"[29] such that if there is an injurious variation, extinction of a species is not an "accident" but a natural and common event.[30] Humans as a species are so pervasive on this planet, and their inclination to interfere with nature is so pronounced, that one may argue that humans have critically impaired the natural selection process.[31]

As humans populated the earth, they used and used up resources to the point that they may have altered natural conditions (i.e., conditions that preceded humans) to the point that life no longer follows the normal rules of evolution. When the natural selection process is disturbed by humans, there is a concomitant disruption of the natural cycle whereby species that can (and should) reproduce themselves then become the species that survive to create future generations. Certain organisms and life systems necessary for species reproduction and survival have been depleted. Natural resources, ecosystems, and various species have been harmed. It may be becoming more difficult for this natural evolutionary progression to take place.[32]

1. NATURAL SELECTION: ADAPTATION TO CHANGE PERMITS SURVIVAL

The theory of natural selection was developed by Charles Darwin in 1859. In its most simple form, it explains both the evolutionary process for all living resources, and the notion that those who reproduce were meant to do so because by their mere existence, they have shown that they are fit enough to perpetuate themselves. Natural selection is considered the mechanism of evolution. It is the process by which organisms that better adapt to an environment survive, reproduce, and create more descendants than other organisms that are not as well-suited to exist and procreate in that environment.[33] Scientists refer to this evolutionary process as follows: "The major tenets of the evolutionary synthesis . . . were that populations contain genetic variation that arises by random mutation and recombination; that populations evolve by changes in gene frequency brought about by random genetic drift, gene flow, and especially natural selection."[34]

---

[29] Charles Darwin, The Origin of Species by Means of Natural Selection 131 (J.W. Burrow ed., Penguin Books 1968) (1859).

[30] *Id.* at 133.

[31] *The Anthropocene: A Man-Made World*, Economist (May 26, 2011) ("scientists warn that if current trends of habitat loss continue, exacerbated by the effects of climate change, there could be an imminent and dramatic number of extinctions before long").

[32] Sustainability or Collapse? An Integrated History and Future of People on Earth (R. Costanza, Lisa Graumlich & Will Steffeneds 2011).

[33] William Gaud, *Natural Selection and Adaptation: Lesson*, Northern Arizona University (2000), *available at* http://www2.nau.edu/~gaud/bio372/class/evolution/lesson3-2-1.htm.

[34] Laurence Moran, *The Modern Synthesis of Genetics and Evolution*, The TalkOrigins Archive (Jan. 22, 1993), *available at* http://www.talkorigins.org/faqs/modern-synthesis.html.

Darwin adopted the idea, originally advanced by Malthus, that there are tremendous external forces that population pressures regularly exert on all organisms all the time.[35] The ability of a population of organisms to expand is infinite, but the resources needed to sustain the different populations of organisms are finite.[36] This dynamic causes a battle for existence between organisms because they must compete for resources. Organisms that survive this competitive setting are those that can command scarce resources better than their competitors; natural selection ensures that only those able to best adapt to the conditions of the natural world are those that should survive to reproduce themselves.[37]

A basic idea of the Darwin theory of natural selection is that variation arises independently of adaptive advantage and selective pressure, which then shapes it and gives it direction.[38] Variation, or influence on organisms, can be helpful to some species who can adapt to the changes, but too much variation can obstruct the natural processes of nature. Darwin hypothesized that variations are caused when environmental stress affects the development of the embryo; he found that variations are triggered when populations of species become out of kilter with their environment.[39]

Darwin saw the world as a machine for producing and then selecting variations; stress on the environment produces flurries of variation, which are then culled by the forces of natural selection. Darwin viewed variation and natural selection, operating over extremely lengthy periods of time, as a unitary process.[40] It is the evolutionary process of natural selection that then occurs and weeds out the weakest species. Variations arise in species by chance, and those variations are not necessarily there to promote survival; instead, the variations occur because of natural laws, such as natural selection. If the natural laws of the environment are abused and interfered with, such that variations either become too abundant or too limited, then natural selection cannot function as intended. If one species (humans) imposes dramatic changes on nature and natural processes, if humans "extend our wills over [natural] things, to objectify them [and] manipulate them,"[41] then this purely anthropocentric effect on nature could distort the normally slow process of natural selection. Natural selection cannot work if there is not sufficient time for variations to develop.[42]

If the pressure cooker created by population pressures, especially human population pressures, eliminates the opportunity for many critical species to naturally "select" a variation that can survive, nature and the natural order of evolution are disrupted, and critical species are adversely affected. Presently, humans have changed

---

[35] DEPEW & WEBER, *supra* note 25, at 122.

[36] *Adaptation by Natural Selection, available at* http://www.wwnorton.com/college/anthro/bioanth/ch1/chap1.htm.

[37] *Id.* DEPEW, *supra* note 25, at 123.

[38] DEPEW, *supra* note 25, at 113.

[39] *Id.* at 128.

[40] DARWIN, *supra* note 29, at 152 (Natural selection "will always act with extreme slowness.")

[41] Christopher Stone, *Should Trees Have Standing?—Toward Legal Rights for Natural Objects*, 45 S. CAL. L. REV. 450, 495 (1972).

[42] DARWIN, *supra* note 29, at 153.

and continue to alter "natural conditions."[43] Humans disturb that which is ordinarily present in the absence of humans by (1) depleting resources, (2) using them in the wrong way, or (3) destroying crucial environmental conditions necessary for the survival and regeneration of resources and organisms. This human-based interference may so alter natural processes to the point where natural selection cannot operate at all, or at least not as it did prior to such human interference.

2. NATURAL SELECTION: THE CONSEQUENCES OF HUMAN INTERFERENCE

For life to evolve, flourish, and become sustainable, it needs to be left alone by and free from externally destructive forces, such as human intervention. When life-forms are not affected by human use demands, another prime directive, natural selection, will determine that only the most robust resources and organisms survive to perpetuate themselves. That process only occurs when there is an environmental context consisting of natural, non-human-altered conditions. It is commonly understood that organisms' overall competitive advantage may be attributed to their heritable traits.[44] This belief is central to the theory of natural selection. Human intervention may have created exogenous dyfunctionality with respect to the natural environment and evolutionary processes. Humans could be short-circuiting the naturally occurring process by which life evolves by destroying those organisms with the strongest genetic traits (e.g., the world has lost an estimated 90 percent of the global shark population due to the shark fin trade). When these living organisms are removed, the natural selection process is unable to function, because of the impact human beings have made on the environment.

The human population has also disrupted variations among species, which is another component of natural selection. Humans have interfered with natural conditions to the point that certain organisms either cannot function while growing to maturity, or cannot survive to reproduce at all. Such organisms would have created variations, an essential component of natural selection. Nature without natural selection is not functional; all life suffers accordingly.

Human activity, such as oil drilling, pollution, and unsustainable extraction of resources, has so abrogated the natural selection process that populations of organisms have died out. The evolution or adaptation of organisms often fails when their environment is dominated by human encroachment. A species may be harmed little by little, or it may be wiped out entirely.[45] An example of such failure is the population of the dark moths that existed in 19th-century England. Their population rose and fell in parallel to the Industrial Revolution. Human interference, in this case because of newly developed industrial processes, had such a great impact on this organism that it could not survive. Similarly, deforestation of the monarch

[43] John Beatty, *Chance and Natural Selection*, 51 PHILOSOPHY SCI. 186 (June 1984); *The Anthropocene, supra* note 31 ("humans are bringing about an age of planetary change").

[44] Mohan Matthen & Andre Ariew, *Two Ways of Thinking about Fitness and Natural Selection*, 99 J. PHILOSOPHY 56 (Feb. 2002).

[45] *Understanding Evolution*, http://evolution.berkeley.edu/evolibrary/article/evo_25.

butterfly's winter base in Mexico makes it difficult for this species to colonize there while awaiting the warmth to return so it can migrate north to reproduce. When forests are lost to humans, other species inevitably become stressed.

For natural resources and organisms to have the opportunity to live and thrive in the face of such a powerful force as the human population, resources need to be left undisturbed (or at least more undisturbed than they are now) so that species may either adapt or die out, according to the evolutionary standards of natural selection. Prior to human interference, evolution and species creation functioned pursuant to predictable rules; some organisms adapted to variations in their environment and were thus able to continue as part of the natural world. Only the best suited could perpetuate themselves, ensuring that the world would be inhabited by the preeminent and strongest species. In order to promote this elemental natural process, human intrusion should be moderated, lessened, or made more accountable. Humans in some ways have become a disruption in the natural order. Although humans are a part of the natural world, they are so dominant a species that they have become an impediment to the environmental processes traditionally relied on by natural resources and organisms. The evolutionary processes that customarily guide nature should be reestablished.

A vestigial structure is a feature that was an adaptation for an organism's ancestor, but which has become nonfunctional because the organism's environment changed, which makes the feature no longer useful. Sadly, humans are changing organisms' environments so much that the adaptations that previously benefited organisms and helped them remain capable for survival are eventually becoming vestigial structures. Shockingly, often there are no adaptations that can protect an organism against the powerful force of human tampering and interference. Human resource use, contamination, and exhaustion occur at such a startlingly fast pace that organisms cannot keep up by simply adapting.

Take the case of the Maldives, a series of coral island atolls in the Indian Ocean. Originally the Maldive islands were completely founded on the remains of living coral reefs, one of the most complex ecosystems on the planet, with the highest biodiversity of all marine habitats. Historically, low human population densities resulted in large areas of coral reefs where the influences of humans were low and barely perceptible. But as humans increased in numbers, and tourism dominated resource use decisions, human impacts on the reefs became more pronounced. Previously healthy and sustainable coral have been damaged and killed by eutrophication (caused by sewage outlets), sedimentation (caused by dredging), oil pollution (caused by boat engines and sun oils), garbage (caused by resort operations), and destructive fishing (caused by night fishing boats whose anchors and fishing lines break coral).

The human population has adapted to numerous variations over the centuries and continues to reproduce and survive. However, because of severe interference in natural environmental processes inflicted by humans, it can be hypothesized that if something is not done to stop this abuse, humans may ultimately be the cause of their own destruction. Humans have consistently shown, and continue to demonstrate, that they are the most adaptable species and the species that is the best suited for survival. But as resources are so removed, contaminated, or environmentally challenged that they are unable to cope with growing human interference, humans may soon find themselves altering the elemental substances required for their survival. If this inclination to use and abuse the natural environment is not limited or checked, there may be such a deficiency in or corruption of resources that the human population may not be able to adapt. Homo sapiens as a species then will be destroyed little by little, or wiped out completely.

When nature is permitted to function with less disturbances or interference from humans, Darwin established that the strongest species and organisms will then survive and perpetuate themselves. With humans so dominate, this essential evolutionary order is now threatened. To reestablish and re-create the natural way of things, humans should assist resources so that natural selection of species can thrive again. Natural selection is, after all, the process that created humans and their world. All natural resources subject to natural selection should be provided some way to resist the seemingly insatiable use demands of this most dominant species—homo sapiens. These natural resources should be respected and heard when they call out to humans bent on overusing them: *leave me alone.*

C. The Right to Privacy

To return to more natural conditions, resources should be unhindered so that they can do what they did before humans—rely on natural selection, the competition for food and reproductive success, and evolution, which helps to determine survival and the ability to perpetuate a species. If the human population refrains from interfering with natural resources, and if resources have autonomy relatively free from human use desires, then variation may return to ensure that species evolve consistent with natural selection, not human selection. For species to regain this necessary independence, one should contemplate a way to encourage humans to refrain from intervening with natural processes. One human-developed method for furthering natural autonomy revolves around the concept of privacy. Similarly, natural resources might be provided a protective right similar to the legal concept of privacy. Just as humans are thought to be in a better condition when they are "left alone" consistent with a "right" of privacy, perhaps so too may natural resources be able to return to a more natural condition if they have a right to ask, or perhaps even demand that, humans recognize their privacy interests—interests that require humans to leave them alone.

1. THE RIGHT OF PRIVACY FOR HUMANS

The human population may have the ability to articulate the nature of privacy, because there is an intuitive understanding of why individual autonomy is important.[46] The concept of privacy began in the 19th century, when wealth abounded in an age of industrial growth. As a result of the economic gains enjoyed by so many,

---

[46] *See* STANFORD ENCYCLOPEDIA OF PHILOSOPHY (Sept. 2006), *available at* http://plato.standford.edu/entries/parivacy/.

private living arrangements started to become the norm, as more and more people moved to urban areas. Organized living in urban areas meant that people began to notice that they had lost some of the aloneness they previously enjoyed in more rural areas. Urbanized dwellers needed explicit protections in order to preserve their privacy. Due to the developing closeness of human beings to one another, it became necessary to define a boundary between the community and the self so as to protect the privacy expectations intuitively valued by individuals in an organized society.

Although there is no one accepted definition of privacy, the general concept is often articulated as a means of individual autonomy and freedom from societal interference.[47] It is, in short, a value associated with a need for individuals and entities *to be left alone*. Governmental protection of privacy rights is a measure of a commitment to personal liberty, and most importantly, to individual autonomy.[48] Privacy advances the liberty a society bestows on its members to make decisions and choices free from the will of others.[49] Privacy represents a variety of values and concerns[50] such that when a right to privacy is bestowed by positive law, it should continue to evolve. At first it may be defined by courts through the common law, and later through lawmaking institutions such as legislatures and constitutional conventions.[51]

In 1890, Louis Brandeis and Samuel Warren published one of the most influential articles on privacy.[52] The article argued that common law states should recognize a "right of privacy" or a "right to be left alone." Brandeis and Warren contended that the common law could initially provide a means for creating and recognizing privacy rights. Even though the article was chiefly concerned with protecting intellectual privacy rights, it advocated the idea that humans needed to be able to be free from the activities and pressures of others. A legally recognized right to privacy has continued to develop through the U.S. common law and state constitutional law. In America it has been recognized as a constitutional right by the U.S. Supreme Court.[53] The legal right to privacy is also primarily acknowledged by the American federal judiciary rather than through Congressional acts.[54] Congress has enacted laws that create rights and duties concerning the gathering, maintenance, and dissemination of

---

[47] Ronald J. Krotoszynski, *Autonomy, Community, and Traditions of Liberty: The Contrast of British and American Privacy Law*, 1990 DUKE L.J. 1401–02 (Dec. 1990).

[48] *Id.* at 1398.

[49] *Id.*

[50] *Id.* at 1401.

[51] *See id.* at 1402.

[52] Louis Brandeis and Samuel Warren, *The Right of Privacy*, 4 Harvard L. Rev. 193 (1890); Nicholas D. Bieter, *Minnesota's Right of Privacy Torts: Expanding Common Law beyond Its Reasonable, Constitutional Bounds in* Lake v. Wal-Mart Stores, *Inc.*, 20 HAMLINE J. PUB. L. & POL'Y 177, 181 (1998).

[53] Krotoszynski, *supra* note 47, at 1400.

[54] *Id.* at 1433.

information regarding individuals, but these laws typically do not concern individual autonomy.[55] It is the federal judiciary that traditionally vindicates privacy rights.[56]

Beginning in the 1920s, the Supreme Court used the Liberty Clause of the Fourteenth Amendment in the U.S. Constitution to assert privacy rights as a legitimate expectation.[57] Using long-standing traditions of liberty enshrined in American society through the U.S. Constitution, the Supreme Court found that an individual family's right to be left alone with its decisions trumped a state legislature's determination that certain languages should not be taught in public schools, or that parents were raising their children improperly.[58]

The Supreme Court next recognized the creation of a constitutional right to privacy in a 1965 case named *Griswold v. Connecticut*.[59] Some justices on the Court characterized privacy as "a penumbra created by express textual provisions of the Bill of Rights and the fourteenth amendment."[60] Other justices labeled privacy as a kind of liberty interest, implicitly, if not explicitly, protected by the Ninth or Fourteenth Amendments.[61] *Griswold* established the Court's authority to look beyond the literal language of the Constitution to guarantee that states did not arbitrarily contravene an individual's basic autonomy interests.[62] The constitutional right to privacy may not always override state interests or regulations, but *Griswold* required courts to weigh societal demands against claims of individual choice and autonomy.[63] The common law development of the right to privacy and then the constitutional acknowledgment of privacy meant that in America, individuals were entitled to protection from unwarranted governmental regulation of certain uniquely personal decisions in private life.[64]

Subsequently, the Supreme Court, in such decisions as *Roe v. Wade*,[65] reaffirmed that there is a constitutional right to privacy, protecting individuals who wish to have the liberty to make certain choices free from legislative interference. Although the word *privacy* is not found in the Fifth or Fourteenth Amendment's right to not be deprived of "liberty," the Supreme Court has consistently determined that the

---

[55] *Id.* at 1433–34.

[56] Eisenstadt v. Baird, 405 U.S. 438, 454, n.10 (1972) ("The makers of our Constitution...conferred...the right to be let alone...").

[57] *Id.* at 1435.

[58] Krotoszynski at 1436; Meyer v. Nebraska, 262 U.S. 390, 399–400 (1923); Pierce v. Soc'y of Sisters, 268 U.S. 510, 534–35 (1925).

[59] Griswold v. Connecticut, 381 U.S. 479 (1965) (describing the penumbral zones of privacy implied by the rights guaranteed by the Bill of Rights, as well as Justice Harlan's belief that a right of privacy can be found within the term "liberty" of the Due Process Clause of the 5th and 14th Amendments).

[60] Krotoszynski, *supra* note 47, at 1436.

[61] *Id.*

[62] *Id.* at 1436–37.

[63] *Id.* at 1437.

[64] *Id.* at 1438. Gonzales v. Carhart, 550 U.S. 124, 146 (2007).

[65] 410 U.S. 113 (1973) (the right of privacy is "founded in the 14th Amendment's concept of personal liberty"); Alexander Rosenberg, *Privacy as a Matter of Taste and Right, in* THE RIGHT TO PRIVACY 68, 74 (Ellen Frankel Paul ed., 2000).

Constitution includes an implicit constitutional right to privacy.[66] The notion of "Liberty" in the Due Process Clause of the Fifth and Fourteenth Amendments[67] guides courts in making decisions that recognize an individual's right of autonomy, and society's willingness to permit individuals to make their own moral decisions, even when others in decision-making positions wish to intrude on a person's freedom to be left alone.[68]

The right to privacy has been recognized, accepted, and legitimated within the United States. A precedent has been set that individuals can expect privacy interests to be honored and legally legitimated.[69] This legal acknowledgement of a "right of privacy" granted to humans was built upon a philosophical concept of privacy that laid the foundation for a later common law and constitutional law acceptance of privacy. As a matter of conceptual belief, privacy derives from the advantages of autonomy—the benefits that flow when external forces do not interfere with one's decisions, choices, and exercise of liberty as one proceeds through life.

2. PHILOSOPHICAL BASIS FOR THE RIGHT TO PRIVACY

The human-developed right to privacy stems from several factors, the most important of which is the notion that humans develop, evolve, and exist best when they are not unduly influenced by outside pressures that seek to affect or change them.[70] All individuals have a desire to have some "space" where they are autonomous within the community in which they live.[71] Like the related concept of private property, privacy defines a sphere of individual dominion into which others cannot intrude without an individual's consent or some other sufficient justification.[72] Dominion and autonomy over oneself includes a locus of self-control, a sphere of decision-making authority about oneself, and the ability to exclude others from participating in one's life's choices.[73] An individual's autonomous rights are negative rights, imposed on other individuals so that they may not interfere with those rights.[74]

---

[66] *See id.*

[67] Krotoszynski, *supra* note 47, at 1439.

[68] Rowan v. U.S. Post Office, Dep't, 397 U.S. 728 (1970) (acknowledging the "right of every person to be let alone").

[69] *See* Michael H. v. Gerald D., 491 U.S. 110 (1989) (stating that "in an attempt to limit and guide interpretation of the due process Clause, we have insisted not merely that the interest denominated as a 'liberty' be 'fundamental'. . . but also that it be an interest traditionally protected by our society").

[70] Lloyd L. Weinreb, *The Right to Privacy*, *in* THE RIGHT TO PRIVACY 25, 31 (Ellen Frankel Paul ed., 2000); *See also* Daniel R. Ortiz, *Privacy, Autonomy, and Consent*, 12 HARV. J.L. & POL'Y 91 (1988); STANFORD ENCYCLOPEDIA OF PHILOSOPHY (Sept. 2006), *available at* http://plato.standford.edu/entries/parivacy/

[71] Weinreb, *supra* note 70, at 31.

[72] Ortiz, *supra* note 70, at 92.

[73] *Id.*

[74] R.G. Frey, *Privacy, Control, and Talk of Rights*, *in* THE RIGHT TO PRIVACY 45, 49 (Ellen Frankel Paul ed., 2000).

Negative rights, or rights of noninterference, are thought to be natural rights.[75] Additionally, privacy is a conventional social right; it is a product of human agreement to aid desirable consequences.[76] Privacy provides individuals with the choice of engaging, or not engaging in, mutual participation. This choice helps define the boundary between the community and the self.[77] Individuals will only respect others' autonomy if theirs is respected in return. This mutuality condition provides each of us with grounds for acknowledging certain boundaries of noninterference in our respective lives.[78]

Because privacy is an ambiguous concept, and because there are many ways individuals seek to be left alone, and many reasons that individuals may want to be left alone, legal institutions in the United States determined that privacy needed relatively broad protection.[79] Privacy allows individuals to preserve authority over themselves regarding certain aspects of self-awareness and identity. It permits individuals to grow and reach their potential without outside pressures. This sense of privacy includes more than just an individual interest in secluding oneself from observation, or in restricting access to personal data; instead, it limits public power to invade one's fundamental decisions about one's self, and prevents governmental entities wishing to interfere in private, consensual choices and associations. It permits individuals to do as they wish, and interrelate to others they choose, without fearing consequences from intrusive third parties.

The restrictions on external forces imposed by the right to privacy permit individuals to function and live their lives according to their individual context-based choices, and to thrive knowing that they are entitled to a certain amount of noninterference by others. A right has thereby been acknowledged that shields them from interference by the government, others in society, and invasions deemed to impede their personal growth and autonomy. As a result of this protection, humans can carry on as individuals infused with inherent liberty to make decisions and choices that can improve their lives and permit them to evolve more naturally.

D. A Right of Privacy Held by Natural Resources?

The right for humans to left alone has been legally recognized for over a century in the United States. If natural resources were similarly allowed to flourish without extensive human intervention, it may be possible to preserve the autonomy of natural resources and organisms. Such a return-to-natural-conditions status might allow natural resources to thrive again consistent with the laws of natural selection.

---

[75] *Id.*

[76] *Id.* at 60.

[77] Ortiz, *supra* note 70, at 97.

[78] Frey, *supra* note 74, at 58.

[79] H. Tristram Engelhardt, Jr., *Privacy and Limited Democracy: The Moral Centrality of Persons, in* THE RIGHT TO PRIVACY 120 (Ellen Frankel Paul ed., 2000).

Nature can adapt to certain levels of ecological invasions.[80] But when living organisms find that fundamental processes of evolution are impeded by human interference, they may no longer be able to change to meet these new conditions. There is then less chance for the operation of normal forces of evolution; instead, resources and organisms may become overpowered by human-caused variations. Humans become an obstruction to evolution and an impediment to the natural selection process. Because resources and organisms cannot designate their own spheres of privacy in the face of overwhelming human dominance, some intervention is necessary in order to create privacy and space-to-evolve.

In order to repair the harm to multiple forms of life engendered by humans' obsession with resource use, the autonomy of natural resources should be recognized. We can begin by acknowledging the legitimacy of natural resources to have some right of independent existence apart from humans. For natural resources to continue to survive and evolve as nature intended, we could then legitimate the notion that true nature can only survive on this planet if it has the ability sometimes to resist extreme human use demands. If human resource use needs can be tempered with a countervailing right, asserted by resources, to *not* be used by humans, ecological survival and natural selection become possible again.

Such mandated noninterference has moral credibility because it is intended to bring about a natural condition—it is the way living things were before humans became obsessed with their use function. Essentially, a right to nonuse, or in effect a right of privacy - the right for natural resources to be left alone, would help to rein in and temper human desires to exploit and affirmatively and recklessly, use natural resources. A return to normal rules of evolution and natural selection might permit the earth to reacquire the conditions that permitted humans to evolve and to get to where we are today as a species.

The environment became available to humans because of the natural progression of evolution that governed survival and species continuation/extinction for billions of years. If the human population is aggressively harming the natural selection process by its fervor to use resources, a right of nonuse held by natural resources and organisms may prevent further harm and allow for the rejuvenation of what was once a veritable Garden of Eden for humans to enjoy. Natural selection might then take place the way it did before humans interfered.

---

[80] Alexander Rosenberg, *Privacy as a Matter of Taste and Right*, *in* THE RIGHT TO PRIVACY 68, 74 (Ellen Frankel Paul ed., 2000); EDWARD O. WILSON, SOCIOBIOLOGY: THE NEW SYNTHESIS 25–78 (1975).

14 The Science of Resource Nonuse

A. Introduction—The Three Physical Characteristics of Natural Resources in the Absence of Humans—Symmetry, Equivalence, and Conservation

Symmetry, equivalence, and conservation are qualities inherent in the physical laws of our natural universe, qualities which have enabled us to understand and predict how our universe operates.[1] Ascribing use and nonuse components to natural resources imparts the fundamental physical qualities of symmetry, equivalence, and conservation to them. These three simple rules describe how the known universe operates, and permit us to anticipate how nature works.

Resource use and nonuse can be conceived as symmetrical mirror reflections, with one component balancing the other, imparting strength. Use and nonuse are not merely separate, but also equal halves. In nature, the presence of symmetry alerts us to another singular underlying property—an equivalence—where the symmetrical halves cannot exist alone, but are instead created by the presence of, and the tension with, the other half.[2] Mathematicians have also proven that symmetry demands a corresponding conservation law, one requiring that the symmetrical property exhibits an

[1] Symmetries in Physics: Philosophical Reflections 23 (Katherine Brading & Elena Castellani eds., 2003); Richard Phillips Feynman, Six Not-So-Easy Pieces: Einstein's Relativity, Symmetry, and Space-Time 23 (1997); Mario Livio, The Equation that Couldn't Be Solved: How Mathematical Genius Discovered the Language of Symmetry 43 (2005).

[2] Livio, *supra* note 1, at 217.

unchanging quality.[3] Understanding natural resource use and nonuse as manifestations of a singular essence also alerts us to nature's conservation demand; the demand for conservation ensures that the essential quality or quantity of the physical entity must remain unchanged.[4] If the essential symmetry and equivalence of nature are lost, so too is nature's need for conservation, and then the resource itself is lost.

B. Three Fundamental Laws of Nature

1. SYMMETRY

Symmetry is a fundamental property in nature, giving nature's physical beings strength derived from balance.[5] Symmetry is not only a property of the organic plant and animal world, it is also fundamental in the nonliving world of distant space and within subatomic particles. In mathematics and physics, finding symmetries has similarly increased our understanding of how the physical world works.[6] Symmetrical forces should likewise be present in the laws governing natural resources and their use by humans. A consideration of these symmetrical forces will afford a more accurate understanding of how best to maintain the strength and resilience of the natural resource system, where all resources have symmetrical use and nonuse functions.

Symmetry can also identify an equivalence in natural phenomena, that is, symmetry reveals where two seemingly disparate or even opposing qualities may instead be manifestations of a single essence. Symmetry can tell us how certain fundamental essences are conserved, so long as these opposite-but-equal forces are kept in balance. Symmetry provides strength; symmetry unifies disparate forces into a single system; symmetry helps bring about conservation of the fundamental components of the observable universe, of which this planet is a part.

Symmetry in organic life—strength from evolutionary adaptation

The symmetry in living organisms is everywhere, from the bilateral symmetry of most animals, to the symmetry of life's smallest building block, the DNA strand. The prevalence of symmetry in nature illustrates its importance as an evolutional adaption.[7] Small floating organisms, those that live suspended in water or some other media, are little affected by gravity because of their size and suspension. Symmetry in three dimensions—up-down, left-right, and front-back—is typical for

---

[3] Steve Adams, Frontiers: Twentieth Century Physics 235, 443 (2000); Peter Atkins, Four Laws That Drive the Universe 45 (2007); Feynman, *supra* note 1, at 29.

[4] Adams, *supra* note 3, at 235, 443.

[5] Brian R. Green, The Fabric of the Cosmos: Space, Time, and the Texture of Reality 219–20 (2004).

[6] Symmetries in Physics, *supra* note 1, at 29; Feynman, *supra* note 1, at 77; Etienne Klein & Marc Lachieze-Rey, The Quest for Unity: The Adventure of Physics 88, 91 (1999).

[7] Timothy H. Goldsmith & William F. Zimmerman, Biology, Evolution, and Human Nature 119 (2001); Livio, *supra* note 2, at 6–7.

these organisms.[8] Add the force of gravity and larger terrestrial life adapt to symmetry also. Trees are symmetrical all around a vertical axis—all left-right, front-back reflections, but they are not up-down symmetrical. A tree's symmetry is that which provides the greatest strength, given its life in a gravitational field.[9] If a tree had all its branches and all its roots on one side, gravity would easily pull it over.[10] But add another outside force, wind, for example, and now the strongest symmetrical adaptation may be bilateral symmetry, with all branches oriented downwind. The wind for the tree is a force in the horizontal plane, equivalent to movement for animals. Like our windswept trees, large terrestrial animals employ bilateral symmetry, best adapted for locomotion and for an existence adapted to both the vertical force of gravity and the horizontal force of movement.[11]

Strength imparted by symmetry provides an obvious evolutionary advantage in nature's engineered structures. Resilience to natural forces requires that organic life take its strongest and most efficient form, and this form universally employs symmetry. Test the strength that symmetry imparts in a thin eggshell. Place an egg on your fingers, wrap it in your hand, and squeeze it uniformly.[12] The thin eggshell achieves its strength through its symmetry, spreading the pressure into equally opposing forces.[13] The hexagonal honeycombs of beehives or the six-sided symmetry of snowflakes are other well-known examples.[14]

Symmetric forms occur for organic life because nature demands the most economical, most efficient structure able to withstand outside forces.[15] DNA strands evolved their symmetrical double helix form as the result of a wide range of forces acting upon that molecule.[16] Chemical molecules and crystals have symmetry as a result of nature's demand for a stable, strong, efficient form.

The bilateral symmetry found in animals is not mere redundancy; rather, the symmetry is part of, and essential to, a single working system. Our eyes and ears illustrate this property. The slightly different angles at which our eyes perceive an object allow our brains to gauge the distance to that object—depth perception. Similarly, the slightly different times for a noise to reach our separate ears allows our brain to

---

[8] LIVIO, *supra* note 2, at 6–7. STEVEN VOGEL, LIFE'S DEVICES: THE PHYSICAL WORLD OF ANIMALS AND PLANTS 281–82 (1988).

[9] LIVIO, *supra* note 2, at 6–7

[10] VOGEL, *supra* note 8, at 58, 277–80.

[11] Magnus Enquist & Rufus A. Johnstone, *Generalization and the Evolution of Symmetry Preferences*, 264 PROCEEDING OF THE ROYAL SOCIETY LONDON 1345 (1997), *available at* http://www.ncbi.nlm.nih.gov/pmc/articles/ PMC1688578/pdf/6N2VRTWKHMQ43B5F_264_1345.pdf; JULIAN HUXLEY, EVOLUTION IN ACTION 132–33 (1953); VOGEL, *supra* note 8, at 145.

[12] VOGEL, *supra* note 8, at 252–53; *How to Squeeze an Egg without Breaking It,* Wikihow http://www.wikihow.com/Squeeze-an-Egg-Without-Breaking-It (last visited Apr. 25, 2011).

[13] VOGEL, *supra* note 8, at 252–53.

[14] LIVIO, *supra* note 2, at 10.

[15] *Id.* at 205.

[16] P.F. Baisnée et. al., *Why Are Complementary DNA Strands Symmetric?* 8 BIOINFORMATICS 1021–33 (Aug. 2002), *available at* http://www.ncbi.nlm.nih.gov/pubmed/12176825.

determine the location of the sound's source. The symmetry of our senses is not only an adaptation that provides the strength and resilience necessary for survival, but also indicates the presence of an underlying single system where the two parts are interwoven. Each is equally essential to the full functioning of the whole. A similar symmetry exists in natural resources. A natural resource has the potential to be used by humans, but it has an equally valuable nonuse component—this component is valuable to ecosystems and planetary processes when humans do *not* use the resource.

Symmetry in structural engineering—balancing the load

What works for nature similarly works for humans and their buildings. Like nature's engineered forms, human engineers give structures stability and resilience through symmetry. An arch is a ubiquitous example, where the stacked stones join together to perfectly offset the force of gravity pulling the stones toward earth.[17] With the opposing stone blocks perfectly balanced and the keystone set, not only can the arch stand, it can support its own weight. Without symmetry distributing and directing the weight atop the arch, the structure topples.[18]

Symmetry in mathematics—group theory

Great breakthroughs in mathematics occurred through the employment of symmetry. Group theory is used to describe and understand geometric shapes, chemical molecules, and crystal structures.[19] By recognizing the symmetry contained in a set, or group, of geometric or chemical changes, mathematicians are able to understand the functioning of an entire system and can calculate the physical properties of natural materials and predict how they will function. By using properties inherent in symmetry, group theory can identify the building blocks of mathematics and unify previously unrelated mathematical fields, such as geometry and algebra.[20] By identifying the amount of symmetry in a number system, group theory can determine whether an equation can or cannot be solved.[21]

Group theory works by identifying symmetries, that is, transformations or manipulations of an object or system that result in an identical object.[22] For example, the geometry of an equilateral triangle can be described in group theory as a set of rotations of the triangle around its central axis that result in an indistinguishable triangle.[23] Highly complex chemical molecules, algebraic equations, and even rules

---

[17] Colin O'Connor, *Roman Bridges* 129, 187 (1993).

[18] *Id.*

[19] Livio, *supra* note 2, at 246; Roger G. Newton, What Makes Nature Tick? 216–17 (1994).

[20] Livio, *supra* note 2, at 193.

[21] *Id.* at 171.

[22] Newton, *supra* note 19, at 206, 215–16.

[23] Livio, *supra* note 2, at 47; *See generally* R. McWeeny, Symmetry: An Introduction to Group Theory and Its Applications (2002).

of social behavior can be fully described through the symmetries those systems contain.[24] Distilling an object's complex geometry into a finite symmetrical set has been a powerful tool in our understanding the universe and was an essential component to Einstein's General Theory of Relativity.[25]

Symmetry in astrophysics

Einstein famously advocated deductive, rather than inductive, reasoning.[26] Rather than sorting through mountains of observational data hoping to shake out a working theory, he would first seek out nature's inherent qualities, chiefly symmetry, and then ask how nature *should* function in light of these qualities.[27] Einstein deductively believed that nature required time and space translational symmetry. That is, nature's laws must be the same everywhere in the universe, and they must be verifiable by all observers.[28] From the demands of nature's symmetry he developed both the Special and General Theories of Relativity.

Einstein's Special Theory of Relativity rebuilt the symmetry initially shattered by the discovery of light's constant speed.[29] In 1887, the Michelson-Morley experiments measured light speed and found that it did not change even if the light source was speeding closer or the light receiver was speeding away.[30] These measurements conflicted with classical physics, where speeds are additive.[31] When we throw a beer can from the window of a moving car, the can travels with both the speed of our throw plus the speed of the car—creating a dangerous projectile and wasting beer. That light does not obey this same rule created absurd results in classical physics, where Newtonian laws would break down based on the speed and motion of the observer.[32] The pursuit of symmetry in physical laws—that is, the insistence that the same laws apply for all observers in all states of motion—led to the recognition that distance, space, and time were interdependent concepts.

A similar quest to remove an asymmetry resulted in Einstein's formulation of general relativity. In classical physics, the force of gravity operates instantaneously, requiring no time to traverse space, as if the sun holds Earth by a rope.[33] In contrast,

---

[24] Adams, *supra* note 3, at 233–24; Livio, *supra* note 2, at 47.

[25] Livio, *supra* note 2, at 197.

[26] Alan Lightman, Great Ideas in Physics: The Conservation of Energy, The Second Law of Thermodynamics, The Theory of Relativity, Quantum Mechanics 171 (2000).

[27] Livio, *supra* note 2, at 205, 231.

[28] Jean Eisenstaedt, The Curious History of Relativity: How Einstein's Theory of Gravity Was Lost and Found Again 24–25 (Arturo Sangalli trans., 2006); Green, *supra* note 5, at 9, 221–22; Livio, *supra* note 2, at 207.

[29] Eisenstaedt, *supra* note 28, at 4; Lightman, *supra* note 26, at 136–42.

[30] Adams, *supra* note 3, at 249, 255; Green, *supra* note 5, at 43–44; Werner Heisenberg, Physics and Philosophy 110–12 (1999); Newton, *supra* note 19, at 89, 127–29.

[31] Lightman, *supra* note 26, at 136–42; Newton, *supra* note 19, at 128.

[32] Adams, *supra* note 3, at 263, 265.

[33] Braine Green, The Elegant Universe, Superstrings, Hidden Dimensions, and the Quest for the Ultimate Theory 67 (2000).

light speed is limited and not instantaneous. Einstein realized this was an asymmetry.[34] If the sun was suddenly plucked from the sky, gravity would cease and Earth would fly off course the instant this rope was cut, but for several minutes the sun's light would still be traversing our sky, and would be observed on Earth as if all were well. Building on special relativity's space-time relationship, Einstein's General Theory of Relativity describes the universe's warped topography, where gravity bends space-time like a bowling ball bends a trampoline.[35] Einstein calculated that, unlike cutting a rope, the space-time trampoline was limited in how fast it could bend and warp—limited to exactly the speed of light.[36] This new, more accurate understanding of the universe was the result of Einstein's recognition that physical laws tend to require symmetry, and are incomplete when the physical or mathematical models predict anomalous or asymmetrical results.[37]

Einstein's recognition that nature demands certain symmetries, reflecting our humanity's dissatisfaction with chaos and imbalance, enabled a vastly more complete understanding of universal forces. A symmetry between ecocentric resource *nonuse*, and human-centric natural resource *use*, might similarly permit us to understand the complex natural system by a more accurate model that reflects nature's fundamental structure. Our natural resource model achieves greater predictive strength by realizing that use-nonuse symmetry must be a driving force underlying all natural resources.

Symmetry in quantum mechanics and subatomic particles

Special relativity produced new laws of motion with universally applicable mathematical equations. Just as special relativity reconfigured the equations governing the mass and speed of Newton's apple, physicists sought to apply special relativity to the mass and energy of subatomic particles described by quantum mechanics.[38] When the equations of quantum mechanics and special relativity were successfully unified by physicist Paul Dirac, an unexpected symmetry was revealed—one that predicted the existence of antimatter. Like the square root of four, which can be both positive and negative two, Dirac's equations gave symmetrical solutions.[39] One solution described the known positive energy, and negatively charged electrons; the other predicted a mirror image, negative energy, and a positively charged electron. Rather than ignoring or throwing out a seemingly absurd result, Dirac believed that

---

[34] EISENSTAEDT, *supra* note 28, at 24–25; GREEN, *supra* note 33, at 84.

[35] GREEN, *supra* note 33, at 69–70.

[36] *Id.* at 73–74.

[37] Giora Hon & Bernard R. Goldstein, *How Einstein Made Asymmetry Disappear: Symmetry and Relativity in 1905*, 59 ARCHIVE FOR HISTORY OF EXACT SCIENCES 437, 475–76 (2005); EISENSTAEDT, *supra* note 28, at 24–25.

[38] ROBERT L. FORWARD & JOEL DAVIS, MIRROR MATTER: PIONEERING ANTIMATTER PHYSICS 22 (1988); GORDON FRASER, ANTIMATTER: THE ULTIMATE MIRROR 55 (2000).

[39] *The History of Antimatter*, European Center for Nuclear Research (CERN) http://press.web.cern.ch/livefromcern/antimatter/history/a.m-history01.html (last visited May 24, 2011).

this symmetry must have a real, physical meaning.[40] In 1936, several years after Dirac published his equations, the antielectron, or positron, was detected in the laboratory.[41]

Antimatter is created by the conversion of energy into mass. Einstein's equation, $E = mc^2$, relates mass and energy, telling us that mass is fundamentally a form of energy, like heat, light, or motion. When energy is converted to mass, it forms matter and antimatter in exactly equal quantities.[42] Though antimatter was unknown when Dirac proposed its existence, the symmetry of his result fit the expectations of physicists, who held that symmetry is a fundamental property of the universe.[43] So scientists accepted Dirac's equations and set to the task of proving antimatter's existence, not only as a mathematical result, but also as a physical entity. Today, positrons, antiprotons, antineutrons, and many other antiparticles have been detected in space and have been created in particle accelerators. Physics predicts that every subatomic particle has its mirror-symmetrical, oppositely charged antiparticle, and most have been detected. Antiparticles are identical, mirror images of our more familiar particles in all their properties. Indeed, scientists have predicted the feasibility of, and have later created, mirror chemical elements, for example antihydrogen.[44]

Antimatter owes its discovery to symmetry. Although its existence is only fleeting, as antimatter and matter instantly annihilate each other, and although the concept initially strikes us as remote from everyday existence—limited to cosmic rays and particle accelerators—antimatter is both real and essential to understanding our world. Antimatter is the key element in the PET scan, a medical imaging technique.[45] Antimatter is also known to be created in earth's thunderstorms.[46] Accepting symmetry as a fundamental property of the universe was a key part of the scientific revolution of quantum mechanics. Although at the time of Dirac, antimatter had never been observed or seriously postulated, his equation's symmetrical result was reason enough for scientists to seek to detect antimatter's concrete existence. Resource nonuse would be a symmetrical, mirror-image twin of resource use, with which humans are most familiar. If nonuse is similarly acknowledged, it is apt to reveal previously undetected realities of natural resources systems, and the effect that human over use has on them.

2. EQUIVALENCE

The observable laws of physics illustrate that materials and forces in the natural universe contain, within a single entity, properties that are seemingly in tension or in

---

[40] FRASER, *supra* note 38, at 55.

[41] FORWARD & DAVIS, *supra* note 38, at 30

[42] *Id.* at 64.

[43] *Id.*

[44] FRASER, *supra* note 38, at 169, 178–80.

[45] *Antimatter Everyday,* European Center for Nuclear Research (CERN), http://press.web.cern.ch/livefromcern/antimatter/everyday/a.m-everyday01.html (last visited May 24, 2011).

[46] *NASA's Fermi Catches Thunderstorms Hurling Antimatter into Space,* NASA (Jan. 10, 2011), *available at* http://www.nasa.gov/mission_pages/GLAST/news/fermi-thunderstorms.html.

opposition with each other, but which are necessary to make that entity whole. That physical materials and natural systems do contain seemingly opposing but equivalent forces (referred to here as their "dual essence") is consistent with the physical laws of nature. A natural system is always directed toward equilibrium. If a natural resource is made up of both a use and nonuse component, symmetrically equivalent, then it would follow that there would be an imbalance, and a lack of equilibrium, when a resource's human-use component is so dominant that it overwhelms its eco-centric nonuse component.

The term *equivalence*, or the "equivalence principle," is borrowed from Einstein's General Theory of Relativity.[47] In general relativity, Einstein's equivalence principle was the recognition that gravity and acceleration were indistinguishable forces. With this realization, Einstein could discern that gravity exerts its force by warping and curving the space-time topography.[48] This is the concept of equivalence and unification. In identification of symmetries—such as the equivalent feel of gravity and acceleration, or the space-time topography—an underlying, single, physical essence is revealed. Equivalence suggests that natural resources are comprised of both a use and nonuse quality, not just the use component that humans are eager to exploit.

Unification in special relativity

Einstein's search to establish symmetry in the equations describing light and electromagnetism in the face of constant light speed led to his discovery of the equivalence relationship of space and time.[49] This discovery of special relativity revealed that space and time cannot be decoupled; rather they are part of a single entity, poetically summed up by Einstein colleague and physicist Herman Minkowski: "Henceforward space on its own and time on its own will decline into mere shadows, and only a kind of union between the two will preserve its independence."[50]

After special relativity, one must also add the dimension of time to our Cartesian world of length, width, and depth. For example, if I describe my location as the intersection of 34th Street and Vine on the fourth floor, I must also specify what time I am there—two o'clock on Tuesday, for example. But in special relativity time and space are not merely independent coordinates, they are connected in a manner such that to change one is to change the other.[51] They are unified such that space and time become space-time. Similarly with natural resources, if one changes, or overuses, the use component, one simultaneously also changes, and possibly overwhelms, the nonuse dimension of a resource.

---

[47] Green, *supra* note 5, at 67.

[48] Eisenstaedt, *supra* note 28, at 77–78; Green, *supra* note 5, at 69.

[49] Adams, *supra* note 3, at 296 (quoting Albert Einstein in "On the Electrodynamics of Moving Bodies," Annalen der Physik 17 (1905): "light is always propagated in empty space with a definite velocity *c* which is independent of the motion of the emitting body.")

[50] Green, *supra* note 33, at 66.

[51] Adams, *supra* note 3, at 295, 299, 303; Symmetries in Physics, *supra* note 1, at 396; Heisenberg, *supra* note 30, at 114–15.

Time and space do not have independent meaning; one must always be interpreted in relationship to the other. The constancy of light speed has two significant side effects—increasing speeds slow time and contracts distance. Moreover, the unity of space-time is not merely a mathematical construct to balance an equation or an idiosyncrasy of light speed in distant space. Space-time has been experimentally verified.[52] Physicists have measured the decay of subatomic particles as they zip around particle accelerators and have confirmed that their decay, akin to human biological aging, slows down as speed increases.[53] Special relativity's unification of space-time not only repaired the symmetry of the physical laws of motion, it enabled a more complete depiction of the universe's topography as set out in general relativity.

Equivalence in general relativity

The term *equivalence principle* describes a specific concept within Einstein's General Theory of Relativity. The world in a gravitational field is equivalent to a world under matching acceleration.[54] Einstein's well-known thought experiment identifies this equivalence by describing familiar sensations. When an elevator accelerates at the start of its descent, we feel this force. The elevator is closed, so we do not see the motion. Einstein realized that the sensation we feel could be caused either by our accelerating decent or by a reduction in gravity.[55] Similarly when the elevator accelerates to rise, the force we feel could equally be an increase in gravity. Although this equivalent feeling does not mean gravity and acceleration are expressions of a singular force, the equivalence enabled Einstein to understand how gravity operates. Applying the equations of acceleration to gravity enabled Einstein to uncover the physics of general relativity that accurately map the universe. Similarly, a more accurate "mapping" of our universe of planetary natural resources could occur if we recognize and respect the equivalent forces of *use*, available to humans since we first emerged, and *nonuse*, available to the planet, and its biosphere, irrespective of humans.

3. CONSERVATION PROPERTIES

Symmetry and equivalence not only reveal an underlying single essence in virtually all natural phenomena, they also show that nature wants to conserve that essence.[56] Conservation is the quality that describes something that does not change when the system is manipulated or transformed.[57] We demand that our physical laws work equally well anywhere and everywhere in space. We demand that they work not only today, but tomorrow and next week; otherwise they are not laws.[58] Physicists call

---

[52] LIGHTMAN, *supra* note 26, at 120.

[53] GREEN, *supra* note 33, at 40–43; LIGHTMAN, *supra* note 26, at 159.

[54] ADAMS, *supra* note 3, at 295; ATKINS, *supra* note 3, at 45; EISENSTAEDT, *supra* note 28, at 77–78.

[55] ADAMS, *supra* note 3, at 295 GREEN, *supra* note 5, at 67; EISENSTAEDT, *supra* note 28, at 77–78.

[56] ADAMS, *supra* note 3, at 235; FEYNMAN, *supra* note 1, at 29; KLAUS MAINZER, SYMMETRIES OF NATURE: A HANDBOOK FOR PHILOSOPHY OF NATURE AND SCIENCE 296, 339 (1996); NEWTON, *supra* note 19, at 225.

[57] ADAMS, *supra* note 3, at 443; KLEIN & LACHIEZE-REY, *supra* note 6, at 87.

[58] LIGHTMAN, *supra* note 26, at11; LIVIO, *supra* note 2, at 199; NEWTON, *supra* note 19, at 223.

this "invariance," highlighting the presence of a fixed, unchanging property. A sphere has continuous invariance because it is identical under all reflections or rotations across its center. Newton's laws of motion have continuous invariance because they apply identically whether we observe objects while standing, while moving, or while spinning, giving rise to the conservation of momentum.[59] The energy contained in a system also possesses continuous invariance because, if the system is isolated, or closed, the total quantity of energy we observe today will still be found tomorrow and next week, if we understand its many forms.[60]

For a natural resource system, conservation properties alert us to our limits. The essence of a natural resource is its connection to an underlying *conserved* quality of the system. Both use and nonuse are naturally conserved within resources, and this essential quality should guide our appreciation of the system. If humans recognize the benefits of nature's conserved quality, that realization affords an accurate projection of the negative results that certainly have been, and will be, created by our overdevelopment or exploitation of the use component of the natural resources.

Newton's Laws of Motion and the conservation of momentum

Newton's Laws of Motion are that (1) a body in motion will stay in motion and a body at rest will stay at rest unless acted on by an outside force; (2) force equals mass times acceleration; and, (3) to every action there is an equal on opposite reaction.[61] These classic Laws of Motion encapsulate symmetry, equivalence/unification, and conservation. The symmetry of the collision—that every force is exactly matched by an equal force acting in the exactly opposite direction—states that the system exists as a balance of opposing forces. No unidirectional forces exist in nature.[62] And we understand that these two opposing but equivalent forces are part of a singular essence—momentum, or mass times acceleration.[63] Finally, we note that the system's momentum is conserved.[64] As billiard balls crash, move, spin, and change direction atop a pool table, some essential quality is unchanged—momentum.[65] The term *momentum* encompases the direction, rotation, mass, and speed of objects. If a small, light ball collides with a large, heavy ball, their resulting motions are dramatically different. But we understand that the two balls' different motions reflect the conservation of the underlying momentum inherent in them.

---

[59] SYMMETRIES IN PHYSICS, *supra* note 1, at 97; GREEN, *supra* note 5, at 223; NEWTON, *supra* note 19, at 223–24.

[60] CHRISTOPHER J.T. LEWIS, HEAT AND THERMODYNAMICS: A HISTORICAL PERSPECTIVE 72 (2007); NEWTON, *supra* note 19, at 222–23; RICHARD EDWIN SONNTAG & GORDON J. VAN WYLEN, FUNDAMENTALS OF THERMODYNAMICS 90 (1982).

[61] DAVID BERLINSKI, NEWTON'S GIFT: HOW SIR ISAAC NEWTON UNLOCKED THE SYSTEM OF THE WORLD 98, 100, 103 (2000); NEWTON, *supra* note 19, at 24.

[62] *Newton's Law's of Motion*, WIKIPEDIA (Feb. 11, 2011 11:00 a.m), http://en.wikipedia.org/wiki/Newton's_laws_of_motion.

[63] NEWTON, *supra* note 19, at 35.

[64] *Id.*, at 223–24.

[65] BERLINSKI, *supra* note 61, at 103–105; LIVIO, *supra* note 2, at 217.

The first law of thermodynamics and the conservation of energy

The first law of thermodynamics states that energy can be neither created nor destroyed; it only changes form. Because of this conservation law, we understand the relationship between all observed forms of energy—heat, light, a falling object, a compressed spring, a chemical bond.[66] We realize that when one form of energy is transformed into another, some essential quality remains constant. Einstein related mass and energy through $e = mc^2$, where e is energy, m is mass, and c is the speed of light.[67] This conservation can also be viewed as symmetry and equivalence across time.[68] If we have a closed system, with no mass or energy entering or leaving it, we expect the quantity of energy present today to still be present in a year.[69] Similarly, in the closed system of natural resources, if the use and nonuse components are in balance, then the entity itself—the resource—is conserved for the future. When use dramatically exceeds nonuse, then the resource is not conserved; it first becomes damaged and then eventually lost. This inherent restriction should alert us to our limits when we seek to use, and then overuse, natural resources.

C. When It All Goes Wrong: Asymmetry, Imbalance, and System Loss

The absence of symmetry, equivalence, and conservation can have ruinous effects. If we destroy symmetry, we lose strength. If we create an imbalance in the unity or equivalence of a system's essence, this action can (1) threaten the integrity of the system, and (2) cause us to lose our ability to understand its behavior and correctly predict the outcomes of outside perturbations. If humans deny the demands of conservation, we risk collapse of natural systems.

1. CONSEQUENCES OF ASYMMETRY

Loss of symmetry is loss of strength

Because symmetry imparts tremendous strength, the loss of symmetry can result in destruction of what is otherwise held together by symmetry. Should we pluck away stones from only one side of our arch, the structure it supports crashes down. If, rather that wrapping our fingers around our egg, we place it between two flat boards, it splatters with minimal pressure. And if an animal with bilateral symmetry highly adapted for forward motion, becomes stationary, the absence of front-back symmetry now becomes a vulnerable blind-spot. When a football running back charges forward, his bilateral symmetry is perfect for the task. However, a quarterback planted to throw

---

[66] Atkins, *supra* note 3, at 25–27; Lightman, *supra* note 26, at 11; Sonntag & Van Wylen, *supra* note 60, at 90.

[67] Green, *supra* note 33, at 51; Heisenberg, *supra* note 30, at 114–15.

[68] Newton, *supra* note 19, at 225.

[69] *Id.* at 222–23.

has a vulnerable blind spot—his left-right symmetry lacks a critical front-back symmetry. His blockers must provide the strength by creating radial symmetry—the pocket. The failure of this radial symmetry results in a sack, and maybe a concussion.

If natural resources are likened to the arch, our plucking away at only the human-use value of a natural resource undermines the system's strength and resilience, eventually causing collapse of the resource itself. If most natural resources are overused, we risk a planetary collapse. By analogy to the football team, our human drive for natural resource use has made the resource's blind side—its nonuse side—vulnerable to a sack, and a catastrophic planetary concussion.

2. IMBALANCES

The perils of ignoring equivalent/unified forces

Newton's laws of motion and Einstein's General Theory of Relativity provide accurate predictions of how objects and forces must travel and interact in the physical universe. Both are built upon an understanding of the unity and equivalence of the underlying forces—that a singular quantity of momentum predicts the speed and direction of colliding objects, and that the equivalence of gravity and acceleration accurately maps the space-time topography to predict the paths of moving objects.

By relying on the laws of general relativity, and then measuring the behavior of our universe's matter and energy, physicists have identified "dark matter."[70] Though undetectable by emitted or reflected light, or radiation, dark matter is inferred from its gravitational effects on visible matter.[71] Its existence is known because the measured gravitational effects of an observed object exceed that which is attributable to its visible "luminous" matter.[72] Both matter and dark matter must be accounted for to calculate an object's true gravitational effect; similarly, both use and nonuse are essential in grasping the essence of a natural resource system. Although humans have traditionally only measured, and valued, a resource's use qualities, a natural resource's nonuse component equally contributes to its essential composition. If we chart a course across the universe without factoring in how dark matter may warp the time-space fabric and impart a different trajectory, we will lose our way. If we chart our course on this planet that focuses only on resource use, but is blind to nonuse, we will adversely affect the world of natural resources.

3. LOSS OF ESSENCE—THE ABSENCE OF CONSERVATION

Entropy and asymmetry in time reversal

Whereas the first law of thermodynamics, derived from symmetry across time, demands that energy be neither created nor destroyed, the second law of thermodynamics

---

[70] GREEN, *supra* note 5, at 294–95.

[71] *Id.*

[72] *Id.*

describes an asymmetry in time reversal, or entropy.[73] The concept of entropy is a measure of the disorder in a system. The second law of thermodynamics states that the entropy of a system can never decrease. Or, to put this law in other terms, when energy is transformed from one manifestation to another, the resulting disorder must either increase or be constant.[74] As a result, our quest for a perpetual motion machine must inevitably fail. For example, we cannot construct a machine able to capture the energy of a falling ball by catching it on a spring.[75] In an idealized, frictionless world, where we lose no energy to air resistance as the ball falls, or to heat as metal spring compresses, the ball would drop, compressing the spring, and the spring would recoil, tossing the ball back to its original height. This energy conversion might continue forever, but the second law of thermodynamics tells us that it cannot.[76] Entropy will exact its fee. Not all of the energy is converted to work because, even in our idealized game of catch, some small portion of the spring-loaded ball is converted to disorder. Increasing entropy bleeds off some of the system's work.

In the case of natural resources, entropy is the transactional fee that must be paid whenever the nonuse potential of a resource is not conserved, but is instead converted into human use. Because the resource itself is made up of both use and nonuse capabilities, allocation of a resource's essence strictly to human use will inevitably drain it of its ecocentric nonuse capability. This loss is the resource's entropy, and the antidyne of conservation.

When conservation is ignored

When we know a conservation property exists, we know we must account for the entire quantity of the conserved essence, not just a portion of it. If we lead a field trip of preschoolers to a museum, the "conservation of preschoolers" tells us to bring back the same number we took, no fewer. And, of equal importance, no more preschoolers should be collected because we know an additional preschooler is not a windfall gain, but instead indicates a loss from another museum group. A surgeon will likewise employ a "conservation of tools" approach during an operation—all that goes in must also come out. In a natural resources context, a similarly critical accounting is accomplished through the conservation of mass and energy. We must account for the dissipation, dilution, concentration, and transformation of all the ingredients we know to be present. If we burn ten tons of coal containing ten ounces of mercury, to believe that the mass of mercury within the burned coal is simply lost forever is not only an incomplete understanding, it is a misunderstanding inviting peril.[77]

---

[73] GREEN, *supra* note 5, at 160–62; NEWTON, *supra* note 19, at 229.

[74] LIGHTMAN, *supra* note 26, at 99–100; SONNTAG & VAN WYLEN, *supra* note 60, at 216–17.

[75] NEWTON, *supra* note 19, at 76; SONNTAG & VAN WYLEN, *supra* note 60, at 177–78.

[76] ATKINS, *supra* note 3, at 77–78; LEWIS, *supra* note 60, at 108–09; LIGHTMAN, *supra* note 26, at 91–98; SONNTAG & VAN WYLEN, *supra* note 60, at 216–17.

[77] ANTHONY DEPALMA, *Mercury's Harmful Reach Has Grown, Study Suggest,* N.Y. TIMES, SCIENCE (JAN. 31, 2012).

Equally perilous would be ignorance that the ten ounces of mercury is present in the fuel in the first place.

Our knowledge that all mass and energy must be accounted for alerts us to look for a quantity of whatever exists that makes up the whole. Accounting for the whole helps to enforce compliance with nature's laws and to protect the earth's nonuse, ecocentric existence. Ascribing both nonuse and use components to a natural resource provides a complete quantification of the system's entire value, ensuring that all the resource's function is accounted for on our balance sheet. To ignore the nonuse component would be to declare as waste, or nonexistent, a significant purpose of the resource. We have been exploiting the use function of natural resources without exhibiting the curiosity or caution to identify the affected nonuse part.

Asymmetry, imbalance, and loss—imposing new equilibriums

An isolated system will always find equilibrium.[78] Imbalance occurs when an outside force acts on the system, creating a perturbation. For example, our conception of subatomic particles pictures an atom in the classic solar system model, with protons and neutrons clustered in the nucleus and electrons orbiting at multiple distances like the planets, where the orbits occupied by the electrons describe the energy state of the atom.[79] But, when a photon of energy hits this atom, the atom absorbs the energy by bumping its electrons into a higher energy orbit, where a new equilibrium is established.[80] One may continue this atomic analogy for natural resources. The pressure of human use serves as a perturbation, forcing the earth's resources out of a prior equilibrium, like our electron absorbing energy by finding a new orbit. The natural resources on this planet, like our atom, can try to adapt to a new energy state, but because humans seem intent on exploiting or capturing only a resource's use state, there is less likelihood that an equilibrium, or sustainable state, can be attained over the long run.

D. Symmetry, Equivalence, and Conservation—Recognizing the Essence of a Natural Resource

The recognition that symmetry reveals fundamental properties of the physical world has enabled remarkable scientific and mathematical progress in the last two centuries.[81] Our understanding of the universe would be incomplete without relativity, quantum mechanics, group theory, thermodynamics—physical laws founded in symmetry. That physical laws demand symmetry, and that symmetry reveals the conjoined qualities of equivalence and conservation, should also govern our

---

[78] *Id.* at 84–85.

[79] ADAMS, *supra* note 3, at 136–37.

[80] *Id.* at 11–13.

[81] FEYNMAN, *supra* note 1, at 77; GREEN, *supra* note 5, at 219; KLEIN & LACHIEZE-REY, *supra* note 6, at 88, 91; LIVIO, *supra* note 2, at 231.

understanding of natural resources. Symmetry, equivalence, and conservation in physical laws mean that those laws are fixed; they are constant and predictable, based on the intrinsic essence of natural goods.

Relativity is not relative. Einstein was motivated by a profound, and very human, dissatisfaction with the asymmetries found in classical physics, where different observers achieved different results using the same laws. Just as we do not accept arbitrary results in our legal system, Einstein did not want results to vary based on situational context. Relativity, incorrectly understood, means that observers see things differently, each in their own way, and that every perspective is equally valid. Correctly understood, relativity eliminates viewpoint asymmetry, revealing a singular essence that is the same and symmetrical for all observers.

The fundamental "law" of natural resources, correctly understood, incorporates a symmetrical nonuse component that parallels and is equivalent to the better-known use component. Both serve our planet and our species. Nonuse in not a competing interest with human use, and nonuse is not a proxy for a competing intergenerational future human use interest. Like space-time, nonuse and human use exist as different manifestations of a unified essence. To fully understand a natural resource, to correctly predict the outcomes of our manipulations of a natural resource, and to establish the most effective laws for managing a natural resource, we must take account of the equal and equivalent nonuse component.

15 The Economics of Resource Nonuse

A. Introduction

Historically, two interests have played a role with respect to natural resources. First, "users" of the resource wish to exploit the resource in some way. They may wish to extract it, develop it, alter it, dump emissions and waste into it, or even just enjoy it. Second, "nonusers" of the resource wish to leave the resource alone. These interests value a resource for its nonuse qualities. For example, most humans enjoy *indirect use value* from public environmental goods (such as the air, water, and underground resources) when those goods are not used as a dumping ground for wastes, but rather are appreciated for providing the necessities of a healthy life. Nonusers also benefit from the *existence value* that humans experience when natural objects, such as wild lands and wildlife, are preserved and protected from the consequences of human use.

Several conflicts may arise between these two interests. Among the class of users, conflicts sometimes occur between those who wish to use the resource for one purpose and those who wish to use it for a conflicting purpose. For example, a field may be valuable for either crops or forage, but not both simultaneously. Farmers may thereby find themselves in conflict with ranchers. Similarly, land may be valuable for either mining or recreation, but not at the same time; miners may find themselves in conflict with motorized recreationists for the same public land.

There also may exist conflicts between users and nonusers. One type of conflict involves users and nonusers who wish to prevent a specific use because it interferes with a resource's indirect use value that is particularly appreciated by nonusers. For example, use of the atmosphere as a depository for sulfur dioxide emissions from coal-burning power plants can create acid rain. While power plants emit toxins into the atmosphere, the resulting acid rain adversely affects the indirect use value enjoyed by humans when the air is clean. Another class of user/nonuser conflict is between resource users and nonusers who benefit from the existence value of objects preserved in a natural state. Resource use may destroy wild landscapes or wildlife species, thereby degrading the existence value enjoyed by humans who desire that the existence of these objects remain undisturbed by human use.

The conflicts between users and users, and users and nonusers, raise interests for essentially anthropocentric ends. Users wish to use resources to maximize human welfare. Nonusers wish for resources to be unused by these users, either because of indirect use value or existence value, both of which are enjoyed and measured by humans. Rarely do nonusers wish to proscribe use of resources for purely selfless, nonanthropocentric reasons, or for reasons reflecting the intrinsic value of natural resources.

The lack of a nonanthropocentric nonuse consideration in conflicts between users and nonusers is the premise of this chapter. Purely anthropocentric considerations neglect the resource interest and will likely result in an environmentally unsustainable end. This chapter will therefore not only focus on the conflict between users who wish to use a particular resource and nonusers who wish to prevent a specific use, but also consider ways to infuse the resource interest itself into the negotiations. In order to do so, the chapter first applies game theory to outline a noncooperative bargaining structure using the Prisoner's Dilemma. This "dilemma" occurs when resource users and nonusers fail to cooperate, resulting in efficiencies. It describes next a coordinated bargaining structure in order to highlight the difficulty in achieving efficiencies when a user-nonuser resource conflict either ignores, or fails to adequately account for, the interest of the resource itself. The chapter concludes by considering the likelihood of an efficient outcome when the natural resource itself is empowered with a right of nonuse, in both a three-player game among user, nonuser, and resource, and a simpler game between a user and a coalition of nonusers and empowered resources.

B. The Inadequacy of Noncooperation

1. THE PRISONER'S DILEMMA[1]

The Prisoner's Dilemma (PD) is perhaps the most often referenced and pervasively understood game theory model. It provides a viable starting point for demonstrating the societal benefits of cooperation.[2] In the theoretical setup for PD, a prosecutor suspects two prisoners of committing a felony. The prosecutor offers the prisoners the option to confess to the crime and receive a lesser punishment or not confess. If the prisoners choose to both confess, they each receive a punishment of only four years in prison. If one prisoner confesses and the other remains silent, the prisoner

---

[1] *See generally*, JOHN VON NEUMANN, PRISONER'S DILEMMA: JOHN VON NEUMANN, GAME THEORY AND THE PUZZLE OF THE BOMB (1992).

[2] Ian Ayres, *Playing Games with the Law*, 42 STAN. L. REV. 1291, 1294–95 (1990) (book review) (footnote omitted).

		Prisoner 2	
		Cooperate	Defect
Prisoner 1	Cooperate	1, 1	6, 0
	Defect	0, 6	4, 4

FIGURE 15.1 The Prisoner's Dilemma.

who confessed will receive no prison time and the prisoner who remained silent will receive six years in prison. However, if both prisoners choose to cooperate with each other by remaining silent the prosecutor will not have enough evidence to charge them with a felony and will settle for a misdemeanor charge carrying a punishment of only a year in prison. The prisoners are not allowed to communicate with one another while deliberating on whether or not to confess.

The PD introduces the concept of Pareto optimality. A situation is Pareto optimal if no player can be made better off without worsening the situation of another player. The Pareto optimal option in the prisoners' situation is to cooperate with each other and remain silent; however, because neither prisoner is able to communicate with the other, by remaining silent each prisoner faces the risk that the other prisoner will confess. Accordingly, the prisoner's dilemma is that each can choose to remain silent with the hope of achieving the Pareto optimal outcome, or each can make the "safe" choice of confessing and avoid the most severe punishment of six years in prison. This dilemma would of course not exist if the prisoners were able to *coordinate* strategies. Unfortunately for the prisoners, the PD structure emphasizes cooperation and not coordination. In order to cooperate each player must make a blind leap of faith that the other player will do the same. Because the ability to achieve the cooperative and Pareto optimal outcome requires a high level of risk tolerance, the prisoners are both likely to take the risk-averse position and confess, resulting in a less efficient non-Pareto optimal result.

The PD demonstrates that the cooperative result is usually the most bilaterally beneficial; however, a cooperative strategy is difficult for risk-averse participants to achieve without coordination between the parties. As coordination is impossible in the PD game, the two players will inevitably choose a suboptimal result and have to spend four years in prison instead of the one year that would have been possible if they could have cooperated, or if they had been able to coordinate their strategies.

2. PD GAMES FOR RESOURCE USERS AND NONUSERS

The PD is an example of how noncooperation often produces an inefficient and suboptimal outcome. It also demonstrates the difficulty associated with achieving a cooperative result without coordination between parties who find themselves as players in a game where there maybe a better outcome with bargaining. These inadequacies reveal themselves when some humans wish to use a resource while others value nonuse.

Consider a theoretical dispute between EarthJustice, an environmental association whose members benefit from resource nonuse, and Consolidated Clearcutting Corporation ("Consolidated"), a resource user. The red-cockaded woodpecker is an endangered species whose natural habitat exists only in the forest Consolidated owns and wishes to log. The legal issue is whether Consolidated's resource use actions will threaten the nonuse values associated with the endangered red-cockaded woodpecker. EarthJustice, being an environmental advocacy agency, attempts to protect these nonuse values on behalf of the red-cockaded woodpecker.

The variance between the archetypal PD model and the Consolidated-EarthJustice conflict is that of goal alignment and transparency of information. In the PD model, although each player has the same goal of little-to-no prison time, they are both unaware of the other player's strategy in getting there. In a hypothetical resource use-nonuse situation, EarthJustice seeks to maintain the endangered red-cockaded woodpecker's habitat through nonuse, while Consolidated seeks to maximize its profit by logging in the forest (using the timber resource) at a minimal cost. These goals cannot both be reached simultaneously.

To simplify the situation, we assume that there will be no underhandedness by either of the parties, and that both parties have only two strategy options: either litigate or do not litigate. If both parties do not litigate (i.e., they instead choose to cooperate), a percentage of the woodpecker species, but not all of them, will be saved, while a certain amount of logging, but not of the entire tract, will be undertaken. Conversely, if one party chooses to litigate and the other chooses not to litigate, the litigating party will, by default, achieve its goal uncontested. This result means either that Consolidated will log the entire forest at its lowest possible cost, or EarthJustice will be able to prevent logging while protecting the forest and the woodpecker.

The state of affairs gets even more complex when considering the most likely strategy, in which both parties choose not to cooperate and instead decide to litigate. If this situation fit perfectly into the PD model, the dual litigation strategy would result in both parties getting close to their goal (i.e., some of the forest would be saved and some logging would be allowed). Although, due to the costs associated with litigation, this outcome would not be as mutually beneficial as the cooperative outcome, it would result in both parties being relatively better off than the outcome where one chooses to litigate and the other defaults.

In reality, a dual litigation strategy is likely to result in one winner taking all because courts generally assign a winner and a loser. Accordingly, a dual litigation strategy would have a similar outcome to that which would occur if one party chose to litigate and the other chose not to. The variance is, of course, that in a dual litigation strategy one party attempted to get its way but failed.

Figure 15.2 below demonstrates the conflict between EarthJustice and Consolidated as described above. Instead of setting forth the potential outcomes in terms of years in prison, Figure 15.2 applies the concept of utility. If EarthJustice and Consolidated cooperate, some of the woodpecker species will be saved while Consolidated will still be able to do some logging. If the maximum utility for each entity is arbitrarily

		Consolidated	
		Cooperate	Defect
EarthJustice	Cooperate	350, 350	700, 0
	Defect	0, 700	250, 250

FIGURE 15.2 The Prisoner's Dilemma as applied to EarthJustice and Consolidated.

assumed to be 700 utils,[3] a cooperative approach in which the habitat is split between the parties, so that some woodpeckers survive and some trees are logged, would allow 350 utils for each party. This result, of course, implies that if only one party litigates and the other party concedes, the litigating party will receive the entire maximum assumed utility of 700 utils. A simplified dual litigation strategy in which an equitable outcome is possible, as opposed to one winner taking all, would result in an equal division of the total potential utils with the addition of the litigation costs. Accordingly, the dual litigation strategy would result in 250 utils for each party.

In a noncooperative framework, the players will most likely choose the dual litigation strategy because they will act independently and self-interestedly. By contrast, a cooperative game avoids litigation and maximizes total payoff. As with the PD game, the most effective manner in which to reach a cooperative result is by introducing the concept of coordination. Part C explores how the conflict between nonusers and users can be restructured so as to achieve an optimal, cooperative result through player coordination.

C. The Potential for Coordination

The PD helps demonstrate that coordination[4] is as important as cooperation in attempting to reach an optimal result.[5] However, coordination problems arise when the players can reach some mutually desired outcome—or avoid some mutually undesired outcome—only by the strategy of combining their actions in a

[3] *Utils* is a commonly used but only hypothetical measure of utility.

[4] Indispensible works describing coordination are DAVID K. LEWIS, CONVENTION: A PHILOSOPHICAL STUDY 5–51 (1969); THOMAS C. SCHELLING, THE STRATEGY OF CONFLICT 89–99 (1963); BRYAN SKYRMS, THE STAG HUNT AND THE EVOLUTION OF SOCIAL STRUCTURE 31–44 (2004); ROBERT SUGDEN, THE ECONOMICS OF RIGHTS, COOPERATION AND WELFARE 36–91 (Palgrave Macmillan 2004) (1986); EDNA ULLMANN-MARGALIT, THE EMERGENCE OF NORMS 74–133 (1977).

[5] Richard H. McAdams, *Beyond the Prisoner's Dilemma: Coordination, Game Theory, and Law*, 82 S. CAL. L. REV. 209 (2009).

certain way.[6] Coordination games depart from the PD in that they allow for some level of transparency between actors. Transparency and communication allow players to more successfully coordinate strategies, and therefore increase the chance of reaching a cooperative result as the players do not have to rely on uninformed hunches or guesses in applying their cooperative strategy. However, there are certain circumstances where players may still coordinate strategies without communicating with each other. The archetypal coordination game is the Stag Hunt game.[7]

1. STAG HUNT GAME

To represent the parties' strategies and the respective outcomes as a result of coordination, one can consider the "Stag Hunt" game as conceived by Jean-Jacques Rousseau in *A Discourse on Inequality*.[8] A Stag Hunt game is a story that turned into a game and represents a "prototype of the social contract."[9] The game illustrates a situation in which two parties go on a hunting expedition. Each party may choose to hunt a stag or a hare. The parties can successfully bag a hare independent of each other; however, in order to successfully hunt the stag, the parties must assist each other, because no hunter can autonomously bag a stag. The stag is, of course, more valuable than the hare, even when shared between two hunters.

In Stag Hunt games, there are two Nash equilbria[10] in which no player wants to switch sides; equilibrium is achieved either when both players cooperate or when both players defect. In addition, each player's individual rational choice depends on what that player expects the other to choose, allowing for the potential that the players will simultaneously choose the same strategy. Although in a Stag Hunt game there are two Nash equilibria, one is risk averse (focusing on the inherent risk), and the other is payoff dominant (focusing on the potential payoff). A payoff-dominant Nash equilibrium is Pareto superior. In the Stag Hunt game, the choice of both parties to hunt a stag is payoff dominant and therefore Pareto superior; however, a player who chooses to hunt the stag takes a risk that the other will choose not

---

[6] *See, e.g.*, LOUIS KAPLOW & STEVEN SHAVELL, FAIRNESS VERSUS WELFARE 15–38 (2002); JOHN RAWLS, JUSTICE AS FAIRNESS: A RESTATEMENT 39–40, 150–52 (2001).

[7] *See, e.g.*, Brian Skyrms, *The Stag Hunt*, 75:2 PROCEEDINGS & ADDRESSES OF THE AMERICAN PHILOSOPHICAL ASSOCIATION 31, 31 (2001); DENNIS CHONG, COLLECTIVE ACTION AND THE CIVIL RIGHTS MOVEMENT 103–07 (1991); Gary Bornstein & Zohar Gilula, *Between-Group Communication and Conflict Resolution in Assurance and Chicken Games*, 47 J. CONFLICT RESOL. 326, 327–31 (2003); Amartya K. Sen, *Isolation, Assurance and the Social Rate of Discount*, 81 Q.J. ECON. 112, 112–15 (1967).

[8] JEAN-JACQUES ROUSSEAU, A DISCOURSE ON INEQUALITY 111 (Maurice Cranston trans., 1984) (1755).

[9] SKYRMS, *supra* note 4, at 31.

[10] "Nash equilibrium is [t]he central solution concept in game theory. It is based on the principle that the combination of strategies that players are likely to choose is one in which no player could do better by choosing a different strategy given the ones the others choose. A pair of strategies will form a Nash equilibrium if each strategy is one that cannot be improved upon given the other strategy. We establish whether a particular strategy combination forms a Nash equilibrium by asking if either player has incentive to deviate from it." DOUGLAS G. BAIRD, ROBERT H. GERTNER & RANDAL C. PICKER, GAME THEORY AND THE LAW 1 (1994).

Player 2

Player 1		Stag	Hare
	Stag	a, a	c, b
	Hare	b, c	b, b

FIGURE 15.3 The Stag Hunt game.

to cooperate. Conversely, the player who chooses the risk-averse strategy and hunts the hare need not worry about the other player's cooperation, but forgoes the potential payoff of a higher-valued stag.

The lesson of the Stag Hunt game is that the greater the level of uncertainty or the lesser amount of transparency between the players, the more likely it is that players will choose the risk-averse strategy, despite the fact that such a choice means the players will fail to acquire the higher-valued stag. In the Stag Hunt game, a strategy to select a risk-averse Nash equilibrium means the choice of both parties is to hunt a hare. Figure 15.3 illustrates the Stag Hunt game in which a>b>c.

Figure 15.3 demonstrates that the stag can be successfully hunted, and a Pareto optimal result can be achieved, only when both parties cooperate. This cooperation in turn is achieved through *coordination* of strategies. Conversely, successfully hunting a hare is a solitary endeavor. In a noncooperative uncoordinated game, the most likely outcome is the risk-averse strategy in which both players hunt the hare. This result ensues because without coordination, neither party can be assured that the other will cooperate. Although hunting the hare is a Nash equilibrium result, neither player reaps the more universally beneficial Pareto optimal result.

Another notable aspect of the Stag Hunt game is that it is a PD invoking the "Shadow of the Future" concept.[11] This concept causes players to consider the future implications of their noncooperative actions: "Hence I learn to do a service to another, without bearing him any real kindness; because I foresee, that he will return my service, in expectation of another of the same kind, and in order to maintain the same correspondence of good offices with me and with others."[12] The Stag Hunt game is simply the PD where some level of transparency exists between the players as they are aware of a possibility of another trial. If both players can anticipate each other's motives, they are essentially silently communicating and therefore reducing the level of uncertainty associated with a particular strategy. The Shadow of the Future concept thereby introduces the possibility of coordination into the PD game structure and transforms it into a Stag Hunt game.

---

[11] SKYRMS, *supra* note 4, at 33–34.

[12] DAVID HUME, A TREATISE OF HUMAN NATURE 521 (Gutenberg eBook 2003), ebooks.adelaide.edu.au/h/hume/david/h92t.

Although the "Shadow of the Future has not solved the problem of cooperation in the PD, it has transformed it into the problem of cooperation in the Stag Hunt."[13] What this means is that rational, self-interested players engaged in a PD are more likely to achieve a cooperative, optimal outcome, and transition the game structure to that of a Stag Hunt game, by considering the future implications of their decision. Coordination simply makes a Pareto optimal cooperative result more likely to occur.

2. COORDINATION WHEN USERS AND NONUSERS CONFLICT

The Stag Hunt model demonstrates the core problem between human resource use and anthropocentric resource nonuse: Without cooperative coordination, the two players in that game will likely choose a lower-payoff risk-averse strategy. If we return to the situation described above, in which Consolidated desires to log a particular area of forest and EarthJustice seeks to protect the forest's nonuse value, the Stag Hunt model demonstrates how coordination between these two players is likely to result in a more optimal outcome. Coordination facilitates cooperation by allowing for transparency between the players so that they can confidently cooperate. Under the Stag Hunt model, the players know each other's strategy and operate based on that knowledge. These strategies incentivize cooperation.

Coordination might be facilitated by the addition of a new factor—the concept of mediation. Recall that coordination requires transparency. Adversarial parties, such as in litigation, are generally diametrically opposed. Such oppositional hostility and adverseness undermines the possibility of coordination. But mediation offers an alternative to litigation. The players may then work together to determine a resolution either independently or through a mediation process. The players can achieve Nash equilibrium by matching strategies (i.e., both could go to mediation or both could agree to a resolution without the help of a third party).

Under this new model, the players' coordinated Pareto optimal result is represented by both players agreeing to a resolution without going to mediation. This resolution would allow the players to arrive at a solution where Consolidated may log some trees and EarthJustice may maintain some habitat for the endangered woodpeckers. This solution is Pareto optimal because it does not entail the financial cost and opportunity cost of undergoing a potentially lengthy mediation process. A solution achieved with a coordinated mediation strategy would probably still allow Consolidated to log and EarthJustice to protect the endangered woodpecker, but with the added cost of mediation. Both of these strategies imply coordination, but a resolution without mediation involves cooperative coordination and affords a much better overall result.

Assume, then, that the two user-versus-nonuser players in the Stag Hunt model both prefer the coordinated non-mediation strategy to the mediation strategy. If, however, the players choose not to cooperate with each other and not coordinate

---

[13] SKYRMS, *supra* note 4, at 34.

		Player 2	
		No Mediation	Mediation
Player 1	No Mediation	a, a	c, b
	Mediation	b, c	b, b

FIGURE 15.4 Stag Hunt applied to Consolidated and EarthJustice.

strategies, one player may end up with a much less valuable result. Specifically, if one player chooses to mediate while the other chooses not to mediate, the player not participating in the mediation process will not have its interests represented. Figure 15.4 illustrates this adaptation of the Stag Hunt game in which a>b>c.

As demonstrated in Figure 15.4, the most universally beneficial (Pareto optimal) strategy is cooperation combined with non-mediation. However, this cooperative outcome requires trust and some level of transparency on behalf of both players. To achieve such transparency and trust, coordination is critical. Coordination can then lead to cooperation. The next section discusses how resource users and nonusers, players who have historically been in opposition to one another, might come to agree on a coordinated strategy, which might then lead to a cooperative outcome.

D. How to Garner Coordination: The Natural Resource as a Focal Point for Coordination

It is mutually beneficial for the participants in a natural resources game to cooperate and coordinate strategies; however, the users and nonusers, raising their own anthropocentric interests, are likely to be adversaries with a propensity for noncooperation. One way to avoid continued conflict and encourage cooperation is to provide the resource itself with some legal stature and legitimacy. This goal can be accomplished by assigning it a legal right, so that its interests cannot be overlooked by users or nonusers.

So far our simplified analysis has identified game structures in which there are two Nash equilibria. Nobel Prize winner Thomas Schelling has pointed out that in such game structures in which there are multiple equilibria, one equilibrium stands out—is salient—due to some characteristic recognizable by all players.[14] This type of equilibrium is a *focal point* to which each player aligns its strategy, expecting the other players will do the same.[15]

---

[14] THOMAS SCHELLING, THE STRATEGY OF CONFLICT 57 (1960).

[15] Judith Mehta, Chris Starmer & Robert Sugden, *Focal Points in Pure Coordination Games: An Experimental Investigation*, 36 THEORY & DECISION 163, 163 (1994). *See also* Maarten C.W. Janssen, *Focal Points*, *in* 2 THE NEW PALGRAVE DICTIONARY OF ECONOMICS AND LAW 150 (Peter Newman ed., 1998); Maarten C.W. Janssen,

When there is a use-nonuse conflict, resource users and nonusers have different interests with respect to natural resources. Accordingly, a pure coordination game in which there is no conflict of interest does not apply. However, although the interests of the direct participants are in conflict with each other, the natural resource itself, although not directly participating in the game at this point but nonetheless having an obvious interest in the outcome, may help to achieve some sort of agreement. If it had some legal credibility, a legitimized natural resource may function as a focal point and unify the interests of the users and nonusers.

In order for a focal point to operate effectively it must be adequately prominent or conspicuous for the game participants to recognize it and to expect other actors affected by the game to recognize it as well. By way of example, Schelling set up an experiment where he asked participants who were unable to communicate with one another to select a place in New York City to meet.[16] Although seemingly an impossible task, the majority of Schelling's respondents selected the same location: Grand Central Station. Similarly, an environmentally conscious resource-using industrialist ought to be cognizant of the natural resource affected by the industrialist's activities, permitting it to be a de facto focal point. However, although resource users "ought to" take into account resource nonuse values, users often do not engage in this calculation if natural resources can be used without cost to the user. Accordingly, the natural resource will require some legitimacy to function as a Schelling-style focal point.

The natural resource's own intrinsic interest in nonuse need not be precisely defined in each application of this model. In fact, it is generally understood that it is each player's description of its own particularized options that is relevant.[17] Players may choose between different ways in which to describe their options. "In making this choice, and then in choosing between the options themselves, rational players follow a 'principle of coordination,' which roughly corresponds with . . . [the] principle of 'payoff dominance.'"[18] The payoff-dominant position ensures Pareto optimal outcomes.[19] Therefore, the mere *threat* of the resource asserting its own nonanthropocentric right of nonuse may be sufficient, because this threat will shape and align the players' own description of their options.

Of course, a theoretically legitimized resource interest might be inadequate to reliably shape the actions of the otherwise opposed players in the resource game. To prevent marginalization of the resource's interest, the resource's right of nonuse ought to function similarly to a state usury law—only when ignored would it trump previous agreements. Contracting parties typically avoid interest rates that constitute usury because, were the parties to write usurious contracts, a court would invalidate

---

Rationalizing Focal Points, 50 THEORY & DECISION 119, 119–22 (2001); Robert Sugden, *A Theory of Focal Points*, 105 ECON. J. 533, 533 (1995).

[16] SCHELLING, *supra* note 14, at 57.

[17] D. Gauthier, *Coordination*, 14 DIALOGUE 195–221 (1975).

[18] Robert Sugden, *A Theory of Focal Points*, 105 ECON. J. 533, 535 (May 1995).

[19] Janssen, *Focal Points*, *supra* note 15, at 150.

their contractual terms by applying the provisions of usury law. Such could be the effect here if the resource itself had legal legitimacy: Parties in natural resource negotiations would have to take into account the resource's right of nonuse, because if they failed to do so, that right could be applied to invalidate the result of the negotiation. A right of nonuse held by the resource could also be asserted if the users and nonusers could not coordinate their strategic decisions at all, resulting in a noncooperative game without resolution.

A law that recognizes the resource's own interest in nonuse may bring about coordination by defining the equilibrium points of the users and nonusers. Recall that coordination facilitates cooperation, and will, in this context, permit the two players to choose strategies that result in a more optimal equilibrium with higher payoffs. And, by creating a focal point, this third party—the natural resource—wields influence on the behavior of the players.[20] However, bargaining under a correlated equilibrium defined by a focal point is guided by each party's expectations of what the other party would accept. Because the well-funded capitalist users are likely to have the strongest bargaining position based on legal resources and political relations, nonusers would require legal clout equal to, if not greater than, the users in order to be able to counteract this user advantage.

Users will likely be in an advantageous bargaining position, and this reality will result in "lopsided" bargain benefitting users over nonusers, even when the resource serves as a focal point as a means to bring about coordination. Accordingly, the concept of the resource-as-focal point, as conceived by Schelling, will likely not be successful as a way to achieve optimality between the human players. Although the usury law structure might in theory appear viable in application, it is unlikely that such laws would be adequately protective of resource interests.

As there appears to be a flaw in application of a resource focal-point model to user-nonuser conflicts, the next section discusses the possibility of other gaming structures in the natural resource use versus nonuse game. These structures continue to apply the concept of *resource legitimization*, but allow the resource itself to function not just as a focal point, but as a fully recognized player in the negotiations.

E. Cooperative Games Where the Resource Has Legal Legitimacy within a Three-Player Grand Coalition

We have considered scenarios in which resource users and nonusers try to cooperate to achieve a Pareto optimal result regarding their divergent interests. Although a two-player coordination game is superior to a noncooperative game, a game between just human users and nonusers does not reflect the interests of all relevant parties. What follows is an exploration of the benefits and pitfalls of allowing the natural resource itself to participate as a legally recognized individualized player in the

[20] McAdams, *supra* note 5, at 228.

game structure. Of course, for this structure to be successfully applied, it would require formal legal acknowledgment of the intrinsic worth of the natural resource.

Imbuing natural resources with their own legal rights that are not derivative of human rights would be unprecedented. The idea of resources having rights would be an extension of conferring standing to animals.[21] Commentators have advocated animal standing by way of protecting social and environmental welfare in those common situations when no human can meet the injury-in-fact requirement of establishing constitutional standing.[22] Commentators have also suggested that natural resources, such as trees, should have standing to assert their own unique nonhomocentric interests.[23] Because humans have typically raised only their own interests that would be benefitted by resource nonuse, natural resources have not had their own nonanthropocentric nonuse interests adequately protected from excessive and destructive human use. Resources should not only have standing to raise their own interests, they should have a substantive right to assert a nonuse interest—the right to be left alone. It is then that the resource game involving user, nonuser, and natural resource can yield an efficient result.

1. GRAND COALITION AMONG PLAYERS

The resource itself may be legitimized and assigned its own legal right, but without some actor to function on its behalf, that legal right is basically useless. Because of this peculiar limitation inherent in a nonverbal resource, all players in a cooperative game may form a coalition that enforces cooperative behavior by way of a common strategy. One may assume in a cooperative game that any group of players may form a coalition. Rational actors, of course, will choose not to engage in a coalition unless it is seen to improve payoffs to its members. Applying a cooperative game structure to a conflict between resource users and humans with a propensity for resource nonuse will lead to a more sustainable result if the natural resource is allowed to participate as a legally legitimized player.

The first step to creating any type of game framework is to identify the parties involved.

Let A represent the resource nonuse interest
Let B represent the user and
Let C represent the natural resource itself.

A functioning coalition relies on two necessary, but not sufficient, conditions: (1) players can reliably make commitments to carry out particular strategies; and

---

[21] Wesley J. Smith, *So Three Cows Walk into Court…*, Weekly Standard, July 20, 2009, at 1: *see also* Stephen R.L. Clark, Animals and Their Moral Standing (1997).

[22] Isa E. Hafalir, *Efficiency in Coalition Games with Externalities*, 61 Games & Econ. Behavior 242, 242–44 (2007).

[23] Christopher D. Stone, Should Trees Have Standing? Toward Legal Rights for Natural Objects (1974). *See also* chapters 17 and 18.

(2) commitments are carried out even when they are suboptimal for a given player. Furthermore, in order to bargain effectively, each of the parties must assess its individual benefits and risks. The sufficient condition reflects a truism: rational participants would only agree to cooperate in a coalition if they perceived a combined bargaining position to be more beneficial than a singular position.

If one applies the concept of coalitions, a Shapley value determines an equitable division of a grand coalition among the user, nonuser, and resource interest.

2. THE SHAPLEY VALUE

Once a coalition among players is formed, one must determine the manner in which to allocate the generated value. Von Neumann and Morgenstern attempted to allocate the value of the grand coalition so that no sub-coalition player could expect to do better alone.[24] However, this outcome is not always possible. Another manner in which to fairly allocate the value of the coalition is to evaluate the expected marginal contribution of each of the players.[25] This is the Shapley value.

The Shapley value determines the payoff share of a party by the contribution that party makes to a "grand coalition." It applies the concept of a transferable utility game in which a grand coalition divides the game's worth.[26] For the Shapley value to function successfully, a coalition must be feasible. Communication among the players must therefore be practicable, and no institutional constraints can exist.[27] For demonstration purposes, assume that communication among the participants (including the legitimized resource interest) is possible and that there are no institutional constraints. There is an obvious pitfall in attempting to realistically apply this model based on this assumption, because the participants in the particular grand coalition are unlikely to bargain among themselves.

Consider the characteristic transferable utility game function:

$$G = (V, N) \text{ where } N = \{1,2,3,4, \ldots, n\}, V{:}2^N \rightarrow IR + (V(\phi) = 0)$$

One should apply the interpretation of V identified by Faruk Gul in his paper studying how an agent holding a resource used in combination with the resources of other agents create value.[28] Within Gul's system each of the players owns a valuable resource, and the different combinations of these resources (termed resource bundles) creates utility according to the function *V*.[29]

---

[24] *See generally* JOHN VON NEUMANN & OSKAR MORGENSTERN, THEORY OF GAMES AND ECONOMIC BEHAVIOR (Princeton University Press 2004) (1944).

[25] U. Faigle & W. Kern, *The Shapley Value for Cooperative Games under Precedence Constraints*, 21 INT'L J. GAME THEORY 249, 250 (1992).

[26] Jean Derks & Hans Peters, *A Shapley Value for Games with Restricted Coalitions*, 21 INT'L J. GAME THEORY 351, 351 (1993).

[27] Gauthier, *supra* note 17.

[28] Faruk Gul, *Bargaining Foundations of Shapley Value*, 57 ECONOMETRICA 81, 82 (1989).

[29] Derks & Peters, *supra* note 26.

In Gul's framework, a random meeting may occur between players and the probability of this meeting is $(2/n_t(n_t-1))$ (n_t represents the number of players in the game at time t).[30] Applying this framework to our model. we can simplify the probability of meeting to be $(2/3(3-1))$ or $1/3$. It ought to be noted that we have eliminated the time element because this is a singular static meeting and we have three identified players in the game (i.e., the nonuse proponents, the use proponents, and the legitimized natural resource). Accordingly, the meeting is no longer random and has a $1/3$ probability of occurring because any of the three players can decide not to cooperate, thereby voiding the entire coalition.

Gul's framework becomes especially useful to our analysis in that it reasons that the resources create streams of utility, "hence, each agent derives $(1 - \delta)V(M)$ from holding the initial resources of the agents in M for one period, where δ denotes the common per period discount factor."[31] According to this model, eliminating the time variable, the utility for Player A, the player representing resource nonuse interest, is:

$$U^A = \Sigma[(1-\delta)V(M^A)-r^A]\delta$$

where $M^A \subset N$ is the player whose initial resources are owned by A after the bargaining process is complete.[32] A's strategy is $\sigma^A \in \Sigma^A$.

Gull's approach concludes that a coalition may be stable if the payoffs constitute "an equilibrium of the associated bargaining game."[33] In other words, use proponents, nonuse proponents, and the resource interest can and will form a stable and reliable coalition when doing so will result in equilibrium under a noncooperative bargaining structure. Therefore, we need only look at the Pareto optimal result of a noncooperative bargaining structure to determine the potential result of the coalition, and then apply the derived Shapley value to split up the coalition's overall worth. Shapley's formula for doing so is:

$$\mathrm{v} = \Sigma_{\mathrm{T}}(\Sigma_{\mathrm{S}\subseteq\mathrm{T}}(-1)^{|\mathrm{T}|-|\mathrm{S}|}\,\mathrm{v}(\mathrm{S}))\,\zeta_{\mathrm{T}}$$

Premised on the assumption that a grand coalition can be formed among the use proponents, nonuse proponents, and resource interest, the Shapley value offers a manner in which to divide the total value of their cooperation. This result, however, is based upon an unreasonable assumption, which is that the three parties would ever willingly form a coalition. The interests of the nonuse proponents—the resource nonuse interest and the resource—are diametrically opposed to that of the users of

[30] *Id.*

[31] *Id.* at 83.

[32] Gul's model incorporates the time variable because he is replicating the functioning of an actual free market with multiple bargaining scenarios. This utility function has been altered so as to represent a one-time bargaining situation.

[33] Derks & Peters, *supra* note 26, at 87.

the resource, making a working coalition unlikely. Furthermore, although we have legitimized the resource, viable means of communication between the resource itself and the use proponents are lacking, especially considering those two parties' opposing goals. Accordingly, the total value of this coalition's cooperation is effectively zero. The following section explores the more likely and more workable coalition between just the nonuse proponents and the resource interest, as well as the operation of this coalition in the overall game with the resource user.

F. The Resource and Resource Nonuser Coalitional Approach

While the human nonusers and the natural resource interest may not have perfect goal alignment, it can be reasonably presumed, and therefore stipulated, that these two players seek similar results in the game. If one assumes that the resource can be legitimized so as to function actively in the game and not simply be represented by nonusers, then nonuse proponents may function on the resource's behalf through a two-party coalition. After establishing the terms of this initial coalition, the nonuse proponents, represented by the nonuse interest and the legitimized resource interest, can then bargain with the use proponents.

1. FORMATION OF THE NONUSE RESOURCE COALITION

In order to conserve and ensure sustainability of the natural environment the resource interest itself must be adequately represented in the natural resources game. The obvious conundrum in such a proposal is how to structure a bargaining model in which the resource interest can sufficiently express itself. One way is to structure a coalition between the nonuse proponents and the resource interest based on the resource interest's own supply function and the nonuse proponents' utility function. This rudimentary framework for such a coalition can later be expanded by exploring more precisely defined variables.

Because the resource interest can be viewed as a producer of goods (i.e., the environmental products that emerge from the resource), it can be represented by a simple supply function:

$$r = E - e$$

Where:
r is the resource interest;
E is the total value of the resource if left alone;[34] and

[34] This value is from the resource's perspective. Therefore, this variable does not consider anthropocentric social welfare gains that would follow if one were to permit resource exploitation. It assumes that the most valuable outcome from the resources perspective would be for it to be left completely alone.

e represents *"pollution,"* which includes not only environmentally detrimental negative externalities, but also simple anthropocentric *use* of the resource.

E, the value of the resource if not used, can be further defined as:

$$E = G + r^\wedge(t/2)$$

Where:

G is a constant that represents the environment as originally endowed at the creation of time;

r is the marginal value of the natural resource that is likely to increase or decrease over time if left alone; and

t is time.

Next we derive the nonuser utility function. We borrow the consumer utility function as proposed by Gregory Chow, who has explained how economic analysis can be applied to understand environmental problems.[35] We adapt it to represent the nonuse proponents in our model. Specifically, let the nonuse proponents have the utility function:

$$\log c + \theta \log(M - e)$$

Where:

c represents the consumption;

e represents pollution, which includes not only environmentally detrimental negative externalities, but also simple human resource use, and M represents more than the maximum amount of resource use that nonusers are willing to tolerate.[36]

According to this utility function, a large value for θ means that pollution is very important when compared to consumption. A large value for e means reduced overall utility. Holding θ constant, a larger M reduces the impact of pollution.

Like Chow, assume consumption equals output (i.e., c = Y) and that use relates to output by e = ayd.[37] The inverse of this equation is Y = Aeδ, with δ = 1/d. Based on these parameters, Chow derives the optimum amount of pollution to be:[38]

$$e = M\delta/(\theta + \delta)$$

Because the nonusers are proponents of environmental nonuse, we can expect the optimum e to decrease with θ because a large θ means nonusers intensely dislike pollution.

---

[35] Gregory C. Chow, *Economic Analysis and Policies for Environmental Problems*, CEPS Working Paper No. 152 (Aug. 2007).

[36] *Id.* at 2–3.

[37] *Id.* at 3.

[38] *Id.*

In his paper, Chow introduces the concept of an all-knowing government or a market economy where consumers have natural capital property rights to achieve the optimum amount of pollution.[39] Although preferable to the current resource market where users and nonusers do battle in court, these solutions may not adequately represent the resource interest. Accordingly, one should apply the legitimized resource interest in a two-party coalition to determine the optimum amount of pollution and resource use.

Based on the optimum amount of pollution from the nonuser's consumption,[40] and with our setting that quantity equal to the amount of pollution represented by the resource interest, the following equation emerges:

$$-r + E = M\delta / (\theta + \delta)$$

When solving for M, which represents the maximum amount of pollution tolerable by the nonusers, we obtain:

$$M = (-r + E)(\theta + \delta) / \delta$$

We now have a value for M that in the resource nonuse coalition represents *both* the interest of the resource and the nonuser. This value can be inputted into the original nonuser utility function ($\log c + \theta \log (M - e)$), making the utility function represent the coalition between the resource interest and nonuser in terms of the maximum amount of pollution that the nonuser is willing to tolerate (this number also represents the amount of pollution the resource interest is willing to tolerate).

2. COORDINATED BARGAINING BETWEEN THE NON-USER COALITION AND THE USE PROPONENTS

That the benefits of a coordinated cooperative bargaining model outweigh the benefits of a noncoordinated bargaining model (i.e., the Stag Hunt Game compared to the Prisoner's Dilemma). The Shadow of the Future concept forces coordination between the parties and takes the bargaining structure being considered from a PD structure to a Stag Hunt structure in which a Pareto optimal cooperative outcome is more likely to occur. Government should be a compelling feature in the resources game, requiring the relevant parties to bargain first, prior to resource use. Use projects should not be undertaken without first coming to an agreement with the coalition of resource nonuse interests. This compulsion forces users and nonusers to be aware of future bargaining situations, making a Pareto optimal coordinated result more likely.

---

[39] *Id.* at 4. *See also* Wade E. Martin and Holly Wise Bender, *Modeling Public Land-Use Decisions as a Cooperative Game*, 12 INT'L J. ENVIRONMENT AND POLLUTION 224–29 (1999).

[40] *Id.* at 39.

Based on the parameters of a bargaining structure where nonusers and the resource itself are aligned, the nonuse proponents and the resource interest's desired output is:

$$Y = Ae\delta, \text{ with } \delta = 1/d$$

Where:

$$e = M\delta/(\theta + \delta)$$

and:

$$M = (-r + E)(\theta + \delta)/\delta$$

Conversely, acting as a profit maximizing entity, the users' production function is the standard profit-maximizing function of:

$$\pi = R - c$$

Where:

$$R = P * Q$$

and:

$$P = MR = MC$$

Pareto Optimality-Obviously, the coalition of nonusers and the resource is attempting to reduce pollution, whereas the users are attempting to maximize profit by reducing costs. Based on the Stag Hunt structure, these parties can coordinate their efforts and perhaps achieve a Pareto optimal result. In this context, the nonuse coalition will be a significant variable cost to the users' production, whereas the users will be a large contributor to the coalitions' pollution concern. Therefore, the Pareto optimal pollution amount will be represented by the equation $M = (-r + E)(\theta + \delta)/\delta$, because this total is the maximum amount of pollution tolerable by the coalition, and most likely represents the lowest cost (regarding pollution) to the profit-seeking user.

Nash Equilibrium-Based on the Stag Hunt model, the bargaining parties may choose not to coordinate efforts but still cooperate. While government is attempting to ensure that the Shadow of the Future concept remains relevant, if the parties see no benefit to coordination, they will simply just cooperate without coordinating strategies. The sacrifice to the user will be that it will not know the maximum amount of pollution tolerable by the coalition, in addition to the opportunity cost of bargaining. The coalition will endure greater costs associated with prolonged bargaining and will risk being forced to concede on its maximum tolerable pollution value. This bargaining scenario will, however, still result in a Nash equilibrium.

Non-Cooperation - The final possibility in this Stag Hunt bargaining structure is for complete noncooperation. However, because government is playing a role in this bargaining model by seeking to force cooperation, the government should act to avoid this result by sanctioning the noncooperating party or parties.

G. Concluding Remarks

A workable and efficient framework for a bargaining situation in the natural resource gone is one in which resource interests are legitimized, and therefore able to participate in the bargaining activities. To achieve such a result, the interest of the resource itself cannot be represented only by nonusers: the interests of the resource itself need to be legitimized. This addition of a third player, the resource itself, is counter to the current bargaining structure, which is typically dominated by human resource users and human nonusers. In order to achieve a Pareto optimal solution, the resource requires its own right, a right of nonuse, so that it can align with human resource nonusers and engage in a bargaining game with resource users where all the pertinent interests are represented.

PART V

Toward a Legally Acknowledged Right of Nonuse

PARTS II, III, AND IV have argued that both social and legal history, as well as the hard disciplines of biology, science, and economics, seem to point toward natural resources being recognized for their inherent nonanthropocentric value. This recognition would, and should, take the form of a legally acknowledged "right," held by the resources themselves, to at times be left alone and free from human interference. As a matter of theory, such a right of nonuse should, when reasonably asserted, bring about some balance to this planet, where resources can compete with an otherwise overwhelming human need to use them. But how might this theory play out in practical terms? The chapters of Part V take up this question, and address the three central issues that a right of nonuse will pose.

First, can legal institutions, particularly regulatory regimes traditionally associated with protecting resources for anthropocentric use or human nonuse purposes, ever be commandeered to protect nonuse values for natural resources? Chapter 16 shows how modern regulations have already started to acknowledge purely ecocentric goals whose aim is not simply to benefit humans. Second, how does one go about creating a legal right for natural resources, and what should be the power of such a right? Chapter 17 explores the parameters of the natural resources that might be provisioned with a legal right, the justifications for such a right, and the limits that would follow if such a right were created. Third, if natural resources are conferred a right of nonuse, how would they be able to assert it? Chapter 18 reviews the law of "standing," which as a matter of generally accepted theory permits *only humans* to assert their own anthropocentric injuries, even when the real or threatened harm is to natural resources. Chapter 18 considers the idea of nonanthropocentric standing, where the party bringing the action is the injured or threatened natural resource itself.

16 The Problem of Government Regulation

THE EMERGING SHIFT FROM ANTHROPOCENTRIC TO ECOCENTRIC NONUSE LAWS

A. Introduction

Traditional land use planning regulations tend to put limits on use of land by owners. Similarly, environmental laws restrict uses of land and nature that cause harm. Both kinds of laws assume that land and natural resources will be used, and the only question is how much to limit the usage and extent of that use. But there is another component of land and environmental use that presumes just the opposite—that resource *nonuse* should also be protected, encouraged, and legitimated. In other words, instead of beginning with the assumption that resource use is the norm, where laws either secure use rights or chip away at only those uses that produce social and environmental costs, one should realize that there is an alternative starting point. In this parallel world, resource and property nonuse has independent value, equally worthy of legal acknowledgement. Such a focus on nonuse would not only be contrary to classic beliefs about the utilitarian role of land, natural resources, and environmental goods, it might also provide a different rationale for the deployment of resource-protective laws. Rather than adopt laws that advance only the human interests that are benefitted when resources are used or not used wisely, we might create legal rules ensuring resource nonuse for more ecocentric values. Those nonuse-protective laws would further the interests of nature that are then allowed to flourish when resources are left alone by humans.

B. Three Tales of Resource Nonuse

In 2009, the U.S. Fish and Wildlife Service was successful in beating back a challenge to its proposed Neches Wildlife Refuge in East Texas. The City of Dallas had wanted to use the site of the refuge as a potential reservoir to serve the growing Dallas/Fort Worth Metroplex. The U.S. Court of Appeals for the Fifth Circuit concluded that the Fish and Wildlife Service had not unconstitutionally invaded a traditional area of state sovereignty in violation of the Tenth Amendment.[1] The site along the upper Neches River, which would have stored water for the burgeoning Dallas/Fort. Worth population, was instead going to retain its native bottomland hardwood forest and wetlands and provide an important wintering habitat for migrating waterfowl.

In 2010, the U.S. Forest Service rejected the Crested Butte Mountain Resort's proposed expansion onto neighboring Snodgrass Mountain. As a result, rather than becoming an extension of the Crested Butte Ski area, Snodgrass Mountain would remain a conifer- and ponderosa-covered Colorado alpine peak.[2] Instead of being festooned with chairlifts, Snodgrass Mountain would be a base for lodgepole pine and winter snow.

Also, in 2010, the Shell Exploration and Production Company dropped a bid for a fifteen-billion-gallon water right on Colorado's Yampa River. This staggering amount of water would have comprised nearly 10 percent of the Yampa River's average spring flow, and would have been shipped to the White River basin for use in Shell's oil shale program. Citing a slowdown in its oil shale development activity, Shell made the business decision to forego its bid for Yampa River water. The news delighted National Park officials because the Yampa flows through Dinosaur National Monument, and Shell's plan would have affected the river's natural peak and low flows.[3]

These three stories mirror the twin themes of this chapter: (1) we increasingly recognize the value of intentional nonuse by humans of natural and environmental resources, and (2) such resource nonuse has worth far beyond the benefit that may be enjoyed by humans; when humans do *not* use resources, the natural world experiences its own nonanthropocentric benefits. In each of the three examples, humans wanted to use a natural resource in some way—to create a reservoir, to expand a ski resort, or to remove water for oil shale development. In each case, as result of a court, a federal agency, or a business decision, the proposed human use of the resource was defeated, neglected, or abandoned, and the resource's nonuse values survived. The site along the Upper Neche River could remain a refuge for wildlife; Snodgrass Mountain trees would grow to maturity and not be cut to create ski slopes, and the water in the Yampa River could still flow through Dinosaur National Monument, with its natural peaks and low flows intact.

---

[1] City of Dallas v. U.S. Dep't of the Interior, 562 F. 3d 712 (5th Cir. 2009).

[2] Jason Blevins, *Crested Butte Resort's Plea Rebuffed*, DENV. POST, May 11, 2010, at 313.

[3] Mark Jaffle, *Shell Drops Bid for Water*, DENV. POST, Feb. 24, 2010, at 513. The page number is A 13.

C. A New and Different Nonuse Paradigm

The fact that these natural resources were spared human use inclinations is a relatively new outcome historically, which may have been driven by a motive that is different from past nonuse decisions. Resource nonuse is a new approach because humans have traditionally viewed nature as an asset to exploit and transform and develop. Over time, it has seemed almost inconceivable that natural resources would have any merit if humans simply left them alone. Moreover, the motive underscoring the absence of human use is also different than past nonuse decisions; instead of counting the ways by which humans would benefit from the nonuse, there is growing recognition that natural conditions have value independent of the value that nonuse has to humans.

Use versus Nonuse—The notion of resources having worth when they are not used is a quite modern development. This country has had a history of aggressive resource usage, which in turn was completely consistent with classical utilitarianism.[4] Utilitarian rationales justified self-interested resource exploitation. All decisions were judged in relation to the general human welfare, where wealth maximization was the primary means of achieving this goal. An unlimited right to exploit nature is in keeping both with the idea of utilizing nature and with enhancing personal wealth and human welfare production.[5] By contrast, stock and renewable commodity resources, such as minerals, coal, timber, fish and wildlife, and land, when left alone, seemed to provide no benefit whatsoever. Utilitarianism flatly rejected the notion that humans could or should have an interest in the preservation of nature.[6]

Of course, a utilitarian-based foundation for natural resource existence meant that resources in America, and elsewhere, would be captured, extracted, developed, and consumed. By the beginning of the 21st century, about 40 percent of the world's land surface had been converted from its natural state to cropland and grazing so as to be a source of food supply for humans.[7] The ocean's aquatic life had been fished and overfished, to the point where the long-term sustainability of the planet's fisheries was now in question.[8] Deforestation throughout the world had removed forest cover and entire ecosystems while adding carbon dioxide emissions.[9]

---

[4] ALASDAIR MACINTYRE, *Reformers, Utilitarians, Idealists, in* A SHORT HISTORY OF ETHICS 227, 232 (1966).

[5] JEREMY BENTHAM, AN INTRODUCTION TO THE PRINCIPLES OF MORALS AND LEGISLATION 11–12 (J.H. Burns & H.L.A. Hart eds. 1970) (1789); RICHARD POSNER, THE ECONOMICS OF JUSTICE 74, 76 (1983). *See generally* THE CLASSICAL UTILITARIANS: BENTHAM AND MILL (John Troyer ed. 2003).

[6] Indira Carr, *Saving the Environment—Does Utilitarianism Provide Justification?*, 12 LEGAL STUD. 92, 94–101 (1992). *See also* Chapters 5 and 9, *supra*.

[7] WORLD RESOURCES INSTITUTE ET AL., WORLD RESOURCES 2005: THE WEALTH OF THE POOR 216 (2005).

[8] Overfishing – Plenty of Fish in the Sea? Not Always, http/:www.ocean.nationalgeographic.com (Dec. 25, 2011); *Extinction on the High Sea*, 277 SCI. 486, 488–9 (1997); Anne Swardson, *Fishing Crisis in the World's Oceans: 90 Nations at U.N. Conference to Consider Limits*, INT'L HERALD TRIB., Aug. 15, 1994.

[9] Shi-Ling Hsu, *The Case for a Carbon Tax 1-2* (2011); THOMAS L. FRIEDMAN, HOT, FLAT, AND CROWDED 148 (2008).

It was inevitable that a utilitarian approach to natural resources management would result in a diminishing and then a non-sustainable supply. The earth's natural resources are in a zero-sum condition: as the world's population grows exponentially, our demand for resources increases, and resource availability falls.[10] And as humans continue to dominate nature, there is a proportional drop in the benefits provided by nature when humans do not use natural resources.[11]

Some degree of resource conservation was inevitable, if humans were to survive. However, in light of this long history of human use, which has characterized the entire scope of human presence on this planet, the idea of intentional nonuse seems both new and almost counterintuitive. Deliberately choosing not to use an available resource seems directly at odds with humanity's tendency to treat the earth and its resources as a pantry, playground, and endless place to dump our waste and garbage.[12] It seems contrary to both human inclination and history that humans would make the decision either to refrain from using available environmental space or to resist exploiting planetary resources. But what is even more unprecedented is an attitude about resource nonuse that fails to reflect normal species chauvinism.[13] The typical anthropocentric assumption is that if resources are not to be used, it had to be because humans would somehow be better off. But what if the nonuse was not to protect or benefit humans, but to benefit nature by protecting it from humans?

Anthropocentric versus Ecocentric Nonuse Laws—Utilitarianism was anthropocentric in that it reflected humankind's interest in using land and the natural environment in order to advance human self-interest (primarily for economic purposes). When humans so overused natural resources that the land and resource base began to contract, and environmental costs began to mount, Americans enacted a number of conservation laws designed to ensure that humans would not exhaust the stock of valuable resources.[14] Then we embraced a number of legal doctrines that restricted private land use, such as zoning codes,[15] the public trust doctrine,[16] and conservation easements.[17] Finally, to protect humans from health hazards associated with

---

[10] Nathan KeyFitz, *The Growing Human Population*, SCI. AM. 119 (Sept. 1989).

[11] Peter M. Vitousek, Harold A. Mooney, Jane Lubchenco & Jerry M. Maelillo, *Human Domination of the Earth's Ecosystems*, 277 SCI. 494 (July 25, 1997). *See* Chapter 13, *supra*.

[12] TOM HAYDEN, THE LOST GOSPEL OF THE EARTH; A CALL FOR RENEWING NATURE, SPIRIT, AND POLITICS (2006).

[13] Richard Routley & Val Routley, *Human Chauvinism and Environmental Ethics*, *in* ENVT. PHILOSOPHY 96, 136 (Don Mannison et al. eds. 1980).

[14] For example, to regulate the deforestation of America's forest, the United States enacted these timber conservation laws: the Organic Act of 1897, 15 U.S.C. § 473; the Multiple Use Sustained Yield Act of 1960, 16 U.S.C. § 528–531; and the National Forest Management Act, 16 U.S.C. § 1600–1614 (1979).

[15] *See, e.g.*, Village of Euclid v. Ambler Realty Co., 272 U.S. 365 (1926).

[16] Illinois Cent. R.R. Co. v. Illinois, 146 U.S. 387 (1892).

[17] Jean Hocker, *Land Trusts: Key Elements in the Struggle against Sprawl*, 15 NATURAL RES. & ENV'T 244 (2001).

unchecked use of the environment as a repository for our emissions, we adopted antipollution regulations.[18]

Although all of these legal devices halted untrammeled land and resource use, they did so for the same reason—to somehow benefit *humans* who would otherwise be harmed by the particular use contemplated. The same anthropocentricism that originally drove utilitarian decisions (and laws) has now inspired various nonuse policies. This attitude, however, may slowly be changing. Decisions by courts, government agencies, and corporations are beginning to reflect another different nonuse rationale,[19] one that rejects a restrictive definition of value in terms of utility only for humans. This different nonuse paradigm acknowledges an intrinsic value of nature, apart from and not dependent on the worth imparted to natural objects and natural resources by humans.[20] When humans do not use natural resources, when nature is left alone, or when humans have such de minimus contact that the resource mimics its value in the absence of humans, there is benefit beyond human interest in the nonuse. This nonanthropocentric interest in resource nonuse is critical for humans to recognize because it adds yet another layer of justification for nonuse when humans are considering whether to use land or natural resources.

The idea that nonanthropocentric interests have merit in their own right is not new. For many years some environmental ethicists have expressed the view that all living things, not just humans, have inherent worth.[21] Moreover, this belief holds that no species or living organism is special or superior, including humans. Some have even taken the view that the concept of nonanthropocentrism encompasses the assumption that all things in nature, living or nonliving, have intrinsic instrumental value.[22] It follows that from this ecocentric perceptive that we occupy no privileged place in nature; humans are no longer seen as "apart from nature," but simply as "a part of nature."[23]

If resource nonuse has enjoyed legal stature and legitimacy when nonutilitarianism serves human ends, then the next step in protecting nonuse values is to acknowledge as a matter of law that land and environmental resources may have intrinsic,

---

[18] W. Paul Gormley, *The Legal Obligation of the International Community to Guarantee a Pure and Decent Environment: The Expansion of Human Rights Norms*, 3 GEO. INT'L ENVTL. L. REV. 85 (1990). See generally, Part III of this book, particularly chapters 9 and 10.

[19] *See supra* notes 1–3 and accompanying text.

[20] *See* MARK SAGOFF, PRICE, PRINCIPLE, AND THE ENVIRONMENT 2 (2004) ("there is an important difference between saying something is good for me, and something is good in itself . . . or good because of its intrinsic qualities.").

[21] *Anthropocentric vs. Non-Anthropocentric Environmental Ethics* (Paul Taylor—Biocentric Egalitarianism), http://ocw.capcollege.bc.ea/philosophy/phil-208-environmentalethics/non-anthropocentric (2007) (*Anthropocentric* v. *Non-Anthropocentric*).

[22] ECCY DE JONGE, SPINOZA AND DEEP ECOLOGY 15–29 (2004).

[23] Bill Devall, *The Deep Ecology Movement*, in ECOLOGY 132–34 (Carolyn Merchanet ed. 1999). Nonanthropocentric environmentalism is frequently called "deep ecology." Arne Naess, *The Shallow and the Deep, Long-Range Ecology Movement. A Summary*, 16 INQUIRY 95 (1973) (Deep ecology takes a nonanthropocentric approach to land and environmentalism whereas "shallow" ecology assumes a traditional anthropocentric approach). See also Chapter 17, *infra*.

purely ecocentric value when humans leave them alone. Legal recognition of an ecocentric nonuse approach can occur either by imposing *duties* on humans to override purely utilitarian considerations and preserve the intrinsic worth of land and resources,[24] or by granting *rights* to resources themselves, to be raised when humans threaten to alter resources in an unused, natural condition.[25] It is appropriate to critically examine this potentially game-changing shift in the law, because both a duty to protect resource nonuse values and right of nonuse held exclusively by the resource will have important implications for those wishing to use land and resources.

D. Anthropogenic Nonuse as a Protected Right

The idea of land and resource nonuse is not a new concept among local planners and regulators.[26] In zoning and land use protocols, requirements for residential and commercial nonuse of space and land are common. Courts have long recognized that governmental impositions of setback requirements on land development for aesthetic and safety reasons is an appropriate, noncompensable exercise of the police power.[27] Similarly, height restrictions are considered acceptable as a matter of both law and taste.[28] Setbacks and height restrictions prevent maximum economic use of land surface and airspace, but such nonuse is seen as furthering various public functions—such as safety and psychological health—and are therefore commonplace. Similarly, open and green space laws have been a feature of city and county planning for decades.[29] These land-and-space nonuse laws have been seen as providing real economic benefits to nearby property owners; property values tend to rise near unused natural parcels, and communities tout open space as an alternative to urban sprawl and a reason to resettle or transfer there.[30]

Both land trusts and land conservations transactions also represent ways to protect natural resources from traditional use interests. Land trusts permit organizations to purchase land and interests in land to preserve ecological communities and historic sites in order to benefit those who value natural scenery and unused resources.[31]

---

[24] John Chipman Gray, The Nature and Sources of Law 43–45 (2d ed. 1963); Robert Elliot, *Environmental Ethics*, in A Companion to Ethics 284 (Pete Singe ed. 1993).

[25] Christopher D. Stone, Should Trees Have Standing? Law, Morality and the Environment (3d. ed. 2010).

[26] G. Cornelius Van Kooten & Erwin H. Bulte, The Economics of Nature: Managing Biological Assets (2000); John Randolph, Environmental Land Use Planning and Management (2003).

[27] Goreib v. Fox, 274 U.S. 603 (1927); *In re* Letourneau, 726 A. 2d 31 (Vt. 1998).

[28] Welch v. Swasey, 214 U.S. 91 (1909); Thompson v. City of Denver, 958 P. 2d 525 (Colo. 1998).

[29] Joseph Arnold, The New Deal in the Suburbs: A History of the Greenbelt Town Program (1971).

[30] William R. Travis, David M. Theobold & Daniel B. Fagre, *Transforming the Rockies: Human Forces, Settlement Patterns, and Ecosystem Effects*, in Rocky Mountain Futures: An Ecological Perspective 1–2, 16 (Jill S. Baron ed. 2002).

[31] Hocker, *supra note 17*.

Because land trusts usually required their owners to buy land they wished to preserve, most state laws now recognize an alternative route to land and resource nonuse that does not necessitate purchase and acquisition of the fee simple—conservation easements. These negative servitudes allow an owner of land to transfer to another the right to prevent the owner (and all its successors in title) from taking specific use actions on the land, such as subdivision, construction, or resource extraction. Like land trusts, most conservation easements are created to "protect . . . natural, scenic, or open-space value of [human-owned] real property."[32] Both legal inventions preserve land because humans are seen to derive some personal pleasure in the nonuse of a particular space.

On a national level, the U.S. Congress has adopted legislation that enshrines large areas for nonuse. Federal statutes acknowledge that humans in America can and do derive satisfaction from land and natural resources without actually directly using them. National monuments are created by the Antiquities Act of 1906, which permits the president of the United States to designate parcels of land for federal protection if they are deemed to be "objects of historic or scientific interest.[33] The National Park Service Organic Act of 1916 conserves as national parks "scenery and the natural and historic objects and the wildlife therein' so that they will be 'unimpaired for the enjoyment of future generations."[34] Many national forests have their nonuse potential preserved as federal wilderness areas, "roadless" areas, or wilderness study areas that may qualify for future wilderness designations.[35] Federal land under the control of the U.S. Bureau of Land Management may similarly be set aside as wilderness study areas where their nonuse potential is preserved by a management directive ordering the BLM to "not . . . impair their suitability for wilderness."[36] When the Federal Wilderness Act was passed in 1964, Congress was more concerned about the anthropocentric virutes of wild lands rather than the benefits yielded from conserving nature for nature's sake.[37]

Even certain constitutions seem to embrace nonuse attributes by disallowing uses of the environment that produce harm to human health. The Montana constitution gives to all persons a constitutional and "inalienable . . . right to a clean and healthful environment."[38] The Chilean constitution provides to its citizens a "right to live in an environment free from contamination."[39] The Indian Supreme Court has stated in dicta that the people of India have a right "to live in [a] healthy environment"[40] These constitutional provisions and judicial statements suggest that resource nonuse

[32] Uniform Conservation Easement Act, § 1 (1) [Definitions].

[33] 16 U.S.C. § 431.

[34] 16 U.S.C. § 1.

[35] 43 U.S.C. § 1131 *et. seq.*

[36] 43 U.S.C. § 1782 (c).

[37] Sandra Zellmer, *A Preservation Paradox: Political Prestidigitation and an Enduring Resource of Wilderness*, 34 Envtl. L. 1015, 1040 (2004).

[38] Mont. Const. art. II, § 3.

[39] Constitución Potítica de la República de Chile [C.P.] art. 19(8).

[40] A.I.R. 1985 S.C. 652, 656.

should be preferred (or mandated) when use of the environment produces pollution or negative externalities that are deleterious to human welfare, especially human health.

E. The Surprising Reality behind Resource Nonuse Laws

Although the law books and regulations are full of requirements commanding the nonuse of land and resources in order to protect them, a closer examination of these laws reveals that often the policy underlying the rule assumes (1) some use of the resource (2) the maximization of the welfare of humans who benefit from an altered use of the resource. In other words, seemingly nonuse decisions are embodied in law because humans can use the ancillary benefits that flow from these decisions.

1. NONUSE AS USE

A glance at federal public land law statutes suggests that what might appear to be a congressional statement about the virtues of nonuse may in fact belie an intent to continue resource use, albeit with a uniquely anthropocentric focus. Take, for example, the Organic Act of 1897,[41] a response to the pleas of conservationists for greater protective measures for federally owned forest land, which had been decimated by indiscriminate timber cutting.[42] Legislative debates show that Congress did not intend for the new national forests to be preservationist reserves; indeed, "[t]hey are not parks set aside for nonuse, but have been established for economic reasons."[43] The U.S. Supreme Court later concurred when it stated in *United States v. New Mexico*[44] that "[n]ational forests were not to be reserved for aesthetic, environmental, recreational or wildlife-preservation purposes."

Similarly, when decades of unregulated livestock grazing damaged the public rangelands, Congress responded by enacting the Taylor Grazing Act of 1934.[45] One of its central purposes was "to preserve the land and its resources from injury due to overgrazing."[46] However, when a modern Secretary of Interior, Bruce Babbitt, created a "conservation use rule" authorizing the placement of some overgrazed land in a "non-use" category, the courts invalidated this action: "This [the non-use category] is an impermissible exercise of the Secretary's authority.... Congress intended [in the Taylor Grazing Act] that once the Secretary [has] established a grazing district... the primary use of that land should be grazing."[47]

---

[41] 16 U.S.C. § 473 *et seq.*

[42] J. Ise, The United States Forest Policy 62–118 (1972).

[43] 30 Cong. Rec. 966 (1897) (Cong. McRae).

[44] 438 U.S. 696, 707 (1978).

[45] 43 U.S.C. § 315.

[46] Public Lands Council v. Babbitt, 167 F. 3d 1287, 1290 (10th Cir. 1999), *rev'd on other grounds*, 529 U.S. 728 (2000).

[47] *Id.* at 1308–09.

Apart from statutes, significant environmental policy drivers also presume the value of natural resources when they are used. The concepts of "ecosystem services" and "natural capital" are grounded in the realization that when natural ecosystems are permitted to flourish, they provide valuable, and even quantifiable, utilitarian services.[48] These ecosystem services are thought to be embedded in the human economy—there is no known substitute for them at any price, and humans cannot live without them. The accompanying school of ecological economics believes that if natural capital is properly harnessed, and ecosystem services appropriately valued, then not only will the biosphere be protected, but profits and productivity will rise.[49] Both ideas—ecosystem services and natural capital—start with the same premise: If natural resources are not overused by humans, these resources perform services that are enormously useful to humans.

2. ANTHROPOCENTRIC NONUSE

The second truth about laws requiring land and resource nonuse is that when there is a decision not to use resources, that decision is inevitably motivated by the needs and wants of humans, not the environment. The concern addressed in these laws is not that the resource itself may be impaired or destroyed by use: the rationale for the nonuse rule is either that (1) humans will be harmed by the resource use, or (2) humans will benefit from the resource's nonuse.

Both land-use ethics and earlier land-reforms call for land practices that are primarily anthropocentric. They demand a change in our behavior so as to prevent harm to humans. In the past, land degradation caused by destructive agricultural activities or unsightly urban sprawl brought about laws to reduce the distribution of *bads*, or hazards to the health and safety of humans.[50] Environmental pollution has similarly been seen historically as primarily a threat to humans, and not to the air, water, or land that was being contaminated. The driving force behind environmental laws, constitutional provisions, and international resolutions has been the protection of the physical and mental well-being of humans.[51]

---

[48] Robert Costanza et al., *The Value of the World's Ecosystem Services and Natural Capital*, 387 NATURE 253 (1997); GRETCHEN DAILY, NATURE'S SERVICES: SOCIETAL DEPENDENCE ON NATURAL ECOSYSTEMS (1997).

[49] ROBERT COSTANZA ET AL., AN INTRODUCTION TO ECOLOGICAL ECONOMICS 77–83 (1997); AMORY B. LOVINS, L. HUNTER LOVINS & PAUL HAWKEN, *A Road Map for Natural Capitalism*, *in* HARVARD BUSINESS REVIEW ON GREEN BUSINESS STRATEGY 65–69 (2007).

[50] TIMOTHY BEATLEY, ETHICAL LAND USE: PRINCIPLES OF POLICY AND PLANNING 3–4 (1994).

[51] G.A. Res. 2398 (IX), GAOR 23d Sess., Supp. No. 21, at 2, Dec. 3, 1968., *reprinted in* I INTERNATIONAL PROTECTION OF THE ENVIRONMENT 99 (Bernd Ruster & Bruno Simma eds.) ("concerned about the consequent effects of [pollution] on the condition of man, his physical mental and social well-being"); Susan Emmenegger & Axel Tschentscher, *Taking Nature's Rights Seriously: The Long Way to Biocentrism in Environmental Law*, 6 GEO. INT'L ENVTL. L. REV. 545, 550–55 (1994) ("immediate human self-interest" was the early anthropocentric rationale for environmental protection); CONSTITUCION POLITICA DE COLOMBIA [C.P.] art. 79, *translated in* 4 CONSTITUTIONS OF THE COUNTRIES OF THE WORLD 20 (Rudiger Wolfrum & Rainer Grote eds. 2005).

Broad official pronouncements about why nature should be protected typically explain that it is, in fact, human welfare that justifies resource nonuse policies. For example, one can compare Principles #7 and #1 from the United Nations Conference on Environment and Development of 1992 ("The Rio Declaration"). Principle #7 requires that member "[s]tates shall cooperate . . . to conserve, protect and restore the health and integrity of the Earth's ecosystems." Principle #1 explains why: "Human Beings are at the centre. . . . They are entitled to a healthy and productive life in harmony with nature." American law tracks this anthropocentric focus. The National Environmental Policy Act (NEPA) recognizes "that each person should enjoy a healthful environment."[52] The Forest Service"s Organic Act reserved national forests "to furnish a continuous supply of timber for the people."[53] Although resource nonuse (or regulated resource use) is definitely embodied in positive law, it is apparent that most of these laws justify these limits in very anthropocentric, almost hedonistic terms. Moreover, when nonuse is expected or mandated, the resource itself has no legal rights; only the people who are the beneficiaries of the nonuse decision have the legal ability to halt resource exploitive actions.

F. The Limits of Protecting only Anthropogenic Interests

1. THE BACA NATIONAL WILDLIFE REFUGE

Laws typically protect the human-driven use, or nonuse, interests in natural resources. The most obvious value of land and resource is the value that is derived from *using* the natural world for direct human benefit, usually economic. As noted above, certain resource *nonuse* functions are also considered valuable to humans—there are health advantages to ridding land, water, and air of pollution, and there are measurable economic attributes that are enjoyed by humans when ecosystem services and natural capital are preserved.[54] But we universally ignore, or discount, the nonuse potential inherent in the nonanthropocentric worth of natural resources. In other words, when land and resources are neither affirmatively used by humans, nor desired by humans when they are in a nonuse state, we tend to forget that these resources still have worth and value.

A lawsuit involving the Baca National Wildlife Refuge in southern Colorado illustrates the three different ways that a natural resource has a human use value, an anthropocentric nonuse value, and an otherwise forgotten purely ecocentric nonuse function. Surprisingly, mineral exploration and development is permitted in wildlife refuges so long as wildlife habitat is protected.[55] In the Baca National Wildlife Refuge, Lexam Explorations, Inc. has valid mineral rights, worth almost $10 million.

---

[52] 42 U.S.C. § 4331(c).

[53] United States v. New Mexico, 438 U.S. 696, 707 (1978).

[54] J.B. Ruhl, Steven E. Kraft & Christopher L. Lant, The Law and Policy of Ecosystem Services 6 (2007) (global ecosystem services have been estimated to be over $30 trillion).

[55] Watt v. Alaska, 451 U.S. 259 (1981).

The U.S. Fish and Wildlife Service had approved Lexam's plan to drill for oil and gas there, to exploit the land's *use* value.[56]

The Baca National Wildlife Refuge is itself part of the National Wildlife Refuge System (NWRS). The NWRS is not a pure wildlife resource preservation system. Rather, wildlife refuges are managed "for the conservation . . . of the fish, wildlife and plant resources and their habitat . . . for the benefit of present and future generations."[57] These "present and future generations" are allowed many human use activities in wildlife refuges, where "wildlife-dependent recreational uses" receive the highest priority. Among these very human-centric uses include "hunting, fishing, wildlife observation and photography."[58] Because it is part of the Refuge System, the Baca National Wildlife Refuge may be protected from the Lexam Corporation's resource use plans to drill there for oil and gas because the *anthropomorphic nonuse* value of this refuge benefits the "generations" who can enjoy the resource's "wildlife-dependent recreational uses."

Conservation groups sued based on a *nonanthropocentric* nonuse interest to block Lexam's plans to drill. The lawsuit claimed that drilling for energy minerals there would irreparably harm the refuge because it is the home to several colonies of Gunnison prairie dogs, a candidate species for the endangered species list.[59] These prairie dogs do not directly benefit humans. Their continued existence provides ecocentric value, however. If they become extinct because Lexam's resource use activities destroy them, then their role in the ecosystem of the Baca National Wildlife Refuge will be extinguished forever. The prairie dogs facilitate access of water to the water table, protect against erosion, and mitigate soil compacting resulting from grazing.[60] In other words, the prairie dogs perform a strictly ecological role when the wildlife refuge is not only not used by Lexam, but when its nonuse benefits flow to the refuge's ecosystem, and not the humans who wish to take advantage of the refuge's "wildlife-dependent recreational uses."

The lawsuit against the Lexam Corporation's drilling activities is not intended to halt a business wishing to extract use value from the Baca National Wildlife Refuge in order for humans to enjoy an anthropocentric benefit that will follow from the refuge's nonuse by Lexam. Instead, the lawsuit is designed to protect the purely ecocentric nonuse values that will continue if Lexam's use interests in the resource are successfully enjoined. As such, the litigation over this wildlife refuge is one of the rare examples of where the legal system has to consider whether a natural resource's nonuse value for *non*anthropocentric purposes outweighs its obvious and measurable use value as a source for energy minerals.

[56] Judith Kohler, *Deal Pending in Refuge—Drilling Suit, Group Says*, The Denver Post 6B (June 21, 2010).

[57] 16 U.S.C. § 668 dd (a)(2).

[58] 16 U.S.C. § 668dd(a)(4)(5).

[59] Judith Kohler, *Deal Would Block Drilling on Refuge*, Denv. Post, June 22, 2010, at 2B.

[60] John Hoogland, Conservation of the Black-Tailed Prairie Dog: Saving North America's Western Grasslands (2005).

2. ANTHROPOCENTRIC VERSUS ECOCENTRIC NONUSE VALUE

One attractive quality of anthropocentric nonuse value is that it is possible to measure the benefit to humans in not using a natural resource. Natural capital and ecosystem services worldwide are thought to be worth $30 trillion—these are the economic benefits that accrue to humans from maintaining land and resources in a natural, unused condition.[61] By contrast, it is difficult, if not impossible, to place some quantitative value that accrues to nature if a resource is not directly used by humans. Even the U.S. Supreme Court has, in apparent frustration, characterized such "non-use benefits" to be "of indeterminate value."[62] As a result, both land-use laws and resources policies tend to be primarily anthropocentric—they demand a change in our resource use behavior either to prevent harm to humans or bring about benefits for people. Nonanthropocentric, or ecocentric, approaches to natural resources create legal and moral imperatives not for the sake of human well-being alone, but also for the good of the land as a whole, apart from human interests. Although humans are included in the biosphere, legal rules restricting resource use that are directed at maximizing the good of the whole biosphere would not necessarily be the same as anthropocentric regulations that attempt to benefit the welfare of only one subset of inhabitants of the biosphere—humans.[63]

Because land and natural resources are not seen as having any intrinsic value that is independent of human use or nonuse value, humans are viewed as being a special, superior role with respect to land and resource regulation. Because humans are usually deemed superior to, and functionally elevated above, the land or resource that is the subject of the law, the legal rule providing protection from use tends to focus only on the anthropomorphic dimensions of the natural resource. The purely ecocentric components of the resource are either ignored or marginalized.

But is this assumption true—do humans occupy a privileged place in nature? If the contrary is the case, if human interests count for no more than the interests of any other living thing, system, or resource found in nature, then it follows that the interests and needs of nonanthropomorphic components of the world should also be taken into account when resource use decisions are being made.[64] The Baca National Wildlife Refuge should be protected from the Lexam Corporation's drilling operations not only because such resource use will harm human recreational interest in the refuge, but because those operations might adversely affect and even wipe out the endangered Gunnison prairie dog.

Anthropomorphism that advocates resource nonuse also may be faulted because it presumes that what is best for humans is the best for the resource being protected. However, the interest of humans and a natural resource are not always synonymous,

---

[61] ROBERT COSTANZA ET AL., *supra* note 38.

[62] Entergy Corp. v. Riverkeeper, Inc., 129 S. Ct. 1498, 1509 (2009).

[63] Kristin Shrader-Frechette, *Four Land Ethics: An Overview*, *in* LYNTON K. CALDWELL & KRISTIN SHRADER-FRECHETTE, POLICY FOR LAND: LAW AND ETHICS 57–58 (1993).

[64] Mary Anne Warren, *The Rights of the NonHuman World, in Environmental Philosophy: A Collection of Readings* (R. Elliot & A. Gare eds. 1983).

especially if policy makers are advancing a regulatory use regime that seeks to prevent only uses that harm humans. If an ecosystem is preserved only up to the point that humans may enjoy the economic benefits of ecosystem services, then that may not be the same nonuse point that the ecosystem needs in order to function as an integral part of the larger biosphere. Furthermore, if the focus is primarily resource nonuse to ensure the quality of human health, substantial environmental degradation can occur before there is harm to any human.[65] These nonanthropocentric virtues of nonuse can only be protected if the law recognizes the intrinsic worth of land and natural resources in an unused condition irrespective of any human interest.

G. Recognition of Nonanthropocentric Values in Resource Nonuse Laws

There appears to be a need to rethink the usual ways by which we interrelate with land and natural resources. First, we need to consider that the planet's resources are not present simply to be actively used by humans, either as a commodity to extract and develop or as a garbage dump for our wastes. Resources also have significant nonuse value, and this nonuse quality is in some ways as important as the resource's use function. Second, when land and natural resources are required by the law to remain unused (e.g., as open space or wilderness), or when harmful uses are prohibited (e.g., by antipollution laws), the motivation for these rules is almost always anthropocentric. The nonuse is designed, and eventually adopted, to benefit humans.

Nonuse policies motivated by nonanthropocentric interests are the exception. However, as noted above, when land and natural resources are left alone, the primary beneficiary is the planet. Its processes can function properly, and naturally, when the focus is not just the human-centric interests that enjoy the benefits of land and resources that are in a natural state. When the focus of legal rules is on the ecocentric interests that flourish in the absence of human beings, then the planet as a whole benefits, and so too do humans, because they are one of many occupiers of the planet.

Despite the relative rarity of policies that support or require nonanthropocentric nonuse values, there are some notable examples of such laws in America and elsewhere. The federal Endangered Species Act (ESA)[66] is the most familiar and heralded statute whose primary purpose is not to benefit humans, but to protect living things that inhabit the planet's biosphere alongside humans. The objective of the ESA is "to provide a means whereby the ecosystems upon which endangered species and threatened species depend may be conserved."[67] The Act does not state or imply that the ultimate motivation for the law is the value that humans experience when

[65] Judith I. McGeary, *A Scientific Approach to Protecting Biodiversity*, 14 J. NAT. RESOURCES & ENVTL. L. 85, 92 (1999).

[66] 16 U.S.C. § 1531 *et seq.*

[67] *Id.* at § 1531(b).

species do not become extinct; rather, the survival of plant and animal species is an end in itself, irrespective of any "existence value" that humans may experience knowing that a species, otherwise threatened with extinction, now survives.

Another federal statute that prioritizes the conservation of wildlife is the National Wildlife Refuge System Improvement Act of 1997.[68] Apart from the ESA, this is the only federal land management statute that places nonhuman interests at the forefront of its agenda. Although it is true, as noted above, that the entire National Refuge System was created "for the benefit of present and future generations,"[69] the highest priority within refuges is wildlife conservation. This fact has meant that nonuse of wildlife is always preferred over human uses of land that may interfere with the wildlife's nonuse value.[70]

Perhaps the most striking example of legislative and executive protection of nonanthropocentric values is found in a wildlife refuge at the very northernmost tip of the United States. The Alaska National Wildlife Refuge (ANWR) consists of 19 million acres in a location that is virtually inaccessible to most human populations. According to the U.S. Geological Survey, there may be over 10 billion barrels of recoverable oil there, making ANWR a natural resource rich in use potential.[71] However, the primary nonuse purpose for the establishment of ANWR is to conserve populations of fish, wildlife, and natural habitats.[72] This nonuse purpose has been deemed by the Ninth Circuit Court of Appeals to be more powerful than the obvious use values located in ANWR, even though there are marginal anthropocentric reasons for protecting remote musk ox, porcupine caribou, and polar bears.[73]

One purely environmental protection statute, the Comprehensive Environmental Response, Compensation and Liability Act (CERCLA),[74] contains a powerful provision protecting the nonuse value of natural resources. CERCLA makes parties responsible for land or resource contamination liable for "damages for injury to, destruction of, or loss of natural resources."[75] The words *natural resources* are broadly defined to include "land, fish, wildlife, biota, air, water. . . ."[76] Such natural resources damages claims are designed to restore nature to the same kind of not-used state it was in before humans dumped hazardous substances there.[77]

International law similarly supports the notion that nature has worth in an unused condition, where that nonuse value is not dependent on the instrumental function of untouched nature for humankind. In 1982, the General Assembly of the United Nations adopted the World Charter for Nature, which includes the provision that

---

[68] 16 U.S.C. §§ 668dd–668ee.

[69] *Id.* at § 668dd(a)(2).

[70] Wilderness Society v. Babbitt, 5 F. 3d 383 (9th Cir. 1993). (cattle grazing must give way to wildlife welfare).

[71] Kenneth Bird, *U.S. Geological Survey: Fact Sheet* 2005 (May 2005), http://pubs.usgs.gov/fs/2005/3043.

[72] Alaska National Interest Lands Conservation Act of 1980, 94 Stat. 2371, 2384 (1980).

[73] Alaska Wilderness League v. Kempthorne, 559 F. 3d 916 (9th Cir. 2009).

[74] .42 U.S.C. § 9601.

[75] *Id.* at § 9607(a)(4)(c).

[76] *Id.* at § 9601(16).

[77] Ohio v. Dep't of Interior, 880 F. 2d 432 (D. C. Cir. 1989).

"every form of life is unique, warranting respect regardless of its worth to man."[78] Ten years later, in 1992, the United Nations approved the Convention on Biological Diversity. The preamble to this document decreed that the signatory countries were "conscious of the intrinsic value of biological diversity."[79] Biocentric and ecocentric laws are emerging; there is slow but steady recognition that nonused land and natural resources are critical to the planet for nonanthropomorphic intrinsic reasons.

H. Some Concluding Thoughts

We must face the sad reality that our current system of laws does not necessarily protect, or even address, a significant component of land and natural resources—the value provided to the ecological health of the planet, irrespective of humans, when nature is not used, when it is left alone. Laws tend to favor the use dimensions of land and resources, and when nonuse is protected, the motive inevitably is anthropomorphic. Put another way, if resource nonuse benefits humans, it is only then that legal systems typically acknowledge a countervailing nonuse right that could supersede otherwise dominant use interests.

If nonanthropocentric nonuse values are to be recognized, the looming question is: How should legal rules reflect this new purely ecocentric interest? This question is huge, and it is discussed more fully below in chapters 17 and 18.[80] Some tentative models, advanced primarily by academics, have been discussed previously in this book in Part III, Chapter 12.

One possibility would empower private parties to act as private attorneys general to enforce public environmental actions directed at safeguarding ecological health.[81] The public trust doctrine might be also expanded to allow states to protect ecocentric interests.[82] Alternatively, states may have *parens patriae* standing to pursue common law public nuisance claims in the interest of protecting their natural resources.[83] Some commentators have even suggested that the concept of private property should be modified so that owners have a duty to consider the nonanthropocentric values inherent in their property when making decisions affecting their land or natural resources.[84]

---

[78] World Charter for Nature, G.A. Res. 3717, U.N. GAOR, 37th Sess., Supp. No. 51, pmbl. Para 3 (a) at 17, U. N. Doc. A/37/51 (1982).

[79] United Nations Environment Programme Convention on Biological Diversity 5 (June 1992).

[80] *See, e.g.*, Burns H. Weston & Tracy Bach, Recalibrating the Law of Humans with the Laws of Nature: Climate Change, Human Rights, and Intergenerational Justice (2009).

[81] William B. Rubenstein, *On What a Private Attorney General Is—And Why It Matters*, 57 Vand. L. Rev. 2129 (2004); Barton H. Thompson, Jr., *The Continuing Innovation of Citizen Enforcement*, 2000 U. Ill. L. Rev. 185 (2000).

[82] Robin Kundis Craig, *A Comparative Guide to the Western States' Public Trust Doctrines: Public Values, Private Rights, and the Evolution toward an Ecological Public Trust*, 37 Ecology L.Q. 53 (2010).

[83] Connecticut v. Am. Elec. Power Co., Inc., 582 F. 3d 309 (2d Cir. 2009*), rev'd* American Electric Power, Inc. v. Connecticut, 131 S. Ct. 2527 (2011).

[84] Eric T. FreyFogle, *Property and Liberty*, 34 Harv. Envtl. L. Rev. 75 (2010).

The most dramatic, and possibly the most efficient legal change, would be to give land and natural resources their own legal rights. Under this model, resources would have the ability to enforce ecocentric nonuse values, irrespective of the consequences of such enforcement actions on any human. If lawsuits were brought, the suit would be in the name of the land or resource, damages would be calculated by loss to that component of nature bringing the suit, and any judgment would be for the benefit of the land and the natural resource, not the humans affected thereby.[85] Such a right of nonuse, held by the resource, would certainly mark a new age of land and resource protection. With current legal regimes seemingly powerless in the face of global climate change and mounting environmental catastrophes, perhaps that new age's time has come.

---

[85] STONE, *note* 25, at xii.

17 The Problem of Rights Creation

CAN NATURAL RESOURCES HAVE LEGAL RIGHTS?

THE CENTRAL ARGUMENT of this book is that natural resources should be protected by conferring on them a legally cognizable "right of nonuse." Such a right would legitimate the nonuse component of natural resources. This nonuse part of resources permits all natural organisms and entities to thrive, evolve, or play some role in the environmental health of this planet, *independent of value to humans*. In the absence of a right of nonuse, natural resources are, and have been, exploited, exhausted, polluted, and otherwise *used* in some way by humans. To prevent the depletion, degradation, or eventual demise of natural resources, it has been argued in these pages that something dramatic is now needed for the planet's resources—(1) an acknowledgement that resources perform a critical function for the earth apart from human benefit when humans do not use them, and (2) a grant of legal empowerment to resources so that they may affirmatively assert, from time to time, a legal right not to be used by humans.

However, the creation of a right of nonuse, held by natural resources, assumes that nature is capable of possessing a legal right that is not derivative of some human right. It also assumes that one would be able to determine which parts of nature could and should have rights. And, even if a non-human-centric right could in theory exist, and even if one could decide which assets of nature should hold the right, one would then need to decide the underpinnings, source, and scope of such a right. Questions that come to mind about a legal right of nonuse include the following: Why should this right exist, and what would be its source? What nonuse rights would natural resources have, and what would be the effect on the exercise of traditional human use rights if the nonuse right were asserted? Would humans have a concomitant *duty* to protect nonuse rights, or would the natural resource simply have a *right* not to be used by humans?

To address these issues, one must first consider the relatively recent field of *environmental ethics*—theories of moral philosophy concerning nonhuman nature. The topic of environmental ethics is consistent with one of the central themes of this book, which is that humans are not necessarily the only components of the earth that are inherently valuable and worthy of some measure of legal protection. Rather, nonhuman entities and natural objects free from human interference are also intrinsically important to the existence and survival of this planet, and hence are deserving of legal recognition (and rights) *irrespective of human needs and wants.*

Second, one must also take into account theories of *political and legal morality.* This discipline asks the fundamental, and difficult, questions about rights creation. Although most of the thinking and writing about rights have been done in relation to legal rights, with those rights being for humans, the normative standards advanced for humans have relevance also to the many nonanthropocentric dimensions of the natural world.

Section A takes up the idea of environmental ethics, and applies its teaching to the theme of this book—that natural resources are capable of being protected by right of nonuse. In this section we will review the reasons rights creation has historically been human-centric, and then summarize the countervailing argument advanced by environmental ethics, which is that there is intrinsic value in nonhuman natural entities. These objects morally and ethically also deserve legal recognition and protection. Section A then asks and answers these important questions: Can rights be granted to anyone other than humans? Which entities of nature can have rights? Should the focus be on the obligations of humans to nature, or on the original rights of nature? Section B considers the larger issue of how the law, and legal institutions, might create a right of nonuse, held by natural resources, consistent with established theories of political and legal morality.

A. A Right of Nonuse and Environmental Ethics

1. THE WESTERN TRADITION OF ANTHROPOCENTRIC ETHICS

The history of the Western intellectual and ethical tradition has been primarily anthropocentric—centered on humans exclusively. Moral philosophy has focused on human culture, not wild nature, as yet unaffected by humans wishing to use natural resources. To the extent Western ethics contemplated nature at all, it was to justify and encourage humans to exploit it.[1] It was thought that humans were destined to transform nature, because in so doing they would change and better themselves.[2] Natural resources and ecological systems should be protected only if the preservation

[1] John Passmore, Attitudes in Nature, In Nature and Conduct 259 (R.S. Peters ed. 1975).

[2] David Rothenberg, Hands End: Technology and the Limits of Nature 19 (1993).

of nature was beneficial to humans.[3] In other words, nature and natural resource were thought not to have intrinsic value, but rather only instrumental or derivative value.

For centuries, anthropocentric philosophical and religious thought held that only human beings had any intrinsic worth, whereas nature, being nonhuman, had value just for its ability to serve human ends.[4] This utilitarian view of natural resources viewed human interests as paramount,[5] such that human needs always overwhelmed the needs or interests of anything found in nature. When there was a conflict between human desires and nonanthropocentric values, the hierarchical balance ensured that human interests prevailed.[6] The only obligation that humans had to nature was occasionally to preserve it on aesthetic grounds because humans benefit when surrounded by natural beauty.[7] Such anthropocentrism was at the heart of the Rio Declaration of 1992, when as part of the United Nations Conference on Environment and Development, Principle I was that "[h]uman beings are at the centre of concerns for sustainable development."[8]

2. ENVIRONMENTAL ETHICS AS AN ALTERNATIVE TO ANTHROPOCENTRISM

By the later part of the 20th century, moral philosophers and ethicists began questioning the validity of anthropocentrism. Some wondered why humans were the only living organisms worthy of independent value. As environmentalism revealed the human dependence on nature and ecological systems, a new moral philosophy emerged—environmental ethics—that was premised on two assumptions: (1) Nature also has intrinsic, not just instrumentalist, value; and (2) humans, as moral agents, have obligations to natural nonanthropomorphic entities, and not only to other humans. The class of entities worthy of moral consideration could not be limited to just one species, *Homo sapiens*. Indeed, perhaps natural organisms and resources that were not even living also deserved to be recognized and protected.[9]

In 1972, two important events occurred that were to cast doubt about traditional human-centric thought and have long-lasting influences among ethicists. Arne Naess delivered a lecture at the Third World Future Research conference during which he argued for a concept he called "deep ecology." The concept of deep ecology was a realization that environmental issues should not just be framed in terms of human efforts (i.e., "shallow ecology"); instead, thought Naess, nonanthropocentric

---

[3] John O'Neill, *The Varieties of Intrinsic Value*, 75 MONIST 119–38 (1992).

[4] J. Baird Callicott, *Non-anthropocentric Value Theory and Environmental Ethics*, 21 AM. PHILOSOPHICAL Q. 299 (Oct. 1984).

[5] DONALD K. ANTON & DINAH L. SHELTON, ENVIRONMENTAL PROTECTION AND HUMAN RIGHTS (2011); JOHN PASSMORE, MAN'S RESPONSIBILITY FOR NATURE: ECOLOGICAL PROBLEMS AND WESTERN TRADITIONS 187 (1974).

[6] Donald Van De Veer, *Interspecific Justice*, 22 INQUIRY 72–73 (Summer 1979).

[7] EUGENE C. HARGROVE, FOUNDATIONS OF ENVIRONMENTAL ETHICS 191–98 (1989).

[8] U.N. Doc. A/Conf. 151/26; 31I.L.M. 874 (1992).

[9] *See, e.g.*, Holmes Rolston III, *Is There an Ecological Ethic?*, 85 ETHICS 98 (1975).

nonhuman natural resources were deemed also to have inherent, noninstrumentalist value.[10] Second, Professor Christopher Store published a law review article, famously entitled "Should Trees Have Standing?,"[11] which argued that existing and forthcoming legal environmental principles be expanded to cover nonhuman natural objects.[12]

Other philosophers soon joined in, challenging the traditional tendency of humans to make normative judgments about nonhuman nature. Some called this historic anthropocentric approach "homocentric imperialism"[13] or "species chauvinism."[14] Many embraced a purely nonanthropocentric theory where all living things, not just humans, were said to have intrinsic value independent of human existence.[15] Yet even this theory of biocentrism was seen by some to be too confining. They instead expanded nonanthropocentrism to include ecosystemic wholes—ecocentrism—which found intrinsic value in natural resources and ecological systems, living or otherwise, that provided the necessary framework for life to flourish.[16] This nonanthropocentric approach, which finds worth in all natural resources and systems in which they exist, was partially endorsed in the beginning of the United Nations Charter for Nature in 1982. This Charter stated: "Every form of life is unique, warranting respect regardless of its worth to man." But, whether nonanthropocentric theories are biocentric or ecocentric, one question remains, which is: Should the use of legal rights be given to anyone, or any thing, other than humans?

3. THE PROBLEM OF NATURE'S RIGHTS

One difficulty facing nonanthropocentrists is that nonhuman living organisms, as well as nonliving natural resources, do not have free will as humans do. These parts of nature cannot usually make choices that determine their fate or shape their identity.[17] As a result, moral philosophers and ethicists have argued that such nonhuman

---

[10] Naess published his lecture in 1973: Arne Naess, *The Shallow and the Deep, Long-Range Ecology Movement: A Summary*, in 16 INQUIRY 95–100 (1973).

[11] Christopher Stone, *Should Trees Have Standing? Toward Legal Rights for Natural Objects*, 45 SO. CAL. L. REV. 450 (1972).

[12] Stone's article was referenced by Justice William O. Douglas in his dissent in Sierra Club v. Morton, 405 U.S. 727 (1972), where he concurred that "protecting nature's ecological equilibrium should lead to the conferral of standing upon environmental objects to sue for their own preservation." *Id.* at 743. Justice Douglas went on to state that "valleys, alpine meadows, rivers, lakes, estuaries, beaches, ridges, and groups of trees, swampland, on even air" should be able to challenge "the destructive pressures of modern technology and modern life."

[13] John R. Rodman, *The Liberation of Nature*, 20 INQUIRY. 83, 87 (1977).

[14] Alan Boyle, *Human Rights or Environmental Rights? A Reassement*, 18 FORDHAM ENVT'L L. REV. 471, 484 (2007).

[15] Richard Sylvan [Routley], *Is There a Need For a New Environmental Ethic?*, PROCEEDINGS OF THE XV WORLD CONGRESS OF PHILOSOPHY 205–210 (1993); HOLMES ROLSTON III, ENVIRONMENTAL ETHICS: DUTIES TO AND VALUES IN THE NATURAL WORLD (1998).

[16] J. BAIRD CALLICOTT, IN DEFENSE OF THE LAND ETHIC: ESSAYS IN ENVIRONMENTAL PHILOSOPHY (1989); ALDO LEOPOLD, A SAND COUNTY ALMANAC AND SKETCHES HERE AND THERE (1949).

[17] ROLSTON, *supra* note 15, at 68.

natural entities are not moral agents and therefore legal rights cannot be assigned to them.[18] Consistent with this view, the prerequisite of a right is some measure of cognitive awareness, or reflective capacity about one's own good, and this quality belongs only to humans, not plants, nonliving natural resources, and ecological systems.[19] Accordingly, because natural resources do not have the capacity to have rights, any nonanthropocentric approach must focus on human duties toward nature rather than the rights of nature.

There are, however, powerful refutations of the notion that nonhuman entities are incapable of possessing rights. Restricting rights to living beings who are aware of their interests would make it conceptually impossible to accord any rights to late-term fetuses, newborns, or humans who cannot speak intelligibly on their own behalf in court.[20] Moreover, if capacity to understand or rudimentary cognitive awareness is a precondition to the conferring of legal rights, then irreversibly injured "vegetating" humans cannot have rights, which is inconsistent with most rights approaches at a moral and international level.[21] Moreover, a natural resource will not be seen to have value for itself, independent of human instrumentalist value, until humans agree to give it rights.[22]

4. WHICH PARTS OF NATURE SHOULD HAVE RIGHTS?

Even if nonhuman entities of nature are conceptually capable of having rights on their own, another issue that arises is deciding what is "nature" and which of its many components are deserving of, or appropriate for, legal rights. If one is prepared to conclude that rights are not exclusively anthropocentric, then the forms of nonhuman entities that are potentially able to have rights include: (1) sentient living animals, that is to say, animals capable of conscious thought and feelings, such as dogs or dolphins;[23] (2) all animals, from whales to cockroaches to protozoa;[24] (3) all living things, including plants (biocentrism);[25] (4) all parts of non-human-built wild nature, irrespective of whether it is living (deep ecology, which would include rocks,

---

[18] Joel Feinberg, *The Rights of Animals, and Unborn Generations*, *in* PHILOSOPHY AND ENVIRONMENTAL CRISIS 46–51 (William T. Blackstone ed. 1974); RODERICK FRAZIER NASH, THE RIGHTS OF NATURE: A HISTORY OF ENVIRONMENTAL ETHICS 126 (1989); H.L.A. HART, ESSAYS ON BENTHAM 185 (1982).

[19] JOHN STUART MILL, NATURE, THE UTILITY OF RELIGION, AND THEISM (1874); WILLIAM A. EDMUNDSON, AN INTRODUCTION TO RIGHTS (2nd ed., 2012); Leif Weinan & Stephen Macedo, *The Diversity of Rights in Contemporary Ethical and Political Thought*, *in* THE NATURE OF RIGHTS AT THE AMERICAN FOUNDING AND BEYOND 286 (B. Shain ed. 2009).

[20] Stone, *supra* note 11, at 488–89.

[21] JOEL FEINBERG, RIGHTS, JUSTICE, AND THE BOUNDS OF LIBERTY 159–84 (1980). *See also* KENT GREENAWALT, RELIGIOUS CONVICTIONS AND POLITICAL CHOICE, chs. 6 &7 (1998) (borderlines of rights status include fetuses, animals, and even vegetation and inanimate matter).

[22] Stone, *supra* note 11, at 456.

[23] PETER SINGER, ANIMAL LIBERATION (2002).

[24] TOM REGAN, THE CASE FOR ANIMAL RIGHTS (2nd ed. 2004).

[25] PAUL W. TAYLOR, RESPECT FOR NATURE: A THEORY OF ENVIRONMENTAL ETHICS (1986).

mountains, and lakes);[26] and (5) all of the preceding parts of nature *and* the systems of nature, such as ecosystems, that permit life to first arise and then flourish (ecocentric holism).[27]

Not only must the debate over nature's rights concede and resolve the matter of *which* entities of nature have the capacity for rights, but it must also address the ethical question of *equality* of moral worth. For example, if one espouses a purely biocentric view, which posits an ethic centered only on living beings, then the issue is whether all living beings, from humans to one-celled organisms, have equal value.[28] The problem with such a biocentric egalitarianism is that it ignores that one form of life, humans, has a near limitless capacity to negatively alter things such as the earth. Humans cause the extinction of species and change the earth's ecology. No other species is as destructive to the planet's natural health as humans, so all living species cannot be equal in terms of their effect on the planet's survival as a source of life.[29]

Nor are all living things equal in terms of how they are programmed to live their life. The protozoan that causes malaria, as well as the mosquito that transmits the malaria parasite, infect and kill humans by the very act of carrying out their normal life functions. If all living things are equal in terms of moral worth, then is it impermissible for humans to protect themselves against such harmful organisms by destroying them? These kinds of objections to biocentric egalitarianism have led to an alternative ethic—hierarchical biocentrism—which both acknowledges an ontological divide between human and nonhuman living organisms and asserts that while all biota have intrinsic value, they are not equal in intrinsic value.[30]

Another critical debate concerning equality within nature's parts involves the issue of whether individual organisms and natural resources should be thought of as having intrinsic value (and rights), or whether an organism or resource has value only to the extent it contributes to the overall integrity, stability, and sustainability of the larger community or system in which it exists. If environmental ethics locates ultimate value in the ecosystem as a whole, then one does not accord equal moral worth to every part of the whole; only those individual resources that benefit the ecosystemic whole have value. If a natural resource or individual organism imperils the whole, then those individuals have negative value.[31] Consistent with this view,

[26] Arne Naess, *The Deep Ecology Movement: Some Philosophical Aspects*, 8 PHILOSOPHICAL INQUIRY 10 (1986).

[27] CALLICOTT, *supra* note 16; LEOPOLD, *supra* note 16.

[28] BILL DEVALL & GEORGE SESIONS, DEEP ECOLOGY: LIVING AS IF NATURE MATTERED (1985); Paul Taylor, *The Ethics of Respect for Nature*, 3 ENVTL. ETHICS 197 (Fall 1981).

[29] Richard A. Watson, *A Critique of Anti-Anthropocentric Biocentrism*, 5 ENVTL. ETHICS 245, 253 (Fall 1983). *See also* Elizabeth Weise, *Higher Temps Push Species Northward or to Higher Ground*, USA TODAY, Aug. 19, 2011, at 6A).

[30] Warwick Fox, *Transpersonal Ecology and Transpersonal Psychology*, in TOWARD A TRANSPERSONAL ECOLOGY: DEVELOPING NEW FOUNDATIONS FOR ENVIRONMENTALISM 197–215 (1990); Frederick Ferré, *Persons in Nature: Toward an Applicable and Unified Environmental Ethics*, 1 ETHICS & ENV'T 15 (1996).

[31] CALLICOTT, *supra* note 16, at 25, 28.

sometimes referred to as ecocentric holism, rights should be assigned not to individual natural resources, but to ecological wholes.[32]

5. NATURE'S RIGHTS VERSUS HUMAN DUTIES TO NATURE

Once environmental ethics made the moral leap beyond anthropocentrism, it meant that nonhuman natural entities had intrinsic worth and humans had a philosophic choice: Did humans have duties toward nature, or did nature have original rights?[33] Although the difference between duties and rights will be explored more thoroughly in section B, below, it is useful to summarize some of the critical differences between the two approaches. It is helpful to also explain why when a right of nonuse, held by natural resources, is compared to a human-duties-to-nature-concept, it is more closely linked to the assumption that nature has intrinsic value.

First, one should realize that to acknowledge human duties to nature does not therefore mean that nature has correlative rights that flow from these duties. On the other hand, if nature has a right of nonuse, humans have a duty to respect that right, although the right might need to be asserted before the duty is triggered.[34] Second, environmental ethics is premised on the notion that humans are *moral agents*, and as moral agents (1) they are aware of the fact that they have moral obligations, and (2) they have obligations to entities in nature other than humans.[35] This duty is grounded on the status of natural resources possessing inherent worth. However, if the only protection afforded nature is that humans have some kind of duty to it, then the only recourse for nature when it is threatened by human use-of-nature decisions is to allege that there has been a failure to perform a duty. If nature has a right of nonuse, it would become the subject of the protection provided by the right, rather than an object of human consideration in the context of a duty to nature.[36]

There are two other differences between human duties and rights of nature that suggest that the latter is preferable. If humans have some duty to nature, then it will be important to impose real restrictions around the extent and scope of this obligation. Otherwise, some humans may believe they have been sanctioned to engage in ecological sabotage in order to prevent wilderness destruction, deforestation, or decreasing species. Groups such as Greenpeace and Earth First! might assume that a human duty to nature necessarily means that direct action is thereby justified.[37] However, the paramilitarism of ecological sabotage is often more criminal than civil. Moreover, sabotage for ecological ends seems closer to terrorism than civil disobedience.[38] A second argument favoring a rights approach is that a duties concept continues to revolve around humans. A right of nonuse held by nature's

---

[32] Naess, *supra* note 26; CALLICOTT, *supra* note 16; LEOPOLD, *supra* note 16.

[33] Robert Elliot, *Environmental Ethics*, *in* A COMPANION TO ETHICS 284 (Pete Singer ed. 1993).

[34] Weinan & Macedo, *supra* note 19, at 296; *Feinberg*, supra note 18, at 45.

[35] TAYLOR, *supra* note 25, at 13.

[36] Stone, *supra* note 11, at 456, 488.

[37] Dave Foreman, *Earth First!*, 45 PROGRESSIVE 39 (Oct. 1981).

[38] Eugene Hangrove, *Ecological Sabotage: Pranks or Terrorism?*, 4 ENVTL. ETHICS 291 (Winter 1982).

components places the focus not on humans, but on the intrinsic worth of a natural entity that may now assert its own right to be left alone.

B. The Creation and Nature of a Right of Nonuse

1. THE SOURCE OF NATURE'S RIGHTS

If nature is to be given rights, especially a right of nonuse (i.e., a right held by natural resources not to be used by humans), then what would be the source of such a right? Although scholars do not agree where rights come from, there are perhaps three possible sources: (1) contractual rights (a product of a mutual agreement), (2) created rights (an act of positive law designed to create entitlements for identified groups or entities), and (3) natural rights (inherent rights).[39] Of the three, natural rights seem most akin to the theoretical conception of nature's rights discussed in section A. Natural rights consist of entitlements and protections held by the recipient of the right simply by virtue of their fact of existence. Nature preceded humans, and nature is the precondition to humans; nature, in a prehuman state, was the reason that humans could arise and evolve. It follows then that if humans have rights simply because of their inherent nature as human beings, then that which was, and is, responsible for human existence—nature—should have rights, too.[40]

Indeed, one theoretical justification for presuming that humans have "natural" rights is to posit that rights should be recognized that existed in a "state of nature." By imagining how humans would exist in such a state (e.g., no one, or no group of humans, would have obvious title to rule others) one can postulate a consequential right (e.g., humans should have equal rights).[41] Similarly, in a prehuman world, nature, natural resources, and systems of nature were able to create, over time, the virtual Garden of Eden (compared to other planets) that permitted *Homo sapiens* to initially evolve. Those same natural entities should now have a right, derived from natural law, to protect that natural status that existed before humans began to systemically and relentlessly destroy it.

2. THE RIGHTS OF NATURE

If nature has rights, and if those rights have as their source natural law, then what are those rights? This interesting question is in turn answered by considering the equally interesting, and fundamental, question: What is a "right"? A right granted by nature is bipolar: it is both permission to do a range of things that the right-holder is able to do, *and* it is also the right not to do something.[42] In the case of natural resources,

---

[39] RAYMOND WHITING, A NATURAL RIGHT TO DIE 52 (2002) (quoting from Alasdair MacIntyre).

[40] Weinar & Macedo, *supra* note 19, at 286.

[41] Henry C. Mansfield, Jr., *Responsibility versus Self Expression, in* OLD RIGHTS AND NEW 97 (Robert A. Licht 1993).

[42] *Id.*

the right of nonuse would be the right not to be used by humans. This division of roles is sometimes thought of as between rights that are positive and those that are negative. Negative rights are the classic rights against interference—the right to be free from certain kinds of acts by other humans or government.[43] Ronald Dworkin argues, for example, that when we say that something or someone has a right to do something, what we are really saying is that it would be wrong for the government, or individuals, to interfere with that something or someone doing it.[44] Positive rights require that government provide methods and services for the right-holder to benefit from and by the right.[45] But, whereas nature's rights demand protection, the provisioning by government should not just be patronizing, such that the rights of nature are intended mainly, or entirely, for human benefit.[46]

What would then be the positive and negative rights of nature? If one were to analogize to the rights held by humans, one sees that there is general agreement that among these rights are (1) a right to life; (2) a right of personal protection; (3) a right to liberty; and (4) a right to not just hold these in the abstract, but also to secure these rights from a government.[47] The first three of these are "negative" rights in the sense that they may be raised by natural resources when humans seek to interfere with them when exercising their right to use the resource. The last is "positive" because the government must procure it.

As applied to the right of nonuse, one can argue, first, that living natural resources would hold a biocentric right to live when confronted with human actions that seek to destroy that which is alive in nature. A right to personal protection would be an ecocentric right held by all resources, living or otherwise, to be protected from certain human use decisions that would destroy the resource's nonuse component. A right to liberty would be another ecocentric right to be able to perform ecosystem or planetary services that the resource otherwise supplies in the absence of human intervention. And a right to secure some measure of assistance from government would be both the granting to natural resoources a right of nonuse by positive law as well as the establishment of some way for resources to assert that right before legal institutions when that right is threatened. The next chapter considers mechanisms for resources to assert their own rights.

3. WHAT IS A "RIGHT" COMPARED TO A "DUTY"?

If natural resources are granted a right of nonuse, which is a legally recognized right to not be used by humans, then the right will be most significant with respect to

---

[43] *Id.* ("Rights are rights against the interference of other human beings, not against the motions of nature.")

[44] RONALD DWORKIN, TAKING RIGHTS SERIOUSLY 188–89 (1978).

[45] STEPHEN HOLMES & CASS SUNSTEIN, THE COST OF RIGHTS: WHY LIBERTY DEPENDS ON TAXES 46 (1999).

[46] Mansfield, *supra* note 41, at 105–06.

[47] William A. Galston, *Between Philosophy and History - The Evolution of Rights in American Thought, in* OLD RIGHTS AND NEW, *supra* note 41, at 68–69. *See also* STEPHEN HOLMES, BENJAMIN CONSTANT AND THE MAKING OF MODERN LIBERALISM, chs. 1–2 (1984).

resolving the central conflict between these two parties: natural resources and humans. These two are the relevant players in the resources game because natural resources have experienced anthropocentric degradation of their "nonuse" component. Nonuse is the part of a natural resource that benefits the planet as a whole when the resource is not being exploited or transformed by humans. Nonuse does not necessarily benefit the utilitarian needs and interest of humans. The resource "use" component is what historically has been the central focus of humans, not the resource's nonuse dimension.

Take the case of natural grasslands for example. When *not* used by humans, grasslands perform significant ecological functions that do not have direct bearing on humans, such as the prevention of soil erosion and the creation of wildlife habitat.[48] By contrast, humans have traditionally ignored the nonuse component and viewed grasslands as valuable primarily for its use component—cattle and sheep grazing. When humans overwork this grasslands use component, the nonuse component is adversely affected, and the result can be ecological catastrophe.[49]

Granting natural resources a right of nonuse that may be asserted in the face of human use desires creates a classic Hohfeldian rights-duty dichotomy between natural resources and humans.[50] This dichotomy is revealed after a rigorous examination of this phrase:

"Natural Resources (NR) have a right to non-use (X) with respect to humans (H)."

If NR have a right (X) that affects H, then the right may convey any (combination) of the following Hohfeldian meanings:

1. NR's right to X means that H has a *duty* to let NR do, or benefit from, X. The existence of such a duty means that humans must let natural resources enjoy their nonuse component when resources assert the nonuse right. This view of the right of nonuse is consistent with Jeremy Betham's account of legal rights. Betham said that an entity (such as the natural resource) can be said to have a right if someone else (e.g., humans) has a duty to either perform some act, or not undertake an act (e.g., do not use the resource), which is in the right-holder's interest.[51]
2. NR's right to X means that NR has the *power* to alter existing legal relations when X is exercised. If NR asserts the right to X, it may bring about a change in legal relations between H and NR. Without X, NR may have been powerless

---

[48] NATURAL GRASSLANDS MANAGEMENT: A PRIMER, Natural Resources Division, Office of General Counsel, U.S. Dept. of Agriculture (Nov. 1997).

[49] W. GARD, FRONTIER JUSTICE 81–149 (1949) (overgrazing of grasslands in the early 20th century left vast landscapes in a devastated condition with severe damage to forage, soils, and habitat).

[50] WESLEY N. HOHFELD, FUNDAMENTAL LEGAL CONCEPTIONS AS APPLIED IN JUDICIAL REASONING (1919). *See also* JOEL FEINBERG, SOCIAL PHILOSOPHY, ch. 4 (1973).

[51] H.L.A. Hart, *Bentham on Legal Rights*, in OXFORD ESSAYS IN JURISPRUDENCE, 2d series 171–79 (A.W.B. Simpson ed. 1973).

to prevent H from exercising various legally acknowledged use rights over NR. By asserting X, NR can affect those use rights held by H.[52]

3. If NR's right to X ends up as a constitutional right, then X is not only an expression of a power, it may also connote an *immunity* from legal change. If NR has an immunity with regard to X, then H lacks the power to alter H's legal position with respect to X. A natural resource's right of nonuse, and the human duty to respect that right when humans wish to raise use interests, would then be immune from alteration.[53]

4. THE LEGAL FORCE OF A NATURE-HELD RIGHT OF NONUSE.

Rights are provided, granted, or recognized because they have strength and peremptory character; when exercised they dominate subordinate interests or claims. In the case of a right of nonuse held by natural resources, the obvious question that arises is the extent to which that right should dominate the traditional contrary right, held by humans, to use natural resources.[54] If, for example, a human has a private property right in a wetlands, and if that human right-holder wishes to dredge and fill that wetlands, what would happen if the wetlands itself had a right of nonuse?[55] Could the wetlands assert that nonuse right so as to prevent the exercise of the human use right?

Rights-based theories have distinguished three ways in which the special weight of rights may be understood. Each model offers a different answer to the question of what follows when the exercise of one right, such as nature's right of nonuse, conflicts with the exercise of another right, such as a human's right of use. The implication of each should be considered if a right of nonuse is to be recognized for natural resources.

1. The first model holds that the right is nothing more than an important interest, which as a matter of law needs to be considered before there can be an exercise of a countervailing right. The right is assigned no greater weight than other conflicting interests. The purpose of the right is simply to ensure that it is *taken into account* before one asserts a parallel and possibly contrary right. This is the kind of right held by the "human environment" within the

[52] A human use right may be affected by the assertion of a nonuse right in several ways. The use may be studied, delayed, conditioned, scaled back, or perhaps even halted.

[53] *See* JEREMY WALDRON, THEORIES OF RIGHTS 5–7 (1984).

[54] As discussed in section A(4) above, it would have to be determined if "natural resources" holding a right of nonuse need to be sentient animals, any animal, anything living, any part of non-human-built wild nature, or just one of the systems of nature.

[55] In addition to taking into account a right of nonuse theoretically held by the wetlands, if the wetlands were considered "waters of the United States" under the Clean Water Act, the private property owner would also have to receive a "Section 404" dredge and fill permit from the U.S. Army Corps of Engineers. 33 U.S.C. § 1344.

National Environmental Policy Act.[56] This statute creates a right in the human environment but only requires that federal agencies contemplating some action at least consider the impact of the proposed action on these environmental interests. If the agency engages in adequate consideration, the proposed action can still occur, even if it has an adverse impact on the "human environment."[57] Under this first model it would be sufficient if the property owner merely considered the effect of dredging on the wetland's nonuse rights.

2. In the second model, the interests protected by the right are given priority, or preference, over other interests.[58] However, the right is *not* absolute. It is only to be protected and promoted to the extent possible after balancing and taking into consideration interests that may be contrary to the right. This "*balancing of interests*" judgment would be done by some official decision maker, a court or a special agency or tribunal. If the interests of the right-holder prevail, the right can then halt the exercise of a countervailing right.[59] Consistent with this second model, the wetland's right of nonuse would be able to prevent the property owner's dredging operation after a court or some other official tribunal determined that nature's nonuse value outweighed the human use value of the dredged and filled wetlands.
3. The final, and most extreme, model is one where the right is not just considered or balanced, but where its exercise is the basis for constraining action or preventing altogether certain decisions. Such rights are *absolute* in that they sharply define the borders of another's action that might affect the right.[60] In the unlikely event that this third model was adopted, the wetlands confronted by the prospect of being dredged could raise its right of nonuse to prevent that human use, and the human would-be wetlands user would have no recourse.

[56] 42 U.S.C. §§ 4331–4370.

[57] Robertson v. Methow Valley Citizen Council, 490 U.S. 332, 350–51 (1989) ("NEPA merely prohibits uninformed—rather than unwise—agency action").

[58] *See, e.g.*, John Rawls, A Theory of Justice 42–45 (1971).

[59] *See, e.g.*, Robert Nozick, Anarchy, State and Utopia 28 (1974).

[60] Alan Gewirth, *Are There Any Absolute Rights?*, in Waldron, *supra* note 53, at 91; Nozick, *supra* note 59, at 28–51.

18 The Problem of Standing

MAY NATURAL RESOURCES RAISE THEIR OWN RIGHT OF NONUSE?

IN ORDER FOR natural resources to assert for themselves a right of nonuse, two prerequisites are required: (1) the natural resource must have a legally cognizable right—either by statute or some other positive law; and (2) the courts must recognize that the underlying injury need not be to a human, but can be to the natural resource itself. The process of how legal rights and remedies might be defined for natural resources was discussed in the Chapter 17. It was determined that the legal right of nonuse should be for, and held by, the natural resource. The location of the right should be within, and the beneficiary of the right would be, the natural resource itself. The natural resource should be able to assert its own intrinsic value, and not simply have an interest that is derivative of some human right to nonused resources.

There is, of course, already considerable environmental protective legislation in the United States, primarily at the federal level, but also at a state and even municipal level. But most such environmental legislation, such as the Clean Air Act, the Clean Water Act, or even the Endangered Species Act, was created with human interests in mind. As a result, only humans have standing to bring lawsuits adjudicating their rights to an environment that is not being used as a garbage dump, or that is free of activities that wipe out habitat, landscapes, and species.

This chapter seeks to establish that, in the United States, a standing test for natural resource protection should not necessarily be based only in terms of an *injury* to a human being. In federal courts, the Article III "case or controversy" requirement has demanded that the judiciary be confronted with an injury that is experienced by a *human* (or a "person") before a right can be asserted. In state courts there is a similar anthropocentric bias for plaintiffs that are human, and who have been injured.

Rather than require humans to demonstrate their uniquely human injury in order to raise the rights of a natural resource, it should be acceptable for a natural resource to allege that its own cognizable right of nonuse has been violated, and to show that it (and not a human) has suffered an injury-in-fact, which in turn permits it to assert its rights in court.

A. The Traditional Anthropocentric Approach to Standing

The concept of standing, as a threshold jurisdictional element, requires a litigant to show an entitlement to judicial action that is separate from proving the substantive merits of the claim advanced. However, this need for plaintiff standing did not exist in American jurisprudence until the 20th century. In the 1920s, the U.S. Supreme Court decided two critical cases, holding that individual citizens could not challenge the constitutionality of statutes unless they held a *personal stake* in their implementation.[1] That personal stake constituted standing to be the plaintiff. For federal courts, the Supreme Court grounded this requirement in the Article III "case or controversy" language of the Constitution. This requirement for a real "case" involving an underlying "controversy" acts as a restraint on the federal judiciary, allowing it to determine only specific disputes affecting individuals seeking redress for their injuries. It also ensures a proper separation of powers.[2] If a plaintiff in federal court lacks Article III standing, Congress may not confer standing by statute.

Standing in state courts does not have the same Article III limitations. As a result, the requirements to establish standing in a state court vary by jurisdiction. Although state courts may impose their own standing rules,[3] most follow the federal requirement that the plaintiff demonstrate some harm to the plaintiff's legal interests.[4]

---

[1] Fairchild v. Hughes, 258 U.S. 126, 129 (1922); Massachusetts v. Mellon, 262 U.S. 447 487–89 (1923). *See also* Bradley S. Clanton, *Standing and the English Prerogative Writs: The Original Understanding*, 63 BROOK. L. REV. 1001 (1997).

[2] Arizona Christian Sch. Tuition Org. v. Winn, 131 S. Ct. 1436, 1442 (2011) ("For the federal courts to decide questions of law arising outside of cases and controversies would be inimical to the Constitution's democratic character. And the resulting conflict between the judicial and the political branches would not, in the long run, be beneficial to either.") (internal quotation marks omitted).

[3] *See* Lansing Schs. Educ. Ass'n v. Lansing Bd. of Educ., 792 N.W.2d 686, 699 (Mich. 2010) ("Michigan Constitution's reference to the judicial power does not inherently incorporate the federal case-or-controversy requirement, and . . . importing this requirement is inconsistent with this Court's historical view of its own powers and the scope of the standing doctrine."); Sierra Club v. Dep't of Transp., 167 P.3d 292, 311 (Haw. 2007) ("the courts of Hawaii are not subject to a 'cases or controversies' limitation like that imposed upon the federal judiciary by Article III"); Provo City Corp. v. Willden, 768 P.2d 455, 456 (Utah 1989) ("the federal rules of standing . . . are not binding on state courts").

[4] *See, e.g.,* Neeley v. West Orange-Cove Consol. Indep. Sch. Dist., 176 S.W.3d 746, 774 (Tex. 2005) ("we may look to the similar federal standing requirements for guidance").

1. THE LUJAN STANDING TEST

The modern, and most restrictive, test for standing in federal courts was announced by the Supreme Court in an opinion by Justice Scalia in *Lujan v. Defenders of Wildlife*.[5] The *Lujan* standing test requires a litigant to show (1) an injury-in-fact, which is concrete and particularized, and is either actual or imminent;[6] (2) causation or traceability; and (3) redressability.[7] The "injury-in-fact" requirement has been the biggest obstacle for establishing standing in environmental litigation because the Supreme Court and lower courts have focused their inquiry on whether human plaintiffs have suffered an injury as a result of alleged harm to the environment, rather than focusing on the injury to the environment itself.[8] In addition, the Court has held that the injury-in-fact has to be to the party bringing the lawsuit, and cannot be asserted on behalf of others.[9]

The Supreme Court has effectively concluded that only persons who have suffered some demonstrable injury to themselves can establish standing. As a result, natural resources, environmental goods, entities in nature, and animals cannot themselves seek redress in federal courts for their injuries because they cannot establish Article III standing under the traditional standing doctrine. Instead, human plaintiffs have to bring claims alleging anthropocentric injury before a court will hear these human litigators make arguments on behalf of the natural entity that is being threatened or that is harmed. This requirement of human injury extends to actions seeking injunctions for protection of natural resources. Plaintiffs would have to assert actual and

[5] 504 U.S. 555 (1992). Cass R. Sunstein, *What's Standing after* Lujan? *Of Citizen Suits, "Injuries," and Article III*, 91 MICH. L. REV. 163 (1992).

[6] New York Reg'l Interconnect, Inc. v. FERC, 634 F.3d 581, 586 (D.C. Cir. 2011) ("the irreducible constitutional minimum of standing [is that] . . . a petitioner must show an actual or imminent injury in fact . . . [where] an injury in fact is an invasion of a legally protected interest which is . . . particularized, . . . [i.e.] it affects the plaintiff in a personal and individual way") (internal quotation marks and citations omitted).

[7] 504 U.S. at 562.

[8] Summers v. Earth Island Inst., 129 S. Ct. 1142, 1148 (2009) ("In limiting the judicial power to 'Cases' and 'Controversies,' Article III of the Constitution restricts it to the traditional role of Anglo-American courts, which is to redress or prevent actual or imminently threatened injury to persons caused by private or official violation of law."); Friends of the Earth, Inc. v. Laidlaw Envtl. Servs., Inc., 528 U.S. 167, 180–81 (2000) ("the relevant showing for purposes of Article III standing . . . *is not injury to the environment*, but injury to the plaintiff.") (emphasis added); Am. Bottom Conservancy v. U.S. Army Corps of Eng'rs, 650 F.3d 652, 657 (7th Cir. 2011) ("a plaintiff, to establish Article III standing to sue, must allege . . . that the relief he seeks will if granted avert or mitigate or compensate *him* for an injury . . . ."); Francisco Benzoni, *Environmental Standing: Who Determines the Value of Other Life?* 18 DUKE ENVTL. L. & POL'Y F. 347, 356 (2008).

[9] This requirement, however, is not an Article III restriction, but rather a prudential limit on standing. *See* Warth v. Seldin, 422 U.S. 490, 499 (1975); United Food & Commercial Workers v. Brown Group, 517 U.S. 544, 557 (1996) (discussing the bar against third-party standing as prudential); Wilderness Society v. Kane Cnty., 632 F.3d 1162 (10th Cir. 2011) (the Wilderness Society did not have prudential standing to sue to enforce federal government's property rights).

imminent irreparable harm to an anthropocentric interest to be able to seek an injunction preventing harm to a nonanthropocentric interest.[10]

2. ALTERNATIVES TO LUJAN

There are some alternatives to this most restrictive standing test. However, they all still require an injury to a person. An *association* may have standing to sue in federal court if (1) one of its members would have standing in his or her own right; (2) if the interest the association seeks to protect is "germane to [its] purpose," and (3) if the claim or the relief requested does not require the participation of individual members in the lawsuit.[11] Because only persons can be members of associations, associational standing still requires that one or more of its *human* members show an injury-in-fact.

Similarly, for *jus tertii* standing, the person who is bringing a lawsuit on behalf of a third party has to show that (1) the person has suffered an injury, in addition to showing injury to a third party; (2) the presence of some substantial relationship between that person and the third party; (3) the impossibility for the third party to be able to assert its own constitutional rights; and (4) the need to avoid a dilution of the third party's rights that would result were the assertion *of jus tertii* not permitted.[12] For *jus tertii* standing, the plaintiff has to show anthropomorphic injury before the plaintiff can assert a third-party interest.

3. PRUDENTIAL LIMITS ON STANDING

In addition to Article III standing, there are prudential limits established by the Congress, or by the Court, which act as further barriers to bringing claims to federal courts. One such prudential limit is the "zone of interest" test, requiring that the plaintiff's asserted interests be related to or consistent with the purposes implicit in a statute or constitutional provision that is the basis for the cause of action.[13] Congress has the power to waive this requirement through "citizen suit" provisions, granting a statutory right to sue to enforce the statute.[14] However, such "citizen suit" provisions narrow down the class of permissible entities by only allowing anthropocentric

[10] A party seeking an injunction also needs to establish that "he is likely to succeed on the merits . . . that the balance of equities tips in his favor, and that an injunction is in the public interest." Habitat for Horses v. Salazar, 745 F. Supp. 2d 438, 447 (S.D.N.Y. 2010) (plaintiff had to show that due to a decision of the Bureau of Land Management to move wild horses, he would suffer the aesthetic injury of not being able to watch them).

[11] United Food & Commercial Workers Union Local 751 v. Brown Group, Inc., 517 U.S. 544 (1996).

[12] *See* Note, *Standing to Assert Constitutional* Jus Tertii, 88 Harv. L. Rev. 423, 432 (1974).

[13] Clark v. Secs. Indus. Ass'n, 479 U.S. 388, 399 (1987); *see also* Am. Independence Mines v. Dep't of Agriculture, 733 F. Supp. 2d 1241 (D. Idaho 2010) (the mining company did not have standing under the National Environmental Policy Act as it asserted an economic injury that did not fall within NEPA's "zone of interests" of preservation of the environment).

[14] *See e.g.*, Endangered Species Act, 16 U.S.C. § 1540(g); Bennett v. Spear, 520 U.S. 154 (1997).

"persons" to bring an action for violation of the statute.[15] Moreover, the federal courts, consistent with *Lujan*, have held that "citizen suit" provisions are not sufficient to confer standing, because Congress cannot create Article III standing by statute.[16] Plaintiffs seeking to bring lawsuits under "citizen suit" provisions for violations of a particular statute must first establish that they have standing, and an anthropomorphic injury, to sue under *Lujan*.[17]

B. Establishing Standing for Natural Resources

A closer look at how standing issues are adjudicated in courts reveals fundamental flaws in the *Lujan* rationale, and in its requirement, generally followed in most courts, that there must always be a human injury before harm to a natural resource may be adjudicated.

1. THE PARADOX

Numerous statutes have already been enacted vesting natural resources, especially animals, with legal rights requiring protection of their interests. The Endangered Species Act,[18] Animal Welfare Act,[19] Marine Mammals Protection Act,[20] and National Environmental Policy Act[21] all provide that courts may halt human activities that threaten the environmental viability of resource interests. But standing requirements are entirely focused on *human* injury. As a result, the rights created by these statutes for *natural resources* do not get litigated in court in the absence of some, however attenuated, *human* injury.[22]

A closer look at the Endangered Species Act (ESA) demonstrates, by one statutory example, just how illogical this approach has become.[23] To be able to enforce a legally protected right—the statutory rights of endangered animal and plant

[15] 16 U.S.C. § 1540(g).

[16] Lujan v. Defenders of Wildlife, 504 U.S. 555, 578 (1992).

[17] In *Lujan*, the Court stated "[b]ut the "injury in fact" test requires more than an injury to a cognizable interest. It requires that the party seeking review be himself among the injured. . . . [R]espondents had to submit affidavits or other evidence showing, through specific facts, not only that listed species were in fact being threatened by funded activities abroad, but also that one or more of respondents' members would thereby be directly affected apart from their 'special interest' in the subject." 504 U.S. at 563 (internal citations and quotation marks omitted).

[18] 16 U.S.C. §§ 1531—1544.

[19] 7 U.S.C. §§ 2131–2159.

[20] 16 U.S.C. §§ 1371–1421h.

[21] 16 U.S.C. §§ 4321–4347.

[22] Michelle P. Bassi, *La Naturalezza O Pacha Mama De Ecuador: What Doctrine Should Grant Trees Standing?* 11 OR. REV. INT'L L. 461, 475 (2009) ("Requiring that humans somehow be harmed by the loss or destruction of the environment is an egocentric requisite and one that makes very little sense for environmental protection.").

[23] Although the Endangered Species Act is used as an example to illustrate the paradox of the current standing doctrine in environmental litigation, the paradox also arises under other statutes granting natural resources with

species—plaintiffs have to demonstrate a very human injury *to themselves* to be able to gain standing. No matter how egregious the alleged harm is to the animal, failure to demonstrate human harm will cause a court to dismiss the case for lack of standing.[24] However, the ESA statute is not aimed at protecting an individual's rights or interests with regards to animals, but at protecting endangered plants and animals from harm or extinction. The requisite injury-in-fact that should be established should be with regard to an injury to the plant or animal, not to the person seeking to prevent or remedy that injury.

The anthropocentric approach of the standing doctrine has led plaintiffs who seek to enforce the legal rights of plants or animals to resort to an array of absurd claims of injury to themselves, in an attempt to establish standing. For example, the members of a conservation group, who sought protection of marine mammals from excessive hunting, had to allege an injury to its members' enjoyment of watching whales to establish standing.[25] To bring their claims, other plaintiffs wishing to acquire standing have to travel to the areas that they seek to protect from excessive hunting, or pollution, and then show "credible plans" of going back, to allege recreational or aesthetic injuries.[26] Plaintiffs have to resort to similar techniques to establish injury to some attenuated human interest in order to have standing to bring claims under other environmental statutes.[27]

---

rights of protection, such as the Wild Free-Roaming Horses and Burros Act, 16 U.S.C. § 1331. *See* Habitat for Horses v. Salazar, 745 F. Supp. 2d 438, 447 (S.D.N.Y. 2010).

[24] *See* American Society for Prevention of Cruelty v. Feld, 659 F. 3d 13 (D.C.Cir. 2011) (plaintiff failed to establish an "emotional attachment to any particular elephant [being harmed]" and therefore plaintiff failed to establish "concrete and particularized" injury); Joanna B. Wymyslo, *Standing for Endangered Species: Justiciability Beyond Humanity*, 15 U. BALT. J. ENVTL. L. 45 (2007).

[25] Japan Whaling Ass'n v. Am. Cetacean Soc'y, 478 U.S. 221, 230–31 (1986).

[26] *See, e.g.*, Animal Welfare Inst. v. Martin, 623 F.3d 19 (1st Cir. 2010) (animal protection organizations brought claims under Endangered Species Act to prevent state of Maine's authorizing trapping activity that affected threatened Canadian lynx; however, to establish Article III standing, the plaintiffs had to show that their members frequently visited the wildlife refuges and tried to observe the lynx); Coalition for a Sustainable Delta v. McCamman, 725 F. Supp. 2d 1162 (E.D. Cal. 2010) (environmental coalition brought action to protect striped bass population under the Endangered Species Act, but needed to establish that one of its members had visited the delta more than two hundred times, had engaged in recreational activities, and had "concrete plans" to visit it again); Forest Serv. Emps. for Envtl. Ethics v. U.S. Forest Serv., 726 F. Supp. 2d 1195 (D. Mont. 2010) (organization claiming violations of the National Environmental Policy Act and Endangered Species Act by the proposed use of chemical fire retardants on Forest Service lands had to establish that they engaged in recreational activities in areas containing species affected by the proposed action, had an active interest in the species, and had "credible plans" to continue their use and enjoyment of the species in question).

[27] *See, e.g.*, Am. Bottom Conservancy v. U.S. Army Corps of Engs., 650 F. 3d 652, 657–58 (7th Cir. 2011) (standing established if plaintiffs attest that they would be "upset" by the diminution of their bird-watching activities caused by a permit allowing for the construction of a waste disposal facility on a tract containing wetlands subject to the Clean Water Act); W. Watersheds Project v. Kraayenbrink, 632 F.3d 472, 484 (9th Cir. 2011) ("an individual bringing a substantive claim related to environmental harms may establish an injury in fact by showing a connection to the area of concern sufficient to make credible the connection that the person's life will be less enjoyable—that he or she really has or will suffer in his or her degree of aesthetic or recreational

For the rights created by these and other similar statutes to have any meaning, there needs to be a remedy and opportunity to enforce them. The natural resources themselves should be able to establish the injury-in-fact prong of standing, if their rights under the statute have been affected. The mechanics of how to establish injury are discussed in section 3 below.

2. ARTICLE III HAS NOT ALWAYS BEEN APPLIED TO REQUIRE HUMAN INJURY

Purely anthropocentric standing mistakenly assumes that the U.S. Constitution, particularly, Article III, requires the presence of human injury as a precondition to the assertion of rights. In fact, standing has been conferred in the absence of particularized human harm.

Standing for nonhuman entities

Various artificial legal creations, such as corporations, trusts, municipalities, and joint ventures, are considered "persons" for Article III standing and other purposes.[28] Even boats and ships have been conferred standing.[29] If a legal fiction or a ship can have standing, one should not be shocked by a suggestion to extend the doctrine of anthropocentric standing to vesting natural resources and animals with standing to raise their own rights.

Massachusetts v. EPA—Standing for states

In 1999, several environmental organizations filed a petition with the Environmental Protection Agency seeking regulation of carbon dioxide as a pollutant under the

---

satisfaction—if the area in question remains or becomes environmentally degraded.") (internal quotation marks omitted); Gulf Restoration Network v. Hancock Cnty. Dev., 772 F. Supp. 2d 761 (S.D. Miss. 2011) (environmental group seeking to prevent sediment pollution caused by the dredging of a wetland had to show that the dredging would adversely affect their recreational activities involving the wetland); Theodore Roosevelt Conservation v. Salazar, 616 F.3d 497 (D.C. Cir. 2010) (environmental groups brought actions challenging the natural gas field development project in Wyoming as a violation of the National Environmental Policy Act; however, they had to submit declarations from their members regarding their past and future intended recreational use of the land); Heartwood, Inc. v. Agpaoa, 628 F.3d 261, 268 (6th Cir. 2010) (environmental plaintiffs who seek to establish Article III standing must identify particular segments and subsections of a forest, a river, or a mountain range that they use and will continue to use); Ohio Valley Envt'l Coalition v. Hobet Mining, 702 F. Supp. 2d 644 (S.D.W. Va. 2010) (in a suit by environmental organizations against a mining company for discharging selenium in amounts that violated state and federal law, the environmental organization had to show for standing that its members used the affected area and had suffered aesthetic and recreational injury).

[28] Christopher Stone, *Should Trees Have Standing—Toward Legal Rights for Natural Objects*, 45 So. Cal. L. Rev. 450, 452 (1972) ("The world of the lawyer is peopled with inanimate right-holders: trusts, corporations, joint ventures, municipalities, Subchapter R partnerships, and nations-states, to mention just a few.").

[29] United States v. Cargo of the Brig Malek Adhel, 43 U.S. (2 How.) 210 (1844) (proceeding against a ship that was seized by pirates).

Clean Air Act. In August 2003, the EPA denied the petition, concluding that it did not have the authority to regulate carbon dioxide under the Clean Air Act. Shortly thereafter, a group of states, cities, and environmental groups filed a lawsuit to challenge the denial of the petition. As a threshold matter, the plaintiffs that were states had to overcome a significant barrier: Did the states have the ability to establish standing? The Supreme Court recognized that Massachusetts, as a sovereign state, had a "well-founded desire to preserve its sovereign territory" from the rise in sea level, resulting from global warming.[30] Then the Court found that the requisite standing tests of injury-in-fact (rising sea level), causation (global warming due, among other things, to increased carbon dioxide levels in the atmosphere), and redressability (regulation of new vehicle emissions, although an incremental step, would be sufficient for standing purposes) had been satisfied.

Massachusetts v. EPA presents a pivotal decision for environmental litigation. In this case, the Supreme Court recognized purely environmental injury to be sufficient, and granted standing to a state, a nonhuman, to litigate its claim to redress its purely ecocentric harm.[31]

Cetacean Community v. Bush[32]

An environmental organization brought a lawsuit under the Endangered Species Act, the Marine Mammal Protection Act, National Environmental Policy Act, and Administrative Procedure Act in the name of the cetacean community of whales, dolphins, and porpoises. The claim alleged that proposed deployment by the Navy of low frequency active sonar (LFAS) had violated the environmental statutes. In a thorough and detailed opinion, the Ninth Circuit discussed the animals' standing to assert the rights granted to them by the statutes. Although the court recognized that there was no Article III barrier to standing,[33] it concluded the animals nevertheless lacked standing under the statutes because the statutes either (1) did not include the animals within the class of entities that could bring suit under the "citizen suit" provision of the statute,[34] or (2) failed to provide a "citizen suit" provision or another clause granting the animals standing to sue on their own behalf.[35] Despite its ultimate outcome, which was based on an interpretation of a statute's "citizen suit" provision, the *Cetacean Community* case recognized that animals could adjudicate their own rights separate from and without regard to human injury or interest. The Court

[30] Massachusetts v. Envtl. Prot. Agency, 549 U.S. 497, 518 (2007).

[31] *See* American Electric Power, Inc. v. Connecticut, 131 S. Ct. 2527 (2011) (an equally divided Court affirms the proposition that States have standing to bring a common law action to protect the interests of the State); Andrew Long, *Standing & Consensus: Globalism in Massachusetts v. EPA*, 23 J. Envtl. L. & Litig. 73 (2008).

[32] 386 F.3d 1169 (9th Cir. 2004).

[33] *Id.* at 1175.

[34] *Id.* at 1176–78 (under APA and ESA, animals did not have statutory standing to sue on their own behalf).

[35] *Id.* at 1178 (there was no "citizen suit" provision in MMPA authorizing standing).

of Appeals held there was no Article III standing barrier for the animals because Article III does not explicitly limit standing to humans.[36]

3. ARTICLE III DOES NOT REQUIRE THE PRESENCE OF HUMAN INJURY

Nothing in the text of the Constitution indicates that Article III courts are limited to adjudicating only controversies focusing on injuries to people.[37] The language of Article III, Section 2 only specifies that the judicial power "shall extend to all Cases, in Law and Equity, arising under this Constitution, the Laws of the United States, and Treaties made." The most obvious interpretation of this language is that courts have the power to adjudicate any and all violations of the federal law, regardless of the injured party, if there is a "case." Furthermore, the U.S. Supreme Court has never explicitly held that a "case or controversy" is limited to humans.[38]

A look at the background of the "case or controversy" language of Article III supports a broader interpretation of standing. Historically "cases" meant any actual infringement of a legal right that a plaintiff could adjudicate in court.[39] Plaintiffs could not invoke the courts' jurisdiction as part of a deliberate litigation strategy.[40] Private plaintiffs could only adjudicate their own private rights, leaving public actions to the government, and restricting private parties from adjudicating generalized claims.[41] But as long as there was an infringement of a right, in common law or a statute, plaintiffs, whether human or otherwise, had the right to seek a remedy in court.[42]

This approach also addressed separation of powers concerns. As Congress would be able to define the rights and laws, the executive branch would administer the law

---

[36] The court, however, in the same opinion dismissed as dictum an earlier decision explicitly recognizing a bird as a "plaintiff in its own right." *Id.* at 1173; *see* Palila v. Hawaii Dep't of Land & Natural Res., 852 F.2d 1106, 1107 (9th Cir.1988).

[37] *Id.* at 1175; Cass R. Sunstein, *Standing for Animals (with Notes on Animal Rights)*, 47 UCLA L. REV. 1333 (2000); Katherine A. Burke, *Can We Stand For It? Amending the Endangered Species Act with an Animal-Suit Provision*, 75 U. COLO. L. REV. 633 (2004) (same).

[38] Although there is some language in *Summers* and *Laidlaw* that refers to the "relevant injury to a person, or plaintiff," it is not clear if the Court used this language in the restrictive sense, confining standing only to "persons" or "plaintiffs" that must be defined as humans. Summers v. Earth Island Inst., 129 S. Ct. 1142, 1148 (2009); Friends of the Earth, Inc. v. Laidlaw Envtl. Servs., Inc., 528 U.S. 167, 180–81 (2000).

[39] Robert J. Pushaw, Jr., *Limiting Article III Standing to "Accidental" Plaintiffs: Lessons from Environmental and Animal Law Cases*, 45 GA. L. REV. 1 (2010).

Thoughtful judges have argued that "[s]ome of the most frequently mentioned grounds for the constitutional doctrine of standing are tenuous . . . ." See Am. Bottom Conservancy v. U.S. Army Corps of Engs., 650 F. 3d 652, 655 (7th Cir. 2011) (unanimous opinion written by Judge Posner). Reputable scholars have similarly advocated that standing should not be interpreted narrowly. *See* 13A CHARLES ALAN WRIGHT ET AL., FEDERAL PRACTICE AND PROCEDURE § 3531.1, pp. 56–57 (3d ed. 2008); Daniel E. Ho & Erica L. Ross, *Did Liberal Justices Invent the Standing Doctrine? An Empirical Study of the Evolution of Standing, 1921–2006*, 62 STAN. L. REV. 591 (2010); Robert J. Pushaw, Jr., *Article III's Case/Controversy Distinction and the Dual Functions of Federal Courts*, 69 NOTRE DAME L. REV. 447 (1994).

[40] *Id.* at 74.

[41] *Id.* at 69.

[42] *Id.* at 76.

exercising its broad discretion to determine enforcement priorities, and the judiciary would exercise its power only if there was an infringement of a plaintiff's legal rights.[43] All of the conditions to separation of powers would be satisfied if plaintiffs were not human beings.

C. How Would Natural Resources Bring a Lawsuit?

If natural resources are granted standing, and are able to sue on their own behalf without proving a corresponding human injury, the next question is *how* a natural resource would be able bring an action on its own behalf. A number of approaches have been proposed by judges and scholars to accomplish the mechanics of having the natural resources adjudicate their own rights in court. All of the proposed methods are purely procedural devices, and do not affect the fundamental principle of this chapter—natural resources should have standing to adjudicate their rights.

1. GUARDIANSHIP MODEL

The first major critique of the issue of standing for nonhuman plaintiffs is still the most frequently cited work on the matter of nonhuman standing—Professor Christopher Stone's 1972 law review article, "Should Trees Have Standing?"[44] Stone argued that the environment should be given standing in its own right in the courts to protect its procedural and substantive rights against the effects of human resource use activity. To accomplish this goal, the environment should be given its own legal rights which in turn could be represented in court by a guardian, similar to a guardian ad litem. Stone noted that to grant a natural object standing in court through a guardian is not much different than to do so with other nonhuman entities, such as corporations, states, estates, municipalities, trusts and ships, which have been given legal standing to adjudicate their rights in courts. To avoid multiple inconsistent judgments concerning the same environmental entity, the system could be set up to have the natural object "be bound" by the judgment, and for it to have res judicata effect for the purposes of possible subsequent lawsuits regarding the same object by other guardians.[45] The traditional system of appointment, substitution, removal, resolving of conflicts of interest, or termination of guardians could easily be adopted for this purpose. Moreover, existing environmental organizations seem more than capable of representing the best interests of the natural resource.[46]

In *Sierra Club v. Morton*,[47] Justices Douglas and Blackmun in separate dissents supported the notion of standing for the environment, although their models of

---

[43] *Id.* at 77.

[44] Stone, *supra* note 28.

[45] *Id. at* 470.

[46] *See, e.g.*, Forest Guardians v. U.S. Forest Serv., 641 F.3d 423 (10th Cir. 2011) (raising the interests of the Abert's squirrel); Sierra Club v. Wyoming Dep't of Envtl. Quality, 251 P.3d 310 (Wyo. 2011) (raising the quality of the air).

[47] 405 U.S. 727 (1972).

how to accomplish it were slightly different.[48] Justice Douglas argued that the environment should have its own rights and be granted Article III standing, and the court should, as Stone recommended, appoint a guardian ad litem to enforce those rights.[49] Some scholars criticized this model as impractical and vague.[50] Indeed, it seems impossible for the court to sua sponte select and appoint a guardian for the environment without a designated plaintiff who could initiate the claim. But, consistent with standard judicial practice, the Supreme Court (or any other court) may designate an attorney to represent an "orphaned" argument—one that is essential to the outcome of the case, but has been abandoned by both parties.[51] The same practice could be adopted if rights are conferred on natural resources. A court could designate a guardian to intervene when a proposed action is threatening the recognized rights of the environment. The primary difficulty with this position, however, is that this approach would be effective only when there is pending litigation affecting a particular natural resource, and it would be inapplicable when the offending conduct goes unchallenged.

Justice Blackmun's dissent in *Sierra Club* seemed to offer the more practical solution—organizations or private individuals could apply to be appointed legal guardians for a particular resource and be able to litigate its rights.[52] This approach also is based on the idea that the natural resource would have both a cognizable legal right and Article III standing, and the guardian would simply effectuate the mechanics of bringing the claim to court. This technique would also eliminate the concern that courts might become embroiled in a "political question" argument.[53] Under Blackmun's proposal, the court would simply be adjudicating the legal rights recognized by all branches of the government.

2. USE OF PUBLIC TRUST DOCTRINE TO INVEST STATES WITH GUARDIANSHIP OF THE ENVIRONMENT

The public trust doctrine could be used to enable the states to act as proxy for the environment in any type of proceeding.[54] The states could become the guardian for the natural resources within their borders to represent their rights. The state

---

[48] *See* Marguerite Hogan, *Standing for Nonhuman Animals: Developing a Guardianship Model from the Dissents in* Sierra Club v. Morton, 95 CAL. L. REV. 513 (2007).

[49] Sierra Club v. Morton, 405 U.S. 727, 749 n.8 (1972) (Douglas, J., dissenting).

[50] Peter Manus, *The Blackbird Whistling—The Silence Just After: Evaluating the Environmental Legacy of Justice Blackmun*, 85 IOWA L. REV. 429, 446 (2000).

[51] Brian P. Goldman, *Should the Supreme Court Stop Inviting* Amici Curae *to Defend Abandoned Lower Court Decisions?* 63 STAN. L. REV. 907 (2011).

[52] Sierra Club v. Morton, 40 U.S. 727, 757–58 (1972) (Blackmun, J., dissenting).

[53] *See* Jeremy Hessler, *A Temporary Solution to Climate Change: The Federal Common Law to the Rescue?* 38 HASTINGS CONST. L.Q. 407, 412 (2011) (discussing invocation of political question doctrine by the courts in environmental litigation).

[54] Mary Christina Wood, *Advancing the Sovereign Trust of Government to Safeguard the Environment for Present and Future Generations: Ecological Realisms and the Need for a Paradigm Shift*, 39 ENVTL. L. 43 (2009); George P. Smith II & Michael W. Sweeney, *The Public Trust Doctrine and Natural Law: Emanations Within a Penumbra*,

legislature would statutorily define the resources to be protected or conserved by the public trust. Once the trust has been created, the state could request a court to review the potential effects on the environment that a proposed action or exploitation would present.[55] The biggest concern for this expansive use of the public trust doctrine to protect the resources of the state is its interaction with the Fifth Amendment. An expansion of the state's control over the protection of natural resources through an expansion of the public trust doctrine could deprive property owners of the right to just compensation under the Takings Clause.

3. AN ARTICLE I TRIBUNAL FOR ADJUDICATING ENVIRONMENTAL CLAIMS

Several scholars have proposed creating or expanding the jurisdiction of current Article I courts to allow for adjudication of certain environmental claims.[56] These proposals would entail bringing environmental claims under existing "citizen suit" provisions in Article I, as opposed to Article III courts, because restrictive Article III standing requirements then would not apply.[57] Because Article I courts are created for adjudicating "public rights" cases, environmental claims would fit within the established uses of Article I tribunals.[58] Shifting environmental claims to an Article I tribunal would be constitutional, as (1) the plaintiffs would no longer have to state their claims in terms of their own "private rights" in order to establish standing, as they have to do for Article III courts;[59] and (2) claims would be focused on the rights of the environment itself, thereby eliminating the concern that removing jurisdiction from Article III courts over these claims would threaten "the institutional integrity of the Judicial Branch."[60]

A significant limitation for using an Article I court for environmental claims is the fact that it can be used only for adjudicating rights grounded in federal statutes, thus closing the door on claims arising out of state law or some other positive law.[61] In addition, concerns may arise regarding the independence of Article I tribunals.

---

33 B.C. Envtl. Aff. L. Rev. 307 (2006); W. Earl Webster, *How Can Mother Nature Get to Court? The Status of the Standing Doctrine in a Post* Laidlaw *Landscape*, 27 J. Land Res. & Envtl. L. 453, 466 (2007).

[55] Webster, *supra* note 54, at 467.

[56] Preston Carter, *If an (Endangered) Tree Falls in the Forest, and No One is Around . . . .": Resolving The Divergence between Standing Requirements and Congressional Intent in Environmental Legislation*, 84 Notre Dame L. Rev. 2191 (2009); Timothy C. Hodits, *The Fatal Flaw of Standing: A Proposal for an Article I Tribunal for Environmental Claims*, 84 Wash. U. L. Rev. 1907 (2006).

[57] Carter, *supra* note 56, at 2212.

[58] *Id.* at 2214 (discussing N. Pipeline Constr. Co. v. Marathon Pipe Line Co., 458 U.S. 50, 67 (1982) (establishing "public rights" adjudications as examples of permissible Article I tribunals)).

[59] *See* Lujan v. Defenders of Wildlife, 504 U.S. 555, 578 (1992).

[60] Carter, *supra* note 56 at 2215–16 (discussing the four-factor test of determining when the integrity of judicial branch is threatened by removing jurisdiction from Article III courts, adopted by Commodity Futures Trading Comm'n v. Schor, 478 U.S. 833).

[61] Hodits, *supra* note 56, at 1937 ("pure public rights originate in a statute enacted by Congress") (internal citations omitted).

Article I judges lack the "bedrock" characteristics of Article III independence—life tenure and salary protection. Therefore it is possibile that the judges would be reluctant to make politically unpopular decisions. These concerns, however, appear minor, as there is evidence that differences in life tenure for Article I and Article III judges does not result in considerable differences in decision making.[62]

4. FEDERALLY CHARTERED CORPORATIONS

Yet another approach that has been suggested is vesting environmental resources with the right to bring citizen suits to enforce environmental statutes, drawing on the paradigm of federally chartered corporations.[63] Congress creates federal corporations to pursue certain policy goals, from building and managing dams to providing mentors to socially challenged individuals. Each corporation is granted a set of purposes, powers, and restrictions, and is created by legislation. Because these corporations have a legal existence, they can vindicate their rights in court. Congress could create groups or categories of environmental resources, designate them as federally chartered corporations, and endow these groups with the power to sue in federal court. The definition of "persons" in citizen suit provisions would have to be expanded to include these newly chartered corporations. Any attorney meeting the factors of Federal Rule of Civil Procedure 17(c) would be empowered to represent the chartered group in court.

This proposal could create fierce competition between various environmental groups, which might then rush to ascertain their eligibility under F.R.C.P. 17(c). Such a race for legitimacy could potentially replace standing litigation with litigation to determine F.R.C.P. 17(c) eligibility. As an alternative, the U.S. Secretary of the Interior could appoint an attorney to represent the interests of the environmental charter in court. This approach would also have its complications due to its potential to politicize the process.[64]

Perhaps a better model would be to combine the idea of the chartered environmental corporation with Justice Blackmun's model of guardianship. The organization or private party that is able to demonstrate the strongest ties and interests in the particular chartered resource would be granted the guardianship to represent it in court. In the long run, though, creating a chartered corporation may unnecessarily complicate the process. If one assumes that the courts eventually accept that natural resources should have standing as other nonhuman entities do, then the statute or the law vesting them with rights should also vest them with a cause of action and standing to sue. Existing citizen suit provisions could be amended to include the objects of the statute's protection within the class of entities that can enforce the statute.

---

[62] Carter, *supra* note 56, at 2219–20 (citing Bruce A. Carroll, *The Possible Impact of Article I Judges: Collective Analysis of Judicial Decision Making between Article I and Article III Judges*, 15 TRINITY L. REV. 50 (2008).

[63] *Id.* at 2227.

[64] *Id.* at 2232–34.

5. CHANGE PROPERTY LAW TO RECOGNIZE RIGHTS OF NONHUMANS

Some scholars have proposed a change in modern property law that would redefine the boundaries of private property rights.[65] Such a new version of property would limit the rights of owners to specific uses and locations "tailored to recognize ecological dependencies and avoid impacts."[66] Laws would be changed so that ecosystem boundaries could be established, within which caps could be set on the use of resources and ecologically centered land within the property.[67] Once these rights of the natural resources are established, then the guardianship or public trust models discussed above could be used to find representation for these resources in court.

6. ACTIO POPULARIS

Under the doctrine of *actio popularis*, anyone could bring an action to defend the natural resource's rights, as long as the person could show actual or imminent injury to the resource's need to be left alone. This group of representatives of nature's rights would include companies, individuals, or even foreign entities. However, permitting anyone to sue on behalf of the resources carries several risks. There is the potential that an insufficiently prepared representative would litigate the case, thus creating bad precedent and further harm the rights of the resources; some litigants could use the lawsuit to pursue their own agendas under the guise of protecting the rights of the resources.[68] Actio popularis could also create a "race to the court" by various parties seeking to enforce the rights of the resources, and potentially create much litigation on the subject of who-is-able-to-bring-which-claims? Although allowing the broadest possible vehicle for enforcing nature's rights, actio popularis could potentially create more harm than benefit to the resources.

7. ACTIO POPULARIS COMBINED WITH "SUFFICIENT INTEREST"

A concept discussed in the English case of *Regina v. H.M. Inspectorate of Pollution and Ministry of Agric, Fisheries and Food (Greenpeace)*[69] suggests that if the range of potential representatives eligible under actio popularis could be somehow linked to those with "sufficient interest" in the affected resource, then litigation raising the interests of resources would be more manageable. "Sufficient interest" refers to the interest and degree of responsibility a party takes in the particular resource or the environmental object that is worthy of a legal challenge asserting its rights.

In the *Regina* case, Greenpeace, an environmental rights organization, sought judicial review challenging the British Nuclear Fuels Company's application to

---

[65] *See, e.g.*, Lee P. Breckenridge, *Can Fish Own Water? Envisioning Nonhuman Property in Ecosystems*, 20 J. LAND USE & ENVTL. LAW 293 (2005); Webster, *supra* note 54, at 467.

[66] Breckenridge, *supra* note 65, at 307.

[67] Webster, *supra* note 54, at 467.

[68] Bassi, *supra* note 22, at 465–66.

[69] [1994] All E.R. 329 (Q.B.).

discharge radioactive waste into the aquatic environment. The High Court granted Greenpeace standing, finding that it was "eminently respectable and responsible" and had a "genuine interest in the issues raised."[70] Borrowing from that concept, a proper representative for the rights of a natural resource would be an individual or an entity that: (1) has knowledge of the injured resource or ecosystem; (2) has a genuine interest, apart from its own interests, in protecting the resource, and (3) has adequate resources and expertise to adequately represent the resource in litigation.[71] Well-established environmental organizations should easily be able to meet this standing requirement;[72] however, it would be difficult, but not impossible, for individuals to establish standing, especially with regard to the last prong of this approach, which requires the representative to demonstrate sufficient resources to efficiently pursue the litigation.

D. Implications of Expanding Standing to Natural Resources

1. HOW WOULD THE NATURAL RESOURCE BE DEFINED?

Professor Stone called this problem an "ontological" issue—defining the boundaries of the "natural object" granted standing would present certain difficulties.[73] Because any natural resource often represents a part of a larger natural system, how narrowly does the resource need to be defined so that it can be given rights and gain standing for an actual case or controversy? The most obvious example is a stream, or a small portion of a river, where one might be concerned only with harmful use of that portion of the stream. When does the concern broaden to the entire river, or the lake or the sea into which the river flows? Would the right of nonuse, or standing to raise it, differ based on how the resource was defined? These issues have been raised in part in Chapter 17.

2. EXPANDING STANDING TO OTHER NONHUMAN, NONNATURAL RESOURCES

Even in 1972, Stone recognized that expanding standing to the natural objects could lead to the slippery slope expansion of standing to other nonhuman entities, such as computers.[74] Can we envision a future where our laptops or smart phones or other wonders of modern technological advances could bring claims against humans,

---

[70] *Id.* at 96, 102.

[71] Bassi, *supra* note 22, at 473.

[72] *See supra* note 46, *supra*.

[73] Stone, *supra* note 28, at 456, n.26.

[74] *Id.* ("I trust that the reader will be able to discern where the analysis is appropriate to advancing our understanding of what would be involved in giving 'rights' to other objects not presently endowed with rights—for example, not only animals (some of which already have rights in some senses) but also humanoids, computers, and so forth.").

or one another, in courts? Could a virus-infected operating system bring a lawsuit against the programmer who created the virus? And, most certainly, expanding nonhuman standing could have huge effect on the abortion question and fetus rights adjudication. Although attempts to create a guardianship for embryos and fetuses in order to represent rights of the unborn is not a novel idea, expanded standing for resources grounded on the existence of a newly recognized legal right, coupled with the elimination of an anthropocentric injury-in-fact requirement, could conceivably give those zygote-embryo-fetus claims momentum. The right of nonuse proposed here should be limited to natural and environmental resources whose nonuse component is endangered by human use.[75] Neither computers nor embryos have a similar nonuse dimension, and therefore the arguments advanced here do not logically extend to nonnatural resources.

[75] Christopher Stone, *Should Trees Have Standing? Revisited: How Far Will law and Morals Reach? A Pluralist Perspective,* 59 S. Cal. L. Rev. 1 (1985); David N. Cassuto, *The Law Of Words: Standing, Environment, and Other Contested Terms,* 28 Harv. Envtl. L. Rev. 79 (2004); W. Earl Webster, *How Can Mother Nature Get To Court? The Status of the Standing Doctrine in a Post Laidlaw Landscape,* 27 J. Land Resources & Envtl. L 453 (2007); Preston Carter, *If An (Endangered) Tree Falls In The Forest, And No One Is Around . . . : Resolving The Divergence Between Standing Requirements And Congressional Intent In Environmental Legislation,* 84 Notre Dame L. Rev. 2191 (2009).

Table of Cases

Index